THE AFTERMATH OF SOVEREIGNTY

DAVID LOWENTHAL, a geographer and historian, has devoted twenty years to research on the West Indies. He has taught at Vassar College and has been visiting professor at a number of universities in the United States and at the University of the West Indies, where he was Fulbright Research Fellow at the Institute of Social and Economic Research (1956–57). During 1961–62 he worked in the Lesser Antilles with the assistance of a Rockefeller Foundation Research Grant and later received a Guggenheim Fellowship. Until 1972 he was Secretary and Research Associate at the American Geographical Society, and he is currently Professor of Geography at University College, London. His most recent book is *West Indian Societies,* a comprehensive study of the non-Hispanic Caribbean.

LAMBROS COMITAS is Professor of Anthropology and Education, Director of both the Center for Education in Latin America and the Center for Urban Studies and Programs, and Associate Director of the Division of Philosophy and Social Sciences at Teachers College, Columbia University. He is also Associate Director of the Research Institute for the Study of Man, an institution for research and scholarship of the Caribbean. Mr. Comitas was awarded a Fulbright Graduate Study Grant (1957–58) and a Guggenheim Fellowship (1971–72) and has done field research in Barbados, Jamaica, Bolivia, and the Dominican Republic. He has written numerous articles, was editor of *Caribbeana 1900–1965: A Topical Bibliography,* and serves as consultant or editor for several publishing projects.

Four books, edited and introduced by David Lowenthal and Lambros Comitas, provide a broad variety of material for the West Indies as a whole; each has the subtitle *West Indian Perspectives:*

SLAVES, FREE MEN, CITIZENS
WORK AND FAMILY LIFE
CONSEQUENCES OF CLASS AND COLOR
THE AFTERMATH OF SOVEREIGNTY

THE AFTERMATH OF SOVEREIGNTY

West Indian Perspectives

Edited and Introduced by
David Lowenthal and Lambros Comitas

Anchor Books
Anchor Press/Doubleday
Garden City, New York, 1973

The Anchor Books edition is the first
publication of *The Aftermath of
Sovereignty: West Indian Perspectives.*

Anchor Books edition: 1973

ISBN: 0-385-04304-X
Library of Congress Catalog Card Number 72–83153
Copyright © 1973 by David Lowenthal and Lambros Comitas
All Rights Reserved
Printed in the United States of America

CONTENTS

EDITORS' NOTE

The West Indies, the earliest and one of the most important prizes of Europe's New World and the first to experience the full impact of the black diaspora from Africa, were also the most enduringly colonized territories in the history of the Western Hemisphere. Here more than anywhere else masters and slaves constituted the basic ingredients of the social order; here more than anywhere else class and status were based on distinctions of color and race. Yet out of that past, here more than anywhere else societies with black majorities have emerged as self-governing, multiracial states.

This collection of four volumes—*Slaves, Free Men, Citizens; Work and Family Life; Consequences of Class and Color;* and *The Aftermath of Sovereignty*—chronicles the remarkable story, played out on the doorstep of the North American continent, of transitions from slavery to freedom, from colonialism to self-government, and from self-rejection to prideful identity.

The West Indies face a host of continuing problems—foreign economic domination and population pressure, ethnic stress and black-power revolts, the petty tyranny of local rulers and an agonizing dependence on expatriate culture. For these very reasons, the West Indies constitute an exceptional setting for the study of complex social relations. The archipelago is a set of mirrors in which the lives of black, brown, and white, of American Indian and East Indian, and of a score of other minorities continually interact. Constrained by local circumstance, these interactions also contain a wealth of possibilities for a kind of creative harmony of which North Americans and Europeans are scarcely yet aware. Consequently, while these volumes deal specifically with the Caribbean in all its aspects, many dimensions of life and many problems West Indians confront have analogues in other regions of the world: most clearly in race relations, economic development, colonial and post-colonial politics and government, and the need to find and express group identity.

It can be argued that the West Indies is a distinctive and unique culture area in that the societies within it display profound similarities: their inhabitants, notwithstanding linguistic barriers and local or parochial loyalties, see themselves as closely linked. These resemblances and recognitions, originally the product of similar economic and social forces based on North European settlement, plantation agriculture, and African slavery, have subsequently been reinforced by a widespread community of interest, along with interregional migration for commerce, employment, marriage, and education. These volumes focus mainly on these underlying uniformities. Within the Caribbean itself, however, one is more conscious of differences than of resemblances. While each Caribbean land is in part a microcosm of the entire archipelago, local conditions—size, resources, social structure, political status—also make it in some significant fashion unique.

The range of these essays is the entire non-Hispanic Caribbean, but most of the material that is not general in character deals with the Commonwealth Caribbean, a preponderant share of this specifically with Jamaica and Trinidad. This reflects neither a bias in favor of these territories nor a belief that they are typical, but rather the fact that most recent scholarly attention has concentrated on, and literary expression has emanated from, the Commonwealth Caribbean. Closer understanding of, and expression in, the smaller French and Netherlands Caribbean and larger but less well-known Haiti lie in the future.

In the Caribbean, a real understanding of any problem

requires a broad familiarity with all aspects of culture and society. Thus the study of economic development relates intimately to that of family organization, and both of these interlink with aspects of political thought, systems of education, and patterns of speech. Consequently, the subject matter of this collection lies in the domains of history, geography, anthropology, sociology, economics, politics, polemics, and the arts. For example, essays on work and family life by economists and anthropologists are complemented by other studies tracing the historical background and sociological interplay of these with other themes. Throughout these volumes economists and geographers indicate how social structure bears on and is influenced by economy and land use, and linguists, *littérateurs,* lawyers, and local journalists provide insights on the impact of these patterns in everyday life.

The reader will find here not a complete delineation of the Caribbean realm but rather a sketch in breadth, with fuller discussion of significant themes, given depth and personality by picaresque flavor. He may gain a sense of what West Indians were and are like, how they live, and what problems they confront; he can see how their own view of themselves differs from that of outsiders; he will know where to look for general studies and for more detailed information. And if there is such a thing as a regional personality, this collection may enable him to acquire a sense of it.

What is currently available to most students of Caribbean affairs is woefully inadequate by comparison with many other regions of the world. A few general histories, technical analyses on particular aspects of Caribbean society or culture, and detailed studies of one or two individual territories comprise the holdings of all but the best-equipped libraries. Moreover, no book has yet been published that includes a broad variety of material for the area as a whole, and few studies transcend national or linguistic boundaries. We therefore aim to make available a wide range of literature on the Caribbean that is not readily accessible anywhere else.

Most of this collection is the work of West Indians themselves, for they contribute forty-five of the seventy-two selections. Seventeen of these are by Trinidadians, fifteen by Jamaicans, four by Guyanese, three each by Vincentians and St. Lucians, two by Martiniquans, and one by a Barbadian. Non-West Indian writers contribute twenty-seven selections: fourteen by Americans, ten by British, two by Canadians, and one by a French author. Many of the North American and European contributors either have been permanent residents in the West Indies or have worked there for long periods of time.

Editorial comment has been held to a minimum, but readers will find three levels of guidance. An introduction to each of the four volumes summarizes the general implications of the issues therein surveyed. A paragraph of topical commentary together with a few lines identifying the author introduces each selection. Finally, a selected West Indian reading list appears at the end of each volume, and a general comprehensive bibliography is appended to *The Aftermath of Sovereignty*.

The papers and documents included here have been altered only for minimal editorial consistency and ease of reference. All original titles of articles have been retained, but where none appear or where book chapter headings do not identify the contents of excerpted material, we have added descriptive titles, identified by single asterisks in the text. Series of asterisks also indicate the few instances where material is omitted. When required in such cases, we have completed some footnote references. Otherwise, only obvious typographical and other errors have been corrected. Our own two translations from French sources adhere to the originals as closely as possible, within the limits of comprehensibility.

The editors are grateful to those who have assisted them in this enterprise, both in and out of the Caribbean. We owe special thanks to Marquita Riel and Claire Angela Hendricks, who helped with the original selections and styled the references. Miss Riel also made the original translations from the French. We are indebted to the Research Institute for the Study of Man, and its Director, Dr. Vera Rubin, to the American Geographical Society, and to Teachers College of Columbia University, and notably to their library staffs, for many facilities.

Our main gratitude goes to the contributors represented in these pages and to their original publishers, who have in most cases freely and uncomplainingly made available their work and have helped to correct errors. We are particularly obliged for cooperation from the Institute of Social and Economic Studies and its Director, Alister McIntyre, and to the Department of Extra-Mural Studies, both at the University of the West Indies, under whose auspices a large number of these studies were originally done. We are also obligated to M. G. Smith for encouragement throughout the course of selection and composition.

David Lowenthal
Lambros Comitas
March 1972

INTRODUCTION:
The Aftermath of Sovereignty

"Government is not politics," warned a Trinidadian re-
former. It is not enough merely to elect leaders who reflect their point of view; West Indians themselves must
share in the process of decision making. This is a hard
lesson to learn after four centuries of subordination to imperial overlords and to local elites, expatriate in feeling if
not in geographical fact. Subordination did not end with
West Indian emancipation in the mid-nineteenth century;
freedom left most ex-slaves still voteless and voiceless.
Not until the mid-twentieth century did all West Indians
gain the right to vote, let alone to hold office; and only in
the past decade have large numbers of West Indians really
begun to participate in government and politics.

Popular participation in representative institutions, opposed almost every inch of the way by entrenched elites,
was won less by mass protest than by the efforts of the
middle classes, who had long been deprived of place and
prestige by racial and ethnic prejudice. In recent years, an
increasingly numerous and prosperous middle class has
almost entirely superseded expatriate and local white elites
in government. But popular participation in public affairs,
notwithstanding local autonomy and universal suffrage,
remains weak and sporadic, while mass dissatisfaction with
the new leaders is as widespread as with the old and is
often more violently expressed.

Caribbean political forms, transplanted from Western
Europe, still formally resemble those of the metropolis but

have become quite different in function. Most British West Indian political parties, for example, stem from trade union bases and avow a Labour Party, working-class orientation; but they are also infused by authoritarianism, a tenacious legacy of the colonial era. Whatever their social origins and professed aims, most present-day West Indian leaders maintain an elitist bias toward their followers. They welcome mass participation as a route to political power but discourage mass participation, let alone criticism, in the actual process of government. Similarly, most Commonwealth Caribbean countries maintain legislative systems with government and opposition parties and a full panoply of cabinets and shadow cabinets, but there is a marked tendency toward one-party states, and in several islands the party in power holds every legislative seat. Thus Caribbean circumstances have transformed the content of colonial institutions while leaving their structures substantially intact.

The advent of formal self-government has intensified other stresses and strains. The small size and weak infrastructure of most West Indian societies intimately involves governments in every aspect of local life and make personalism, nepotism, corruption, and tyranny ever-present dangers. Yet efforts to counteract these risks through regional linkages and interisland collaboration continually founder on the shoals of insular rivalries. One need only cite the short history of the late West Indies Federation (1958–62) and the recent (1967) secession from St. Kitts of tiny Anguilla (population 6,000), followed by its reversion to colonial status in 1971. Personal ambitions, local needs, and the demands of regional cooperation are more apt to put West Indian states in conflict than in concert.

The ideological consequences of past dependence are likewise at odds with newly gained freedom. Some West Indians are now attempting to transform the steeply stratified social systems inherited from the colonial past into more egalitarian and dynamic forms. But this impulse is less locally inspired than it is animated by the worldwide thrust toward social justice and mass self-determination. West Indian social reform requires constant nourishment from external sources, underscoring old patterns of dependency. Owing to lack of indigenous models, the West Indies, more than other ex-colonial areas, remain bound to colonial habits. And owing to inherited patterns of production and marketing, reinforced by smallness and isolation, they also remain economically and strategically dependent on former imperial overlords.

Formal self-government and independence, moreover, divide those who still wield economic control from those who now possess political power. Old elites and multinational corporations dominate the productive resources of West Indian societies, whereas formal political control and governmental services are in the hands, respectively, of new popular leaders and the old middle class, themselves at odds with each other. The dilemma this poses for rational planning and implementation was succinctly put by a West Indian premier who, after electoral victory in the late 1950s, noted that "my party is in office but not in power."

Yet a felt need for self-assertion commensurate with political independence drives West Indians increasingly to reject the consequences of these realities and to press for reorientations of society as a whole. In this process, reformers repudiate the present political leadership as unable, if not unwilling, to transform West Indian states into self-respecting autonomous entities. Nationalist impulse focuses on redressing past social and racial imbalances, which are seen as both causes and consequences of imperialism. The local governments themselves, whether emphasizing local cultural forms or African roots, continually proclaim intentions to nationalize this or that, to rediscover and elevate West Indian heroes—a Marcus Garvey in Jamaica, a Cuffy in Guyana—to replace old ceremonial forms with new ones—a Trinidadian Order of the Balisier instead of an Order of the British Empire.

Such activities, however, are often more symbolic than substantive. As some West Indians themselves remark, the

search for West Indianness today is in many respects quix-
otic for small islanders whose social ramifications and cultural linkages span both hemispheres. The risks and promises, the imaginative extensions and practical limits, of
emphasizing what is local or what is West Indian constantly shift, depending on relationships among West Indians and between them and the world outside.

The present volume considers aspects of all these questions under two broad rubrics: government and politics
and national and personal identity. The first section,
"Freedom and Power," considers the institutional dimensions of West Indian government and politics. The opening selection surveys the broad transition from subjugation to independence, with the author—a West Indian
prime minister—proclaiming the end of the bad old days
of master and slave, ruler and ruled, empire and colony.
A detailed account of the growth of electorates and the
development of representative institutions in the various
territories follows. Responding to these opportunities for
participation, and agitating for their extension, West Indians have formed certain characteristic political alignments. These are studied in the next two selections, the
first focusing on the origins and traits of parties in the
larger territories, the second examining a case study of
personalistic small-island politics. The stress between ma-
joritarian rulers and administrative cadres is the subject of
the next selection, which describes some of the political
pressures West Indian civil services are subjected to and
how they are fended off. A case study of a Trinidad election casts into high relief the interplay of all these political
forces with race and ethnicity. Finally, four selections deal
with the hopes and disappointments of regional association: first, a critique of the former West Indies Federation by an uncompromising Jamaican nationalist; second,
an explanation of the causes of its collapse by a Barbadian
architect of the federation; third, a vivid account of vain
efforts by a St. Lucian to salvage a small-island grouping
from the federal ruins; and fourth, a recent plea by a
Guyanese East Indian for a greater West Indian political

entity to be grounded on realistic economic and social premises.

The second section, "On Being a West Indian," opens with a critique of the West Indian search for racial identity: Frantz Fanon, the best known of Caribbean radical writers, scores the new West Indian attachment to Africa as no less visionary and romantic than the old West Indian tie to Europe. The three following selections focus on specific aspects of the search for identity: one by a black Vincentian determined to redress the pro-European bias of the West Indian colored middle class; a second by a Trinidadian East Indian determined to resist the submergence of his own ethnic identity in a predominantly black West Indian world; a third by an eminent St. Lucian economist who deplores West Indian xenophobia and argues that the search for uniquely West Indian traits is a dead-end street. The West Indian identity crisis is next seen in the context of a specific contemporary event—black-power manifestations in Trinidad culminating in a 1970 mutiny of the armed forces. This story is examined in socioeconomic perspective by a local radical leader, followed in the next selection by an eloquent plea on behalf of a convicted ringleader in that mutiny, here portrayed as an idealistic dupe of a corrupt colonialist society. The following two articles graphically express the limits and ineffectiveness of protest in societies as small and poor as the West Indies: a Guyanese economist discounts his government's nationalization of the bauxite industry as mere window-dressing, and an internationally famous Trinidadian novelist views the West Indian black power movement as a theatrical substitute for reality. But a creativity that is uniquely West Indian plays a valuable role in local political and social life; in proof of this, an equally eminent Trinidadian political activist in the final selection acclaims the contributions of the most celebrated of contemporary calypsonians.

I FREEDOM AND POWER

1.

This essay by the Prime Minister of Trinidad and Tobago is a classic example of history in the service of politics. Delivered as a partisan tract, with characteristic West Indian invective, it sketches the transition from subjugation to freedom. Dr. Williams contrasts the colonial West Indies, dominated by a parasitic master class, with the new order in which the West Indian people, thanks to autonomy and responsible government, have in his view come into their own heritage. The extent to which political change has in fact affected underlying economic and social realities is an issue hotly debated in most of the essays in this volume.

DR. ERIC WILLIAMS is the epitome of the West Indian scholar-politician. After winning a prestigious Trinidad Government Scholarship, he took a First (in History) at Oxford, went on to teach at Howard University in Washington, D.C., and subsequently became the senior West Indian staff member of the Caribbean Commission, established the metropolitan countries to coordinate their various affairs in the West Indies. In 1956 he resigned to found and lead the People's National Movement, which has governed Trinidad for the past sixteen years. Dr. Williams has served as Pro-Chancellor of the University of the West Indies and is the author of numerous books, including *Capitalism and Slavery, British Historians and the West Indies, The History of the People of Trinidad and Tobago,* and *From Columbus to Castro.*

Massa Day Done
Eric Williams

On December 4, 1960, the *Trinidad Guardian* announced
that Sir Gerald Wight had joined the Democratic Labour
Party. The announcement was presented in such a way as
to suggest that this was a feather in the cap of the Democratic Labour Party, and therefore the citizens of Trinidad and Tobago should follow the lead of Sir Gerald
Wight. Consequently, in my address here in the University†
on December 22, in which I reported to the people the outcome of the Chaguaramas discussions in Tobago, I poured
scorn on the *Guardian*, reminding them that our population of today was far too alert and sophisticated to fall for
any such claptrap. I told the *Guardian* emphatically:
Massa Day Done. In other words it was the *Guardian* I
attacked for its slave mentality. But if Sir Gerald Wight
and his admirers thought that the cap fitted him too, that
was nothing over which I should lose any sleep.

The Scribes and Pharisees had a field day. Someone
wrote to the *Guardian* to say what a gentleman Sir Gerald
was, ever since he was a boy of eight on horseback. Another one wrote to say that Sir Gerald had got him a job.
Farquhar, that notorious sycophant, called my statement

*Massa Day Done: A Masterpiece of Political and Sociologi-
cal Analysis,* Port of Spain: P.N.M. Publication Co., 1961. Reprinted with permission of the author, Dr. Eric Williams.

† [Williams was referring to the "University of Woodford
Square," the name he gave to regular gatherings for speakers
and audiences in Woodford Square, Port-of-Spain.]

mischievous and accused me of responsibility for all the evils of Trinidad society which he, from his pulpit, had not been able to exorcise. Finally the DLP in a statement which appeared in the *Guardian* on March 5, 1961, called on me to withdraw what it called the wicked statement Massa Day Done, and to make an unqualified apology for introducing it.

I categorically refuse to withdraw my statement or to make any apology for it, qualified or unqualified. I repeat, more emphatically than when I said it the first time, Massa Day Done. I accuse the DLP of being the stooge of the Massas who still exist in our society. I accuse the DLP of deliberately trying to keep back social progress. I accuse the DLP of wanting to bring back Massa Day. Tonight I shall explain to you fully just what is meant when I say, Massa Day Done, and by the same token just what the DLP means and stands for when they not only object to the statement but even ask me to withdraw it.

This pack of benighted idiots, this band of obscurantist politicians, this unholy alliance of egregious individualists, who have nothing constructive to say, who babble week after week the same criticisms that we have lived through for five long years, who, nincompoops that they are, think that they can pick up any old book the day before a debate in the Legislative Council and can pull a fast one in the Council by leaving out the sentence or the paragraph or the pages which contradict their ignorant declamations —for people like these power is all that matters. They have not the slightest idea as to the constituents of progress in our society and the elements of our historical evolution. All that they can see in the slogan, Massa Day Done, is racial antagonism. This is characteristically stupid. Massa is not a racial term. Massa is the symbol of a bygone age. Massa Day is a social phenomenon: Massa Day Done connotes a political awakening and a social revolution.

What was Massa Day, the Massa Day that is done? Who is Massa?

Massa was more often than not an absentee European planter exploiting West Indian resources, both human and economic. I had particularly referred in my address in the University before Christmas to a book well-known to students of West Indian History written by an absentee English landlord who visited his plantations in Jamaica for the first time around 1815. The author's name was Matthew Lewis. He has written a Journal of his visits to Jamaica, and in my address I referred to one passage in the Journal when, as he went around the plantation, the slaves ran up to him with all sorts of complaints, saying "Massa this, Massa that, Massa the other". Massa lived in England off the profits of West Indian labour. He became a big shot and ostentatiously flaunted his wealth before the eyes of the people of England. He was a big noise in the House of Commons in the British Parliament. He could become a Lord Mayor of London. A famous play entitled "The West Indian", presented in Drury Lane in London in 1776, portrayed Massa as a very wealthy man who had enough sugar and rum to turn all the water of the Thames into rum punch. Massa's children were educated in England at the best schools and at the best universities, and it was openly and frequently claimed in the long period of the British controversy over the abolition of the slave trade and abolition of slavery that Oxford and Cambridge were filled with the sons of West Indian Massas. When things got bad and sugar ceased to be king in the West Indies, Massa simply pulled out of the West Indies, in much the same way as the descendants of Massa's slaves today pull out from the West Indies and migrate to the United Kingdom.

We have a record of one such Massa in the small poverty-stricken island of Nevis. He arrived in Nevis about 1680 with ten pounds, a quart of wine and a Bible. He developed into a big shot, became planter, merchant, and Legislator, and when things turned sour in the 19th century, he invested all his wealth derived from the West Indian soil and the West Indian people in railways and canals and harbours in Canada, India and Australia. He went back to live in the old County of Dorset in England from which his ancestors had migrated to the West Indies,

and his biographer tells us that today the same family occupies the same pew in the same church in the same village. What he does not tell us is that it was as if Massa
had never emigrated to the West Indies. Massa left behind
Nevis as under-developed as he had found it. The wealth
that should have been ploughed back into Nevis to save it
from its present disgrace of being a grant-aided Colony,
went to fertilise industrial development everywhere in the
world except in the West Indies. Today only a beach which
bears his name survives to remind us that this particular
Massa had ever existed in Nevis. His English biographer
tells us that it was as if he had never left his English
County. We tell him it is as if Massa had never been in
the West Indian Island.

On his West Indian sugar plantation Massa employed
unfree labour. He began with the labour of slaves from
Africa, and followed this with the labour of contract workers from Portugal and China and then from India. The
period of Massa's ascendancy, the period of Massa's domination over workers who had no rights under the law,
the period of Massa's enforcement of a barbarous code of
industrial relations long after it was repudiated by the conscience of the civilised world, lasted in our society for almost 300 years.

To his slave workers from Africa the symbol of Massa's
power was the whip, liberally applied; records exist showing that 200 lashes were not infrequent, and a tremendous
howl was raised by Massa when British law tried to step in
and limit punishment to 39 lashes under supervision. To
his contract workers from India the symbol of Massa's
power was the jail. Massa's slogan was: the Indian worker
is to be found either in the field or in the hospital or in jail.
For such trivial offences as leaving the plantation without
permission, being drunk at work, using obscene language,
encouraging his colleagues to strike, the Indian worker,
who was paid a legal wage of 25 cents per day, was sentenced to jail by the law of Trinidad and the law of British
Guiana where Indians were employed in large numbers.

Massa's economic programme was to grow sugar and

nothing but sugar. His table, one of the most glaring examples of gluttony that the world has ever known, was
almost entirely imported, and as a Brazilian sociologist, Gil-
berto Freyre, has emphasised in respect of that country, it
was the African slave who kept alive the real traditions of
agriculture in the West Indies and concentrated on the
production of food for his own subsistence. The Indian
contract worker went even further than the African slave,
and it was he who brought West Indian society to its present level in terms of the production of such essential
commodities as rice, milk and meat. Massa's economic programme represented the artificial stunting of West Indian
society, and a powerful Royal Commission sent out from
Britain to the West Indies in 1897 condemned the emphasis put on a single crop peculiarly vulnerable in the markets
of the world, attacked Massa for making it difficult for the
West Indian peasant to get land of his own on which to
grow food crops, and advised that there was no future for
the West Indies which did not put in the forefront of the
programme of economic development the settlement of
the landless labourers on the land as peasant owners.

Massa's day should have been done then. But it was
very easy in those days for Britain to ignore the recommendations of a Royal Commission and Massa was allowed to
perpetuate his uneconomic and anti-social activities until
1938 when another Commission from Britain, at the height
of the world depression, repeated the condemnation of the
1897 Commission almost in the identical language used by
its predecessors. Massa's long economic domination of the
West Indies reduced the population of the West Indies,
whether slave, contract or free, to the drudgery of the
simplest and most unedifying operations, almost unfitting
them totally for any intelligent agricultural activity, and
giving them a profound and almost permanent distaste for
agricultural endeavours.

Massa was able to do all of this because he had a monopoly of political power in the West Indies which he used
shamelessly for his private ends as only the DLP can be
expected to emulate in our more modern times. He used

this political power ruthlessly to import workers for his
sugar plantations with no respect either for elementary
economics of his time or of population problems of the
future. Massa's economy was distinguished by perhaps the
most scandalous waste of labour the history of the world
has ever known. Forty house slaves in a Jamaican slave
household was not unusual, and the domestic female slave
who carried the cushion for Massa to kneel on in church
in Surinam, or kept Massa's cigars lighted while he was
being shaved in Brazil, typifies not only Massa's total contempt for the human personality but also his pathological
unconcern with the most elementary considerations of cost
of production. It was the same with the Indian workers
brought in on contract. They were brought in without any
consideration whatsoever as to the supply that was really
needed, if any was needed at all, and a Commission from
the Government of India which visited the West Indies and
Surinam in 1915 condemned as an unwarranted waste of
labour the importation of four workers to do work which
would have been light labour for three.

Massa was able to do all this because he controlled political power in the West Indies and could use state funds
for his private gain. Whilst he imported African slaves
out of his own personal resources, he dug into the purse
of the West Indies Treasuries for public financing of Indian indentured migration to the tune of about one-third
of the total cost of introducing the workers. This went on
throughout the 19th century on Massa's insistence at the
very period when, as thousands of Indians came to Trinidad and British Guiana, thousands of Barbadians and
Jamaicans went to build the Panama Canal, or migrated
to the United States of America to do unskilled work, or
went to Cuba to work on the sugar plantations in that
Island.

As far as Massa was concerned this organisation of
West Indian economy, this dispensation of political power
was one of the eternal verities. He developed the necessary
philosophical rationalisation of this barbarous system. It
was that the workers, both African and Indian, were in-

ferior beings, unfit for self-government, unequal to their superior masters, permanently destined to a status of perpetual subordination, unable ever to achieve equality with Massa. It was there in all the laws which governed the West Indies for generations—the laws which denied equality on grounds of colour, the laws which forbade non-Europeans to enter certain occupations and professions, whether it was the occupation of jeweller or the profession of lawyer, the laws which forbade intermarriage, the laws which equated political power and the vote with ownership of land, the laws which, consciously or unconsciously, directly or indirectly, attempted to ensure that the non-European would never be anything but a worker in the social scale, the improvement of whose standard of living depended, as a British Secretary of State once told the workers in Jamaica in 1865, on their working on Massa's plantation for wages. That was why, when slavery was abolished in 1833, and Massa was afraid that the emancipated slaves would no longer accept the drudgery and exploitation of the slave plantation but would work for themselves on small plots, Massa in Barbados and Massa in British Guiana destroyed the gardens and food plots which the slaves had been permitted to cultivate during slavery in order to force them, out of the threat of starvation, to accept starvation wages on the plantations.

Massa was determined to use his political power for his own personal ends. He had no sense of loyalty to the community which he dominated or even to the community from which he had originally sprung. When Massa in Haiti found that the French Government was ready to abolish slavery he offered the island to England. When Massa in Jamaica found that the British were ready to abolish slavery he entered into conspiracy with planters in the southern States of America. When Massa in St. Croix in the Danish Virgin Islands found that it was too difficult to deal with the emancipated slaves, he tried to sell the island to the United States of America. When Massa in Cuba on his sugar plantation found himself confronted by a combination of abolitionist forces representing progressive metropolitan opinion, free white planters in Cuba growing tobacco and not sugar, and the slaves themselves, he too turned his eyes to the United States of America and plunged the country into civil war. When Massa in Jamaica in 1865 recognised that it was no longer possible to hold back the tide of constitution reform and deny the vote to the emancipated slaves, he brutally suppressed a revolt among the Jamaican workers and peasants and persuaded the British Government to suspend the self-governing Constitution of Jamaica and introduce the Crown Colony system. And when Massa in Barbados in the 1860's feared that West Indian federation might involve a large redistribution of his land among the workers of Barbados, Massa made official overtures for joining the Canadian Federation. Massa was always opposed to independence. He welcomed political dependence so long as it guaranteed the economic dependence of his workers. He was for self-government so long as it was self-government for Massa only and left him free to govern his workers as he pleased. Our whole struggle for self-government and independence, therefore, is a struggle for emancipation from Massa.

That was the West Indian Massa. There has been slavery and unfree labour in other societies. Ancient Greek society, precisely because of slavery, had been able to achieve intellectual heights that so far have had no parallel in human history. The ownership of a large slave empire in the West Indies did not prevent the flowering of intellect and the evolution of politics in the metropolitan countries of Europe. But the West Indian Massa constituted the most backward ruling class history has ever known. Massa in Jamaica had a contempt for education and the profession of teaching which scandalised even the commentators of the 18th century. A traveller in Haiti before its independence commented caustically on Massa's anti-intellectual outlook. He described the conversation of Massa as follows: It begins with the price of sugar and then goes on to the price of coffee, the price of cocoa, and the laziness of Negroes; and then it retraces the same ground beginning with the laziness of Negroes, and going on to the price of cocoa, the price of coffee and the price of sugar. Massa in Trinidad in the early 20th century asked sarcastically of what use would education be to the children of the plantation workers if they had it. He stated unambiguously in the Trinidad Legislative Council of 1925, in the age of Cipriani, that as long as Trinidad was to remain an agricultural country, the less education the children of the plantation workers had the better. As one of the abolitionists in the Colonial Office recognised a century and a quarter ago, there was no civilised society on earth so entirely destitute of learned leisure, literary and scientific intercourse and liberal recreations.

This was Massa Day. This was Massa—the owner of a West Indian sugar plantation, frequently an absentee, deliberately stunting all the economic potential of the society, dominating his defenceless workers by the threat of punishment or imprisonment, using his political power for the most selfish private ends, an uncultured man with an illiberal outlook.

But not every white man was a Massa. Las Casas, the Roman Catholic Bishop, condemned in Cuba, in Santo Domingo and in Mexico the iniquitous exploitation of the aborigines by the Spaniards. Thomas Clarkson, the humanitarian in England, and Victor Schoelcher, the radical politician in France, dedicated their entire lives to a relentless crusade against slavery. It was Clarkson who, 170 years ago, made one of the finest defences of the African against charges of inferiority, before modern sociological research and modern progressive ideas. It was Victor Schoelcher who provided the abolition programme in France in 1848 with the resounding peroration that the French Republic could not compromise with slavery and tarnish its immortal formula, "Liberty, Equality and Fraternity". It was the white Cuban philosopher, Luzy Cabellero, who coined the famous aphorism that "the blackest thing in slavery was not the black man." It was the white Cuban philosopher, José Martí, who educated Cuba in the view that man is more than white, more than Negro, more than mulatto. It was the white Spanish planters in Puerto

Rico who themselves demanded the emancipation of the slaves. It was a white Danish Governor who on his own initiative abolished slavery in St. Croix and returned home to be impeached for exceeding his instructions. It was the white Missionary, John Smith, who died in imprisonment in Massa's jail in British Guiana because he insisted on educating the Negroes and teaching them to read in order that they could read the Bible. It was the white Rev. William Knibb who organised in Falmouth, Jamaica, a tremendous movement against Massa and swore that he would not rest until he saw the end of slavery, and who, once slavery was abolished, spent the rest of his life in providing schools for the children and in trying to secure land for the people. It was the white Rev. James Phillips in Jamaica who, as far back as 1845, put forward proposals for the establishment of a University College in Jamaica which, if the British Government of the time had had the foresight to accept and to promote, would have changed the whole course of West Indian History in the past 100 years.

Here in Trinidad it was people like the Grants and Mortons who first undertook the education of the children of the Indian indentured workers on Massa's plantation. It was names like Lange which advocated the vote for Massa's workers. It was the Alcazars and the Stollmeyers among others in Trinidad who fought Massa on the question of Indian indenture; it was Sir Henry Alcazar who, in a memorable phrase in a memorandum to the Royal Commission of 1897, stated that the effect of Indian indenture was to keep the ruling class of Trinidad at the moral level of slave owners.

If Massa was generally white, but not all whites were Massa, at the same time not all Massas were white. The elite among the slaves were the house slaves. Always better treated than their colleagues in the field, they developed into a new caste in West Indian society, aping the fashion of their masters, wearing their cast-off clothing, and dancing the quadrille with the best of them. To such an extent did Massa's society penetrate the consciences of these people, that Haitian independence, which began with a fight for freedom for the slaves, ended up with a ridiculous imperial court of a Haitian despotism with its café-au-lait society and its titles, its Duke of Marmalade and its Count of Lemonade, exploiting the Negro peasants. The Maroons in Jamaica, runaway slaves who took refuge in the mountains from the horrors of the plantations and who became the spiritual ancestors of the Rastafarian movement of our time, after waging a successful war against Massa and forcing Massa to recognise their independence and to constitute them a veritable state within a state, accepted a peace treaty which required them to help Massa to put down any other slave rebellions. Emancipation of the slaves led in the smaller West Indian Islands to a gradual transfer of ownership of property to the point where, in such islands as Grenada and St. Vincent, whilst Massa remained, his complexion became darker.

This, then, was Massa in the West Indies. This was Massa Day.

The most savage condemnation of Massa in Trinidad came from the evidence of an Englishman who made Trinidad his home, Mr. Lechmere Guppy, Mayor of San Fernando, before the Royal Commission of the Franchise in 1889. Guppy related to the Commission a conversation between himself and a sugar planter with whom he had remonstrated about the condition of the houses provided for the Indian immigrants. "The people ought to be in the field all day", the planter said. "I do not build cottages for idlers". When the Mayor reminded him that there might be sickness or children or pregnant women, the planter answered, "Oh my dear Guppy, what do you talk to me about lying-in and nursing women; I only want working hands". To which Guppy retorted, "Then you will never have a settled population of labourers on your estates". "A settled population", said the planter: "I want two years of good crops and good prices, and then I will sell my estates and go to live in Europe".

Guppy voiced the growing national and liberal consciousness when he unsparingly criticised the Indian inden-

ture system as a selfish expedient pursued by a few Massas
to the detriment of the community at large. Their chief
aim by the policy, he emphasised, was to keep down the
rate of wages, to force down artificially the price of
labour and to confine it to the cultivation of the sugar cane.
This they did "by importing labourers at the public expense to be indentured to plantations; by taxing the necessary food of the labourer; and . . . refusing to grant
Crown lands to small settlers; by inequitable labour laws;
by encouraging the unjust administration of the laws by
Magistrates devoted to the wishes of the sugar planters; by
refusal of practicable roads other than those required to
convey the sugar planters' produce to the shipping place,
and minor means tending to the same end. During all this
time no men could be more grandiloquent about their intention, in all they proposed to do, being the development
of the resources of the island; no men could be more determined, as shown by their measures, to do no other thing
than bolster up the more or less nominal owners of sugar
plantations".

Life with Massa was summed up by me in a formal
statement I made to an international conference in Geneva
on October 20, 1955, when I acted as spokesman of the
International Confederation of Free Trade Unions at a
meeting of the Committee on Plantations of the International Labour Organisation. In my statement I concentrated particularly on a reply on sick pay for plantation
workers submitted by the Government of Trinidad and
Tobago through its representative at the Conference, Mr.
Albert Gomes. The reply of the Government of Trinidad
and Tobago was as follows: "The sugar employers do not
consider it possible to provide sick pay to plantation
workers".

My formal statement at the Geneva Conference on this
question reads as follows:

> Let me emphasise in some detail the significance of
> this statement from the Government of Trinidad in the
> light of the views which have been expressed from time

to time by the sugar employers of the Caribbean area on social questions and the conditions of the workers. I shall give some specific examples:

1. In 1896, the British Government appointed a Royal Commission of Inquiry to investigate the difficulties then being encountered by the British West Indian sugar industry. The principal sugar employer in Trinidad gave evidence before the Commission to the effect that the plantation workers could live comfortably on 5 cents a day.

2. In 1910, before another Royal Commission of the British Government, this time on the commercial relations between Canada and the British West Indies, Canadian manufacturers and Trinidad merchants and employers indicated how it was possible to subsist on this low wage. They stated that what was rejected as stockfeed in Canada, was imported into Trinidad as flour, which was bought up like hot cakes by the plantation workers.

3. In 1915, a Commission of the Government of India was sent to various Caribbean territories to investigate the conditions of the indentured Indian immigrants. The Commission reported that the protection of the plantation workers against malaria by providing mosquito nets and against hookworm by providing shoes, would only involve unnecessary expenses for the sugar employers.

4. In 1926, in Trinidad, in evidence before a committee of the Legislative Council on the restriction of hours of labour designed principally to prohibit the labour of children of school age during school periods, one of the principal sugar employers stated in the most emphatic way that if they educated the whole mass of the agricultural population, they would be deliberately ruining the country. After this he proceeded to ask, of what use would education be to the children, if they had it?

5. In 1930, on a visit to British Guiana, a well known British Philanthropist, a close friend of the late Mahatma Gandhi, was told unambiguously by one of the sugar employers that the London directors of his company would not provide any money for the elimination of the disgraceful workers' houses,

though they would readily spend money for the installation of new machinery.

6. A Commission of Inquiry, which investigated widespread disturbances in Trinidad in 1937, was advised that sugar employers thought it unnecessary to provide adequate sanitary facilities for their employees, because the workers would not use them.

7. In Barbados in the following year, one of the sugar employers assured the members of the commission of inquiry investigating similar disturbances in that island that the plantation worker in Barbados did not take milk in his tea because he did not like milk!

I just leave to your imagination the conditions which would prevail today in the British Caribbean territories if the views of the sugar employers had received the consideration which they thought should be attached to them.

The Second World War meant the end of Massa Day. Wendell Willkie, the unsuccessful Republican candidate in the 1940 American Presidential Election, issued a general warning in his book *One World,* written at the end of a world tour. Willkie warned the world:

Men and women all over the world are on the march, physically, intellectually, and spiritually. After centuries of ignorant and dull compliance, hundreds of millions of people in eastern Europe and Asia have opened the books. Old fears no longer frighten them. They are no longer willing to be Eastern slaves for Western profits. They are beginning to know that man's welfare throughout the world is interdependent. They are resolved, as we must be, that there is no more place for imperialism within their own society than in the society of nations. The big house on the hill surrounded by mud huts has lost its awesome charm.

They marched everywhere, during and after World War II—in India, in Burma, in Indonesia, in Nigeria, in Ghana, in the Philippines, in Puerto Rico, above all in the United

Kingdom. The counterpart of Massa in the West Indies was the squire in the United Kingdom. The welfare state has been super-imposed on the class society. The age of sweated labour in the factories has been abolished by the British trade unions. Oxford and Cambridge no longer serve exclusively the sons of the ruling class, and Parliament and the diplomatic service are no longer the exclusive preserve of their graduates. Massa Day Done in the United Kingdom too. Here is an advertisement from the *Observer*, one of London's principal Sunday papers, on February 12, 1961:

> BUSINESSES FOR SALE
> AND FROM KENYA, NIGERIA, CENTRAL AFRICA, MALAYA, INDIA and Other Corners of What Was 'The Empire' of Sahib, Boss And Master, come a host of sadly disillusioned one time 'Empire Builders' to face the necessity of providing home and income for self and family—And to this problem the most certain answer is the purchase of A Village Store with maybe an appointment as Sub-Postmaster, or the purchase of a 'Pub, Filling Station, Tea Room or some such business. There is no better thought.

Massa Day Done, Sahib Day Done, Yes Suh Boss Day Done. All decent American public opinion is nauseated by Little Rock. The horrors of the Congo, deplorable though they are, represent the struggle between Massa and Massa's former exploited subjects. Massa is on the run right now in Portuguese Angola. The pressure from India and Ghana, Malaya and Nigeria in the Commonwealth Prime Ministers' Conference has forced the South African Massa out of the Commonwealth.

Massa Day Done everywhere. How can anyone in his senses expect Massa Day to survive in Trinidad and Tobago? That, however, is precisely what Sinanan and the DLP stand for. Because for them to ask me to withdraw the statement, Massa Day Done, and, adding insult to injury, to demand that I apologise for it, is to identify themselves with all the forces of reaction which have been overthrown or are at bay in all the other countries of the world. What they seek, Sinanan and the DLP, is actually to restore Massa Day. For Massa Day Done in Trinidad and Tobago, too, since the advent of the PNM in 1956. Let us assess the position in Trinidad today.

Massa's racial complex stunted the economic development of our territories. Today, with the PNM, the cane-farmer, the small farmer growing cane, pitting his puny weight against the large plantation, is receiving a recognition that he never anticipated, and is coming into his own, a man with a stake in his country, with the legal right to refuse his labour if he wishes to and to work his own land. The sudden and dramatic growth of industry, producing fertilisers, furniture, milk, textiles, paints, cement and a hundred other essential commodities, is vastly different from the monoculture society of Massa Day. In Massa Day the West Indies produced what they did not consume and consumed what they did not produce. Today, under the PNM, the slogan is, "Made in Trinidad".

Massa stood for the degradation of West Indian labour. PNM stands for the dignity of West Indian labour. The symbol of Massa's authority was the whip, his incentive to labour was the lash. Today, with the PNM, the worker's right to establish trade unions of his own choice and to bargain collectively with his employers is recognised by all but the obscurantists who still regard Trinidad, as Massa did, as a place to which the ordinary conventions of human society ought not to apply. Massa passed laws to forbid non-Europeans from being jewellers or lawyers. Today, under the PNM, the right of the West Indian to occupy the highest positions in public and private employment is axiomatic and is being increasingly enforced.

Massa stood for colonialism: any sort of colonialism, so long as it was colonialism. Massa's sole concern was the presence of metropolitan troops and metropolitan battleships to assist him in putting down West Indian disorders. Today, with the PNM, those who were considered by Massa permanently unfitted for self-government, permanently reduced to a status of inferiority, are on the verge of full control of their internal affairs and on the threshold, in their federation, of national independence.

Massa believed in the inequality of races. Today, as never before, the PNM has held out to the population of Trinidad and Tobago and the West Indies and the world the vision and the practice of interracial solidarity which, whatever its limitations, whatever the efforts still needed to make it an ordinary convention of our society, stands out in sharp contrast as an open challenge to Massa's barbarous ideas and practices of racial domination.

Massa was determined not to educate his society. Massa was quite right; to educate is to emancipate. That is why the PNM, the army of liberation of Trinidad and the West Indies, has put education in the forefront of its programme. If Massa was entirely destitute of a liberal outlook and learned leisure, the PNM, come what may, will go down in history as the author of free secondary education and the architect of the University of Woodford Square.

The DLP statement of March 5 reflects the hostile forces which still exist in our society. There are still Massas. Massa still lives, with his backward ideas of the aristocracy of the skin. And Massa still has his stooges, who prefer to crawl on their bellies to Massa, absentee or resident, Massa this, Massa that, Massa the other, instead of holding their heads high and erect as befits a society which under the PNM is dedicated to the equality of opportunity and a career open to talent. Farquhar is one outstanding example of this contemptible backwardness and this slave mentality. The DLP is another. When they ask me to withdraw my banner, Massa Day Done, they are in fact telling the people of the West Indies that they want Massa to continue in social control, monopolising political power, stultifying economic development, disciplining the workers. They are in fact telling us that they are as much the stooges of the Massa of the 20th century as the house slaves were of Massa's 18th century counterpart.

We of the PNM, on the other hand, have been able to incorporate into our people's national movement people of all races and colours and from all walks of life, with the common bond of a national community dedicated to the pursuit of national ends without any special privilege being granted to race, colour, class, creed, national origin, or previous condition of servitude. Some of our most active and most loyal PNM members are indistinguishable in colour from our Massa. In recent weeks I, with several top leaders in the PNM, have had the opportunity to meet privately with many representatives of business and the professions in our community, and we have all been struck, notwithstanding a little grumbling here and a little dissatisfaction there, with the large reservoir of goodwill and admiration which the PNM is able to draw upon. You members of the PNM must understand once and for all that you misunderstand your Party and you do a great disservice to your national cause if you think that every white person or every Indian is anti-PNM or that every black person is pro-PNM. You shall know them not by their colour or their race but their fruit.

When, therefore, I categorically repudiate the DLP's impertinent suggestion that I should withdraw a historical analysis which is the product of more than 20 years of assiduous research on the problems of the West Indies in the context of the international community, I unhesitatingly condemn them for betraying, not for the first time and not for the last time, the vital interests of our national community. I accuse them of an intellectual dishonesty which is prepared to accept any bribe and to commit treason to their country in order to grasp political power for themselves. They serve to remind all of us here in the University, which like all reputable Universities must remain dedicated to the pursuit of truth and to the dispassionate discussions of public issues, of two important considerations which are fundamental in PNM's conception of the national community and in PNM's crusade for the interracial solidarity—first, not every white is Massa, second, not every Massa is white.

If Sinanan attacks me for the statement Massa Day Done, where then does Sinanan stand on the question of the canefarmers of Pointe-a-Pierre, Naparima and Caroni whom PNM has just recognised as a vital force in our society, these canefarmers of today who were Massa's indentured Indian workers yesterday? If Sinanan attacks me for the statement Massa Day Done, where then does Sinanan stand on PNM's programme of housing for sugar workers and canefarmers which has accelerated the elimination of the disgraceful barracks in which Massa housed his indentured Indian workers against all the invectives of the Englishman, Lechmere Guppy? If Sinanan attacks me for the statement Massa Day Done, where then does Sinanan stand in respect of the Indians who, as indentured workers, adopted the slave terminology of Massa and were forced into the social and economic status which Massa carried over from the regime of slavery?

I must ask Sinanan and the DLP to answer these questions in view of their alleged concern with the problem of the small farmers. The DLP has just published a plan for agriculture with the photograph of Stephen Maharaj; in it they ask for a sound credit system for farmers. Bryan and Richardson led last Saturday an agricultural demonstration from the Eastern Counties demanding aid for the farmers.

Let us recognise immediately the right of any group of people to demonstrate peacefully in our community. Let us recognise immediately that the agricultural demonstration was itself a tribute to the political awakening and the national spirit generated by PNM. But when all is said and done, the question remains: Who is the farmer these people have in mind? Massa? It is precisely Massa who has so far directed the operations of the Agricultural Credit Bank set up in 1945 and dominated the facilities extended by it to farmers. Here are some examples of the operations of that Bank:

1. A loan of $10,000 in 1955 for the development of cocoa and citrus; two years later it was ascertained that the estate had a large area in anthuriums, orchids, African violets and roses.
2. A loan of $25,000 in 1954 to pay off a bank over-

draft and for development; this was followed by
another loan for $35,000 a year later again to pay
off an overdraft.

3. A loan of $6,000 in 1955 to extend an estate
   dwelling house; the applicant already owed over
   $30,000 on two previous loans.
4. A loan of $43,500 in 1955 to an employee of the
   Bank to purchase an estate.
5. A loan of $13,000 in 1956 to purchase an estate
   which was sold two months later.
6. Loans of $50,000 and $68,000 in 1955 and 1956
   to a large planter who used the money in part to
   make payments to the press and the church, and
   to pay dividends, income tax and auditors' fees.
7. Loans of $150,000 in each of the years 1955 and
   1956 to a large industrial and commercial concern.

As against this emphasis on large scale agriculture and
the big planter who had sufficient security to approach an
ordinary commercial bank, the small farmers and agricultural societies were pushed into the background by the
Bank. The average loan made to farmers in this category
varied between $110 and $175 from 1950 to 1959. Thousands of dollars were left unutilised each year which could
have been allocated to small farmers. Small farmers waited
months and years for attention, whilst the big farmer was
attended to in a matter of days. One such large farmer,
who received a loan of $40,000 in August 1957, made his
application in July; there were several applications there
pending. A large loan of $26,000 was approved in two
months in 1956; a small loan of $600 took eleven months.

What is the explanation of this system? It is fourfold—(1)
the lack of any precise policy laid down by the Government for the guidance of the Bank; (2) the insufficient
liaison between the Bank and the Ministry of Agriculture,
which is the organ of Government responsible for agriculture in the country; (3) the composition of the Board
and staff of the Bank; (4) the latitude given to all such
statutory bodies to function in independence of the Government.

Bryan must have known all of this; if not, why did he not know? The PNM had to learn it. Yet Bryan did not one single thing to correct it. The PNM has had to take the necessary steps. First we transferred the Agricultural Credit Bank to the Ministry of Finance where, as a financial institution, it properly belongs. Second, as soon as the transfer had been effected, the Minister of Finance instituted an investigation into the operations of the Bank. Third, on the basis of that investigation, we proceeded recently to alter the composition of the Board of the Bank. Fourth, we are proceeding shortly to amend further the Ordinance governing the Bank to make available to it for loan purposes additional capital of $1¼ million provided in the Five Year Development Programme and to enable it to make loans to fishermen out of a sum of $500,000 earmarked in the Development Programme for this purpose. Finally, we have made available subsidies in many forms to the small farmers, and we are concentrating particularly on the prospects and problems in the world market for our export crops, whilst we have already taken large and positive steps to stimulate a greater production of local foodstuffs and fruits. A new market is now being built on the Beetham Highway to improve the distribution system, while, with the active encouragement of PNM's Government, a large new factory, Pacmarine, will shortly be in production on Wrightson Road canning local products and so providing an additional market for the farmers.

Bryan was Minister of Agriculture for six years and did none of these things. Now, as a member of the Federal House with not enough to do, he wants me to agree to a radio debate with him on agriculture. He had six years of radio time; now he wants a little lagniappe. Stephen Maharaj and Ashford Sinanan sat in the Legislative Council for six years before the PNM and did nothing to help the canefarmer or the cocoa farmer over whom they now shed crocodile tears. Richardson was a member of PNM General Council. Apart from lobbying to get a seat in a farming area, none of us in the General Council had any suspicion, either from his participation in the work of the

General Council or from his silly articles in the *Guardian*, that he had any affection for the farmers at all. Now he wants a Small Farmers' Association. Will he please tell the small farmers how much money he has been able to borrow from the Agricultural Credit Bank, so that they can compare the Bank's tenderness to a doctor of medicine doing part-time agriculture with its disregard of the genuine agriculturists of the country? To avoid all further misunderstanding on this question of credit, I shall publish forthwith the investigation of the Agricultural Credit Bank which I was, for various reasons, reluctant to make public. Then the small farmers will be able to judge for themselves.

Why this sudden recognition by Bryan, Richardson, Maharaj, Sinanan and DLP of the existence of the small farmer, when in years gone by they never uttered one single word of condemnation of the Bank's neglect of the small farmer? All that is left for them to do is to blame PNM for the fall in world prices. You know the explanation, Ladies and Gentlemen, as well as I. It is election year, and for guys like these, anything goes. They lack brains, perspective and principle. So they resort to confusion, intrigue and of course the *Guardian*, our old Public Enemy No. 1, whom we sent straight to hell on April 22, 1960.

It has recently been announced that the *Guardian* is to change hands and will hereafter form part of international chain. It is obviously impossible for us to anticipate the line of action that will be taken by the new Canadian owners. We can only wait and see. We note in the meantime that Monday's *Guardian* could find a lot of space for a report on the opening of a DLP office in Gasparillo on Sunday, no space at all for a PNM rally in Morne Diable on the same Sunday, and insufficient space for a truncated report of a monster PNM meeting in San Juan on Saturday night. We can only conclude that the explanation lies in the fact that the DLP function was attended by 125 persons (which no doubt explains the *Guardian's* photograph that suggested a death rather than a birth), while there were at least 5,000 present at PNM's Morne Diablo rally. Monday's *Evening News* reduces the estimated 8,000 at PNM's San Juan meeting to 1,250; I suppose the reporter got tired of counting. We note also that Gomes today writes on everything under the sun except PNM, that Farquhar did not appear last Sunday, that we have been spared for some Sundays Forrester's idiocies, and that the voice in the wilderness of Cassandra seems to have been strangely silent in recent weeks. We watch with interest to see how long the absurd review of the week's news will continue to disgrace the Sunday news. For the rest, as I have said, let us wait and see what the new Canadian ownership will produce. But whilst we wait and see, the danger of a press monopoly continues, with all the evils that that brings in its train even in the advance and diversified United Kingdom society, still more in Trinidad with its legacy of four and a half years of dishonest reporting, deplorably low intellectual standards, and partisan prostitution of freedom of the press. We shall continue our efforts to appraise and to counteract this monopolistic pattern. In these efforts our own Party organ, *The Nation,* has an important role to play as the intelligent voice of the national community, the trumpet of independence, the jealous protector of West Indian interests. In the impending revision of the Canada-West Indies Agreement of 1926, for example, whose side will the Canadian-owned *Guardian* take? The West Indies? or Canada? Now that the principal obstacle to a daily issue of *The Nation* has been removed from the scene, PNM has its own contribution to make to the promotion of political education through the press and to the maintenance of the press from monopolistic control.

Let the DLP know therefore that no amount of attacks on the PNM by Sinanan or the *Guardian* will in any way stop the onward march to national independence and community dignity. No amount of stabs in the back from PNM renegades will stop us either. After all, as a new party, nine months old when we won the 1956 elections, faced with ever-increasing pressures in four and a half years in power as a Government, it was inevitable that scamps and vagabonds and individualists should hop on the band waggon and seek to corrupt the party for their personal ends. We are now finding out those who pretended to support us on Chaguaramas because they thought we would not succeed in our declared policy to tear up the 1941 Agreement. They applauded loudly when I said that I would break the Chaguaramas problem or the Chaguaramas problem would break me; they saw me broken already. Now that I have broken the problem, lo and behold, all the scavenger birds of the PNM suddenly suggest that I have changed my direction and they don't like us West of the Iron Curtain. All those who see in Castro a precedent for a few persons lusting for power to take control suddenly begin to attack us for not emulating Castro; they forget we took power peacefully and did not take it from a fascist dictatorship. All such who wish to confuse, who seek to climb on PNM's backs to achieve their own mental aberrations, who want to abuse me because I refuse to condone corruption in any quarter, all these imps of Satan will be dealt with in due course. C.L.R. James' case has been sent to our Disciplinary Committee for action; when, it is no longer *sub judice* I shall deal with it fully and publicly, and with all those who seek to use him in their struggle to defeat the PNM and to destroy me.

We go on our way, confident and undaunted. We stand here tonight, we the PNM enormously proud of the confidence the vast majority of the people have in us. We have seen it recently for ourselves, in Tunapuna, in Fyzabad, in Point Fortin, in Princes Town, in Sangre Grande, in San Juan, and on Sunday in Morne Diable. If the people wish to abandon that confidence in us, because they don't have a secondary school in Fyzabad, because they don't have price supports in Sangre Grande, because they don't have rental mortgage houses in Princes Town, because they have a dirty drain in San Juan, because the oil companies are reducing their labour force in Point Fortin; if the people want to sell their identification cards to the enemy, or refuse to take their photographs because they have to go to a fete or play cricket or wappie, or can't be bothered to vote, if the people want to sell themselves back into the slavery from which PNM has emancipated them; if the people prefer Massa to PNM—then they have the democratic right to make a history that will be unique in the world. History is full of instances where slave owners restore or try to restore slavery. I know of no instance when the slaves themselves, once emancipated, return voluntarily to their former chains.

If you wish to do that, Ladies and Gentlemen, you must do it without the PNM, certainly without me. We shall continue on the road of national dignity and national independence. It is we of the PNM who brought the United States Government to you to renegotiate in Tobago a treaty negotiated for you in London twenty years ago. It is we of the PNM who gave you your flag and ran it up at Chaguaramas to do the "saga ting" everyday in the breeze. It is we of the PNM who will shortly renegotiate the basis of your relations with Venezuela with a view to removing the discrimination against you that is sixty years old. It is we of the PNM who brought the Secretary of State for the Colonies for the first time in your midst to appreciate at first hand that the future destiny of the West Indies depends on you. With the new Agreement on Chaguaramas, we of the PNM have even been able to welcome Sir Winston Churchill to Trinidad. It is we of the PNM who will take the United Kingdom Prime Minister around when he comes on Friday on his historic visit, and I hope hundreds of you will be at Piarco to welcome him. It is we of the PNM who will show him around some of our development projects, who will take him to Chaguaramas, who will take the lead in making representations to him in respect of West Indian migration to the United Kingdom, protection for West Indian products and economic aid to the West Indies, in order to assure economic stability as the foundation of our political democracy.

It is only left now for Her Majesty the Queen to visit us. After all we are an important part of the Commonwealth, and if Her Majesty can go to Australia, to India and to Pakistan, to Nigeria and to Ghana, she can come also to the West Indies. There will shortly be an appropriate occasion for so distinguished a visit. Her Majesty's sister, Princess Margaret, inaugurated the Federal Parliament on April 22, 1958. The Federation will arrange for its independence at a conference in London scheduled to begin on May 31. I now publicly propose that Her Majesty the Queen be invited to inaugurate the first Parliament of the Independent West Indies on April 22, 1962, at 11 o'clock in the morning.

And so we stand ready to meet the challenge of this year's election. The challenger calls himself the DLP but he goes under many aliases and has no fixed abode. He stands for nothing in particular; he poses as the champion of labour and the small farmer but worships at the shrine of Massa. He has been repudiated by Britain and America and the *Guardian* has sold out under him. He has offices but no party. Like ancient Gaul, he is divided into three parts.

Defending our title is the PNM, the party of principle and not of wealth, the party of the people and not of Massa, the voice of the national consciousness and not of individual or sectional privilege, the mass movement of the national community and not the divisive tendency of an unassimilated splinter group. With our new electoral procedure we eliminate corruption, protect the living from the dead, identify the individual, and ensure free, honest and unperverted elections. With our free secondary education we safeguard equality of opportunity and a career open to talent.

With the University of Woodford Square in the lead, we have called upon the many rather than the few for financial assistance for our cause, to enable the Party as such not the individual candidate to finance the election campaign. By so doing we ensure greater discipline of and control over the elected representatives. The population is contributing magnificently. I have here with me tonight a dollar turned over to Dr. Solomon as a contribution to our Public Appeal for Funds by a young man, a member of the PNM, who was given it by an Opposition Member whom he assisted with changing a flat tyre in the early hours of one morning after a late sitting of the Legislative Council. Once again therefore, tonight, our Women's League will, with the permission of the Police, solicit your contribution in our official receptacles. Tonight of all nights I call on you to help us, for tonight of all nights Massa Day Done.

And so we proceed to the election bearing aloft proudly our banner of interracial solidarity, with the slogan inscribed thereon, Massa Day Done, and below it the immortal words of Abraham Lincoln who dealt Massa in the United States of America a mortal blow:

With malice toward none; with charity for all; with firmness in the right, as God gives us to see the right, let us strive on to finish the work we are in.

2.

The British Caribbean territories achieved self-government piecemeal and over a long period of time. Since the First World War, in stages outlined in this essay, the colonies have gained broader suffrage, more elected representatives in their legislatures, and greater local autonomy. The rise of West Indian trade unionism and labor unrest in the 1930s, followed by the cataclysm of the Second World War, measurably hastened the process. Most present West Indian leaders were born and schooled during this period, when a small number of nationalists exerted constant anti-colonial pressure but before popular feeling had crystallized into mass political action.

JESSE HARRIS PROCTOR, JR., is an American political scientist with degrees from Duke University, the Fletcher School of Law and Diplomacy, and Harvard University. He is presently Professor and Director of Graduate Studies in Political Science at Duke University, Durham, North Carolina.

British West Indian Society and Government in Transition 1920–60
Jesse Harris Proctor, Jr.

There are two principal aspects of the constitutional development of the British West Indies during the period from 1920–60: the advance toward self-government and the achievement of federation. Each is related not only to the other but also to the changes in society which were taking place during these years.

By 1960 each territory had attained "internal self-government" or was only a step away from it, and all the islands except the British Virgins were united into The West Indies Federation which stood on the threshold of independence.

Four decades earlier, the only inter-territorial constitutional links were those which bound Antigua, St. Kitts-Nevis, Dominica, Montserrat and the Virgin Islands into the unpopular Leeward Islands Federation, and those which associated the Windward Islands of Grenada, St. Lucia and St. Vincent under a common governor.

At that time the "pure" Crown Colony system prevailed generally. In most of the islands there were unicameral legislatures which contained a majority of official members, controlled by the governor, and a few unofficials nominated by him. British Honduras varied from this pattern in having an unofficial majority.

Only three of the colonies had elected members in their

Social and Economic Studies, Vol. II, No. 4, December 1962, pp. 273–304. Reprinted with permission of the author and the Institute of Social and Economic Research, University of the West Indies.

legislatures, and these were chosen on the basis of a restricted franchise in elections which attracted little interest. There were fourteen elected members in the Legislative Council of Jamaica, but they were outnumbered by the official and nominated members who voted together when asked to do so by the governor. These elected members did possess a limited negative power, for opposition by any nine of them on financial matters or by all of them on any other question could be overcome only if the governor declared the decision to be "of paramount importance to the public interest." In Barbados alone the Old Representative System still survived; there was to be found a bicameral legislature with an entirely elected House of Assembly and a nominated Legislative Council. The elected element wielded a more effective veto here than in Jamaica since the governor possessed no reserve power to override its opposition, but money bills could be initiated only by the Executive Committee and the Assembly could not secure the enactment of measures it favoured without the approval of the Legislative Council and the governor. British Guiana had a unique system with two partially elected legislative bodies, neither of which contained nominated unofficial members. The Court of Policy, which had power over non-financial matters, contained a majority of officials which could be thwarted, however, if seven of the eight elected members absented themselves and thus prevented a quorum. The Combined Court had an elected majority in which resided the power to raise and appropriate money so long as they did not increase the estimates prepared by the Governor in Executive Council. The governor did not possess reserve powers, but the initiation of all money votes and legislation was vested in him.

Everywhere the executive bodies contained an official majority and were responsible to the Crown. Only in Barbados were elected legislators required to be included, but there they were in a minority and were not responsible to the Assembly.[1]

[1] For a detailed discussion of the constitutions at this time, see H. Hume Wrong, *Government of the West Indies* (Oxford: Clarendon Press, 1923).

The transition from this constitutional order to that existing in 1960 was accomplished in an evolutionary fashion, as the colonies progressed through a complex series of intermediate stages. Gradually the proportion of elected members in the legislatures was enlarged, the qualifications for voters and candidates were lowered, the elected element in the executive councils was strengthened both in numbers and authority, the power of the officials was reduced, and the executives became increasingly responsible to the legislatures. The general trend was clearly toward the British model of cabinet government, but the rate of advance varied and in one case there was a temporary retrogression. The detailed features of each stage were not precisely the same for all.[2] These variations in pace and form reflected in large measure differences in the social environment. There seemed to be a deliberate effort on the part of the United Kingdom to correlate constitutional development with social change, to grant political concessions when the particular local society seemed ripe for such an advance.

The creation of a federal government involved reaching agreement first on the principle of federation and, then, on the provisions of the federal constitution. This, too, was an evolutionary movement, for the sentiment in favour of federation grew gradually over the years and the constitutional draft had to be significantly revised twice before

[2] For comparative studies of these developments, see Morley Ayearst, *The British West Indies: The Search for Self-Government* (London: Allen and Unwin, 1960); Ronald V. Sires, "Government in the British West Indies: An Historical Outline," *Social and Economic Studies,* Vol. 6 (June 1957), pp. 109–32; C. M. MacInnes, "Constitutional Development of the British West Indies," in *Developments Towards Self-Government in the Caribbean* (The Hague: W. van Hoeve, 1955), pp. 3–19; E. W. Evans, "A Survey of the Present Constitutional Situation in the British West Indies," *ibid.,* pp. 23–31; Colin A. Hughes, "Power and Responsibility: A Sociological Analysis of the Political Situation in the British West Indies," *ibid.,* pp. 95–107; Colin A. Hughes, "Semi-responsible Government in the British West Indies," *Political Science Quarterly,* Vol. 68 (September 1953), pp. 338–53.

being finally accepted.[3] Neither the West Indian reaction
to the idea of federation nor the form of the constitution
itself can be understood without reference to the changing
social environment in which these developments occurred.

There were signs of growing discontent with the constitutional order during the early 1920's, particularly among
the small coloured middle class which was then emerging.
Representative Government Associations sprang up throughout the area in the immediate post-war period, often under
the leadership of returning servicemen, to press for the
addition to the legislatures of members elected on a limited
franchise, and for federation. They organized public meetings and prepared petitions to the Colonial Office which
were supported to some extent by the submerged black
working class, although most of the latter remained rather
apathetic. The predominantly white upper class was generally not in favour of such changes for they enjoyed
political supremacy under the existing system due to their
close contacts with officials and their hold over the nominated seats, which were generally occupied by lawyers,
businessmen and planters who were white or who sought
to identify themselves with the élite.

In response to the demand for reform, the Parliamentary
Under Secretary of State for the Colonies, E. F. L. Wood
(later Lord Halifax) was dispatched to the Caribbean at
the end of 1921 to make a comprehensive investigation
and to formulate policy recommendations.

His proposals, which were to serve as a guide to constitutional development during the inter-war period, ap-

[3] For surveys of the federal movement, see Lloyd Braith-
waite, "Progress towards Federation, 1938–1956," *Social and
Economic Studies,* Vol. 6 (June 1957), pp. 133–84; S. S.
Ramphal, "The West Indies—Constitutional Background to Federation," *Public Law* (Summer 1959), pp. 128–51; J. H. Proctor, Jr., "The Development of the Idea of Federation of the
British Caribbean Territories," *Revista de Historia de America,*
No. 39 (June 1955), pp. 61–105; J. H. Proctor, Jr., "The Framing of the West Indian Federal Constitution: An Adventure
in National Self-Determination," *ibid.,* Nos. 57–58 (Jan.–Dec.
1964), pp. 51–119.

peared to be based primarily upon his assessment of social conditions in the area.

Responsible government he regarded as altogether out of the question within the foreseeable future, not only because there was as yet no demand for it, but also because West Indian society was of such a nature as to make it too hazardous. He was impressed by the sharp divisions in the population along lines of colour and religion and by the fact that substantial sections were "backward and politically undeveloped."[4] The level of education was so low and interest in politics was so little diffused that only a small proportion of the electorate could be expected to exercise the franchise. The absence of a class with sufficient leisure to be politically active meant that responsible government might well only open the way to the establishment in power of "a financial oligarchy" which would proceed to promote its narrow class interest. There did not yet exist leadership of sufficient "impartiality or integrity" to which the Crown could in good conscience relinquish its responsibility. The chief burden of government must therefore continue to be borne by officials who possessed the necessary detachment. Thus there did not seem to him to be sufficient change in the West Indian social order to render invalid the classic defence of the Crown Colony system.

He was favourably disposed to the idea of introducing a degree of representative government, however, and accordingly proposed that a few members of the legislative council should be chosen by direct election in Grenada (where such an advance had recently been approved), St. Vincent, St. Lucia, Trinidad and Tobago and possibly Dominica. Room for such new elected members should be made by reducing the number of nominated unofficials. The officials must remain in the majority so that the governor would have the votes to override the unanimous

[4] "Report by the Hon. E. F. L. Wood on his Visit to the West Indies and British Guiana (December 1921–February 1922)," Great Britain, *Parliamentary Papers*, Cmd. 1679, 1922, p. 7.

objection of the unofficials when necessary to enact those measures which he considered essential to sound administration. Mr. Wood did recommend, however, that when faced with such unanimous opposition, the governor should delay implementing the measure until it had been referred to the Secretary of State.

Such modest concessions were favoured partly because of his belief that the demand for elected representation would prove ultimately irresistable. He considered its strength to be presently much less than might be suggested by the mass meetings (for many attended these without really understanding what was at issue), but he predicted that it would grow substantially because the spread of education had produced a coloured and black intelligentsia whose democratic sentiments had been stimulated by the war and by travel abroad and who were now prepared to engage in propaganda among the people.

A further reason for recommending such reform now was that there were among the coloured element "not a few individuals of somewhat exceptional capacity and intelligence, who play a prominent part in the public life of their communities."[5] He evidently felt that the coloured middle class had now developed to such an extent that it would make good use of the opportunities provided by the addition of a few elected seats, and the partially representative institutions would not rest on too narrow a social basis.

Mr. Wood was not prepared to recommend such changes at this time for Antigua, St. Kitts-Nevis, and Montserrat where he felt that the social foundations for the healthy growth of representative government did not yet exist. There was strong opposition to the introduction of the elective principle in those islands on the part of the large planters and most prominent merchants. This he attributed to a more pronounced class cleavage which resulted from the existence of great sugar estates and a numerous agrarian proletariat, in contrast to the large

[5] *Ibid.*, p. 6.

number of small holdings and peasant proprietors in the Windward Islands and Dominica. He was rather reluctant to recommend such concessions for Dominica, however, because of the high degree of illiteracy, the primitive state of internal communications, and the fear that the demand for the same advance would be stimulated in the other Leeward Islands.

Social conditions in Trinidad were said to be such as to make the problem of representative government more difficult there than elsewhere. Its population was exceptionally cosmopolitan and the East Indians, who constituted about 36 per cent of the total, were not effectively integrated. "Socially it is divided into all kinds of groups which have very few relations with one another," he reported.[6] Although change was opposed by the Chamber of Commerce, the Agricultural Society, and some of the East Indians, all of whom argued that the system of nomination was necessary to safeguard their interests, the majority seemed to favour some representation, and Wood was impressed by the argument that education was rapidly expanding and that "the existence of a considerable class of peasant owners afforded a guarantee of stability." He therefore included it in the group for which new constitutions were proposed.

These islands, he suggested, would eventually advance to the next stage of constitutional development at which the elected and nominated members together would hold a majority of seats in the legislature, but the electeds alone would remain in the minority. He considered it likely that the officials would be voluntarily supported by the nominated members since they would be representing "the responsible element in the community"[7] but the governor should be empowered to enact measures essential to good government with the votes of the official minority alone to assure the necessary control by the Crown.

Jamaica, which already had an unofficial majority, now seemed to him ready for a more advanced type of con-

[6] *Ibid.*, p. 23.
[7] *Ibid.*, p. 8.

stitutional structure. Interest in politics was more widespread there than elsewhere, the press was more efficient,
the electorate consisted primarily of coloured or black
smallholders, and the elected members had behaved re-
sponsibly. There he proposed that the number of officials
in the legislature be reduced so as to place the elected
members in a majority. Moreover, the complete liberty of
nominated unofficials to vote as they liked should be definitely established. This would free them of the "stigma"
that they were merely "dummies" of the governor, and
should make it possible to secure the services of better
men for these positions. Power would have to be reserved
to the governor, however, to secure the passage of a bill
essential to the good government of the colony even if
supported only by the officials. In an effort to give the
elected legislators a sense of responsibility, he proposed
that a minority of them be included in a new advisory
executive council and that the governor be directed to
refer a bill opposed by all the elected members to the
Secretary of State for decision. Such an advanced constitution might possibly be anticipated for the other territories in the future, he suggested; but he warned that
"the conditions of Jamaica may be said to be exceptional,
and proposals to meet those conditions may not necessarily
be the best for universal application."[8]

Wood envisaged, then, a cautious constitutional advance
over an indefinitely prolonged period during which deli-
cate adjustments would be made in the composition of the
legislatures and eventually of the executive as well, in
response to appropriate changes in society, but with Crown
control of the governments remaining complete.

As for federation, he concluded that it would be advantageous but that the difficulties in its way were such
as to make it impracticable. Some of the obstacles which
he cited were social in character, particularly the absence
of any real desire for it and the strong "centrifugal tendency" which was deeply rooted in the "astonishing di-

[8] *Ibid.*, p. 9.

versity of . . . language, religion and historical tradition" as well as patterns of land tenure.[9] He therefore felt that "the establishment of West Indian political unity is likely to be a plant of slow and tender growth"[10] and that a move by Britain toward federation at present would only prejudice the development of that local demand which would be essential for its success. He could recommend merely that consideration be given to the early association of the Windward Islands and Trinidad and Tobago under a common governor.

At the request of the Secretary of State, the governors of those islands explored that proposal with their unofficial legislators and with each other, but they concluded that local conditions were such that it could not possibly be introduced for several years, and the idea was dropped.

The Wood proposals concerning the reform of the unit constitutions fared better. Provision was made in 1924 for the addition to the legislative councils of Trinidad and Tobago, the Windward Islands, and Dominica of members elected on the basis of a restricted franchise, the official majority being retained. The representative element was not strengthened in Jamaica, but the nominated members there were encouraged to assert their independence.

No change in the constitution of British Guiana had been recommended by Mr. Wood, but in the years following his visit that system became almost unworkable as the Government increasingly encountered opposition on the part of the elected members which it was unable to overcome. Such a development resulted in part at least from the growth of the coloured middle class element in the legislature due to the extension of the franchise and the rising political consciousness of the coloured and black population. In 1928, therefore, the old constitution was abolished, and a Crown Colony type of legislative council was created with nominated unofficials and elected members together constituting a majority over the officials but with the elected members in the minority. The governor

[9] *Ibid.,* p. 31.
[10] *Ibid.,* p. 32.

in executive council was given the power to certify the enactment of bills rejected by the legislature.

Such changes were recommended by a commission appointed by the Secretary of State as appropriate for the kind of society which now existed in British Guiana. It reported that the population consisted of "a congeries of races from all parts of the world, with different instincts, different standards, and different interests," the great majority of whom were "too indifferent or too ignorant to exercise their political rights."[11] Elections provided such inadequate representation for certain sections of the community, particularly "the small but extremely important European class which still controls the principal agricultural and commercial activities of the Colony"[12] and the agricultural population, that nominated seats should be added for their benefit. The elected members of the Combined Court protested that such changes would place the colony once more under the control of the plantocracy.[13]

This was a constitutional change similar in some respects to that experienced by the islands during the nineteenth century, but the protection of Crown Colony government was now invoked for a different element of the population. Its effect was to bring British Guiana into line with the pattern which now prevailed everywhere except Barbados, and to start it up the same ladder the others were climbing. The Governor, Sir Cecil Rodwell, argued that the old constitution did not offer a path to political advance. "They were really in a *cul de sac*," he said, "and it would be better to back out and enter the main road to responsible government through the various degrees of Crown Colony government."[14]

[11] "Report of the British Guiana Commission (April 1927)," Great Britain, *Parliamentary Papers,* Cmd. 2841, 1927, pp. 8, 51.

[12] *Ibid.,* p. 55.

[13] "Memorandum Prepared by the Elected Members of the Combined Court of British Guiana in reply to the Report of the British Guiana Commission," Great Britain, *Parliamentary Papers,* Cmd. 3047, 1928.

[14] Quoted in Sir Cecil Clementi, *A Constitutional History of British Guiana* (London: Macmillan, 1937), p. 397.

Meanwhile, it had become apparent that the advocates of representative government in the Lesser Antilles were not satisfied with their new constitutions. Elected legislators were for the most part coloured, moderate representatives of middle-class opinion who found the permanent official majority available to the governor quite frustrating. Little comfort could be derived from the fact that the governor was required to report the matter to the Secretary of State when his majority was opposed by all the unofficials or from the fact that Governments sometimes dropped or revised measures which encountered such opposition, for the nominated members were not often inclined to vote solidly with the elected element. The new representatives could only offer advice, and there was no assurance that it would be accepted. They demanded therefore that more, if not all, of the nominated legislators should be replaced by elected members and that there should be at least an unofficial majority in the legislatures.

There were also indications of growing interest in federation. The unofficial members of the executive and legislative councils in Antigua petitioned the Colonial Office in 1929 to combine Trinidad and Tobago, the Windwards and the Leewards under one governor and legislature, and the following year the unofficial legislators in Grenada and Dominica pressed for the union of the Leeward and Windward Islands.

The Secretary of State was prompted by these developments, as well as by representations from officials in the West Indies and members of Parliament, to send Sir Charles Fergusson and Sir Charles Orr to the Caribbean in 1932 to examine the possibilities of closer union between Trinidad and Tobago, the Windward Islands and the Leeward Islands.

To formulate an agreed policy for presentation to this commission, seventeen unofficial legislators and other political leaders from Trinidad, Barbados, Grenada, St. Vincent, St. Lucia, Montserrat, Antigua, St. Kitts-Nevis and Dominica met at Roseau, Dominica, for a six-day conference beginning on October 28, 1932. They agreed that the federation of all the islands represented should be effected, and proceeded to draft and approve a set of constitutional proposals. These provided for a unicameral legislature composed of twenty-seven elected members and six officials, the former being chosen annually by and from the elected members of the island legislatures; an executive council consisting of the governor-general, three officials, and six members elected by and from the federal legislature and responsible to it; and a governor-general who would act upon the advice of the executive council. As for the island constitutions, the conference agreed that the nominated element should disappear from the legislatures and that the number of elected members should be increased so as to give them a majority. In case of a conflict between the Government and the legislature on a matter of primary importance, the issue should be referred to the governor-general. Finally, they proposed that a finance committee should be appointed by each legislature to assist in the preparation of estimates and money votes.[15]

A. A. Cipriani, representing the Trinidad Workingmen's Association which consisted, he said, mainly of "barefooted men," urged that the conference go on record in favour of universal suffrage, but the moderate, middle-class orientation of the others was reflected in their opposition to this idea, and a compromise was reached according to which the definition of the franchise would be left to each local legislature. What they seemed to want was essentially more middle-class representation in the legislatures.

The Fergusson-Orr Commission spent three months in the area in an effort to ascertain local opinion regarding closer union, but they found that most witnesses wished to discuss reform of the island constitutions. Many of them clamoured for a larger voice in the management of their own affairs and complained about the extent to which local opinion was overridden by the official vote, while others were opposed to any change.

The commission concluded that a combined system of

[15] The West Indian Conference, Roseau, Dominica, B.W.I., October–November 1932, *Proceedings* (Castries: Voice Printery, n.d.).

nomination and election was "best suited to present conditions."[16] Elected members should now be introduced into the legislatures of Antigua, St. Kitts-Nevis and Montserrat, lest the mass of the people remain politically apathetic there; but nominated members should be retained everywhere to secure the services of well qualified men who would not be willing to stand for election and to guarantee representation of those interests which might not secure seats through the elective process. The number of nominated members might be reduced in some cases, they suggested. The proportion should vary according to local conditions, being lower where there had been more experience with elections and where "political consciousness" was more developed. Everywhere the nominated member should be entirely free to vote as he wished.

It was also proposed by this commission that the number of officials in the legislatures be reduced to three or four, leaving an unofficial majority. The necessary control could be maintained by authorizing the governor to certify the enactment of measures declared by him to be "necessary in the public interest" over the objection of a majority, subject to approval by the Secretary of State. This would be "more straightforward" than relying upon an official majority in such cases, and would free the officials to devote more time to their departmental duties.[17]

The slightly more liberal franchise which existed in Dominica should be extended to the other islands in the Leeward and Windward groups, but universal suffrage should not be introduced until the level of education had been greatly improved, for the masses were presently unfit to judge political issues and demagogues might come to power.

As for the executive councils, the commission considered retention of the official majority essential, but proposed a

[16] "Report of the Closer Union Commission (Leeward Islands, Windward Islands, Trinidad and Tobago) (April 1933)," Great Britain, *Parliamentary Papers*, Cmd. 4383, 1932–33, p. 17.

[17] *Ibid.*, p. 19.

substantial increase in the number of unofficials chosen by the governor so that the local community could participate as much as possible in the framing of policy. It was hoped that this would engender a "sense of responsibility" and a more co-operative attitude on the part of the people, especially since some of the unofficials might be chosen from the legislature.[18]

These islands seemed no more ripe for federation to Fergusson and Orr now than they had to Wood eleven years previously. They, too, were impressed by the "deep-seated differences" in religion, language and "mental outlook" as well as in geography, economy, and history. They stated:

> Each cherishes its own individuality, the product of its history and traditions . . . To discover a common denominator is a baffling problem. With these differences in view it is small wonder that each community is interested solely in its own affairs and pays scant attention to those of its neighbour.[19]

It was true that the islands "pay lip-service to the general idea of federation," but little real enthusiasm was found for it except in Dominica, and it was clear that such a union would be acceptable only if it produced economy in administration and did not threaten the "individuality" of each unit. There was strong opposition to the idea in Trinidad not only because of the fear that it would involve a financial burden, but also because "in the curious amalgam of races which comprises its population, of which East Indians form a third, it has its own problems, and requires time to settle down into a co-ordinate community."[20]

A "real federation" of the Leeward and Windward Islands was also impracticable because of difficulties of communication among them and because they were quite

18 *Ibid.*, p. 13.
19 *Ibid.*, p. 3.
20 *Ibid.*, p. 6.

unwilling to relinquish control over tariffs or to pool their
customs receipts. The commission could therefore recommend for those two groups only a common governor who
should convene annual advisory conferences of delegates
from each unit to discuss matters of common concern. It
hoped that from such a foundation there might eventually
grow a West Indian federation.

Discussions of this proposal in the West Indian legislatures as well as outside the council chambers revealed considerable opposition primarily on account of the estimated
costs, and the Secretary of State concluded that it would
not be practicable to press it.

The proposals for the reform of the island constitutions
were implemented within the next few years, however. By
1936 provision had been made for the introduction of
elected members into the legislatures of Antigua, St. Kitts-
Nevis and Montserrat, as well as British Honduras. The
franchise was generally patterned after that existing in
Dominica. The official and nominated members were reduced so as to establish an unofficial majority but
an elected minority, thus enabling these territories to skip
the first stage of constitutional advance proposed by Mr.
Wood and proceed directly to semi-representative government. Simultaneously, elected members were increased and
the officials reduced in Dominica and the Windward Islands so as to give them the same status.

With the passing of the official majority in the legislative
councils, the governors gained reserve legislative powers.
Decisions would be left to the elected and nominated majorities as far as possible, but the governors remained able
to secure the enactment of bills which they considered to
be in the interests of public order and good government
against their unanimous opposition.

Meanwhile, as constitutional evolution thus proceeded
rather leisurely, social changes were taking place which
resulted in a series of "disturbances" throughout the area
during the years from 1934 to 1939. These strikes and riots,
which frequently involved the violent destruction of lives

and property, were to mark a major turning point in the history of the British West Indies.

The upheaval seemed to represent essentially a protest on the part of the black lower classes against their living and working conditions. They had, of course, long lived in poverty; but their situation had worsened recently as a consequence of the rise in unemployment and underemployment, which resulted from the fall in the world prices for West Indian exports, and of the sharp increase in the rate of population growth after 1921 due to declining mortality. There had also been a marked increase in urbanization recently. Many of the unemployed drifted to the towns where they were often unable to find work or decent housing and where they, as well as other new townspeople, became more acutely aware of the disparity between their standard of living and that of others. A further explosive element was the substantial number of returning emigrants who had been forced to come back home from the United States or Latin America by the depression and/or discriminatory practices after 1931 and who were particularly conscious of the contrast between West Indian conditions and what might be. The working class generally was also increasingly affected by the spread of education and the mass media of communications which not only increased their knowledge of the outside world but also raised in them hopes and ambitions which could not be fulfilled. For these reasons the apathy which had characterized their attitudes previously now gave way to a demand that something could and must be done.

This growing dissatisfaction erupted into violence partly because there seemed to be no channels through which it might find peaceful expression. Not only was there no recognized collective bargaining machinery, but also the existing governments seemed quite unresponsive to working-class interests.

This proved to be much more than merely a blind and ineffective outburst, for there quickly sprang up trade unions and labour parties throughout the area with leaders who articulated the grievances of the masses in such a way as to give the movement a positive content and direction. They pressed the workers' interests through political action as well as trade union activity. The submerged majority was now at last politically activated and mobilized. W. Arthur Lewis has described this as a "revolution." In 1939 he wrote, "The major issues discussed today no longer revolve round the aspirations of the middle classes, but are set by working-class demands. . . . Initiative has passed into the hands of trade union leaders and the new working-class bodies . . ."[21] Similarly, H. W. Springer has written, "It would be hard to overestimate the profound change of outlook in this period. For the first time the people as a whole were politically awakened."[22]

Some of the new labour leaders emerged from the ranks of the black working class; others were coloured professional people. Whether because they appreciated the great potential political power of the masses or because they were resentful over the discrimination which prevented them from securing the higher positions in society for which they felt qualified, the middle-class leaders now increasingly identified themselves with the black masses rather than with the predominantly white élite.

The new working-class movement demanded not only higher wages, better working conditions and social reconstruction generally, but also radical reform in the constitutions, for they blamed their distress in large measure on the Crown Colony system itself. The existing governments seemed to be too much under the influence of the propertied interests which were well represented in the nominated seats. The addition of a few middle-class representatives elected on a narrow franchise had not been enough to produce measures needed to improve the work-

[21] W. Arthur Lewis, *Labour in the West Indies: The Birth of a Workers' Movement* (Fabian Society Research Series, No. 44; London, 1939), p. 33.

[22] H. W. Springer, "The West Indies Emergent: Problems and Prospects," in David Lowenthal, ed., *The West Indies Federation: Perspectives of a New Nation* (New York: Columbia University Press, 1961), p. 3.

ers' conditions. Paradoxically, as W. A. Lewis has put it, the Crown Colony system was now "detested by those whom it was supposed to protect," and was being defended by "those whom it was supposed to attack."[23] Labour leaders felt that they would have to control the government in order to secure the necessary legislation, and for that, much more was required than simply an increased number of elected members. Their cry was for universal suffrage, entirely elected legislatures, executive councils responsible to the legislatures, and drastic reductions in the governors' powers.

These developments also operated to strengthen the support for federation. The occurrence of "disturbances" throughout the area demonstrated that the several territories shared common problems and interests and constituted a single economic and social community. Moreover, the new labour groups established and maintained contact with one another. In 1938, representatives of organized labour from British Guiana, Barbados, and Trinidad assembled in Port of Spain for a meeting of the B.G. and West Indies Labour Congress and approved a draft constitution for a federal government embracing all the British Caribbean territories. It provided for a federal executive council with an official majority and a unicameral legislature composed of fifty-two members elected on the basis of universal suffrage.

Meanwhile the strikes and riots had so alarmed London that a strong ten-man Royal Commission under the chairmanship of Lord Moyne was directed to investigate social and economic conditions and related matters in the area and to submit recommendations for action. It took evidence in each of the colonies from October, 1938, to April, 1939, and submitted its report at the end of the year.

The Moyne Commission hoped to meet the unrest primarily by bold economic and social measures. It recommended the establishment of a West Indian Welfare Fund to be financed by an annual grant from the British Govern-

[23] Lewis, *op. cit.*, p. 40.

ment of one million pounds and to be administered by a special organization independent of the local governments. The money should be used to finance schemes for the improvement of education, public health services, housing, and social welfare facilities. Moreover, steps should be taken to encourage the growth of trade unionism, the promotion of agriculture, and the settlement of people on the land as smallholders.

The Commission recognized, however, that constitutional development was directly relevant to the problem of social reform and that the latter could not be effectively solved if the former were held back. It stated:

> Rightly or wrongly, a substantial body of public opinion in the West Indies is convinced that far-reaching measures of social reconstruction depend, both for their initiation and their effective administration, upon greater participation of the people in the business of government. . . . Moreover, we are satisfied that the claim so often put before us that the people should have a larger voice in the management of their affairs represents a genuine sentiment and reflects a growing political consciousness which is sufficiently widespread to make it doubtful whether any schemes of social reform, however wisely conceived and efficiently conducted, would be completely successful unless they were accompanied by the largest measure of constitutional development which is thought to be judicious in existing circumstances.[24]

On the other hand, Lord Moyne and his colleagues believed that too great a constitutional advance might hinder the social reform effort. Thus it rejected the demand for self-government primarily on the ground that continuing control by the Crown over the finances of the colonies would be necessary if they were to receive the substantial assistance from the U.K. which was needed to support development and welfare. The problem, as the Commission

[24] "West India Royal Commission Report," Great Britain, *Parliamentary Papers,* Cmd. 6607, 1944–45, p. 373.

saw it, was to define those constitutional changes which would facilitate and not impede improvements in social conditions.

Accordingly it proposed some variation in the composition of the executive and legislative organs, but no fundamental change in their functions or powers. The number of officials in every legislative council should be reduced to three, but the resulting vacancies should be filled by nominated rather than elected members. It was important to make the legislatures "more fully representative of all important sections of the community," and this, it thought, could be better accomplished by wise use of the power to nominate than by the establishment of elected majorities.[25] The elected element itself should be made more truly representative by moving toward universal adult suffrage. Some members of the Commission felt that this should be introduced immediately, but others opposed such precipitate action lest it dangerously accelerate the rapid change which was already underway. They agreed, therefore, that the electorate should be enlarged "to as great an extent as local conditions make possible or prudent," and that fully representative local committees should be set up to consider reducing the present qualifications for voters and candidates.[26] It was clear that one reason leading the Commission to favour an extension of the franchise was that this would expedite the enactment of the necessary social legislation. This point was explicitly stated with reference to the one colony where the elected element had enough power to be obstructive if it wished—Barbados.

The reserve power of the governor must be retained to assure effective control as the unofficial majority developed. Public opinion, the Commission asserted, would provide a safeguard against its arbitrary or frequent use.

As for the executive councils, it was proposed that nominations be made in such a way as to broaden their basis and to provide better representation for all important in-

25 *Ibid.*, p. 377.
26 *Ibid.*, p. 380.

terests (the Commission having found that in only one of them was there a representative of labour) and that, wherever possible, some elected members of the legislature should be appointed. In the larger colonies there should be instituted a system of consultative committees for each of the major branches of administration. They should contain the Department Heads and a majority of members chosen by and from the elected legislators who would thus gain some education in the practical details of government and be in a better position to offer advice. These efforts to associate the elected legislators more closely with the work of the executive would remedy, it was hoped, what seemed to the Commission to be the greatest weakness of the Crown Colony system—the almost constant opposition existing between the Government and the elected legislators.

As for federation, the Commission reported that interest in the idea had grown in the past few years, with some groups—particularly labour organizations—now advocating the union of all the British territories in the Caribbean area, and it predicted that support for such a step would increase with the extension of the franchise. The Commission concluded, however, that West Indian opinion was not yet ready to accept the principle; "local pride" and "insularity" were still too strong to make an attempt at general federation advisable.[27]

The Commission was strongly in favour of federation as a goal however, and proposed that a step might be taken in that direction by federating the Leeward and Windward Islands. Its support for federation was motivated in large measure by the belief that "monies available for social services can be better and more wisely controlled if those services in a large number of islands are made to work to a uniform plan under common direction."[28] Its attitude on this question, too, seemed to be guided by a consideration of what would best promote an improvement in social conditions.

[27] *Ibid.*, p. 327.
[28] *Ibid.*, p. 328.

Social welfare and development measures were implemented in accordance with the Moyne Commission's recommendations, but the constitutional reforms which it proposed proved far too modest. Subsequent political change in the West Indies was much more rapid and radical than might have been anticipated from reading its report. Within a few years, each of the territories had much more advanced constitutions than it recommended and the effort to federate the Leeward and Windward Islands had been overtaken by the march to a general federation.

As the progress toward self-government and federation quickened, it became apparent that these two movements were related to each other in several ways.

The strongest argument in favour of federation so far as many West Indian nationalists were concerned was that it provided the best means for reaching the all-important goal of self-government. No one of the territories could really hope to achieve full independence on its own, they felt.

Others were afraid, however, that federation might impede the attainment of self-government. Some were suspicious that it was an imperialist device to divert West Indian energies into an endless wrangle among themselves over the details of the federal system. Those in the more advanced colonies were afraid that their further progress might be delayed until those units lower in the constitutional scale had caught up with them, or that if federation were achieved in the absence of constitutional uniformity, the federal government itself could be no more representative and responsible than that of the least advanced unit. There was therefore a demand in some quarters for postponing federation until unit self-government had been attained.

In these circumstances it was clear that a federal constitution which provided anything like a "glorified Crown Colony" would be unacceptable and that further reform of the unit constitutions must proceed concurrently with progress toward federation. Such a concurrent movement was dangerous, however, for if the units advanced too far before being united, the difficulty of securing agreement

on federation would be seriously increased owing not only
to the loss of its principal inducement but also to the further growth of vested interests and local nationalism within
each unit.

Although the two lines of development were thus inter-
twined, their relationship to the changing West Indian society can be best examined by tracing the further evolution
of the territorial constitutions before turning to a consideration of the movement toward federation.

The official element in the legislatures was speedily reduced in those colonies where it was still substantial, as
the Moyne Commission had recommended, but the demand for representative government was too great to be
met merely by the addition of nominated members. In
Trinidad and Tobago a large decrease in the number of
officials in 1941 was accompanied by a slight increase in
the elected element and no change in the number of
nominated members, thus giving that island at last
an unofficial majority but an elected minority. In accordance with the prevailing pattern, its governor now also
gained reserve powers. In British Guiana, two nominated
members were added in 1943, but this was so much less
than the number of officials removed that the elected members there were now actually in a majority. When the nominated officials were dropped from the British Honduras
legislative council in 1945, both the elected and the nominated unofficial elements were increased.

Meanwhile, Jamaica had taken a different path to representative government, for in 1944 it secured a bicameral
legislature in which the dominant body was an entirely
elected House of Representatives. All the official and nominated members were concentrated in a second chamber
known as the Legislative Council which could only delay
by one year bills passed by the House. Barbados followed
that lead in 1947 when the legislative authority of its nominated upper chamber, which had previously been equal
to that of the all-elected House of Assembly, was reduced
to a one-year suspensory veto.

Elsewhere elected majorities were soon established in

mixed unicameral legislatures. This form of representative
government was provided for Trinidad and Tobago in
1950; for Grenada, St. Vincent, St. Lucia, Dominica, Antigua, St. Kitts-Nevis, Montserrat, and the Leeward Islands
Federation in 1951; and for British Honduras and the
British Virgin Islands in 1954. The last of these had received a legislative council with an unofficial majority in
1950 after having been without a legislature since 1902.
British Guiana secured in 1953 a bicameral system in
which the predominant House of Assembly contained
twenty-four elected members and three officials, and one-
third of the nominated upper chamber was chosen on the
advice of members of the Assembly; but this was suspended
within a few months in favour of a unicameral body composed entirely of official and nominated members. Its
recovery from this retrogression was rather prompt, however, for a new constitution in 1956 provided for a legislature consisting of fourteen elected members, three officials and not more than eleven nominated members, and
after the 1957 election the governor chose to fill only six
of the nominated seats thus giving it an elected majority.
In Trinidad and Tobago the size of the elected majority
was raised further in 1956, and three years later the legislatures of the Leeward and the Windward Islands were
similarly reorganized. In 1960, moreover, agreement was
reached on the establishment of bicameral legislatures for
Trinidad and Tobago and British Guiana, thus permitting
the complete removal of nominated members from the
principal legislative body in those territories.

Such increases in the strength of the elected element
were accompanied by an extension of the franchise and a
lowering of the qualifications for candidates. Universal
adult suffrage was established first in Jamaica in 1944 and
next in Trinidad and Tobago the following year. Property
and income qualifications were reduced in Barbados in
1943 and in British Guiana in 1945, and the former as
well as the Leeward and Windward Islands advanced to
universal adult suffrage in 1951. British Guiana followed
suit in 1953, and the next year British Honduras required

only that the voter be able to write his name and the date.

As a result of these changes, political power passed substantially to the black workers. Large numbers of them exercised the newly-won franchise, and labour leaders, frequently themselves black and of working-class origin, increasingly filled the legislatures. Most of the old, relatively moderate middle-class representatives were swept out of the elected seats. They, as well as the upper-class spokesmen of the planting and commercial interests, could find refuge only in the nominated seats which remained at the governors' disposal.

The retention of nominated members everywhere, either in weak upper chambers or as minorities in unicameral bodies, was justified as a necessary means to provide representation for those sections of the community which were important but could not hope to win seats in an election conducted on the basis of universal suffrage. Such assurance of minority representation was said to be particularly important in a society such as that existing in the West Indies, where class and colour cleavages were so deep that majority tyranny was a greater danger. This remnant of the Crown Colony system was now to be used, curiously enough, as a safeguard for the interests of that very class against whom it had been originally directed. The rationale for it remained the same, however—to protect the interests of those who would not be well represented through elections.

There was an anachronistic quality about the nominated seat however, and in 1956 a significant transformation of that device began. At that time the governor of Trinidad and Tobago was authorized to make his nominations in such a way as to assure the party which had won most of the elected seats an effective majority of the total legislative council. It was agreed in 1959 that nominated members in the Leeward and Windward Islands would be appointed after consultation with the leader of the majority party and if necessary in such a way as to ensure a working majority for him. A similar provision was made the following year for two of the five nominated members in British

Honduras. Thus the device of nomination was coming to be used at least in part to make party government effective.

But mere "representative government" was not the goal of West Indian politicians in the post-World War II period. An elected majority in the legislature made it possible to frustrate the Government—or at least to force the governor to use his reserve powers—but it did not enable the elected members to play a constructive role since they could not take the initiative in the framing of policy. Their opposition would become not only permanent but also irresponsible unless they could be placed in the position of having to devise practical alternatives.

Nor were the rising labour leaders now prepared to settle for the appointment to the executive council of a few elected legislators chosen by the governor. The Trinidad and Tobago constitution of 1941, which required him to appoint, in his discretion, two elected and three nominated members from the legislative council, did represent a step forward, as did also the British Guiana constitution of 1943 which stipulated that five legislators must be so selected, for in each case the unofficials thus became a majority. The elected members were, however, in a minority and as such were often unable to fulfil their promises to the electorate and were tempted to evade responsibility for unpopular measures approved in executive council. Moreover, they ran the risk of becoming so identified with the official and nominated members as to lose the support of their followers. Finally there was no guarantee under such an arrangement that those chosen by the governor actually enjoyed the confidence of the majority of their elected colleagues in the legislature.

What most West Indian political leaders now wanted was for the executive councils to become responsible to the representative legislatures rather than to the Crown. Such a transformation in the relationship between the executive and legislative organs began with the Jamaican constitution of 1944 which was the first to provide for the introduction into the executive council of persons elected from and removable by the legislature. It was to consist of five members chosen by and from the all-elected House of Representatives, two members nominated by the governor from the Legislative Council, and three officials. The elected members were therefore in a minority, and the governor remained in firm control despite the unofficial majority because he could suspend those chosen from the Legislative Council at will.

Two years later an element of responsibility was introduced into executive-legislative relations in Barbados without any formal change in the written constitution. The governor announced that the four members whom he was required to nominate to the Executive Committee from the all-elected House of Assembly would be those recommended to him by the person best able to command a majority in that House. Such a change was prompted there by the need to resolve the deadlocks which had developed in its Old Representative System as a consequence of the inability of the executive to maintain the confidence of the Assembly following the extension of the franchise and the growth of political consciousness. With this advance Barbados surmounted the difficulty which had produced a reduction in the power of the elected element in B.G. in 1928.

The Trinidad and Tobago constitution of 1950 represented a somewhat different step in this direction, for it permitted a majority of the executive council to be chosen from among the elected legislators by the legislative council as a whole. They could be removed by a two-thirds vote. In view of the fact that eight of the twenty-six members of the legislature were either nominated or official, there was still no assurance that those chosen would be the ones preferred by most of the elected legislators, particularly in view of the underdeveloped state of parties there. Owing their seats to the votes of official and nominated members, their responsibility would be somewhat compromised.

In 1951 each of the Windward and Leeward Islands (but not the Virgins) and the Leeward Islands Federation were brought into this line of development with new constitutions which provided for the addition to the executive councils of a minority of elected members chosen by the legislatures and removable by them. Such an arrangement was established in the Virgin Islands and British Honduras in 1954. In the case of the latter, the legislature was also authorized to name two of its nominated members to the executive and these together with the elected members it chose constituted a majority of that body.

Meanwhile Jamaica had set off a further wave of advance when in 1953 it combined the more progressive features of the Barbados and Trinidad experiments to create an executive council with a majority of elected legislators who would be appointed and removed on the advice of the leader of the majority party to be known as the Chief Minister. By 1957, the Chief Minister was presiding over this body which then consisted of ten members from the House of Representatives chosen by him, two from the Legislative Council appointed by the governor on his advice, and no officials. Finally, in 1959 the council became a cabinet and the Chief Minister a Premier.

The executive council of Trinidad and Tobago was rendered more responsible in 1956 when the last nominated member and one official were dropped and the legislature (in which the elected element had been substantially increased) was authorized to name eight (rather than five) of its own members, one of whom they were to designate Chief Minister. Finally, in 1959, the governor was directed to call upon the elected member most likely to command a majority to form a Government. Removals as well as appointments would be on the advice of the premier, and he would normally preside at cabinet meetings. The two officials were retained as non-voting members, but the following year agreement was reached on their total elimination.

The elected members on the Barbados Executive Committee were increased to five in 1954, and in 1958 the general direction of government in internal matters passed to a sub-committee of that body, to be known as the cabinet, consisting of the premier, four members appointed on his advice from the Assembly, and one chosen by the gov-

ernor from the legislative council. The following year it
was provided that the member from the legislative council
would also be appointed on the premier's advice.

In 1956, each of the executive councils of the Windward
and Leeward Islands gained an elected majority, to be
chosen by unofficials in the legislature, and three years
later it was agreed that they should be selected by the member of the legislative council considered by the Administrator (who was to become the top official in each island
with the abolition of the joint governorships) most likely
to command a majority in that body. By 1960, British
Honduras had an executive body containing a majority of
elected members chosen by the unofficials in the legislature and led by a First Minister.

The advance of British Guiana toward such a semi-
responsible system was delayed, partly at least on account
of British concern over the deeper racial cleavages and
slower economic progress there. Not until 1953 did it secure a constitution which permitted the legislature to name
some of its members to the executive council. The Wad-
dington Commission which recommended such a step
found that racial tension had increased there due to the
growing East Indian demand for equal participation in
Guianese life, but argued that racialism and other un-
wholesome tendencies would be reduced by the grant of a
measure of political responsibility.[29] The new executive
council, which contained a majority of elected members,
was abolished after a short time, however, as the leaders
of the majority party seemed determined to subvert the
constitution, and was replaced by a temporary one consisting of three officials and seven unofficials nominated by
the governor. The Robertson Commission of 1954 urged
a delay in the return to representative institutions because
the social environment did not seem to be one in which
they might be expected to function successfully, citing particularly the increasing racial hostility, the widespread dis-

[29] *British Guiana Report of the Constitutional Commission,
1950–51,* Great Britain, Colonial Office, Col. 280, 1951, pp.
14–15, 25.

satisfaction and frustration, the lack of an informed public opinion and of strong independent voluntary associations, and the absence of that "diversity in the electorate which in Great Britain inevitably provides for the existence of at least two parties of differing outlook with distinctive programmes appealing to different sections of the community and each with a reasonable prospect of power."[30] That Commission recommended therefore marking time for a while, and expressed the hope that during this period the economic and social development of the colony would be vigorously carried forward and that "the gradual improvement of social and economic conditions would help to bring about a change in the political outlook of the electorate."[31]

Within two years, the Secretary of State announced that democratic institutions would be restored, and following the election of 1957 British Guiana was well back on the road to responsible government. The governor named leaders of the majority party to occupy all five of the seats which the new constitution required him to fill from among the elected legislators, and he refrained from making appointments to the two positions for nominated members which had been authorized, thus placing the elected element again in the majority.

Meanwhile, the increasingly numerous elected members of the executive councils gradually gained power over the initiation and administration of policy as they evolved into ministers. In some cases, the committee system recommended by the Moyne Commission assisted in this development. In British Guiana in 1943 and in the Leeward and Windward Islands in 1951, elected members on the executive councils were appointed chairmen of committees which discussed and offered advice on the activities of various departments. A similar arrangement was established in the Jamaica House of Representatives in 1944,

---

[30] "Report of the British Guiana Constitutional Commission," Great Britain, *Parliamentary Papers,* Cmd. 9274, 1953–54, p. 67.

[31] *Ibid.,* p. 70.

the difference being that the chairmen were not executive councillors; more significant in that colony was the authorization, at the same time, of the various elected members in the executive council to represent certain departments in the deliberations of that body and of the legislature. They were quasi-ministers at this stage, as they had no real authority over the departments, but they were able to gain valuable experience. This was also the situation in Barbados in 1946 and in British Honduras in 1955. Ministerial status was achieved by the elected members when they were given effective administrative control over their departments and began to exercise genuine executive functions. The ministerial system was introduced in Trinidad and Tobago in 1950, in Jamaica in 1953, in Barbados in 1954, in the Leeward and Windward Islands in 1956, in British Guiana in 1956 (after an abortive experiment with it in 1953) and in British Honduras in 1960. Originally, only a few of the less sensitive subjects were assigned to the quasi-ministers or ministers, but gradually more and more portfolios were transferred to their hands from those of the officials until eventually they were in administrative charge of all—or almost all—internal matters.

At the same time, the executive council was evolving from an advisory body *vis-à-vis* the governor into a cabinet with effective power over the initiation of public policy. The 1944 Jamaica constitution provided that it should be "the principal instrument of policy" and gave it control over the introduction of money bills and bills to implement government policy. Similar terms were used to describe the position of the executive organ in Barbados in 1946, Trinidad in 1950, British Guiana in 1953, British Honduras in 1954, and the Leeward and Windward Islands in 1956. The governor gradually moved toward the status of a constitutional monarch guided by the advice of his ministers in most cases, and eventually lost his power to certify the enactment of laws rejected by the legislature. He remained able to reserve for the signification of Her Majesty's pleasure only those bills likely to prejudice the Royal prerogative or inconsistent with the constitution or with international agreements. Such a gain was made by Jamaica in 1959 and was agreed to that year for the Windward and Leeward Islands. It was promised the following year to Trinidad and British Guiana.

As internal self-government was thus attained, or brought within reach, power and responsibility were transferred almost entirely to West Indian politicians who represented the working classes. Although opinions differed as to whose interests the Crown Colony system served, it had in any case, as D. G. Anglin has noted, "carried the West Indies through a critical period when premature constitutional reform might have meant restoration of power to the European minority, with results similar to those in East, Central, and South Africa today."[32]

It is possible to establish a rough correlation between social progress and constitutional advance during the period under examination. One can point to certain aspects of West Indian society in the 1950's which indicated that it was now better able to support democratic political institutions than it had been previously. A somewhat more integrated social order was emerging. There had developed a variety of associations which were drawing together hitherto disjointed elements. Class divisions were becoming less rigid and colour was becoming less significant as a determinant of status. The illiteracy rate was falling and the masses were becoming increasingly well informed. The middle class was growing, and becoming less eager to dissociate itself from the masses and from its West Indian heritage. More people were being drawn into the towns, and the rural-urban dichotomy was lessening. The University College of the West Indies was turning out graduates well equipped to fill positions of leadership in politics and the bureaucracy.

On the other hand, however, most West Indians continued to live so near the subsistence level that they were

[32] Douglas G. Anglin, "The Political Development of the West Indies," in Lowenthal, op. cit., p. 37.

not prepared to take an active or responsible part in the political process. The growth in population seemed to cancel out every effort to raise their standard of living. There was still a substantial proportion of illiteracy and many of those who could read were easy prey for demagogues. Many educated West Indians remained quite alienated from the masses. The middle class was not yet substantial or secure enough to function as an effective stabilizing force. Classes were still separated by great cleavages, in terms of social organization and values as well as income, and colour had not by any means lost its importance. Tension between the East Indians and the Negroes seemed to be growing as the former became increasingly self-assertive and the latter felt increasingly threatened.[33]

It could hardly be argued, therefore, that the ideal social prerequisites for democracy had been satisfied or that West Indian society was so clearly ripe for self-government that the transition to that status could take place without misgivings.

Actually constitutional advance in the West Indies cannot be interpreted simply as a response to social advance, particularly in the last decade or two. The desire to synchronize the two, which was expressed by successive

[33] For discussions of recent and contemporary West Indian society, see George E. Cumper, *The Social Structure of Jamaica* and *The Social Structure of the British Caribbean* (*excluding Jamaica*) (Mona, Jamaica: University College of the West Indies, n.d.); T. S. Simey, *Welfare and Planning in the West Indies* (Oxford: Clarendon Press, 1946); H. W. Springer, "On Being a West Indian," *Caribbean Quarterly*, Vol. 3 (December 1953), pp. 181–83; Mary Proudfoot, *Britain and the United States in the Caribbean: A Comparative Study of Methods of Development* (London: Faber and Faber, 1954), Chs. 4, 9–12; the collection of papers ed. by Vera D. Rubin, published under the title "Social and Cultural Pluralism in the Caribbean," *Annals of the New York Academy of Sciences*, Vol. 83 (January 1960), pp. 761–916; A. P. Thornton, "Aspects of West Indian Society," *International Journal*, Vol. 15 (Spring 1960), pp. 113–21; and David Lowenthal, "The Social Background of West Indian Federation," in his *The West Indies Federation*, pp. 63–96.

commissions and Secretaries of State, could not be fully realized. There were so many other factors operating to force the pace that political concessions could not be withheld until all the desired social foundations had been well laid. The demand for self-government on the part of organized labour grew too insistent to resist without creating a situation in which nothing constructive could have been accomplished in either the constitutional or the social realm. The various intermediate forms of rule did not provide effective solutions partly because they did not satisfy the West Indian nationalists but served rather to increase their frustrations by giving them a taste of power but denying them its reality. In addition some of these arrangements were not entirely successful instruments of imperial tutelage; they tended to produce permanent and irresponsible opposition rather than the habits needed for successful self-government. The pace of constitutional change in the West Indies was also accelerated by the pressure for more liberal colonial policies in the U.K. and elsewhere in the world, as well as by progress in other parts of the empire.

It cannot be argued, however, that democracy is any less likely to succeed than it would have been if self-government had been delayed until a more democratic society had come into existence. Indeed, further delay might well have decreased the chances for democracy. There are those who believe that this is the great lesson to be learned from the experience of British Guiana—the one place where things went wrong. Dr. Rita Hinden, who was a member of the commission which recommended the far-reaching concessions of 1953, stated after they had opened the way to power for a party which displayed such undemocratic tendencies that the constitution had to be suspended:

> What then does one conclude? Is it that there should not be adult suffrage and responsible government until all the economic and social conditions predispose to it? My conclusion is just the opposite. The trouble in British Guiana was not that self-government came too soon,

but that it came too late . . . Either one holds back everything—which is no longer possible in a British colony—or one holds back nothing.[34]

[34] Rita Hinden, "The Case of British Guiana," *Encounter,* Vol. 2 (January 1954), p. 22.

3.

The beginnings of mass political participation are outlined here in an essay written before the quickening of British West Indian federation, defederation, and independence. Political parties formed on the British model were used by their leaders to advance themselves rather than to promote any particular credo. Indeed, most parties were alike in opposing colonial authority, in parading radical bona fides, and in their loose organization and modes of electioneering and recruitment. The relationship between political leaders and followers described here is dated, but contains the seeds of much present-day West Indian political behavior.

MORLEY AYEARST, born in Canada, took his undergraduate degree at the University of Ontario and a doctorate at Princeton. He is now Professor of Political Science at New York University. This essay, stimulated by a Fulbright Research Fellowship in the West Indies, was followed by a general study, *The British West Indies: The Search for Self-Government.*

A Note on Some Characteristics of West Indian Political Parties

Morley Ayearst

Political parties, like other institutions, are conditioned by the society in which they emerge and develop. The characteristics, and indeed the significance of West Indian political parties cannot be grasped without some understanding of the West Indian social milieu.

It is beyond the scope of this note to attempt any real social analysis of the West Indies but a few brief observations may be made. It should be kept in view that in the islands and the two mainland colonies there exist societies based primarily, now as formerly, upon the exploitation of export crops requiring an abundant use of low-cost labour; that the Government has always been identified with the land-owning class or the British colonial officials or both; that the land-owning class historically has been self-identified with the "home" country rather than the colony. In some colonies absentee ownership (especially by companies) of the larger estates has become a common situation. As a result of these conditions and of the fact that labour has been provided almost entirely by Africans or East Indians whereas Europeans have owned most of the land and occupied most of the principal official positions, a "plural" society developed; one in which the Negro and coloured majority felt themselves to be less than full mem-

Social and Economic Studies, Vol. III, No. 2, June 1954, pp. 186–96. Reprinted with permission of the author and the Institute of Social and Economic Research, University of the West Indies.

bers of society. Loyalty was often divided, the political loyalty of the masses, in so far as any existed, belonging to the colony, and that of the owning class, white and coloured, primarily to the British connection. It should be noted further that this society was an acquisitive one, devoted almost exclusively to monetary gain, unconcerned with local cultural matters and one in which none of its institutions was organized democratically. The typical institutional pattern was hierarchical: decision and direction at the apex, submission and obedience at the bottom and with no machinery whereby the mass could exert influence upon, much less control over, the leadership. This was true not only of government under the typical Crown Colony system, wherein the Crown-appointed Governor occupies a position somewhat analogous to that of the British monarch after 1689, but also of such popular religious bodies as the Pocomania groups of Jamaica and the Trinidad "shouters". Local government remained under the control of the central colonial administration and provided no real opportunity for the development of self-government at that level.

It was under these adverse circumstances that the postwar changes occurred. The autocratic forms of the Crown Colony system were modified to allow of more and more popular participation in government. These changes came with almost bewildering rapidity considering the inexperience of the newly-enfranchised masses, the considerable amount of illiteracy and the complex linguistic and racial situation in certain colonies, particularly Trinidad and British Guiana. Full adult suffrage in Great Britain was achieved only a few years ago as the climax of a movement going back to the Middle Ages. In the United States, the existence of a plural society in the South meant the much slower development in that area of a complete mass democracy. Today, nearly three generations after emancipation, the Negro and coloured population in the South is not everywhere enfranchised in fact, although rapid progress in this direction is being made. These facts are in sharp contrast with the West Indian situation. Here the enfranchisement of the black and coloured majority has proceeded rapidly under pressure exerted by local politicians, often identified with labour organizations, and acquiesced in by British governments anxious to avoid political and economic dislocation. The small minority, white and coloured, chiefly interested in large-scale agriculture and commerce, could not oppose this trend successfully.

Another important difference between the West Indies on the one hand and Great Britain and the United States on the other, is that the latter are industrialized and started to become so simultaneously with the development of mass democracy. Further, this mass democracy was founded upon a long tradition of earlier semi-democracy. Industrialization meant the growth of a large and influential middle class of technical, professional, managerial, salaried personnel and numerous small entrepreneurs. This has had a stabilizing effect upon politics and has made the two-party system workable. Both parties must find support in all social ranks to be successful. Even the present Labour-Conservative division in British politics by no means represents a separation of the electorate on strictly class lines. There are always a considerable number of voters who are not permanent supporters of any party and who are susceptible to political argument based upon policies. These voters can swing an election and must be wooed by both parties.

In the West Indies, on the other hand, the middle class is numerically important only in a few towns and cities. Broadly speaking the only parties that can win an overall majority based upon universal adult suffrage are those that can appeal to the desires and emotions of the low-income voter. It is hardly astonishing, therefore, to find that most West Indian parties are connected in some way with a labour union or a federation of unions. It is also a fact that the labour unions, another relatively recent West Indian institution, has provided the African or East Indian workman with his only important mass organization. His society is conspicuously lacking in community-wide organizations that he can identify with his needs and aspirations. As soon as labour unions came into being he tended, therefore, to regard them as the general defender of all his interests.

Such a general representation is essentially political, and union leaders were compelled either to play up to this demand or to give way to those who would do so. In certain cases, political leaders came forward first as politicians but soon found that union leadership was the only road to permanent political importance. In Barbados, for example, both the Progressive League and the Congress Party anteceded their labour unions. In both cases the moving spirits were educated middle-class coloured men who saw the colony's problems primarily in political terms but found out that the problems which interested the masses were economic. The only way to achieve a mass appeal, necessary because of universal suffrage, was to organize a labour union and identify the party with it. In Jamaica, Manley's People's National Party was compelled to organize a union base in reply to the Jamaica Labour Party and its Bustamante Industrial Trade Union.

The question may be raised as to why religious organizations have not played a more important part in West Indian politics, for the West Indian is almost always a member of some religious group. The main reason would appear to be the fact that in many colonies the sects are numerous and that even within a particular sect there is little or no administrative or other co-ordination. The Church of England is more or less identified with the Government and has only a moderate following among the African population in most places. The Roman Catholic Church is important in some areas but its leaders have in general exercised a discreet reticence in political affairs. It is by far the most important church in British Honduras where about 90 per cent of the colony's education is undertaken by church schools, chiefly Jesuit. In that colony the influence of Roman Catholic doctrine is strongly evident in the announced policies of the People's United Party. It is said that in Trinidad the Hindu pandits can influence the votes of their congregations and in some cases are willing to sell this influence to candidates for the Legislature. In Jamaica there is alleged to be competition between candidates and parties for the approval of the Pocomania pastors.

All of this is of relatively minor importance and is chiefly a matter of small-scale corruption likely to be found in a politically primitive society where a locally influential person can command a price for delivering a few votes. The exception is in those areas where Roman Catholic adherence is widespread. Here there is no question of corruption but rather of a potentially important influence upon Government policies. This is still potential rather than actual.

The successful West Indian political party, therefore, is typically a labour party, in many cases paying lip-service to socialism and always stressing the "Nationalist" ideal: more self-government for the colony and a rapid advance to political independence, either within the British Commonwealth or otherwise. Thus it is pledged to satisfy the two most urgent demands of the West Indian voter: that his economic status be improved and that he become a full member of his society. That these demands are based upon emotional needs rather than any impartial economic analysis, means that the effective political argument is the emotional one. Party leaders therefore use highly charged emotional language in their electioneering speeches, while at the same time they recognize the practical necessity of compromise and moderation in actual policies. Judged by their deeds, their socialism is very moderate. They can remain as leaders and continue to be elected so long as they voice the emotional demands of their followers and appear to be the people's champion in the struggle against colonialism and capitalist exploitation.

This verbal behaviour is usually combined with a readiness to accept advice from official and conservative sources and to make compromises except in cases where the compromise would flagrantly display subservience to the colonial status. An outstanding exception is provided by the People's Progressive Party of British Guiana. In this case the leadership is avowedly Marxist and, when in office, refused all compromise and even refused to discuss policies in the Executive Council meetings.

Another characteristic of most West Indian parties is that they are very loosely organized. All are provided with constitutions including arrangements for local party groups which are to be represented at party conferences which in turn are supposed to pick leaders and decide high policy issues. In most cases these constitutions remain partly or entirely of the "paper" variety. Local party groups are generally few in number and inactive except immediately before elections. The accepted party leadership decides candidacies and the party structure is hierarchical, with the rank and file voter playing very little part other than by voting at elections. The party structure is demagogic rather than democratic.

This is not peculiar to West Indian parties, of course, but there is no such close and working organization for the re-assessment of leaders and the deciding of issues on a broad party basis as is provided by the structure, for example, of the British Labour Party and the French Socialist Party. Obviously, such organization is the result of time and education. As a broad generalization it may be hazarded that the more outstanding and unchallenged the leader, the less he is disposed to accept direction from his colleagues and the more he depends upon his own charismatic appeal to the electorate.

There is some danger, under these circumstances, that an unusually popular party leader may succumb to the temptations of ambition and seek irresponsible power. In view of the rapid advance of mass democracy in the colonies and the fact that emotional appeals have provided the key to political victory there was the possibility that West Indian political history might reflect the civil-war-to-dictatorship pattern of the ex-Spanish republics and Haiti. The first stages of such a development actually occurred in British Guiana. If it be fair to assume that, all things considered, a slower, more orderly advance to self-government is preferable, the West Indian colonies are more deeply indebted to the restraining influence of the colonial officials than some West Indian nationalists are yet ready to admit.

Apart from the enforcement of public order, what part have the British colonial officials played in the development of West Indian parties? It is difficult to give a simple answer to this question. Most Governors, it may be as-

sumed, are concerned chiefly with the quiet development
of the colony's economic and political life and are inclined
to co-operate with their elected legislators as far as possible
within the limits set by their instructions from the Secretary of State. They assume an appearance of neutrality in
the local political struggle. Nevertheless, they would be
displaying a more than human self restraint if they did not
in various ways try to further the political fortunes of the
leader or party they consider most suitable for power. The
methods employed are seldom overt, although in rare cases
Governors have engaged in what might be termed electioneering. (One is reminded of Sir Charles Poulett Thom-
son, later Lord Sydenham, who as Governor of Upper
Canada over a century ago ran a successful election campaign.) Clearly a public affiliation between the Governor
and a party leader would be disastrous for the latter, in all
probability. Covert aid has been furnished in certain cases,
even to the extent of allowing one party to break up the
meetings of another without police interference. Public
condemnation of a party is rare. A recent example is provided by the attacks on People's United Party leaders carried in the official news bulletin of British Honduras as well
as the investigation ordered by the Governor. The attempt
to destroy the People's Progressive Party in British Guiana
is also overt. Both of these instances emphasize the political ineffectiveness of such open action. Neither the
P.U.P. nor the P.P.P. has appeared to suffer any loss of
popularity as a result. Indeed, the contrary may well be
the case, as the official action taken seems to prove the
sincerity of the parties' claims and makes martyrs of their
leaders.

The most effective influence by Governors upon party
leaders has been private. It takes the form of modifying
ill-advised or extreme policies by private conversation and
by argument in Executive Council. This is the more effective when the Governor is able to win the personal confidence and friendship of local politicians. The discreet
distribution of knighthoods and lesser honours among eminent colonials is another device which can be useful in securing the identification of the local elite with the official

Government and the British connection. This was particularly useful at an earlier period when the struggle for social status within the colonial society was more important than the independence drive. With the coming of mass voting and the strong nationalist, anti-colonial movements of the post-war years the distribution of honours has lost some of its point, although still useful in colonies where radical movements are not dominant.

Indirectly, the colonial governments have done something to provide leaders for the new political parties by granting scholarships for study in England. A majority of the party leaders in most of the colonies have enjoyed such opportunities, with or without scholarship aid.

The presence of the *ex-officio* members in legislatures militates against the development of the party system. It is noteworthy that the oldest and strongest of the West Indian parties have developed in colonies with bicameral legislatures, the primary chamber containing elected members only. When officials are present they are likely to carry the chief burden of introducing and defending legislation and thus to rob the party leaders of an opportunity to shine as legislators. The existence of nominated members also may have the effect of removing certain outstanding figures from party activity. Certain of a dignified place in the colony's political life, they are the less likely to enter party politics. Of course many could not or would not do so in any case, but others might make a valuable contribution to party development were this the only road to political eminence.

The problem of maintaining leadership and party discipline is one which West Indian party leaders must face almost daily. Here again, this situation is not exclusive to the West Indies. To a greater or lesser extent it exists everywhere. All legislators are, at least in their own view, potential Prime Ministers. Their loyalty to the party chief is more likely to be conditioned by political necessity than by anything else. Strong party leaders are those who can maintain their own position in the public eye as the unchallenged and dominating figure in the party and who are also adept at intra-party management, particularly the distribution of posts and other political rewards. Party discipline can be maintained firmly only when the leader is able to control the political future of his supporters. Where, as in Trinidad, the party system is not yet well developed, legislative leadership depends upon personal qualities, the ability by force of personality to dominate an argument and shrewdness in the art of parliamentary intrigue.

Electioneering techniques are similar throughout the area. There is much dependence upon the street meeting. This is characteristically long, with speeches by several party leaders interspersed with singing. The outsider is constantly amazed at the West Indian capacity to endure, and seemingly enjoy, vast quantities of political oratory. Nearly all parties have one or more newspapers to present their viewpoint on current issues. With a mass electorate containing a large number of illiterates one may doubt the effectiveness of the printed appeal. Nevertheless, the party leaders feel the necessity of this medium (and they may well be right) although it is relatively costly.

In general West Indian parties have very limited funds. Their electorates are small, by comparison with the industrialized countries, but they cannot depend upon any financial support from most of their rank-and-file members. Their unions are poor and consist of a high proportion of "free riders" except in times of crisis. Some parties are alleged to enjoy secret gifts of considerable size from merchants or others who are interested in the good will of the party leaders. Occasionally a wealthy candidate will finance his own campaign generously. This is especially true in Trinidad and Tobago where parties are ineffective in most areas.

The question of corruption in connection with West Indian political parties is one of considerable current interest. Certainly, corruption among politicians is no novelty anywhere. Political or official power of any degree gives the holder the ability to distribute favours or withhold them. Even the petty official may delay action which he is legally required to take until a small "present" is forthcoming. This has not been unknown in both European and American countries. Greater power means greater opportunities for the giving or withholding of favours which may have important financial aspects. Certainly the West Indian politician is no exception in being subjected to considerable temptation to accept bribes—the greater in that he has, or expects to have, a higher standard of living than can be maintained on his official income. That local political leaders are corrupt is a belief universally held in the West Indies. In so far as this belief is founded upon fact, the reason for the corruption may be due in some measure to the absence of any considerable well-to-do, public-spirited class with a tradition of political service, as in the United Kingdom. Even in Britain this development is fairly recent. It may be noted that English politics and many English politicians, before the passage of the nineteenth century electoral reform legislation, were notoriously corrupt. Certainly, it would be very rash to assume that such corruption as may in fact tarnish West Indian politics is proof of the inability of West Indians to govern themselves. One result of a mass electorate has been the emergence of a new type of elite (to use Pareto's term). This consists of Negro, coloured and East Indian barristers, teachers, union officials and others, some of them not highly educated, and unskilled in the niceties of parliamentary behaviour. The displaced colonial elite, white and coloured, quite naturally is quick to characterize these upstarts as demagogues and rogues. Perhaps the most disquieting feature of political corruption in the West Indies is the relative indifference of the mass electorate to its exposure.

A word about Communism. The only effective Communist-led party in the area is the Guianese People's Progressive Party. Needless to say, the rank-and-file members are not Marxist, although ready enough to display red banners and other symbols of the Communist fraternity. This party differs sharply from most others in the excellence of its party organization and the tight control over party activities exercised by the five-member "Politburo" through the network of local group secretaries. The appeal to the voter is the one almost universally effective in the colonies: political independence and freedom from the economic controls of the colonial system with a prom-

ise of rapid improvement in the standard of living unde-
terred by crude economic facts. The leaders of this party
are all young, energetic and in some cases, thorough-going
fanatics who give the movement immense drive. As this
party was the first in the colony to hit upon the key appeal
and as it was able to get the support of both the Georgetown Africans and the East Indian estate workers, it was
naturally unbeatable at the polls. The dictatorial ambitions
of the party leadership and their determination to secure
party domination of all branches of the administration became evident after a short period in office. The P.U.P. of
British Honduras is not Communist-led, although the
fanaticism of its leaders on the anti-colonial issue might
produce a crisis in the colony's politics.

Other Communist and crypto-Communist parties in the
colonies are small and ineffective and could be a danger
to the orderly advance toward self-government only in the
event of a serious economic collapse. Elsewhere than in
British Guiana the key appeal has been made already by
non-Communist parties which have become well established.

Irresponsible demagogues preaching non-Communist but
general radicalism based on the universal appeal have had
relatively little success. In the politically primitive island
of Grenada some electoral strength was shown by "Uncle"
Gairy at the last elections, but he was quite unable to preserve party discipline, or loyalty. His chief weapon, strikes
accompanied by intimidation and violence, could be successful only in a near-revolutionary situation.

Up to this point our attention has been directed mainly
to the parties allied with trades unions and with a mass
appeal. How about other parties, notably conservative opposition parties? Some of these are parties which, so to
speak, exist under protest. The old dominant land-owning
and commercial class, which had fought with the Governors and enjoyed near autocratic power under the old
colonial system, finally established a *modus vivendi* with
the Governor and his officials under the Crown Colony
system. This was done by using all necessary pressures to
secure legislative representation by nominated members,

who, acting in concert with the officials, could block radical legislation and preserve the *status quo*. As the franchise was broadened and the number of nominated members reduced, the old dominant class found itself less and less able to govern directly. Even so, the conservatives considered parties premature in colonial politics and were reluctant to form one of their own. They preferred as long as possible to operate as political independents appealing to the voter simply as citizens of repute and standing. The advent of universal adult suffrage made this hazardous in most places where the union-based party with its mass appeal was too strong to be overcome by any but exceptionally popular independents. It is under these circumstances that the National Party in British Honduras and the Electors' Association in Barbados were formed. Both represented a middle-class business interest. Neither has any trades union support. Under the old restricted franchise in 1950 the Electors' Association won 10 out of 24 seats in the House of Assembly. Under universal suffrage its strength dwindled. It is tagged as a white man's and employer class party. This, rather than conservatism in policy, is the reason for its collapse. It has been unable to remove the curse of colour identification. Possible coloured candidates include a number of civil servants who are automatically disqualified. Those who do identify themselves with the party are charged with being the tools of the "Broad Street Bims". This party displays to perfection the problems that beset a middle-class, white-led party in West Indian politics. It is fair to say that white candidates find it difficult to secure election, under universal suffrage, anywhere in the West Indies. Under these circumstances the business community refuses financial support to such candidates and prefers to invest its political funds in the winning party regardless of its radical programme. This, the business men are confident, is the best way to protect their interests. Conservative parties also find it very difficult to organize local groups to work among the voters. Conceivably at some future date, the class-colour question may be resolved so as to eliminate it as an important political factor. Until then, the political talents of the white colonial seem doomed to remain unused for the most part, except when made available in nominated memberships.

An unusually active party of this sort is the Party of Political Progress Groups in Trinidad. As its cumbersome name indicates, it began as a political pressure group rather than a party and still retains an element of this. It is primarily a "clean government" organization but is essentially middle class and conservative in philosophy. While coloured members are welcomed, it remains chiefly a white party. It does not intend to present candidates everywhere but will support worthy candidates of other parties. Partly because of the primitive party situation in Trinidad, the P.O.P.P.G. has so far enjoyed a measure of success and is currently active in the attempt to extend its influence with the voters beyond Port of Spain where it has had most of its followers.

This note would be incomplete without some notice of the African-East Indian struggle for political dominance in Trinidad and British Guiana. In both of these colonies the Africans enjoyed an ascendancy until recently, based upon the fact that they had achieved freedom and a degree of financial and educational advance while the East Indians were still indentured labourers suffering under a system but little removed from slavery. In recent years the East Indians have emerged as a rival group of rapidly increasing numbers. They have become important landowners and business men and have entered the professions and civil service in considerable numbers, thus breaking into what was formerly an African and coloured preserve. At the same time they have become politically active and, because of the tendency of the East Indian elector to vote only for one of his own race, have had a considerable success.

At present this issue is partly hidden in Trinidad, and in British Guiana is eclipsed by the P.P.P. which has united the East Indians under Jagan and Lachmansingh with the Georgetown Africans under Burnham and Chase. This racial rivalry exists however, and in the future may prove to be a seriously complicating factor in the party politics of these two colonies.

4.

The political saga of a small island in the eastern Caribbean exemplifies the problems inherent in attempts to realize the benefits of self-government under economic and social conditions that have little changed since emancipation. The author, himself a Vincentian, shows how small-island circumstances exaggerate the defects of party structure outlined in the preceding essay. Intense personalism, family vendettas, a desperate dependence on government jobs and favors, and the lack of any difference of principle between warring factions are all symptoms of a broader problem: in the absence of basic economic and social change, universal suffrage and internal self-government avail little.

KENNETH JOHN, a graduate of the University College of the West Indies, was a tutor in the University's Extra-Mural Department in Jamaica and, when this article was written in 1966, in St. Vincent, before going to England for postgraduate work.

St. Vincent: A Political Kaleidoscope
Kenneth John

In this article I want to deal with the political situation as it exists in St. Vincent. More particularly I want to stress the unstable nature of the party system, such as it is, and to suggest that the dismal state of the island's political condition will persist so long as we are afflicted with the twin perils of a failure of leadership and the political illiteracy of the masses.

In an article of this sort one is hard put to know where to begin; so many present-day events seem to stem from the past, determined, conditioned, or at least influenced by what went before. The mainstream of my discussion spans the period 1951–66, and there is a reason for this. I want to deal specifically with fifteen years under adult suffrage when, to put it clumsily, Vincentian politics became "nationalized," when the roles of the nascent political party and emergent trade union movement became the most prominent features of the social landscape. But this will not be done to the exclusion of some treatment of the preceding era which has evidently cast a shadow on the present situation. To begin with, political development and constitutional advancement tend to go hand-in-glove and for this reason it will be necessary to give a graphic picture of constitutional development as background knowledge for a better grasping of the subtleties of today's political trends.

Flambeau (Kingstown, St. Vincent), No. 5, July 1966, pp. 1–9. Reprinted with permission of the author.

St. Vincent became a British Colony after the Seven
Years' War, a claim which was confirmed by the Treaty of
Versailles 1783. The imposed constitution was a pocket-
edition of the British with a Governor, Council and Assembly standing as miniature versions of King, Lords and
Commons. But whereas in the British circumstance the
separation of these three organs of Government was more
apparent than real owing to the evolution of a two-party
system and the force of convention, in St. Vincent each
body was sealed off in virtually water-tight compartments.
The hand-picked council was merely advisory to the Governor who ruled as well as reigned. The assembly, like the
Council representative only of the White Planter class, remained a largely ineffective debating society save where it
obstructed in its control over finance. To think of becoming a member of the assembly one first had to own 50
acres of land or a lot in town valued at £50 per annum,
while to exercise the vote one had to own 10 acres of land
or a lot valued at £10 p.a. in the country or £20 in
town. This political system was the handmaiden of colonial
slave society then enjoying its heyday, but it developed
a momentum of its own which spilled over and persisted in
its fundamentals far into the post-emancipation period.
From 1763–1838 Vincentians existed under a very repressive regime dominated by a sprinkling of White Planto-
crats. The slaves, far and away the bulk of the population,
had few rights. They were not human beings, legally speaking; they were mere chattel. After the Emancipation Act
(1838) quite a few of the ex-slaves bought out mountain
lands and by their industry and resource began to qualify
for the franchise. It was this prospect of eventual government by the free Blacks placed against the backdrop of the
Haitian revolution and Morant Bay Rebellion in Jamaica
which prompted the White overlords to surrender the constitution and opt for pure Crown Colony rule in 1877. Thus
a trend which might have developed peacefully into democratic institutions was stunted at its birth; hence the significance of 1951. The new council was wholly nominated
and, not unnaturally, it was constituted of the island's

moneyed men—John Hazell, Cheesman and Kennedy Porter were the unofficial members. It needs no great perceptive mind to observe that political parties had no raison d'être in the prevailing climate. Primitive Crown Colony Government held sway for nearly fifty years. During this period progressive ideas from the large world began to seep through the colonial curtain, news of the proletarian revolution in Russia broke through, and many Vincentians were imbued with libertarian and egalitarian ideas to which they were exposed during overseas fighting in the First World War. Indeed George V himself had declared piously that the successful termination of the war "manifests the victory of the ideals of freedom and liberty for which we have made untold sacrifices." But many colonials were tempted to take the King seriously. In Trinidad Cipriani formed a Representative Government Association with the slogan "Crown Colony rule must Go" and all the smaller islands followed suit. It must be emphasized that the Vincentian counterpart was not a really radical movement. It was for the most part the dissentient voice of a disgruntled middle class which believed that it had mastered all the cultural shibboleths and political idiom of the mother-country to qualify for some measure of constitutional advance. Little thought was directed to the condition of the man-in-the-street. Featuring in the Association were the "nouveaux riches"—C. D. McDowall, F. A. Corea, H. M. Haywood, Alex Fraser, O. D. Brisbane, and intellectuals like George McIntosh and Robert Anderson. The upshot of all this agitation was the Wood Commission of 1922. In his report in 1924 Wood made that famous statement which the British have forged into a handy weapon for use at constitutional conferences, "that democracy is a plant of tender growth," as a fitting preface to the grudging concessions which he recommended. An elected element was reintroduced hedged in by property and educational qualifications. In any event there were to be only 3 elected members who even with the unlikely support of nominated members could be outvoted by the official bloc. As if elected members like Alex Fraser, Walter Grant and Joseph Gray, all men of economic substance, would need curbing in the legislature! The second term under this constitution was dominated by the same stamp of men. Arnold Punnett was nominated in place of Elliott Sprott who had died and A. B. C. DaSantos was returned when J. M. Gray had retired on grounds of ill-health. At its third term the old pattern, as it was no doubt anticipated, persisted with only a slight change in personnel, Agostino DaSilva and Frederick Corea being the new elected members. Obviously some bold break-through was needed lest the system harden into a constitutional dead-end which might frustrate the political aspirations of the great majority of the people. The cue was taken by a group of Windward Islands liberals, spear-headed by Grenada's Marryshow, who clamoured for a self-governing West Indian political community. The St. Vincent Representative Government Association was superseded by McIntosh's Workingmen's Association to which was attached a political wing known as the St. Vincent Labour Party (1932). As a direct outcome of pressure tactics which climaxed at the Dominica Conference at which St. Vincent was represented by Eb. Duncan, a further liberalisation of the constitution was effected. Frankly, it was not much of a muchness, the elected members went up from three to five and the nominated from one to three. It was glowing testimony to the passion of the British for piece-meal, gradualistic, constitutional grants. It meant only that the elected members could now hold the official bloc in temporary deadlock once it had been assured the co-operation of the nominated element. Once again it is necessary to emphasize that with the exception of George McIntosh, who tended to radicalism, the other elected members were conservatives who could reasonably be expected to be cautious in their approach and accommodationist in their outlook. They were Newton Nanton, Alpheus Allen, and Herbert Davis. George McIntosh virtually fought a lone battle in the House championing the cause of the disfranchised class which he tried to shock out of its lethargy and supineness. When economic hardship during the 1930's depression married with political suppression and social degradation the message got through, and the result was the 1935 civil disturbances during which George McIntosh was jailed. The British Colonial Office which believed only in "negotiation after crisis," sent in the celebrated Moyne Commission to investigate and make recommendations.

The Moyne Commission Report was revealing. It provided documentary evidence which read like an indictment against British Colonial policies that exploited a people living in sub-human conditions. It was dynamite and the British withheld its publication until the end of the Second World War. In fact Moyne flattered to deceive, for although he saw clearly the cause for most of the discontent he was diffident in coming up with the real answers. But radical problems need radical solutions, Moyne or no Moyne, and his advocacy of constitutional reform that was "judicious in existing circumstances" only begged the question. By the time of the implementation of his report much water had flowed under the bridge and it was clear that nothing short of adult suffrage with an unambiguous timetable leading up to eventual autonomy would suffice. The new constitution came in force in 1951. The illiterate masses were for the first time made political animals. And there was an elected majority in the House—eight as against three nominated and two officials. A quasi-Ministerial system was set up with three elected members serving as chairmen of various committees which were responsible for the running of the relevant Government departments. It in fact offered a period of apprenticeship for potential Ministers and, given the plums of office offered by the new governmental structure, the idea of the formal political party was born.

With the advent of the universal franchise in 1951 our main story begins. The flood-gates of pent-up frustrations were unlocked and the people channelled all their released emotions into politico-economic movements. Everyone had to be a party man and a unionist in a fashion bordering on the fanatic. A political vacuum was created which sucked

in the charismatic leader to offer a "Father figure" image
to a people still afflicted with the slave mentality of Massa
Day. Political meetings spiced with meaningless sloganising
and empty promises became the chief form of entertain-
ment in a culturally benighted region. Following their local
hero to whom they were often bonded by the spell of persuasive oratory and social identification or by the more
compulsive strangle-hold of economic dependence, the people shifted their support with every move he made. And
the politician, newly arrived, and bewitched by the intoxi-
cant of freshly-won laurels, gyrated between parties,
crossed the floor, and performed all sort of incredible political gymnastics in the haunting desire to consolidate his
acquisition of power. Thus has the political situation in
St. Vincent remained fluid, even amorphous. The game of
party chairs and music has become commonplace and
makes a mockery of the political process; the obstinate
conservatism of an inefficient Civil Service aggravates the
problem; and the intransigency of the Employer-class in
dealing with irresponsible Trade Unions adds to the troubles. When it is recalled that all these problems are located
in a small, backward island, with no clear-cut future, the
political situation seems very bleak and to admit of no
ready answer.

* * * *

The first factor which strikes the eye of any casual observer is the political intensity of present-day St. Vincent.
In the light of what was said before regarding the pro-
tracted political suppression of the people this is not surprising. Precisely because they had been denied a place in
the political process the people got themselves to believe
that politics held the key to all problems and offered the
panacea to every ill. And they were encouraged in this
belief by some political aspirants who regarded the capture of the seat of government as the passport for acceptance on the higher rungs of the social ladder as well as by
those who saw politics purely in terms of job opportunity

and looked upon election campaigns as a veritable life-and-death struggle. Further, the face-to-face relations of our very intimate and compact society has led to the practical personalisation of politics. In this context one can understand the painstaking research which goes into the probing of family histories and private lives of election candidates. Feuds and quarrels as well as personality problems are hammered out and settled on political platforms when not in the Council Chamber. In this way a most vicious circle has been set up, for the people, fed so long on the empty diatribe of irrelevant mudslinging, have acquired a taste for the sordid and the base. The net result is that anyone with pretensions to introducing a rationalistic and intellectual approach to St. Vincent's problems is more likely than not to be hounded out of the political arena, as indeed was the fate of "son" Mitchell when he threatened to launch a third Force and revolutionise politics. Mitchell has had to do some serious rethinking and pool resources with the Labour Party. And it is difficult to cut a path out of this barren political wilderness if only because of the paucity of talent in our midst. Teachers and Civil Servants are rigidly debarred from taking any active part. To the major business houses and commercial banks politics is dirty business, and the message has clearly been transmitted to their staff. This means that a few professionals, Trade Unionists and political careerists share the field of politics along with a handful of professionals some of whom find it difficult to establish an affinity with the masses.

The traditional hostility between the Press and the PPP Government began way back in 1951 when, instead of sympathising with political advance and educating and informing, the Press stood as a cold prophet of doom in the face of changes it was powerless to stay. Indeed the *Vincentian* self-righteously greeted the early political crises in the tone of a "We-told-you-so" editorial, and called for an electors' association of the old, respected, conservative politicians who dominated in the days of pure Crown Colony rule and its several variants. With the liberalisation of the constitution, it was symptomatic of the changing times that the self-made coloured businessman, Marksman, would be preferred on the nominated benches to a mulatto Planter enriched with inherited interests; and it is understandable that the PPP Government was adamant in its stand for a unicameral legislature in the new constitutional arrangements lest the established interests beat a glorious retreat and ensconce themselves in the sanctuary of a Senate.

If we retrace our historical development we can easily account for some of the inter-party animosities and personality conflicts. The parties are based on no ideology or, in so far as they stand for anything, they stand for the same thing. Since one side cannot attack the other side's programme in as much as manifestoes all preach the same story, personalities are assailed. The country is a poor agricultural community divided between the small group of "haves" and a large undifferentiated mass of the "have nots." Since any serious-minded party must minister to the needs of this large category of working (and unworking) people all parties will necessarily use the same basic approach. And since the parties stand for more or less the same thing, and since gainful employment is so hard to come by, it is not surprising (though we might find it distasteful) to find men jumping from one side to the other to get a salary and, incidentally, to get something done for their constituency. For the national cake is so small that the Government in power always sees to it that their supporters are guaranteed at least a small slice.

This very real temptation to change sides is aggravated by the disproportionately strong bargaining power of the Individual. In our small legislature of 9 seats a single politician might easily hold the balance of power and can determine the composition of the Government. Campbell held such a position in 1959 when the PPP made overtures to Young. But Clive Tannis went over and tilted the balance in the Government's favour. In 1965 it was Young who went over to tip the scales once more on the side of the PPP. And if Slater had resigned with Haynes from the PPP in 1962 (as some folk were led to expect) the Government would have collapsed. The politicians are empowered to do these feats of political somersaulting because for the most part they are not indebted to the Party for their seats, though the results of the South Leeward constituency in the coming election may well prompt a revision of this statement. It is of more than passing interest to note that five members of the present legislature—Joshua, Young, Slater, Tannis and Latham have survived four elections under varying labels. After the old 8 Army came tumbling down like the pack of cards it was, Mr. Joshua formed his PPP in whose saddle he has since remained unchallenged. Young went over to PPP in 1954, joined the Labour Party in 1955, departed to lead the PLM in 1957, merged it with the Labour Party in 1957, and defected to become a top brass in the ruling PPP in 1964. Slater has been fairly constant. After the short honeymoon with the 8 Army he remained an Independent until 1957 when he went over to the PPP to whom he has ever remained faithful. After the demise of the 8 Army Tannis also remained fiercely Independent until 1958 when he joined forces with Labour, only to go over to the PPP during the '59 political crisis. Mr. Latham, too, was an Independent member of the House who joined the PPP in 1956, quarrelled with the leadership, and enlisted in the ranks of the Labour Party in 1958. Added to these are George Charles and Afflick Haynes who also share colourful political careers. Charles led the 8 Army in 1951, ran as an Independent in 1954, contested under the PLM banner in 1957, ran on a Labour ticket in 1961, and appears to be a PPPite at the present time. Haynes, on the other hand, was an Independent in 1954, a member of the PPP from 1956–62, a Labourite from 1962–64, and seems to be a PPP supporter at the moment of writing.

There is a lot of talk in St. Vincent that the parties are divided on class lines. This is sheer nonsense. In terms of educational qualification, shade gradation, or economic indices, the country is about eighty per cent lower-class. And since both parties share the country evenly it is obvious that both are supported by a substantial portion of the

working class. But it is true that the foundation membership of the Labour Party was dominated by middle-class
folk, and though that party has come a very long way in
terms of organising and winning support at the grass-root
level it has never been completely absolved of its original
sin. In any event it has been easy for its rival to capitalise
on its leadership by a professional elite and project a
bourgeois image on it. Equally, on the other hand, because politics in a country as poor as St. Vincent is a relatively costly business, even the supposedly lower-class party
has had to compromise itself and seek support from certain
middle-class business men who welcome the opportunity to
exploit the political situation for their own economic ends.
In any event the Planter class always looms in the background to hand out sufficient funds to either side to curry
favour, safeguard their interests, and ensure that neither
party has an overpowering mandate to effect any real radical scheme.

The most frightening thing about the artificial division
of the followers of the two parties is that people living in
squalor, suffering the same stark hunger and economic
distress, will tear each other to pieces and sacrifice each
other on the altar of an ephemeral party difference. Trade
Unions fighting for the same category of workers become
hopelessly splintered and a fractured cooperative and credit
union movement cannot get off ground floor because the
people involved are blinded to their community of interest
by this fictitious concept of different party orientation. All
the while the vested interest in the community back-seat
drive and play the parties off against each other like mari-
onettes dangling on a thread. The trouble is that the reactionary element from which both parties derive their financial sustenance is able to force them away from the
masses spiritually and get them to toe the line of the conservative interests. It is a tragic illustration of "who pays
the piper calls the tune." In the meantime the parties in
their frustration turn inward and engage in dirty in-
fighting, character assassinate, and burn themselves up in
hate accompanied by a studied evasion of the real issues

that confront the society. With no clear objective in sight but at the whim of one of the major political actors mock political battles are staged with demonstrations, counter-demonstrations, placards and highly emotional speeches which drain away the energies of the people apparently to no end. When this phenomenon has been developed into a fine art—and it is fast becoming one—we will have reached a political blind-alley; there will be no move to effect social and economic reconstruction, but manifestoes will continue to parade all sorts of grandiose projects, and all sorts of glittering promises will be made (and believed) but the more things vary the more they will remain the same. Politics will still be of the gutter variety dominated by mudslinging, acts of naked treachery, corruption and posturing, and political life will continue to be fought in a veritable jungle. In Hobbesian language political life will be "poor, nasty, solitary, brutish," if not short. As it is now. Unless there chances some dramatic turn in the current trend of events.

5.

Governments are run by civil servants as well as by elected officials. In small territories like the West Indies, the civil services have a transcendent importance. Traditionally a major avenue for middle-class advancement, the West Indian civil service is apt to contain a large proportion of local secondary school and university graduates. When local elected rulers succeeded colonial officials, relations between the legislative and administrative branches of government came under increasing stress, with civil servants and political leaders each jealous of the power and perquisites of the other. In this article, a Guyanese scholar and administrative authority describes the steps taken by civil-service commissions to regularize recruitment, training, salaries, and other conditions of employment. In the final analysis, however, such regulatory mechanisms do not prevent coercion and politicization in newly independent societies where political and administrative leaders feel they represent clashing interests. Many a civil servant has been summarily dismissed, many a politician subtly destroyed, as a consequence of such rivalries.

B. A. N. COLLINS took his undergraduate degree at the University College of the West Indies, later studied at the Institute of Political Studies of the University of Paris, and received a doctorate in political science and public administration. He returned to the Caribbean to become a tutor in the Department of Extra-Mural Studies and subsequently a lecturer in government at the University of the West Indies. In 1966 he became Professor of Public Administration and Government at the University of Guyana, where he has also served as Dean of the Faculty of Social Science and as Acting Vice-Chancellor of the University. Since 1970 he has been with the United Nations in New York and in Kenya.

Some Notes on Public Service Commissions in the Commonwealth Caribbean

B. A. N. Collins

One feature common to the political institutions of four new nations in the Caribbean—Jamaica, Trinidad, Guyana and Barbados—is the entrenchment in their constitutions of independent Service Commissions which deal with the civil, police and judicial services. These Commissions were instituted by the former ruling power, in the West Indies as elsewhere in the British Commonwealth, in anticipation of independence, in order to secure the careers of members of these services from the control of future political leaders. This paper deals only with the first one of these institutions, the Public Service Commission. The purpose is to comment on the adaptation of the original concept of the P.S.C. to the particular environment of these Caribbean territories, noting in particular those circumstances accompanying independence which compel re-examination of the machinery of government, and raise doubts about the adequacy of the P.S.C. for serving the purposes of good public administration in these new states. Indeed the experience of Jamaica, Trinidad and Guyana already suggests that the terms of reference and consequent procedures of the P.S.C., which seemed appropriate for actual and anticipated conditions when these were British colo-

Social and Economic Studies, Vol. 16, No. 1, March 1967, pp. 1–16. Reprinted with permission of the author and the Institute of Social and Economic Research, University of the West Indies.

nies, might prove quite insufficient for dealing with the current situation in the public services.

The P.S.C. in the Caribbean came about after the British Government had, in keeping with post-war colonial policy, decided to prepare all its territories for eventual independence within the Commonwealth. The Colonial Office White Paper on "Organisation of the Colonial Service" (1946) recommended that in discharging his duties of selecting and appointing candidates to the local service each colonial Governor should be advised in these matters by a P.S.C. "so composed as to command the confidence of the Service and the public."[1] It seemed necessary to create this institution because it was the official view that political independence for the colonies might prove dangerous for the integrity of the public services. The public was only to be assured of civil service neutrality by entrusting the control of careers to a body as non-political and in as high public regard as the judiciary. For, as the report of the 1950–51 British Guiana Constitutional Commission later put it, expressing positive British conviction: "A democratic form of government cannot be sustained unless both the judiciary and the civil service function independently of the Legislature . . . Not only has the civil servant a right to protection against discrimination, but he should be assured that any disciplinary action against him should be taken on the advice of a tribunal, to which no suspicion of political partisanship could justifiably attach." Moreover, the Report added, future Ministers themselves should "as far as possible be protected from the possibility of pressure by unscrupulous persons demanding places or promotion for friends and relatives as the price of their political support." So they recommended a Public Service Commission for British Guiana whose membership "should be entirely outside political activities," as a pre-requisite of internal self-government and eventual independence.[2]

[1] Great Britain, Colonial Office, *Organisation of the Colonial Service*, Col. No. 197 (London: H.M.S.O., 1946), p. 9.

[2] British Guiana, *Report of the Constitutional Commission, 1950–1951*, Col. No. 280 (Georgetown: Government Printer), p. 33.

The P.S.C., then, was born of mistrust of politicians and their friends and the paradox appears of Whitehall agreeing to give the Colonies political independence while revealing the continued distrust for local politicians which had marked the attitude of British officials under the colonial system. English Governors could be entrusted with the care of the civil service, but not local elected Ministers. This view of course was shared by many leaders of local opinion in colonial days. The Correspondent of the "West India Committee Circular" (May 1951) noted a "general outburst of messianic faith in Governors," when Sir Hugh Foot arrived in Jamaica. The Bishop of Jamaica wanted the Governor to know that "in spite of constitutional changes . . . the ordinary Jamaican . . . still expects the Governor to govern . . . and . . . to protect him from the unwise and sometimes unworthy manoeuvrings of party politicians."[3]

It should also be pointed out that in creating the P.S.C. Whitehall was also passing on the benefit of experience of past British politicians. The notorious effects of party patronage on the public service had been criticized in the still influential 1855 Northcote-Trevelyan Report. This Report led to reforms which eventually resulted in the establishment of a Civil Service Commission which preserves the British public from unfit appointees, by testing the qualifications of persons who seek appointment in the Civil Establishment. Not the least of the benefits that Britain could give the young nations, therefore, was the lesson from her historical experience that politicians, unless explicitly prevented by legislative provision, would seek to "interfere" in the public service and that this tendency once developed could be difficult to eradicate.

Another purpose of a P.S.C. which was not equally stressed in Reports, was to offer equality of opportunity and treatment for all public servants on the basis of merit. To emphasize this would be to imply that this was not the case under the system by which the Governor, through

---

[3] Quoted in H. V. Wiseman, *The Cabinet in the Commonwealth* (London: Stevens, 1958), p. 313.

his Colonial Secretary, controlled appointments, transfers, promotions and discipline in the local service. But there had been local criticisms of public service appointments. The pre-war Moyne Commission noted the resentment frequently caused by the appointment of white senior officials from elsewhere to the public services in the West Indies.[4] This resentment seemed to have been strongest in Jamaica. The Jamaica Progressive League called, in the late thirties, for the Jamaicanization of the civil service. One of the League's leaders, W. A. Domingo, called "a breach of the Constitution" the "flagrant discrimination" represented by a Colonial Office advertisement in a London paper for a Medical Officer for Kingston, requiring that the applicant be a "person of European parentage."[5]

Though government service was more open to all talents than many areas of the private sector the civil servants in many West Indian territories were not always convinced that government was an utterly impartial employer and asked for some institutional arrangements to deal with promotions in particular. For example the *Report of the Committee on the Public Service in Jamaica, 1939–1942,* had put forward the suggestion of the Civil Service Association for the appointment of a "Promotions Selection Committee," but recommended that such a body should act only in an advisory capacity.[6] In fact throughout the major West Indian territories the Governor's Deputy, the Colonial Secretary, was his one-man Public Service Commission, assisted by Secretariat or departmental boards. The approach of independence did not mean, however, that the Colonial Secretary's function passed to his civil service successors, the Permanent Secretaries at the head of Ministries or, as in Britain, to a Civil Service Commission composed of civil servants. Local civil servants were not to be en-

[4] Great Britain, *West India Royal Commission Report,* Cmd. 6607 (London: H.M.S.O., June 1945), p. 60.

[5] W. A. Domingo, "A Breach of the Constitution," *Public Opinion* (August 6, 1938).

[6] Jamaica, *Report of the Committee on the Public Service in Jamaica, 1939–1942* (Kingston: Government Printer, 1942), p. 10.

trusted with these personnel functions any more than local Ministers. Even the appointment of a senior establishment officer to the early P.S.C. was only a temporary expedient. The civil servants in general favoured, it seemed, a non-civil-service P.S.C. to deal, not only with recruitment, but with discipline and promotions as well. (In Jamaica, for largely administrative reasons, "discipline" remained with the Jamaica Privy Council until 1956.)[7] The absence so far of powerful departmental traditions governing these matters justified the transfer of such powers to a P.S.C. The public service was so small that no single department could offer a full career to all its members, and none seemed adequately equipped to deal justly with disciplinary matters. An additional reason for a non-civil service P.S.C. was adduced later by the Trinidad Civil Service Association—to protect civil servants from other civil servants. "It is a well known fact that a Civil Servant is much more ruthless and cunning than any Politician could be, when he is in a position to exercise authority arbitrarily and with any degree of finality."[8]

Finally, in commenting on the genesis of the P.S.C. it must be noted that nowhere does one find, as in American writings on Civil Service Commissions, any extensive discussions which indicate the influence of scientific management theories. There is no view expressed that a P.S.C. would lead to more scientific selection and placement, or more precise job classifications, or the application of other modern personnel management techniques. Metropolitan influence had brought such teachings to the American Philippines but the P.S.C. in the British Caribbean, like its model in London, made small pretence about furthering scientific personnel administration. Objectives were limited to ensuring that candidates met minimal educational standards, to preserving the public service from politicians, and to looking after particular cases by applying and extending

[7] B. Hamilton, *Problems of Administration in an Emergent Nation* (New York: Praeger, 1964), p. 97.

[8] Trinidad, Civil Service Association, "Draft Commission for Trinidad" (Unpublished Memorandum, 1962), pp. 3–4.

the elaborate personnel jurisprudence which had developed in the Colonial Secretariat. It was largely, in fact, a system of civil service protectionism.

In due course the P.S.C. was established, either by Public Law passed by the local Legislature, as in Jamaica in 1951, or as part of a newly granted Constitution as in British Guiana in 1953. Initially the P.S.C. was in each territory merely advisory to the Governor, appointed by him in consultation with the Chief Minister, and was assured of the Governor's backing. It got the support of the Staff Associations, which were also consulted on its members' appointment, and had the privilege of access to it. (The Officers of the Barbados C.S.A. were sent copies of the Commission's agenda.) It had a good opportunity to build up its personal prestige, for at this stage public concern about localization increased and the P.S.C. gained credit for appointing "the first local man" in a number of high offices. Conventions had time to form—such as the one forbidding Ministers to deal directly with Commissioners. The Governor remained the intermediary between Cabinet and the Chairman of the P.S.C. Of course the Governor maintained control over the "Secretary of State appointments"—generally the English civil servants whose conditions of service were not to be controlled even by an independent local commission. Indeed the P.S.C. never became "executive" until satisfactory arrangements about careers and compensation for possible loss of service were agreed between Britain and each local territory. The second and executive stage came when the Governor appointed the Commission on the advice of the Premier, and when the Governor's power to reject the recommendations of the P.S.C. was removed, normally (as was the case in every territory save Guyana) previous to the final Independence Conference. Thus the years before independence gave the Commission valuable time to gain experience, to settle on routines and procedures, and to become accepted generally within the community as a normal and essential feature of self-government. Indeed, on the whole it gained much personal prestige for itself, as well as acceptance of its pur-

poses to the extent, as we shall see, that the independence
settlements left its functions unchanged.

Functions and membership combined to achieve and reinforce the original purpose of the P.S.C.—the independence of the public service from politics. The P.S.C. appointed and promoted public officers to vacant posts as
these posts were created by the Government, and it was
concerned with transfers within the service in so far as
transfers affect the career of the civil servants concerned
or of others indirectly concerned. Government, as employer, laid down terms of dismissal and codes of disciplinary action; the Commission ensured that justice was
done within these terms. Since government scholarships
affected recruitment and careers, this touched on the responsibilities of the P.S.C. and the Commission worked
out an appropriate relationship with selection boards. Generally, training activities did not come under the P.S.C.,
since, in the words of a former Commissioner's *Notes for
the Guidance of Members of Commissions*, "it is difficult
for the Commission to maintain its independence" if it
accepts responsibility for activities which cannot be
divorced from ministerial control.[9]

In the West Indies the preferred method of procedure
for recruitment was the interview. There were no entrance
examinations on the English model—evidence of academic
qualifications (certificates or degrees obtained) and a tes-
timonial of good character were sufficient. Once admitted
to the public service the officer's advancement depended
on seniority, on his performance at interviews, and on
his annual confidential report. It was a process designed to
protect his career opportunities, and one presided over by
persons not generally unsympathetic to his point of view.
Indeed in most cases and at most times the chairmen of
the P.S.C. and at least another of the four or five part-time
Commissioners would be retired local senior civil servants
of vast experience and much personal prestige within the

[9] J. A. Mulhall, *The Public Service Commission in Overseas
Territories: Notes for the Guidance of Members of Commissions* (London: H.M.S.O., 1962), p. 12.

public service. Other members would be "dignitaries"—persons of high social standing. Often there was a scholar (schoolmaster or university staff-member) who could be helpful in determining academic qualifications. The author knows of hardly any case where their integrity was questioned but several when their capacity as judges of men was sceptically regarded. In any case it needs to be added that these paragons of integrity were not easily available—businessmen were reluctant to take on the job because of pressure of time and, of course, politically-minded persons were to be excluded. In Guyana, this caused the Governor some difficulty in selecting Commissioners—"a non-political being in Guiana is almost a prehistoric animal" the Leader of the Opposition is reported to have said at the 1962 Independence Conference.[10]

The Commissioners were assisted by a Secretariat headed by a civil servant Secretary sometimes titled Chief Personnel Officer (Jamaica) or Director of Personnel Administration (Trinidad). No doubt the ideal choice would have been a civil servant with formal qualifications in personnel management or industrial psychology in addition to wide administrative experience. The job classification for British Guiana had explicitly, but in vain, required certain formal academic and professional qualifications. Persons in the service with such special qualifications proved hard to find. The Public Service Commissions still do not always have academically-trained personnel specialists as secretaries, nor do they employ staff inspectors. But, as stated before, the P.S.C. considered its duties to be quasi-judicial, not managerial.

The Staff Associations were not too dissatisfied by these arrangements and in any case had a right of appeal to the Governor. This sort of P.S.C. could protect them from consequences of their own apparently political behaviour. Thus there could be little opportunity for victimization by politicians, even after civil servants went on strike in 1962 and 1963 in British Guiana. Generally too, this P.S.C.,

[10] British Guiana Independence Conference, London, 1962, *Report*, Cmd. 1870 (London: H.M.S.O., 1963), p. 12.

very much influenced, it was felt, by its Chairman and its
civil servant Secretary was inclined to give due weight to
seniority in estimating merit, seniority being an objective
and egalitarian criterion much favoured by civil servants
and ex-civil servants. Whatever doubts there were about
the Commission's competence were expressed discreetly.
The biases of Commissioners (in favour of evident social
adjustment or love of sport or of old boys of a particular
secondary school) became quickly known, and as the
writer can attest from experience as a Commissioner civil
servants soon learned the appropriate kind of "Commis-
sionmanship" to be employed. The willingness of the Commissions to fill all possible vacancies with locals, or as a
Colonial Office Report put it, "the need to give expressions
through the Public Service to the new constitutional status
of the country"[11] pleased civil servants as well as the public, even though many were not unaware that this policy
could leave insufficient places open for other local candidates (such as university graduates) who became available
in later years. Some civil servants may even have had the
good luck (from their point of view) of being promoted
beyond their capabilities.

Finally, since the Government was one of the biggest
employers in each country, the P.S.C. system of impartial
selection and promotion became an influential example for
private firms to emulate. To help extend the merit principle
in Caribbean society, in however imperfect a form, was
undoubtedly a great contribution, and gained for the
P.S.C. the favour of enlightened public opinion.

When the time came to prepare draft constitutions for
the Independence Conferences the P.S.C. was already a
positively established feature of self-rule. In the drafts prepared and presented locally (at Queen's Hall, Trinidad or
Queen's College, Guyana) an independent P.S.C. was always featured. There was general agreement on its functions; there were only differences on the procedure for
selecting P.S.C. members. It is to be noted that little

[11] Great Britain, Colonial Office, *Service with Overseas Government*, Cmd. 1193 (London: H.M.S.O., n.d.), p. 10.

was said even at this stage about the qualifications of Commissioners as management experts. The Trinidad C.S.A. Paper referred to earlier would have further limited the choice by excluding not only serving officers but those who had retired less than three years previously. "Civil Service experience is not a necessary requirement for appointment to the Commission and in most cases constitutes a hindrance . . . Although persons of integrity could be found within the civil service, there are many more outside of it who should be given the opportunity to serve the country on this very important body. Any risk of converting the work of the P.S.C. to that of a pensioner's job, should be removed."[12] It was not made plain whether this view stemmed entirely from principle, or from dissatisfaction with an ex-civil service member or members. However, the rule generally established was that an ex-civil servant may serve, but, as in the case of other members, cannot hold any other public office for a fixed time thereafter and, judging from the lists of Commissioners appointed it seemed that civil servants remained more concerned with integrity, than with managerial expertise. Locally-born management experts were in any case rather hard to obtain.

The London Independence Conferences confirmed the functions of the P.S.C. and enshrined the P.S.C., as developed so far, in the constitutions of the four territories. The importance of the P.S.C. was safeguarded by making its powers generally unalterable save by constitutional amendment. Two things seemed to contribute directly to this state of affairs. Firstly, the two-party system ensured that an Opposition played the role of guardian of freedoms at Independence Conferences. To take one example: at the Barbados conference, 1966, the opposition parties wanted to make constitutional provision for C.S.A. representation on the P.S.C.[13] Thus, in effect, political rivalry helped pre-

[12] "Draft Commission for Trinidad," *loc. cit.*

[13] Barbados Constitutional Conference, London, 1966, *Report*, Cmd. 3058 (London: H.M.S.O., 1966), p. 6. This was one of the "Points of Disagreement," left to be settled at the

serve the *status quo ante* independence of the P.S.C. Such
dispute as there was in London centred on the new method
of appointment of the Commissioners. This, it was generally agreed had to be by the Governor-General "on the
recommendation" of the Prime Minister. The attempt to
limit this exercise of political power took the form of ensuring that some recommendations be made by the Prime
Minister in Jamaica and Guyana, "in consultation with"
the Leader of the Opposition. Thus impartiality was to be
sought through some measure of bi-partisanship. Furthermore, some of the Commissioners were to be selected by
the Prime Minister from panels of names put up by Staff
Associations, as in Guyana, where the Prime Minister was
only allowed to recommend one person without consulting
anybody. The Trinidad Constitution alone does not require
the Prime Minister to consult with anyone, though he may,
by convention, consult with the Leader of the Opposition.
Secondly, the dynamics of the Conference situations also
aided the entrenchment of powers and independence of
the P.S.C. after appointment, for Britain, in the last exercise of her authority, was not going to yield the principle
of an independent P.S.C. Knowing this, the governing
parties concentrated on other matters (electoral systems
for example), which were negotiable. Thus the Independence Conference marked full agreement by local political
leaders with the original concept of the P.S.C. The P.S.C.
system received its accolade at its source, Whitehall.

After Independence Day the P.S.C. becomes an important part of the constitutional life of the new nations. The
question that now arises is: How adequate is the P.S.C. today for the purposes of the new states? To answer that we
must first look very briefly at some of the new circumstances obtaining which were not clearly envisaged before
Independence or which, though perceived earlier, did not

Conference. The view of the ruling party (which prevailed)
was that "in practice there would continue to be consultation
with such representatives of public employees as might be appropriate and practicable."

sufficiently alter matters to the point where fresh thinking about the duties of a P.S.C. seemed called for.

Let us consider first the scope for recruitment. Historically, government had been an attractive employer because of its opportunities offered to all comers and because of fringe benefits such as overseas leave and a non-contributory pension. Earlier government reports had seemed to assume that these things would long constitute an exclusive advantage.[14] But, in fact, after Independence, commercial and industrial organizations competing with the governments and each other for good local recruits have been offering better remuneration, speedier opportunities for reaching posts of real responsibility together with good training, pension and health schemes. Some firms even offer generous overseas leave facilities, at a time when the states, partly because of the expense, are cutting back on the leave provisions which had been among the most appreciated of civil service perquisites. The needs of modern industry have compelled local and foreign-owned firms to recruit in a more universalistic manner than before; talent is purchased wherever it could be found, at a competitive price. Government is no longer the only employer which recruits from all classes and shades of West Indians. Even the commercial banks are beginning to place public advertisements in the papers (something never done before) to attract qualified national applicants, with no reference to social background. But the general recruiting style of the P.S.C., to judge from its advertisements, remains that of a body which still seems to believe that its duty is to preserve the service from hosts of patronage-hungry applicants.

Furthermore, government policy in the new states has been to discourage, by work permit and other types of legislation, the importation from abroad of staff for the private sector. The purpose has been to "naturalize" the management of foreign-controlled firms in harmony with

[14] R. O. Ramage, *A Review of the Report of the Working Party on the Government Service of Jamaica* (Kingston: Government Printer, 1955), Para. 16.

the spirit of national independence, and to secure more employment opportunities for local people. A consequence has been the reduction in the potential reservoir from which governments draw their own staff, and also a marked tendency for highly qualified civil servants to resign from public service in order to enter private enterprise.

The creation of public corporations and other quasi-governmental institutions (for example, the National Bank), has also resulted, in Barbados, Trinidad and Guyana, in the loss to the central government of senior staff. For to make a beginning these have had to recruit some of the ablest people in government service. The Bank of Guyana secured the services of the Head of the civil service (the Secretary of the Treasury) as well as a number of other senior persons. The further point to note here is that these staffs were recruited without recourse to the P.S.C., and this afforded an opportunity for "political interference," in the career opportunities of civil servants.

A particular threat to the merit system came in Guyana when the opposition party complained of "racial imbalance" in the public services. A Commission of Enquiry sent by the International Commission of Jurists absolved the P.S.C. of any charge of racial bias, and rejected any suggestion of applying remedial quotas to the recruitment of public servants. But in a perhaps justified breach of the merit principle the International Commission recommended recruitment by racial quotas for a limited time to the police and security forces, as well as an Ombudsman for the investigation of complaints of racial discrimination.[15] The situation did not arise in Guyana and Trinidad where racial or communal quotas had to be initiated in the civil service as in Malaya or Ceylon, but an attempt to allay suspicions may have explained the tendency in these poly-ethnic societies to appoint Commissioners who were themselves representative of the principal racial groupings.

A more general circumstance accompanying independ-

[15] See International Commission of Jurists, British Guiana Commission of Inquiry, *Report: Racial Problems in the Public Service* (Geneva, 1965), pp. 115–21.

ence was the creation of a foreign service. Because of the special nature of this civil service activity a new method of recruiting staff was adopted in Trinidad and Guyana which, in fact, delimited the authority of the P.S.C. In Guyana, the Prime Minister and the Minister of State for External Affairs and the Permanent Secretary of that Ministry sit on an Advisory Committee which recommends candidates for appointment by the P.S.C.[16] Whatever the advantages of this arrangement the fact remains that political persons now have a greater say in careers in a part of the public service. The case in Trinidad is similar. Of course it is accepted practice everywhere that senior diplomatic staff would, like Permanent Secretaries, be posted by the Prime Minister.

Even in the discharge of duties which came solely within its purview, the P.S.C. found itself affected by unanticipated restraints. When governments accept the idea of a P.S.C. to remove the public service from politics, the reasonable *quid pro quo* is that the P.S.C. would assure the governments of sufficient services of public officers to implement government policies. The P.S.C. had consequently to bestir itself to find staff, often in a situation where manpower studies showed serious local shortages. Thus the Barbados P.S.C. had recently to instruct the Chief Personnel Officer to employ part of his leave in the U.K. in recruiting Barbados-born nurses resident there for service at home. An insufficient number seemed to have applied in the normal course. Likewise the Guyana P.S.C., shortly after Independence Day, sent its Deputy Chairman to the West Indies, U.S.A. and Great Britain to recruit doctors of Guyanese and foreign nationality. Some standard procedures for recruitment and appointment had to be modified to allow the mission to succeed.

[16] Guyana, Foreign Service, *Draft Regulations and Rules* (Georgetown: Government Printer, 1966), p. 5. Indeed the Trinidad Constitution (*vide* Sections 94 and 95) in effect gives the Prime Minister wide powers of appointment and transfer, not only to the foreign service, but to the Ministry of External Affairs.

The P.S.C. was also under pressure from within the service to hasten or modify its procedures for appointments and promotions. Many department heads had accepted the idea of leaving to the P.S.C. the responsibility of promoting and transferring staff, for this freed senior civil servants from the allegations of or pressures for favouritism which are only too possible in small or transitional societies. But now the pressure on civil servants came from Ministers anxious to get on with their plans. The P.S.C. often appeared to be a bottleneck—slow to recruit, or to "process" urgently required staff. Delays in appointing the best graduate applicant often ensured his loss to a more swift employer. The elaborate personnel rules which were designed as safeguards often proved to be a hindrance when the accent was on action. Care taken, for example, to preserve the rights of seniority may lead to delayed and eventually unsatisfactory appointments. Ministers, less interested in the control aspects of the P.S.C. and more in the service aspect, cannot but notice these shortcomings and are tempted to seek ways of circumventing the P.S.C., sometimes with the aid of senior civil service advisors. The author has heard in each of the new states of P.S.C. matters that seem to exemplify the triumph of process over purpose. The fault often lay, it must be added, with the staff of the Commission, and their secretariat-styled routines, rather than with the Commissioners themselves.

Direct pressures on the P.S.C. by politicians are of course hard to document. The President of the Jamaican C.S.A., when challenged publicly to prove the allegation that he had made, "of too much ministerial pressures on Service Commissions," did not do so.[17] But interviews with civil servants in all the four territories, not to mention charges by opposition parties, indicate that the services are not always as free from "political interference" as civil servants would wish. Thus as early as July 1963 the Civil Service Association of British Guiana had to bring to the attention of the P.S.C., complaints which it had received

[17] Hamilton, op. cit., p. 190.

that Ministers of Government "were concerning themselves with staffing matters," as the C.S.A.'s Annual Report later put it.[18] The Report continues: "We pointed out that (a) particular Minister concerned himself with the selection, appointment and transfer of personnel at all levels. We advised them (the P.S.C.) that we understood that some of his selections for appointments were later submitted to the Public Service Commission merely for formal approval." Despite reminders there was no reply from the P.S.C. which was, at that time, still "advisory" to the Governor.

A suspicion that governments felt that all was not well with civil service performance seemed justified by the fact that the first three territories to gain independence inaugurated, shortly after freedom day, major studies concerning the efficiency of the public services. In discussing these reports we are concerned, here, only with what was said in direct or implicit criticism of the P.S.C.

Within two years after Independence Trinidad set up a Working Party, chaired by a former head of the civil service and consisting of civil servants and representatives of the Civil Service Association (it was somewhat of an inside job) which reported on "The Role and Status of the Civil Service in the Age of Independence." In an important section of their Report the Working Party found it necessary to consider "to what extent should the politician interfere with the administration of the Civil Service." Evidently this was no dead issue in Trinidad. In answer to the question the civil servants chose a quotation from Laski reiterating the view that "the welfare of the state is best served if permanent officers are free from control from politicians." Otherwise, among other regrettable consequences, "a favourable climate is created for that breed of men who seek to obtain preferment by political patronage without possessing in the majority of cases the necessary training or competence. To achieve their ends they indulge freely in lobbying, news-carrying and sycophancy and the stage

[18] British Guiana, Civil Service Association, *Annual Report, 1963–1964* (Georgetown: Government Printer, 1964), p. 23.

then becomes set for the wholesale destruction of efficiency and morale." . . . "From what has been stated above," the authors conclude, "there can be easily deduced this cardinal principle—that appointments to the public service should be free from political patronage to any degree whatever." The working party felt this principle still needed to be stressed, especially in view of what they described as "the conflict of understanding and outlook between politician and civil servant which still prevails in our country."[19]

The 1965 Report on the public service in Jamaica was written by outside advisers (recruited through the U.N.) and dealt in part with the subject of personnel administration. The experts first paid proper compliments to the "integrity and impartiality" of the P.S.C. whose members and staff "carry out their constitutional office with great thoroughness and care."[20] However, the experts perceived failings in the performance of standard duties, and the need for the P.S.C. to play a larger part in staff development. Indeed the experts noticed "throughout the ministries a general sense, sometimes vague sometimes quite explicit, that the P.S.C. moves in a sphere more remote from day-to-day activities than is consonant with the pressures of current business. It operates mainly in what is for practical purposes a judicial or magisterial capacity upon requests submitted to it by individual Ministries. It has little opportunity of initiating business or playing a generally creative role in the civil service." . . . "True impartiality," the Report goes on to say, in rather oblique criticism, "depends not so much on remoteness or lack of involvement in whatever issues are in question, as on a passionate sense of justice armed with all the relevant information possible,

[19] "First Report of the Working Party, 'On the Role and Status of the Civil Service in the Age of Independence'" (Trinidad: 1964), pp. 28–29.

[20] Jamaica, *Report on Public Administration in Jamaica: Prepared for the Government of Jamaica* (New York: United Nations, 1965), pp. 18 *et seq.* Quotations are from the "Restricted" Report issued April 6, 1965. The final Report was to be published subsequently.

an intimate grasp of the context and a lively concern for the public interest." A remedy lies in creating a full-time Commission—but the experts, relying on information received, no doubt, thought it unrealistic to expect men of the correct calibre and prestige to undertake full-time assignments. (When the author challenged this assumption at a public forum called by the Jamaican C.S.A., another speaker, the Editor of the *Daily Gleaner,* better informed, warned the audience that Jamaica could hardly field such a full-time team. The meeting seemed to agree with his view.)[21] However, the U.N. experts agreed that it was desirable and quite within the constitutional powers of the P.S.C. to enlarge its role to permit it to become, not merely a point of judicial reference, but a source of creative contribution to the civil service. Since the Commissioners could not work full-time, the experts recommended an increase of the Commission's senior staff to whom, under its statutory authority, could be delegated a considerable amount of day-to-day activities in the field of staff development, for example, training, personnel supervision and continued research on man-power needs. The P.S.C. should also delegate much authority to Ministries to promote staff. The P.S.C., freed from minutiae such as the transfer of typists or the formal approval of pensions already computed by the Pensions Branch and audited by the Accountant General, could concentrate on really important issues of policy. Evidently the experts would not hesitate to charge the staff of the P.S.C. with most of the duties of the central personnel agency of the Government Service, and with functions extended "to include the central administration of the whole range of policies and practices regarding general conditions of service (with the important exception of matters relating to pay) which are now under the Ministry of Finance."

The reaction to these wide-ranging proposals from the

[21] Symposium, The Role of the Civil Service in an Independent Jamaica, Holy Cross Church Hall, Half Way Tree, March 15, 1966, reported in the *Civil Service Outlook,* Vol. 7, No. 2, pp. 15–17.

C.S.A. members at this meeting seemed to include some concern about delegating a great deal of power to civil servants. One is reminded of the comment by the Trinidad C.S.A., quoted earlier, about the cunning of the civil servant in authority. It seemed to be the view in Jamaica too that "each junior officer is in need of adequate protection from his seniors and it is in the interest of the service that such protection be given."[22] In the past one could direct appeals through the Governor to the Secretary of State. This external safeguard passes with independence, the P.S.C. takes its place, and the high degree of mistrust evident in West Indian society continues to give the non-civil service P.S.C. a *raison d'être*. However, the Jamaican recommendations have not been implemented in so far as they deal with this extension of P.S.C. power. Meanwhile some of the shortcomings this enlarged P.S.C. was meant to remedy must be presumed still to prevail.

Guyana, as always, seems to offer an extreme case, or rather the same case carried to extremes. Another U.N. team (consisting of two experts with wide experience of Commonwealth countries) was asked a few months after Independence (*inter alia*) to recommend any changes it might consider necessary in the Government's personnel recruitment, promotion and training policies, including the powers, duties and functions of the relevant Service Commissions.[23] In discussing the performance of the P.S.C., their report was as critical as that of Jamaica. They noted "grave dissatisfaction was evinced on all sides at the prolonged delays in disposing of personnel business." Such delays were "said to be a serious source of inefficiency

---

[22] "Draft Commission for Trinidad," *loc. cit.*

[23] It should be noted at this point that, according to the Report of the British Guiana Independence Conference, 1965, the Constitution "will make it clear that the Commissions will not be subject to direction or control in the exercise of their functions . . ." British Guiana Independence Conference, London, 1965, *Report,* Cmd. 2849 (London: H.M.S.O., 1965), p. 16.

throughout the Service."[24] In effect, this was a charge that the P.S.C. procedures could be sometimes dysfunctional to efficient government. Part of the blame, of course, could be attributed to past government policy. The Commission, as fully acknowledged by all interests, was faced with a formidable task when it acquired executive power on Independence Day, May 26, 1966. Almost a total ban had been imposed for two years (1962–64) on the filling of vacancies and a serious backlog had accumulated by December 31, 1964. The vacancies had been unusually numerous too, it appears, because of the high number of resignations from the Service in recent years. The Report of the P.S.C. for 1961 had commented on the tendency for civil servants, especially junior staff, to "look outwards" to other more remunerative employment.[25] There is evidence, too, that the disturbed political circumstances in Guyana—in 1963 and 1964 in particular—led to a loss, through early retirement or resignation, of a high number of senior and middle-grade officers. However, the current delays stem in part from the administrative procedures of the P.S.C. "Parsimonious delegation to Permanent Secretaries is one of the root causes of the delays about which so much is heard—from Ministers, Permanent Secretaries, staff associations and citizens."[26]

Difficulties also stem from the constitutional position of the P.S.C. Basically the P.S.C. in Guyana, as in other countries, is separate, even aloof from departments performing other management functions, and its unique constitutional position makes the co-ordinating of these functions more

[24] Guyana, *Draft Report on Public Administration in Guyana* (Georgetown: Government Printer, November 16, 1966), pp. 50 ff.

[25] British Guiana, Public Service Commission, *Annual Report, 1961* (Georgetown: Government Printer, 1961), p. 9.

[26] *Report on Public Administration in Guyana*, p. 48. Yet when the P.S.C. recently (December 1966) delegated to Permanent Secretaries in Trinidad the power to make acting appointments and to transfer officers within Ministries, many feared (the author was told) that this could facilitate "political interference."

awkward. The U.N. experts on Guyana do not advocate the Jamaican recommendation—enlarging the scope of the P.S.C.—but one already adopted in the other new states of India, Ceylon and Ghana. They proposed creating a Public Service Ministry, preferably under the Prime Minister, which aimed at bringing together all the non-P.S.C. personnel functions—Establishments, Training, Management Services—in a single agency. Indeed, Trinidad by collecting many personnel functions together (in the Ministry of Home Affairs), in a post-election re-shuffle of Ministries in November 1966, seems also to be moving in this direction.[27] Meanwhile, in Guyana the P.S.C. will maintain its constitutional responsibilities, being serviced by a small staff of its own.

The author recalls that his similar suggestion for Jamaica, made in the address to the Jamaican C.S.A., referred to earlier, did not arouse general enthusiasm. However, it is too early yet to see if civil servants in Guyana would welcome the idea of this new Ministry, though it is predictable that the centralization of these functions under the Prime Minister would be viewed suspiciously by the Opposition.

This proposal challenges some previous arguments for a Public Service Commission. For the view that to have an efficient civil service it is desirable that politicians be excluded from personnel functions, is replaced by one which sees the efficiency of the public service as a function of the effective centralization of control under political leadership. The P.S.C. remains, of course, and not merely as an anomalous constitutional relic. From what has been indicated before, it is evident that the watchdog function in the West Indies is not archaic. But modern manage-

---

[27] There seems to be in any case strong opinion among civil servants in the Caribbean that management functions should be removed from the cost-conscious Ministry of Finance. Hamilton recommends the Ministry of Home Affairs (Hamilton, *op. cit.*, p. 162). But Trinidad's Finance Ministry still controls all matters relating to pay and numbers of staff, and deals with disputes between the Government and civil servants. Disputes may be referred to the Industrial Court.

ment practices seem to require either its enlargement (as proposed for Jamaica) or its being supplemented (as proposed for Guyana). The difficulty of constitutional amendment appears to make the latter the easier course.[28]

However, while vigilance continues, all bodies concerned with the efficiency as well as the integrity of the civil service must nowadays be, in the discreet phrase of the U.K.'s Plowden Report, "increasingly conscious of the importance of management."[29] The concerns of public service management, as the Plowden Report succinctly puts it, include "the preparation of material on which decisions are taken; the technical efficiency with which large operations of administration are carried out; the cost-consciousness of staff at all levels; the provision of special skills and services (scientific, statistical, accounting, O. & M. etc.) for handling particular problems, and the awareness and effectiveness with which these can be used; the training and selection of men and women for posts at each level of responsibility."

Where else but from a Public Service Ministry is this drive for improved "management" to come? The P.S.C. is already fully occupied with its special duties. In any case the view is pervasive that the improvement of administrative capacity will be slow, unless, as La Palombara thinks, those in favour of such changes secure "the overt, continuous and single-minded support of central political leadership."[30] West Indian Governments are not unwilling to offer this leadership, within constitutional limits. Constitutional entrenchment protects the P.S.C. from changes, but in any case the ideas and recommendations of U.N. experts do tend to reinforce the P.S.C. concept, while at the same time offering supplementary means of attaining efficiency in the public service. Certainly no support

[28] Whether or not these proposals are to be carried out remains undecided at the time of writing (December 1966).

[29] Great Britain, *Control of Public Expenditure,* Cmd. 1432 (London: H.M.S.O., July 1961), p. 17.

[30] Quoted in Ferrel Heady, "Bureaucracies in Developing Countries," a paper prepared for the Conference of the Comparative Administrative Group, Maryland, April 1966, p. 25.

is given to the view that the P.S.C. is outmoded, and that its functions of recruitment and discipline could now be entrusted to Ministries and Departments. The principle behind the system is reinforced, even as its practical short-comings are noticed.

It is interesting to note that these reappraisals of the personnel function in the West Indies are occurring prac-tically at the same time as in the Mother Country, and for practically the same reasons. Much of the evidence heard in 1964 and 1965 by the House of Commons Committee on Estimates in preparing its Report on "Recruitment to the Civil Service" is echoed in the comments now made about the P.S.C. in the Commonwealth Caribbean. The great difference is that in recent years hardly any authori-tative person in the U.K. expresses fears about political favouritism after initial appointment by the C.S.C. (Ac-cording to a former Civil Service Commissioner there is no mistrust, because "at the higher levels where political influence might be expected to enter in, the tradition of non-interference by Ministers seems to be sufficiently firmly rooted to ensure that, with rare exceptions, it does not.")[31] But the problem of recruiting and holding good staff is similar to the Caribbean. "Part of the difficulty the (U.K.) Commission face when attempting to adapt them-selves to a comprehensive situation is what Professor Mackenzie described as their 'administrative style,'" re-ported the Estimates Committee.[32] "It appears to Your Committee that the Commission's procedures still concen-trate on keeping people out rather than attracting them." In the U.K., too, it seems, the merit system sometimes frustrates the merit principle and methods designed to im-prove the public service by eliminating improper influences on appointments may, in the process, hamper efficiency. Perhaps it is of comfort to know that some of the faults of the P.S.C. in the West Indies are inherent in the merit

[31] A. P. Sinker, "What Are Public Service Commissions For?" *Public Administration*, Vol. 31, Autumn 1953, p. 209.

[32] *Recruitment to the Civil Service*, Sixth Report from the Estimates Committee (London: H.M.S.O., 1965), p. xi.

system and do not represent a failure on the part of its membership, or a reflection on the society it serves. The experience of other new states, such as the Philippines, where merely "formalistic" merit systems seem frustrated by locally accepted patterns of nepotism and favouritism, offers West Indians a wryly gratifying contrast.[33]

The evidence confirms that the P.S.C. remains one of the valuable institutions which have been preserved from pre-Independence days. It had been, when created, a *modern* institution in colonial society, and one with which the Mother Country therefore insisted that new Commonwealth nations must begin their "start in freedom." It survives, because the new nations have learned to accept the virtues of a public service relatively insulated from political influence. After Independence Day therefore, the P.S.C. continues to recruit, appoint, promote and discipline persons within the public service in sole and punctilious discharge of these important parts of the personnel function. But its now constitutionally sacrosanct forms of organization and sets of procedures may sometimes hinder the objective of putting the best men in place quickly and with utter impartiality. Indeed, changing circumstances outside the public service, as well as the complexities in its relations with government departments, increase its difficulties and make it now appear somewhat reactionary. Governments, and, it needs be added, Public Service Commissioners as well, clearly realize that there is a larger problem than keeping out spoilsmen. The over-riding concern is the development of the existing civil service to cope more adequately with the enlarged objectives of Government. Further recommendations have had to be made, and will doubtless continue to be offered, which seek to reconcile the constitutional functions of the P.S.C. with the need to develop the efficiency of the civil service, the emphasis being now at least as much on *performance* as on *integrity*.

The experience of the Caribbean Commonwealth coun-

[33] F. W. Riggs, *The Ecology of Public Administration* (London: Asia Publishing House, 1961), pp. 92–143.

tries, particularly Guyana, which has had to endure the greatest internal stresses, helps to enlarge the body of evidence justifying on balance of advantages over disadvantages the application of the merit principle in the public service by means of an independent P.S.C. But the same experience already indicates that the P.S.C., as constituted today, might be inadequate for dealing with the modernization of the public service. Inefficiency in the public service will not long be tolerated, because for practical even more than moral reasons, governments cannot afford it. The P.S.C. will either enlarge its functions, or yield in some part to a more effective administrative body. Either way the P.S.C. is involved in the diagnosis of the ills of Caribbean administrations, and will be affected by the cures.

6.

The approach of independence in the West Indies brought into sharper focus local social, economic, and ethnic rivalries. Trinidadians, like Guyanese, were divided by ethnic loyalties as well as by partisan philosophies, as shown here by a British political scientist long resident in the Caribbean. The emergence of Eric Williams and his People's National Movement gave extra impetus to Trinidad's transition out of colonialism; the PNM contrasted with other political parties by emphasizing public education, economic rationality, mass participation, and an intellectual approach to politics. Nonetheless, in the electoral battle described here the intensity of individualism and racialism showed that the old order was by no means dead.

GORDON K. LEWIS, born in Wales and educated in history and political science at Cardiff, Oxford, and Harvard, taught at Chicago, the University of California (Los Angeles division), and Brandeis before becoming professor of Political Science at the University of Puerto Rico, where he has taught since 1955. His major works on the area include *Puerto Rico: Freedom and Power in the Caribbean* and *The Growth of the Modern West Indies*.

The Trinidad and Tobago General Election of 1961
Gordon K. Lewis[1]

The Trinidad and Tobago election of 1961, like that of 1944 in Puerto Rico, confirmed the earlier famous victory of a Caribbean nationalist reform movement and consolidated its power; for just as in 1944 the Puerto Rican *Populares* were released from an embarrassing legislative situation in which they had been dependent upon the three votes of an otherwise insignificant political grouping, so, in 1961, the People's National Movement (PNM) replaced a legislative situation in which they had been able to accept the responsibilities of government only by means of the support of nominated members of their own choosing in the old Legislative Council with a new alignment of forces that gave them an overwhelming majority (20 out of 29 seats) in the House of Representatives of the new territorial constitution. In both cases, responsibility was at last matched with the commanding power appropriate to the demands of responsibility. It is still too early to say, of course, that Dr. Williams now stands, as did Governor Muñoz-Marín in 1944, on the threshold of a generation of uninterrupted power. But everything points in that direction, not least of all the presence, in the Trinidadian

Caribbean Studies 2, no. 2, (July 1962), pp. 2–30. Reprinted by permission of the author and the Institute of Caribbean Studies. Copyright by The Institute of Caribbean Studies, University of Puerto Rico.

[1] Dr. Lewis has written on both the Hispanic and non-Hispanic Caribbean. See *Puerto Rico: Freedom and Power in the Caribbean* (New York: Monthly Review Press, 1963).

case, of a thoroughly demoralised opposition face to face with a government and a party characterised by vigor, discipline, driving purpose and intellectual highmindedness.

Other elements of the election were, of course, indigenous to Trinidad. The constitutional framework was novel, in that the new 1961 constitution brought the institutions of local parliamentary government—the office of the Premier, the Governor's office, the new popular chamber abolishing the old colonial device of "nominated members", the new Senate (giving Trinidad for the first time a bicameral legislature)—into line with constitutional advances elsewhere in the former British Caribbean area. It also laid down the constitutional prerequisites for the expected grant of full independence within the near future, following the Jamaican lead. This modernisation of the old Crown Colony institutions was accompanied by (1) the rationalisation of the territorial constituency boundaries by means of the legislation pushed through earlier by the PNM government and (2) a unique voting and registration system, enacted earlier in 1961, the main features of which were the replacement of the ballot box with the mechanical voting machine, a photographic voter registration system believed to be the world's most modern of its kind, and therefore (unlike the British system) a permanent registration process based on the issuance of personal identification cards. Trinidad thus became not only the first country in the world to be fully equipped (as the United States is not quite) with voting machines, thus cutting down the hazards of electoral fraud, but also possessed of the world's most modern permanent personal voter registration system. The Puerto Rican system, by comparison, utterly archaic as it is, breeds large-scale fraud, as the post-electoral legislative investigations into the registration of the *Partido Accion Cristiana* amply show. The revolution thus achieved in the Trinidad electoral mechanism, so noteworthy as it was, even attracted the attention of the United States Senate, Senator Humphrey reading a liberal encomium of it into the *Congressional Record*. Nor should sight be lost of the fact that an elaborate procedure of enumerating, photographing and documenting a total of some 377,000 or more voters, throughout a period of some five months, provided an occasion for a remarkable demonstration of national civic pride, granting, indeed, to the average Trinidadian voter a sense of participation in the pre-electoral process never before offered to him. Not the least interesting of all, perhaps, was the education of the rural voter in the use of the strange voting machine by means of a simple educational film exhibited by mobile projection units. The Opposition's attempt to charge that the machines could be "rigged" (much of it based upon an inaccurate article contained in the *Reader's Digest*) did not seriously diminish the significance of all this. As the event turned out, indeed, the failure of the polling stations to deal sufficiently rapidly with a heavy turnout was due to human rather than to mechanical factors; the Shoup Company expert who headed a team of experts sent down to assist the Government in launching the innovation opined that the voting was slowed down mainly because of unnecessarily complicated procedures at the poll clerks' tables rather than in the polling booth proper. All in all, both from an organisational and a moral viewpoint, the election was a remarkable achievement. The very turnout itself showed that much: 88% of all voters on the electoral list, soaring to over 90% in constituencies like San Fernando West, Fyzabad, Pointe-a-Pierre and Tobago East. The achievement takes on added meaning when it is recalled that, until only yesterday, the corruption and "bobol" of Trinidadian politics were an infamous byword in the region, so much so that the Federal Capital Site Commission of 1956 had refused to accept Trinidadian claims on the ground, partly, that the society's easygoing toleration of corruption in its public life would be a "disquieting augury" for the future of a federal capital located there. Trinidad at that time, in terms of political maturity, was at the bottom of the West Indian ladder. She stands today, incontestably, at the top.[2]

[2] For General Election returns, see *The Evening News* (Port of Spain, Trinidad), December 5, 1961; and *The Nation,* organ

The PNM, both as a party and a government, thus emerged from the election in unassailable control of the Trinidadian situation. Their 1956 victory, coming as it did only a brief nine months after the very birth of the party, had in some sense been premature, for it had thrust power upon a body of men who, with exceptions like Dr. Pat Solomon, were newcomers to politics. By 1961, however, they had become an effectively coordinated team. As a Cabinet, they were in secure control of the legislature. They no longer required the support of nominated members—the "King's Friends" of the old regime—in the popular house; for although their party lost the later election in the Siparia constituency—deferred because of the death of the Democratic Labour Party (DLP) candidate, Mr. Ajodhasingh, the "gentle masseur" of South Trinidad— their solid majority was enough as it stood. In the new Senate, likewise, their constitutional power, through the Premier, to nominate 12 of its 21 members guaranteed executive ability to curb that body should it ever decide to behave like the United States Senate rather than like the British House of Lords. There were 16 newcomers to the House, thus granting the Premier much needed room for manoeuvre in appointments, as the list of his new Cabinet appointments later made evident. The democratisation of the machinery of government, finally freed of the trappings of British colonialism, was thus matched by the emergence of a matured political movement to put it to use. Nor was the change politico-constitutionalist only, for it was itself accompanied by a real change in the sociology of the creole politics. That that was so was evident from the dramatic revolution occasioned by the occupational background of the 12 PNM Senators. For whereas the class of nominated members under the colonial scheme had been drawn, habitually, from the narrow *elite* of the white English residents, the plantocracy and the mercantile oligarchy, their PNM successors included agricultural pro-

---

of the People's National Movement, issues of December 8 and December 15, 1961. For details of the new PNM Cabinet, see *The Nation,* issue of December 22, 1961.

prietors, trade unionists, company managers, solicitors and at least one housewife. The unexpected defeat of Miss Donawa in the Fyzabad arena, it is true, denied to the PNM the opportunity to seat in the House an attractive young woman at once a Muslim Negress and the daughter of one of the old stalwarts of the 1937 oilfield "disturbances"; but the victory of Mrs. Teshea in Port-of-Spain East and the appointment of Mrs. Crichlow to the Senate marked well enough the advent of women into politics *via* the training ground of the PNM Women's League.

The intrusion of the intellectual into a politics previously marked by its absence of trained mind, dramatised in the meteoric rise of Dr. Williams to power, is, of course, too well-known to need explanation; it suffices to say, there, that the election consolidated his own tremendous personal hold over his party, and that much of the enormous PNM plurality must be attributed to his almost superhuman toil during the election, addressing as he did something like 125 meetings all over the territory within a brief four weeks. The 1961 election, all this is to say, must be seen as almost the final culmination of a historical process from colonialism to independence, in which there has occurred a gradual transfer of power from expatriate colonial civil servant to creole political leadership. The process has been maddeningly prolonged—Trinidad did not elect its first local representative to the old Legislative Council until 1925. Since 1956, however, the process has been accelerated under the new impetus given to it by PNM nationalism (it has been a myth of British Colonial Office thinking that independence is always willingly "granted" to patient colonial peoples, whereas in fact it is secured by impatient colonial freedom movements, with much anguish and frustration). So, in the Trinidad case, there is now full internal self-government, the creolisation, in the figure of Sir Solomon Hochoy, of the local governorship, the modernisation of the civil service, the establishment of a new constitutional framework designed for West Indian needs. Much, of course, remains to be done. The 1961 constitution still retains important imperial reserve-powers that could be used—as in the Canadian constitutional crisis of 1926—against a local popular government. The proper lines of jurisdiction between government and party, and the rules governing their connection, especially when the party, like PNM since 1956, is the government party, have yet to be worked out satisfactorily. That problem, indeed, has worried many in the PNM, and it is a safe prophecy that within the next five years the PNM ranks will witness a debate similar to that within the British Labour Party within recent years concerning the basic problem of effective party control, through the device of the annual conference, of the legislative party group. Then, too, the society still awaits the full growth of a two-party system. Inter-racialism, again, is still a consummation devoutly to be wished rather than an achieved reality. For the whole society is one—as the quality of the opposition literature during the election showed—that still lacks common standards rooted in the cement of common social ideals. In all of these respects, 1961 is the promise of things to come rather than their final arrival. But it is, assuredly, an encouraging beginning.

The PNM, naturally, ran on its five-year governmental record. In part, the record was one of planned economic development of the public sector, combined with incentive-encouragement of the private sector, much after the Puerto Rican model. Of a surety, there was much to be proud of, as the party's *Election Manifesto* made abundantly clear: establishment of an Industrial Development Corporation and 32 pioneer industries set up under its auspices; intensification of the exploration of new sources of oil, exemplified in the agreement signed with a consortium of American companies in respect of the East Coast high seas; encouragement of small farming in sugarcane and coffee, as well as food crops; a new loan system for fishermen; the opening up of new and hitherto inaccessible lands by the construction of new roads, especially the new North Coast highway; increased security for tenant farmers through a long overdue Land Tenure Ordinance;

establishment of a Port Authority to modernise the antiquated Port of Spain dock system; and so on. In part, again, the record was one of a burgeoning welfare state aiming at the social protection of the small man, Captain Cipriani's "barefoot man", hitherto the sport of the Trinidadian perverse attitudes to wealth and poverty:

> Poor man say he rich,
> Fabulously rich,
> Rich man say he poor,
> Wanting so much more.

That included a massive privy scheme for the neglected rural areas; the near completion of the Navet Dam scheme to provide an adequate water supply for the growing urban areas; large-scale urban development and slum clearance schemes, hand in hand with a smaller Aided Self-Help scheme; the establishment of the device of the new Employment Exchange, calculated to end the wasteful system of workers tramping from place to place in search of the odd job and to place labour recruitment on a rational basis; and—among much else—hire purchase legislation to protect the poor consumer in an economy traditionally dominated by the small trader mentality. Two additional programs seemed to the PNM platform speakers to be worthy of special merit. The first was the tremendous PNM educational revolution; indeed, all of its items—the construction of the new Polytechnic Institute, the provision of some 17,020 new places in elementary and secondary schools, free secondary education, an increase of college exhibitions from 255 in 1956 to 1000 in 1960, the phenomenal increase in Island Scholarships, hitherto the mark of a small educational *elite,* not least of all, the search, in the Maurice Report, for an educational philosophy properly suited to West Indian needs—bespoke the PNM conviction that the Platonic maxim that the most important minister in the state is the minister of education has a peculiar meaning for the new colonial nationalisms, a conviction not unrelated to the fact, of course, that Dr. Williams is himself an outstanding West Indian Oxonian, as his autobiographical sketch, *A Colonial at Oxford,* sufficiently shows. The second program is related to all this: the PNM emphasis upon national culture and the active promotion by the state of cultural activities to counteract the legacy of cultural imperialism. The building of the new Queen's Hall, to take an example only, has given to Port of Spain a modern center of the arts that San Juan still grievously lacks: while, to take another, the organised improvement of Carnival through the device of a governmental committee (a graduate thesis, indeed, could be penned on the PNM's audacious usage of the *ad hoc* committee) has helped at once to democratise Carnival processes and to give to the calypsonian both a financial reward and a professional status he has hitherto been denied. And, of course, underpinning all this, there was the public image of the PNM as the official custodian, like the PRI in Mexico and the PPD in Puerto Rico, of the national revolution, embodying the new national principle which was seen at once as the outcome and the executioner of British colonialism in the territory and, beyond the territory, in the West Indies as a whole.[3]

Much of this sort of program is, of course, a natural development in colonial-nationalist modern politics. Because the new nativist leaderships do not inherit a matured industrial system, as did, say, British Socialism in 1945, they confront problems of capital accumulation, investment capital and economic productivity unknown to Fabianism. The classic weapon of the metropolitan socialist, therefore—the nationalisation of basic industries—is denied to them because, in Governor Muñoz-Marín's phrase, you cannot share what you don't have. Not only this, but they are also the voices of a nationalism quite alien to the internationalist ethic of metropolitan socialism. The British Labour Party has never had the problem before it of welding together the disparate elements, ra-

---

[3] People's National Movement, *Election Manifesto: General Elections 1961* (Port of Spain, Trinidad: PNM Publishing Company, 1961).

cial, religious, ethnic, of a colonial pluralist society into a sense of harmonious community; yet that is the main task of the new movements of contemporary Caribbean progressive parties. All this explains why, in the Trinidad election, there were "no enemies on the Left" for the PNM, for it is good Marxism to insist, as did Lenin, that the national question must precede the social question in its resolvence. Nothing illustrated that better than the dismal fiasco of the attempt by the ex-PNMite Mr. C. L. R. James to inject the language and strategy of Trotskyite Communism into the Trinidadian debate after his open break with Dr. Williams earlier in 1961. A reading, indeed, of the curious document put out, in characteristic cloak-and-dagger fashion, by Mr. James, *PNM, Go Forward: A Critique of PNM's Internal Party Politics,* shows how much its author was out of place in a constitutionalist-reformist movement, for it bespeaks throughout the outlook of the professional insurrectionary concerned with the organisation of an underground movement dedicated to the forcible overthrow of a repressive and autocratic regime. Only such an outlook, for example, could so distort the inner PNM struggles as to see a mild middle-class party functionary like Mrs. Beckles as the Rosa Luxembourg, as it were, of the movement or to see himself as the Lenin who, at the appropriate moment, would supplant the Kerensky-role of Dr. Williams. To speak, again, of a "revolutionary energy" of the Trinidadian masses that would be channelled into a party organised along lines of military command was completely to lose sight of how much the defiant individualism and the raucous flamboyancy of the Trinidadian character-structure made such a possibility extremely unlikely. The James thesis, indeed committed the cardinal error—as did orthodox Soviet thought after 1917—of trying to impose an absolute theory of action upon all progressive movements irrespective of whether local conditions made the theory applicable.[4]

That it was alien enough to the whole PNM outlook—

[4] C. L. R. James, *PNM, Go Forward: A Critique of PNM's Internal Party Politics* (mimeo; Port of Spain, Trinidad, 1961), Pts. 1, 2, and 3.

apart from its unpleasant aroma of personal vanity—was evident enough from the fact that the document's surreptitious circulation among the membership produced, not the factionalist debate Mr. James's polemical spirit clearly anticipated, but a loud silence. So much so was that the case that not even an Opposition frantically in search of issues felt it was worth using as a stick with which to beat the PNM; and apart from the reading of a few provocative extracts by Mr. Sinanan in the federal Parliament the document passed unnoticed. As a consequence of all this, policy, not doctrine, dominated the electoral debate. The PNM alliance of political radicalism and socioeconomic liberalism made it difficult for its detractors to denounce it as dangerous collectivism. The DLP machine, indeed, could do no better, here, than to advance as "proof" of a collectivist bias the reproduction, McCarthy-like, of an old photograph of Dr. Williams welcoming Dr. Castro in the latter's brief stopover at Piarco Airport. It is true, of course, as all Caribbeanists know, that Dr. Williams is the author of a minor classic in Marxist historical analysis, *Capitalism and Slavery*. But, for good or ill, his party's program is no more the Marxism of that volume than, to take a Victorian analogy, Disraeli's program of 1874 was the romantic Tory Democracy of *Sybil* and *Coningsby*.

But if the modern nationalist movement in the West Indies makes it difficult for the creole Left to find a niche, equally so is it the case with the creole Right. Because the middle class is small in the society a rightwing party cannot obtain many votes. A white skin is a political liability, although the prejudice is visibly declining, as the cases of Mr. Cargill and Mr. Densham in the Jamaican federal election of 1958 showed; conservative fears about the consequences of adult suffrage have not been realised; Froude's pessimistic prophecy, early on, that independence would witness the exodus *en masse* of the white population has not materialised; while the identification, in the popular mind, of the local ruling classes with British colonialism—cleverly exploited in Dr. Williams' election slogan, "Massa Day Done"—makes it difficult, as yet, for those classes to organise their own political expression on native grounds. Once again, the Trinidad 1961 election gave new proof of those generalisations. A creole white like Mr. Bermudez, coming, as he did, from an "old" Port of Spain business family of Venezuelan origins, could become a PNM candidate, and, indeed, make himself personally popular in the proletarian Belmont section, but could not have launched a party restricted to his own ethnic or class group with any success. It is true that the forces of traditionalist Trinidadian society, the white English enclave, the French, Portuguese and Chinese creoles, the Chamber of Commerce, were solidly anti-PNM. But it is equally true that they clearly felt it would have been inexpedient to have openly opposed the ruling party. So, the Chamber of Commerce contented itself with a press release announcing its political impartiality and urging both parties not to alienate overseas investors by any condoning of political violence. The Cane-Farmers Association did likewise, adding a warning to its members that all attempts of politicians to divide their organisation must be resisted. The press, in the form of the *Trinidad Guardian,* and under its new Canadian ownership, also adopted a pose of political neutrality, at least an improvement upon its vicious anti-Williams campaign of 1956. The earlier animosity of the Catholic Church to the nationalist movement was also muted, much of it due to the hierarchy's conviction that the Church-State Concordat of 1960—unlike the neighbouring case of British Guiana—adequately protected the interests of the Catholic parochial schools in the territory. Thus, there was no Trinidadian repetition of the gross tactical mistake of the Catholic Princes of the Church in the Puerto Rican election of the previous year. That fact no doubt contributed somewhat to the PNM victory in the heavily Catholic Arima constituency.

The hostility, or the latent hostility, of all of these groups, this is to say, had no place, politically speaking, to go. That the hostility was there admitted of little doubt. Most of the Trinidadian social well-to-do—in the St. Clair area, for example—evinced, in private, a quite paranoic hatred of Dr. Williams, founded, psychologically, upon their resentment at being dispossessed of the image of prestige and leadership hitherto theirs, as they saw it, almost by a law of natural prescription. Yet they had no mass social base that could be used as the foundation of an openly conservative movement. They were obliged, consequently, to turn to the predominantly East Indian DLP. In one way, naturally so: the quoted remark of one of them—that he would prefer to eat grass with an East Indian rather than be ruled by a Negro—shows how, as a ruling group, they have preferred East Indians because the Indian "coolie" has been more "manageable" than the Negro. Even so, a DLP movement could hardly be a real home for them. As socially respectable citizens, they could support the party clandestinely yet cavil at accepting, socially, a DLP "boss" like Bhadase Maraj with all of his dubious social connections and questionable reputation as an Indian political *cacique*. And even if they went so far as to become DLP-sponsored candidates, they were caught in the trap of being dependent upon an Indian racial base in its own turn deeply suspicious of them. That was the pathos, altogether, of the candidacies of men like Mr. Rostant and Dr. Forrester. And it is only necessary to read the long, sad story of Mr. Gomes's relationships with his former Indian colleagues to realise how much racial animosities make it difficult for the Trinidad creole politician to live amicably with the Indian political set.

The best illustration of this political frustration was to be seen, of course, in the patent difficulties of the DLP opposition in producing any sort of public policy as an impressive alternative to the incumbent administration. For one did not have to be a self-righteous PNM *aficionado* to agree that the DLP manifesto, *Guide to Policy*, was at once inconclusive, vague and insubstantial. Bearing all the marks of a hurried response to the PNM platform, it was a collection of odd recommendations held together by no clearly defined public philosophy. Its suggested national insurance scheme—based, its critics said, upon per-

functory visits to Britain by DLP draughtsmen—made no
effort to examine the financial implications of a scheme
the likes of which not even the federally-supported prosperity of the Puerto Rican Commonwealth has yet been
ready to propose. It spoke of making agriculture the first
industry of the economy; but since, by agriculture, it obviously meant the traditional export crops, it laid its authors
open to the charge that they wished to continue the "Colonial Pact" system in which West Indian agriculturists have
played the role, in the phrase of the Moyne Commission, of
the tropical farms of the British nation. On the public
platform, it is fair to say, Dr. Capildeo, the DLP leader,
had some things to say about the usage in Trinidad of
the eleven-plus school examination, presently under fierce
criticism in the United Kingdom itself, that rang true.
Yet his party manifesto advocated the adoption of a
technical education program which would ensure, in its
words, that migrants to the United Kingdom "are skilled
persons, not only labourers", thus putting Trinidad into
the position of being merely a tropical supply-point for a
cheap labour-force in British industry; and not the least
grossly anomalous aspect of that proposal was that it was
advanced at the very moment when the British Government and Parliament were moving not to accelerate but to
curtail West Indian immigration by means of their immigration control bill. Combined with all this there went the
astonishing suggestion, as a contribution to the economics
of the tourist industry, that a tunnel be built connecting
the capital to Maracas Bay on the north coast; although
it was perhaps appropriate that a party that conducted
much of its campaign underground should also have
wished to drive the American tourist underground. In foreign affairs matters, there was a cryptic declaration that
the party was not satisfied with the present United States-
West Indies Leased Bases Agreement, controlling the local
Chaguaramas US naval enclave; but the manifesto did
not advance reasons for the disagreement nor propound
any alternative terms. That went hand in hand with the
jejune suggestion that the Federal capital be removed

to Tobago, "Robinson Crusoe's island", thus ignoring all the persuasive arguments of the Capital Site Commission report advocating the "twin city" concept with the existing Port of Spain urban complex as its base. To end it all, there were alarming lacunae in a manifesto purporting to serve as a guide to the legislative program of a modern government. There was nothing about bus transport—an absolute top-priority task in Port of Spain as in all the leading Caribbean cities—, finance, population, an economic development program. The civil-service vote, on the other hand—always so important in colonial societies where there has occurred an artificial growth of administrative as distinct from economic institutions—was courted with the retrograde suggestion that the old colonial system of foreign leave travel for civil servants should be restored. Altogether, it was hardly a program calculated to appeal to the surprisingly sophisticated Trinidadian political audience. For many of its critics, indeed—as a reading of "letters to the Editor" suggested—it seemed an insult to the general intelligence; and their feelings were reinforced by the report during the campaign that, requested by a San Fernando audience for his party's manifesto, Dr. Capildeo had replied that he had it with him but that the crowd were too stupid to read it.[5]

All this, naturally enough, is not to say that, thus absolved from the necessity of fighting either a doctrinally leftwing or rightwing opposition, the nationalist liberalism of the PNM style does not face its own intrinsic difficulties. Its leading ideas—economic development, party discipline, a Periclean civic pride, the reorganisation of social institutions, interracialism, an Afro-Antillean nationalism—have been well thought out, not merely as ends in themselves but as means towards the utopia of the new society its members envisage. But their translation into appropriate institutional forms remains still in its infancy. The elec-

[5] Democratic Labour Party, *Know Your Party* (Port of Spain, Trinidad: Rahaman's Printery, 1961); Democratic Labour Party, *Guide to Policy* (Port of Spain, Trinidad: Tri-Color Printery Ltd., 1961).

tion manifesto promise, for example, to set up a new Planning Board after the fashion of the Indian model in New Delhi suggests present inadequacies, as indeed was dramatised by the flood disaster in the Diego Martin valley suburban area some weeks before polling day; for to say, as did the Premier, that that disaster was due to indiscriminate and unplanned private development by unconscionable housing contractors was to overlook the fact that, if that were so, it indicated at the same time an absence of effective governmental control over the anarchy of the private profit-motive in a notoriously speculative field. The PNM emphasis on agriculture, again, is welcome, especially in the light of the pronouncement of the Caribbean Congress of Labour, during the campaign, that no strengthening of the West Indian economies could be expected unless it included a bold program of agricultural rationalisation. Yet it is as yet an open question as to whether that end can best be reached by policies that reinforce the *petit proprietaire* system of West Indian agriculture and that revolve around the idea—which was the leading recommendation of the report of the British Royal Commission of 1897—of the location of landless labourers as small peasant farmers growing their own food and thus diversifying an economy based on sugar monoculture. The various Caribbean agrarian reform programs based upon the idea have not been conspicuously successful, and they now face the competition of the more radical Cuban program. A great deal, again, of Dr. Williams' campaign oratory criticised the Trinidad upper classes and their social privileges. Yet there is no surety that the PNM official policy of bringing in expatriate business corporations by means of pioneer industry and tax-exemption legislation will not itself create new privilege, or that absentee wealth in new industry will be any more sympathetic to West Indian interests than, previously, it has been in sugar or banking or commerce. The white planter or creole merchant "massa" may simply be replaced by the foreign business "massa". The danger is all the more real in the absence of any sort of international

code to govern the behavior of private capital in overseas ventures; and, as a matter of fact, the Swiss Bank
affair during the Trinidad election itself, an affair that at
times read like a chapter out of a Rafael Sabatini novel
of international intrigue, was an ominous warning about
the risks that the governments of "underdeveloped" nations run at the hands of the more unscrupulous elements
of the American and European business classes. What is
more, the recent debate on the hazards of absentee ownership unleashed in Puerto Rico by the speech of the *Popular* Leader of the House of Representatives warning against
the mushrooming of continental supermarkets in the economy suggests that within ten or fifteen years the Caribbean
economies that are eagerly following the Puerto Rican
"Operation Bootstrap" model may themselves be compelled to face up to similar socio-cultural consequences
of too heavy a dependency upon foreign private capital
sources. Those consequences, perhaps, are in the short
run unavoidable so long as those economies cannot turn
to an international public economy for the aid that they
need; and certainly, Dr. Jagan has yet to prove that, in the
case of British Guiana, a local socialist austerity program
will be able to generate sufficiently high rates of internal
savings and capital investment to offset the exclusion of
outside business firms. The dangers are there, nonetheless.
Dr. Williams may discover, as Governor Muñoz-Marín has
discovered, that the reconciliation of the business profit-
motive with the establishment of the good society may be
a Gordian knot that no sword can sever.

The election campaign proper was in many ways characteristically Trinidadian. For not even the PNM espousal of
sophisticated party discipline and machinery could prevent the electoral evocation of the general culture-traits of
this racy, cosmopolitan and Byzantine society. It would be
wrong, of course, to call December 4, 1961, a Caribbean
version of the Eatanswill election. Yet there was much in
it, even so, of that Dickensian farce. There was the steelband. There were the organised parades; sportsmen and

housewives, among other groups, arranged pro-PNM marches. There were the party emblems, the DLP torch and the PNM balisier, the latter decorating colorful party shirts and ties. There was the open-air mass meeting, fast disappearing in the United Kingdom, where raucous heckling, sometimes accompanied with bell-ringing, at other times with egg-throwing, made platform speaking a real hazard. There was the torchlight parade, once, like the Fourth of July picnic, a standard feature of American political campaigns. There was the religious touch: the Baptist church paraded for Miss Donawa in Fyzabad. There was the "small island" touch: the Grenadian colony in Grenada Alley in Laventille voted solidly PNM. Both sides used the street-corner meeting, the motorcade, the poster and the handbill. There were the amateur touches, like the home-made cardboard slogans—"PNM is our help in time of need", "Dr. Williams is our bright light", "We want PNM biscuit, not DLP roti". The calypso note, naturally, was ever-present, for the Trinidadian man in the street, like the king-calypsonians who are his real popular heroes, will "turn ole mas" under the slightest of pretences. There are few Western societies in which at some point God does not become, during election times, a candidate at large; so, the PNM Women's League at one point called for a day of prayer. The West Indian talent for natural oratory, so much like the Welsh, was there, too: to hear the platform chairman, for example, of one meeting in the oilfield area invoking the sonorous Amerindian names of South Trinidad villages was to be reminded, in its moving magic, of Whitman's roll-call of the States of the Union. Above all, there was the frenetic popular enthusiasm, so markedly in contrast to the apathy that has seized the British voter since the nineteen-fifties. It must have been like that, the English observer is tempted to wonder, with British Labour in the early *Clarion* days when socialism was still a passionate religion for its working-class devotees. For there must be few places in the modern democratic world where crowds of thousands will jam a meeting place, like the "University of Woodford Square" in downtown Port of Spain, and listen with an attentiveness worthy of a university classroom to their Political Leader lecture them, in the most rigorous Oxonian fashion, on the most abstruse aspects of their national economics and politics for hours on end.

But there were less attractive features about it all. The bad habits of Trinidad politics, described in Mr. Naipaul's novel, *The Suffrage of Elvira,* were perhaps too strongly entrenched in local culture and personality to disappear completely under the PNM spell. The spirit of acquisitive individualism, nicely summed up in the remark of Macaw's column character that the Government "dey gimme de Las Cuevas Road, is a pity dey din gimme a car too so ah could go an see it", still motivates many voters who have joined the PNM bandwagon as the winning side. The old charge of "bobol", of making money out of politics, was resurrected in the DLP effort to prove that Government Ministers had stored away their spoils in Swiss bank accounts. The vulgar technique of "exposing" the private lives of political opponents was also invoked, although it is doubtful if the DLP attempt to "smear" Dr. Williams by publishing in their party organ United States court documents relating to his Nevada and District of Columbia divorce proceedings could much influence a West Indian public that has always taken a Rabelaisian view of marital difficulties. Tempers flare violently in these circumscribed societies where people live on top of each other: it was reported that the Minister of Home Affairs had threatened to destroy one businessman socially, politically and economically, while it is on record that the DLP leader publicly promised to remove the territorial Governor, Sir Solomon Hochoy, should his party be victorious. The worst offender in all this was easily the DLP. But it is only fair to add that, on at least one occasion, the PNM propaganda technicians sought to spoil Dr. Capildeo's standing with the religiously-minded voter by circulating a report of an Oxford University Debating Union meeting in which, as a youthful undergraduate, he had allegedly defended an atheistical position (it would not have been difficult, after all, to have held up certain PNM chieftains as lapsed Catholics).

This sort of thing is easily the prelude to physical violence, which in fact finally erupted in the Trinidad case in fatal shootings in the El Socorro-Aranguez area and the Governor's declaration of a state of emergency in four electoral districts. The newspaper coverage of the election being unpardonably inadequate and amateurish, it was difficult to determine exact responsibility for the violence. It is probable, however, that DLP *agent-provocateurs* themselves slashed the tyres of their own members' automobiles while a private house meeting was in session in the Woodbrook district, and equally probable that PNM *marabuntas* from the Laventille hills molested East Indian traders at the early morning market in Port of Spain. Be all that as it may, it is certainly beyond question that the public utterances of Dr. Capildeo, unlike those of the Premier, constituted an open and reckless incitement to civil disorder. There could be no other construction put on his widely publicised invitation to his followers to "come forward on election day and smash up a thousand voting machines", or to "get ready now to march on Government House"; and of his threat that "the day we are ready we will take over this country and not a thing will stop us". "The only remedy", he told a private house meeting, "is to adopt the South American method of bloodshed and riot and revolution or civil disobedience until you grind government operations to a full stop and you then get possession". It is small wonder that many of his own colleagues became thoroughly alarmed at their leader's temperamental outbursts and that, according to report, many of the Indian pundits turned against him. Only the notorious credulity of the colonialist mentality, perhaps could persist in acclaiming the author of such irresponsible vituperation as an "intellectual". The PNM adherents who saw in all of this a deliberately calculated strategy to provoke disorders that would in turn provoke British military intervention, after the fashion of the 1953 British Guiana case, might have been taking a melodramatic view. Yet the calling in of British armed forces into the second Guiana crisis, in February 1962, in response to a general strike organised by the opposition forces to Dr. Jagan shows, indeed, that there are still powerful elements in West Indian society that are ready to use outside metropolitan aid in the cause of destroying governments they cannot defeat by constitutional means. And even had there been no violence at all, it would have been difficult for any electorate to take seriously a party whose leader publicly announced before polling day, as did Dr. Capildeo, that he himself would accept no ministry in a DLP government but would make himself available "to check on all Ministers to see that they do their jobs properly and efficiently": a curious concept, to say the least, of public administration in the modern democratic state and one that died, in the British case, with the great Prime Ministership of Sir Robert Peel more than a century ago.[6]

Much of the campaign concerned itself with the discussion of party and its meaning. From the beginning, in 1955, the PNM had made itself the champion of party organisation and discipline. In that field, of course, the two major parties in Jamaica, to make a Caribbean comparison, are about equally developed. In the Trinidad case, however, the 1961 campaign strikingly dramatised how far the DLP lagged behind the PNM pacesetters. Not even the most rationalist of politics, of course, can entirely eliminate the factor of personality. So, in the PNM case, there was the hero-worship of Dr. Williams. No one could have watched the tumultuous reception given to him by the ordinary folk of New Village as he made his triumphant entry into Point Fortin during one of the election highlights and have failed to appreciate the powerful emotional

[6] See, as examples of all this, "PNM Hooligans versus the Rest", *Democratic Labour Party Bulletin*, No. 1; "Quoted Verbatim from the Sunday Guardian", *ibid.*, No. 4; "We Accuse: DLP Design for Violence", *People's National Movement Bulletin*.

electricity that is at work between "the Doctor" and the masses. There is always the danger that the "cult of personality" of this sort can clash with the PNM ideology of party loyalty; the gradual metamorphosis, after all, of Mr. Manley in the Jamaican case from the Fabian intellectual of 1940 to the "Man of Destiny" in 1960 is symptomatic. Yet it has to be said that, so far at least, the mass adulation of the Political Leader has been kept within the limits of a formidable party organisation, strikingly at variance with what has happened with the role of Governor Muñoz-Marín in the Puerto Rican *Popular* party. The group oath-taking of party candidates to party ideals; their required attendance at a pre-election party school; the control of both their platform manners and their speech-content by a firm party code: all bespoke a tight grip on one of the leading Trinidadian traits, a defiant attitude toward any kind of authority.

The DLP, by contrast, although technically a party, was, in behavior, nothing much more than an assorted group of old-style political individualists. One of the most telling of PNM campaign bulletins consisted of a damning collection of quotations, both within the Legislative Council and outside, in which DLP members laid bare their uncomplimentary opinions of each other in a vein of gross scurrility; Mr. Simboonath Capildeo's charge that his colleagues Mr. Maharaj and Mr. Seukeran were seeking to "divide people against people, race against race, and with the evil, malignant, wicked, sinful, vile, despicable and nefarious newsmongering they are trying to divide brother against brother" was typical. As a party, again, the group had little of the respect for the public that a genuine party should surely possess, and not the least fantastic aspect of a generally fantastic election was the fact that, using violence as a pretext, its candidates refused to hold a single public meeting for the last three weeks of the campaign. All this, of course, sprang from the irrepressible adventurism and individualism still rampant in certain sections of the Trinidadian political mind. Its anti-party psychology showed itself, also, in the figure of the political independ-

ent, although his numbers in 1961 (3) were well below
the swarm of 1956 (39). It was there, too, in the independent candidate disguised as "leader" of a "new" party,
such as Mr. Bryan and his United Labour Party and Mr.
Broomes and his African National Congress. The behavior
of some DLP candidates—Mr. Lai-Fook's emphasis, in the
Diego Martin race, for example, upon his Catholicism
rather than upon his party affiliation—betrayed the same
independent mentality; while the broadsheet privately put
out by the former Organising Secretary of the DLP, Mr.
Ramaldo Gomes's *My Relationship with the DLP,* and in
which the author came out in support of the PNM, made
much of the fact that, during the time of his appointment,
he had been prevented by his own leadership from organising DLP party groups. Most pathetic of all, perhaps,
was the lonely figure of the once-great Uriah Butler, "Chief
Servant of the Lord", whose 517 votes in his old La Brea
stronghold underlined so harshly what a political anachro-
nism he had become in a new age that had passed him by.
Nor was public respect for him heightened when it was
learned that his two years' absence in England, away from
his legislative duties in the old Council, had been report-
edly consumed in the composition of a curious thesis seeking to prove the illegal occupation of the British Monarchy
by the Windsor royal dynasty on the basis of a supposed
deathbed conversion to Catholicism by George III. The
eclipse of the independent, in brief, was one of the permanent achievements of the election. Altogether, eleven independents or quasi-independents lost their deposits. So, if
the highlight of the 1956 victory had been Mr. Ulric Lee's
defeat of the old political warrior, Mr. Albert Gomes, that
of the 1961 conquest was Mr. A. N. R. Robinson's defeat
of "Fargo" James in Tobago East. From now on, it is safe
to say, the political independent in Trinidad and Tobago
will remain, in Burke's phrase, an unpitied sacrifice in a
contemptible struggle.[7]

[7] "We Accuse: DLP versus DLP", *People's National Movement Bulletin;* Ramaldo Gomes, *My Relationship with the
DLP* (Port of Spain, Trinidad: Charbol Press, 1961).

The Trinidad election, this is to say, must be seen as the decisive victory of the Burkian idea of party in the territorial life as, indeed, was the victory, on the very same day, of the young Democratic Labour Party in the neighbouring Barbados election. That could be seen in the heavy pluralities of the constituency votes: Mr. Wallace (PNM) polled 80.2% of total votes cast in the San Juan constituency, Mr. Hosein (DLP) polled 72.64% of the votes cast in the Chaguanas constituency. Mr. Granado (PNM) actually polled the astonishing figure of 93.53% of the popular vote in the Laventille PNM stronghold. The lesson was plain that the voter was determined to return a government with no doubts about its comfortable majority support, and the lesson was underlined by the fact that there was only one close contest (so much a constant feature of American elections), Mr. Jamadar's narrow majority of 126 in the Fyzabad district. The era of the private stronghold, Mr. Butler in the La Brea-Point Fortin oil belt (where the PNM could not even hold a meeting in 1956), Mr. James in Tobago (where there has always been a strong tradition of political feudalism in the peasantry), Mr. Bryan in the eastern countries, is almost certainly over and done with, just as, in the United States, the New Deal welfare state undermined the economic bases of the "machine boss" in the big cities after 1933. The process, in Trinidad, involves at the same time a gradual breakdown of the separation between the rural and urban areas. The old charge, that the PNM had always been a Port of Spain urban grouping, falls down in the light of the fact that not only did it win its "safe seat" areas in the capital and the capital periphery, but also rural areas like Toco-Manzanilla, Tobago and Ortoire-Mayaro; while even in the strongly held Indian areas like the three Caroni countries the party managed to obtain approximately half of the total vote polled by the three successful Opposition candidates for that area. Between 1960 and 1961 the PNM party managers had clearly taken to heart the criticism voiced in the declaration of a convention delegate that they had too readily assumed that the territory of Trinidad and Tobago was exhausted by the

University of Woodford Square in Port of Spain and
Harris Promenade in San Fernando.

No one can read the reports of the PNM General
Council or of the Annual Conventions without appreciating how much citizen participation in party life has become almost a new religion with many Trinidadians.
Party politics, perhaps, has worn somewhat thin in the "advanced" Anglo-Saxon societies. But in the newly emergent nations, allied to the new nationalism, it has become
a veritable article of faith. It promises, too, a new intellectual excitement in societies hitherto characterised by a
dismally low level of intellectual life. It is worth noting, in
that respect, that the new leadership of this worldwide
phenomenon, still essentially middle-class, is being recruited from the new groups of economists and political
scientists rather than from the old groups of doctors and
lawyers; and in the Caribbean that can be seen in the
figure of Dr. Williams himself, as well as in those of Mr.
Errol Barrow in Barbados, Mr. Edward Seaga in Jamaica
and, coming back to Trinidad, Mr. Peter Farquhar in
the ranks of the DLP. The old dominion of the legal mind,
so prevalent still in the small islands, is thus replaced by
the new interests of the social-sciences mind. The new
Caribbean parties, again, to take another distinguishing
mark, are post-war in their origins, as distinct from the
pre-war origins of the older parties like the Jamaican PNP
and the Barbados Labour Party. Nor should sight be lost
of the interesting fact that whereas older leaders like Sir
Grantley Adams and Mr. Manley have been nurtured in
the culture of British politics, both Dr. Jagan and Dr.
Williams have had important American experiences. Dr.
Williams, indeed, has cleverly used the dramatic imagery
of the contrast between the New World and the Old (a
theme at the heart of life and thought throughout all the
Americas) to press home the revolutionary scale of the
PNM achievement. "It is a conflict", he has written, "between those who take to the sword and who will perish by
the pen, a conflict between obscene language and univer-

sity analysis, a conflict between *patois* and Latin, between the *mauvais langue* whispered from house to house and the intelligent mass meeting of the age of political education dispensed by the People's National Movement".

Because of all this, and more, it was difficult to accept the official editorial attitude of the West Indian press that in the Trinidad election two major parties in a real two-party system were locked in combat. The Jamaica *Gleaner* opined blandly, a thousand miles away, that the "similarity of temperament" between the two party leaders would give Trinidadians "some safety in their choice in that, whoever becomes Premier should give that territory a thoughtful leadership that contains the minimum of 'old talk'".[8] And not the least comic aspect of the election was the spectacle of the *Trinidad Guardian* gravely pontificating on the claims of the two parties in the manner of the *New York Times* during an American presidential campaign year. For so to view the election was to embrace a palpable fiction. Dr. Capildeo at no point conducted himself as a responsible politician. Indeed, his unsportsmanlike refusal either to concede the PNM victory or to congratulate the winner, combined with the curious fact that it was not he but his lieutenant, Mr. Seukeran, who deported himself as the defeated statesman by issuing that usual congratulatory statement, marked him out as a spirit altogether too jealous to enter a game of politics based upon the gentlemanly conventions of the English constitution. Dr. Williams in Trinidad, it is not too much to say, like Governor Muñoz-Marín in Puerto Rico, still awaits the quality of opposition that he deserves.

Like all West Indian politics, the Trinidad variant has its close associations with race and class. The class-party correlations have already in part been noted. The forces of property and privilege, with single exceptions, were anti-PNM. The social round of the Yacht Club, Government House receptions and tourist-hotel parties that gets re-

[8] *Sunday Gleaner* (Kingston, Jamaica), December 3, 1961.

ported daily in the social columns of the press remained stolidly immune to the PNM magic. At the middle-class level there were clearly conflicting considerations at work during the election year. For although most middle-class creoles, by the nature of their place in the society, were predisposed to PNM, there were discontents working to disrupt their allegiance. There were the discontented ex-party members, the usual human loss in the first years of a new movement, some of whom, it is said, are old Queen's Royal College friends of Dr. Williams peeved at not rising higher in the party councils. There was the ex-Minister like Dr. Winston Mahabir, whose veiled hints about the rise of doctrinal orthodoxy in the party were not neglected by the Government's enemies. More generally, there were entire groups, like the Civil Service Association, whose members were dissatisfied with the procedure adopted by Government in the current regrading and reclassification tasks, as was made evident by the paid publication in the press (an unheard-of procedure in the British Civil Service) of the Association's correspondence with the Permanent Secretary of the Ministry of Finance. Even more, the mass protest march staged by the Association during the election itself indicated that, one, as a self-styled trade union it did not intend to allow political loyalties to interfere with its professional interests and, two, it was learning how to operate as a "pressure group" in a modernising economy instead of remaining, as it has tended to remain in Trinidadian life, an occupational group too timid to speak out lest its members be victimised as, indeed, was always a real possibility under the colonial regime.

That new middle-group militancy must be related to the total class pattern. For although PNM Cabinets remain middle-class in their composition the most important single phenomenon to emerge out of the election was the evidence that, as a mass party, the PNM was shifting slowly leftwards in its social class base. That was evident enough in Dr. Williams' campaign speeches. It was even more evident in the obvious capture of the working-class vote by the ruling party, symbolised in the decisive move of the local National Trades Union Congress to identify itself formally with the PNM and, as evidence of its good faith, to organise a mammoth pro-PNM demonstration in Port of Spain. The new trend—perhaps terminating once and for all the unsuccessful history of trade-union attempts at promoting their own political organisations in the territory—was hardly surprising in the light, once again, of Dr. Capildeo's splendid genius for fighting the wrong war at the wrong time in the wrong place. For his stern rebuke that "any trade union mixed with a political party is a house divided and is bound to fail", coupled with his ominous warning about "too many strikes", was bound to alienate all trade unionists; as in fact it did, with perhaps the exception of the Amalgamated Engineering and Allied Workers union. They felt, not unnaturally, that it presaged repressive anti-union legislation on the part of a DLP government. To demand that unions divorce themselves from politics, the NTUC statement urged, "is in fact asking the workers to tie their hands behind their backs in their struggle, while freeing the hands of the capitalists"; and it is suggestive that the statement called in the aid of the American experience by quoting Mr. Meany's observation that American unions are active in politics because they find that, although the company spy and the professional strike-breaker have about passed from the scene, and although unions have certain protections under the law, the employer has decided that the place to curb the union movement is in the legislative field. Dr. Williams, naturally, welcomed the new support, not surprisingly when his own earlier record of adviser to the Caribbean union movement is called to mind. It remains to be seen whether the local union leadership will stay put with the American labour practice of rewarding political friends and punishing political enemies, or will move forward, after the British fashion, to formal affiliation with the PNM. That this is still an open question shows how much political-industrial developments in Trinidad have followed lines different from those of the neighbouring Jamaican pattern.[9]

This PNM "opening to the left", of course, is empirical rather than theoretical. If it promises a turn to socialism —hardly likely—it will be, at the most, in the French phrase, a *socialisme sans doctrines*. Its real motivation, perhaps, is a growing realisation that, in Caribbean politics, movements with only middle-class bases become rapidly isolated, as the recent difficulties of the Manley party in Jamaica and the National Civic Union in the Dominican Republic illustrate. To that degree, at least, Mr. James' severe strictures on the bourgeois stamp of the PNM ministerial benches (and their wives) ring true. The traits of that class—social careerism, egotistic individualism, personal rivalry and murderous back-biting (the famous Trinidadian *mauvais langue*), the round of social protocol and respectable public service that ends with a citation in the Royal Birthday Honours List (there must be a sizeable number of eminent PNM members who look forward to following Sir Learie Constantine, one of their foundation members, into the ranks of the new West Indian knighthood class)—make a precarious foundation for a progressive nationalist movement. Many of the internal troubles of the PNM certainly go back to all this. New blood, by way of wider class recruitment, should be a necessary medicine. It would help to counteract the class prejudice that so frequently masquerades as "shade" prejudice in the West Indian multi-layered pigmentocracy. It would help, further, to allay the religion of social respectability that has persuaded too many West Indian middle- and lower-class persons that there is a necessary indignity about manual labor, and thereby condemned them, as the

[9] See, for all this: Dr. Capildeo, remarks quoted in *The Trinidad Guardian*, November 8, 1961; Statement of the Amalgamated Engineering and Allied Workers Trade Union, *ibid.*, November 14, 1961; Statement of Communications Workers Trade Union, *ibid.*, November 12, 1961; Statement of Trinidad and Tobago National Trades Union Council, *ibid.*, November 16, 1961; and remarks of Mr. John Rojas, in *The Evening News*, November 27, 1961.

pathetic hero-figure of Mr. Naipaul's large novel, *A House for Mr. Biswas*, exemplifies, to empty and inconclusive lives. The recognition of labour in the new senatorial appointments in Port of Spain is a step in that direction. If this goes well, the PNM promises a social alliance between the socially disinherited and the middle-class groups which no previous movement led by successive Trinidadian politicians—Cipriani, Butler, Rojas, Rienzi, Gomes—has been able to effect.

The Achilles heel of that promise is, of course, the ugly spectre of race. Historically, there has been little race admixture to cement the various ethnic groups—Africans, Indians, Chinese, Syrians, Europeans—into a new Trinidadian whole. It is true that the divisions in Trinidad have not gone as far as in British Guiana, where Mr. Sidney King's sensational proposal for racial partition during that colony's recent election showed the depths of Negro-Indian mutual hatred. It is true, too, that the established occupational differentiations of the Trinidadian social structure, founded upon the traditional economic subserviency of the Indian labourer and the traditional incapacity of the creole for trade, are beginning to break down as, first, the middle-class Negro is getting away from the bias in favor of the "older" professions such as law, medicine and the civil service and, two, the creolisation of the Indian proceeds apace. As a result of all this, there is much to place on the credit side of the ledger. A completely racialist "ticket" has become a serious hazard, so both parties sponsored a racially mixed list of candidates. The PNM ran the personally popular Saied Mohammed in San Fernando West, the DLP ran Negro candidates like Peter Farquhar in Pointe-a-Pierre and James Kelly in Barataria; and the fact that this might be regarded as a slate-making tactic in a multi-group electorate does not detract from its significance. Dr. Williams urged upon his followers the truth that an Indian friend in the PNM was better than a Negro enemy in the DLP. The attempt of the African National Congress to emulate the Garveyite "black nationalism" of the Millard Johnson variety in Jamaica fell on stony ground, if only because the "Back to Africa" slogan meant little to a Trinidad that has traditionally been an importer rather than an exporter of people. To the degree that it is possible to correlate the voting statistics with the 1960 Population Census figures put out by the Central Statistical Office in Port of Spain, it seems likely that the PNM Indian candidates in the three predominantly Indian constituencies of Couva, Chaguanas, and Caroni East polled minority returns higher than the Negro ratio of the population, while Mr. Mohammed in Barataria almost certainly pulled large numbers of Indian voters into the PNM column. On the other hand, the narrow margin of the DLP winner in the Fyzabad constituency reflected rather faithfully the racial composition of that almost equally divided Indian-Negro area; nor did the PNM strategy of running an Indian standard-bearer in the heavily Indian Pointe-a-Pierre constituency prevent the majority of its voters from supporting the DLP Negro candidate. Much of the Indian sense of alienation towards the Trinidad society has been the result, of course, of heightened cultural identification with India since 1947. It was therefore astute of Dr. Williams, to say the least, to head a government mission to New Delhi during the election year and to celebrate the centenary of the Indian poet-philosopher Tagore with a learned disquisition, in his private capacity as scholar and historian, on the significance of that great humanist spirit for the modern nationalist movement both in India and the West Indies.

Yet, when all is said and done, this was a beginning only. The hard, inner core of the voting pattern was undoubtedly racial loyalty. The very failure of a group like the African National Congress could be seen, indeed, in a negative rather than a positive light, for if the Trinidadian Negro vote did not divide along intra-Negro lines between "brown man" and "black man" elements, as in Haiti and Jamaica, the resultant Negro unity could be explained simply as the closing of the race ranks against a felt Indian menace that does not exist in either of the Greater Antillean societies. That probably explains why, so far, race alignments seem more pressing than class alignments, why, for example, the social and economic division between the "barefoot brigade" and what Dr. M. G. Smith has aptly styled the "motorised salariat" has not taken on a political expression in Trinidad as it has done in Jamaica. It is suggestive, to make another point, that the DLP staff organisation did not deem it worthwhile to enter an Indian candidate in any of the four Port of Spain districts, and that not even the most ardent PNMite would have considered a Negro to run the gauntlet in the solid Indian territories of Naparima or Caroni East. It is probable, again, that the Chinese group voted DLP, with exceptions like the business family from which Senator Ronnie Williams comes, although it would be interesting to know how many of them voted PNM in resentment against Dr. Capildeo's threat to depose the Trinidad-Chinese Governor, Sir Solomon Hochoy, should the DLP win the election. Habit, said Plato, is everything. The notorious clannishness of the Indian, based, historically, upon his cultural isolationism, will take a long time to disappear. There are many PNM members, again, for whom, underneath the thin veneer of their ideology, the word "Indian" is still a word of opprobrium. Nor were there wanting signs, in the heat of election, of anti-white, anti-expatriate feelings on the part of the PNM common man, certainly an unhappy fact when it is remembered that there were enclaves of pro-PNM sentiment both in the managerial echelons of the oil companies and in the faculty of the old campus of the Imperial College of Tropical Agriculture at St. Augustine.

Class-race feelings, clearly enough, are in a state of flux in the Trinidadian boiling pot. How far the present situation will change as class loyalties have a chance to replace race loyalties in a rapidly changing socio-economic structure is problematical. There are signs, at least, that the old creole ruling elements will turn to the DLP as their fears of PNM social radicalism swell (the entry of Sir Gerald Wight into the governing councils of the party is a straw in the wind); just as, in British Guiana, there are signs that elements within the East Indian business groups and more wealthy rice producers appear to be forgetting their racial affinity as their apprehensions about Jaganite "communism" increase. Economic rationalism, along class lines, if this process continues, would begin to supplant racial nationalism. If that turns out to be the case, the remedy may well turn out to be as potentially as explosive as the disease it seeks to exorcise, for the hatreds of class are no more pleasing than the hatreds of race. It is at that point that the all-inclusive nationalist *credo* of parties like the PNM would receive its most formidable challenge. Be all that as it may, the gospel of an all-Trinidadian racial solidarity remains, as yet, an aspiration rather than a reality. Negro self-respect, admittedly, has won out, after the sentiment of the calypsonian:

> Soon, in the West Indies,
> It will be Please, Mr. Nigger, please.

But it will surely be some time before the race-mixture theme of *Koon Koon Street Arima*

> They could say ah crazy or ah mad
> But ah love Arima bad,
> It have some Indian mix up wid nigger
> Calling me to plant sweet cassava . . .

becomes equally sovereign in the Trinidadian communal psychology.

The issue of the West Indies Federation, and its place in the election, merits a special note. The election was held in the shadow of the impending dissolution of that unfortunate experiment precipitated by the Jamaican secession: a secession, incidentally, that gave added piquancy to the chapter of Mr. Murray's early volume of 1912 on *A United West Indies* entitled "Reasons for Excluding Jamaica".[10] It is not exaggeration to say that Trinidad in

---

[10] C. Gideon Murray, *A United West Indies* (London: The West Strand Publishing Company Ltd., 1912), Ch. 1, "Reasons for Excluding Jamaica".

1961, like the border states in the crisis of the American federal union in 1861, held in its hands the power to make or break the Federation. As a consequence, the brooding omnipresence of the Trinidad Government's decision, one way or the other, to end it or mend it, coloured the whole electoral campaign. Early on, the PNM decided, in convention, not to make the matter an electoral issue but, rather, to make it a subject of special enquiry once the election was over. The Opposition, in addition to the DLP group of federal parliamentarians whose interest in continued Trinidadian membership was self-evident enough, sought unsuccessfully to compel the government to break its self-imposed silence. For the PNM strategy was surely prudent in the light of the grim price that the PNP Government in Jamaica had had to pay for injecting the federal question into local politics; while the small audience that attended Dr. Elton Richardson's "federal forum" at Queen's Hall during the election indicated that there was little popular demand behind the DLP viewpoint. The PNM decision to leave the Federation was thus left for the General Council and a special convention to announce in early 1962. It has been said that the decision should have been referred to a popular referendum vote. But a referendum frequently fails to deliver a decisive vote on a controversial issue, as the Jamaican referendum itself showed. As a device, it is profoundly alien to the British-West Indian constitutional tradition, which has never accepted the idea of the formal mandate as a guide to governmental policy. And, in any case, the proper answer to the critics is that, if the desirability of a referendum be granted, it should in all logic have been held on the federal level and prior to, and not after, the adoption of the federal constitution, following the example of the Australian federal case half a century earlier.[11]

Three things are noteworthy about the Trinidadian decision, disappointing as it was to those, like Dr. Arthur

[11] Resolution of the General Council of the People's National Movement. Full text reprinted in *The Nation*, January 15, 1962. The Report of the Special Convention of the People's National Movement, reported in *The Nation*, February 2, 1962.

Lewis, who had urged continued Trinidadian membership in a truncated Eastern Caribbean Federation. In the first place, it showed, if further proof were still needed, the utterly artificial character of the federalist sentiment. That sentiment, in the Trinidad populace, has really been fed primarily by Dr. Williams' own educational efforts following his resignation from the Caribbean Commission, and that he could kill it as easily as he could create it was evident in the fact that, Mr. Andrew Rose's pro-Federation motion excepted, the party convention accepted the new policy without any real dissent. "Federation mash up": there was little of regret in the colloquial Trinidadian dismissal of the experiment. In Trinidad as much as in Jamaica, then, the spirit of patriotic nationalism has won out over that of federal unionism. Nor was that PNM sentiment alone, for Mr. Ashford Sinanan of the DLP, like Mr. Robinson of the PNM, resigned his federal seat in order to run as a local candidate. It is doubtful, looking back, if the federal sentiment ever penetrated below the level of the middle-class professional and civil service groups who were prepared, as was the federal establishment itself, to accept the Federation as an instrument representing British sentiments and following (as the federal constitution showed) the predilections of a British constitutional tradition that has never really understood the workings of the federal principle because it has never experienced them. For only those predilections could have been guilty of arguing, as they did in the Rance Committee Report of 1949, that there would occur a quiet and tranquil transfer of unit government powers to the federal centre, when in fact all modern federal experience elsewhere forcibly suggests that such a process of centralisation of powers is always accompanied by bitter and prolonged struggle.

In the second place, the PNM attitude was therefore not so much anti-federal in basic principle as it was against continuing membership of what it viewed as a farcical and not a genuine Federation. It was critical, from the outset, of a Federation in which, to use Bagehot's famous dis-

tinction between the dignified and the efficient elements of
a constitution, the dignified elements were exaggerated
and the efficient elements played down; so that the Federal Government's public image centered upon the Federal Governor-General (an imported party Whip from
the Westminster Parliament), the comings and goings of
the Federal ministers, the aping of House of Commons
ritual in the Federal house, rather than upon regional
economic planning and development. The PNM saw that
in order to meet the clamant needs of an "underdeveloped"
colonial economy the region required a strong federal
government endowed with the necessary legal and financial powers to integrate the economy, fatally decentralised
as it was; and such a program was set out in the exhaustive studies sponsored by the Trinidad Government: *The
Economics of Nationhood, The Case for United Kingdom
Assistance, European Integration and West Indian Trade,*
in addition to monographs on the comparative cases of
Puerto Rico and Nigeria. Yet the Federal Government
never looked like undertaking such a scheme at any point;
even more important, the British Government and Parliament utterly failed to guarantee the sort of continuing
economic aid that West Indians surely had a moral right
to expect after three centuries of colonial exploitation.
There was little to suggest, indeed, that in 1962 British
leadership had in any way changed its view, set out in an
infamous passage of the Rance Committee Report, that
economic aid saps the "self-respect" of a politically independent people, penned at the very moment (1949) when
Britain itself was receiving massive economic aid from the
United States without any visible effect upon the "self-
respect" of the British people. In the light of all this, Dr.
Williams and his colleagues clearly felt that it was not
the historic function of Trinidad to take over obligations
in the grant-aided economies of the Leeward and Windward Islands that were inescapably the responsibilities of
the British people and the British Government.

Thirdly, and finally, then, the Trinidad attitude was
at once negative and positive. Negative, in that the PNM

modernising oligarchy were unwilling to give time and
energy to the creation of their kind of federation with
the remaining units, for everything about the "small island" mentality strongly suggested that such a course
would have meant another prolonged fight for the acceptance of their ideas. The period 1956–61 had witnessed
an enervating and wasteful struggle between the Trinidad-
Hamiltonian thesis of a strong central government and
the Jamaica-Jeffersonian thesis of a weak federal centre.
Trinidadian leadership of an Eastern Caribbean Federation would quite certainly have meant another such struggle with "small island" leaderships jealous of their costly
and top-heavy governmental structures. It is true that the
decision was a harsh one, harshly worded, and an un-
deniable retreat from the earlier magnanimity of PNM
attitudes: the General Council resolution setting out its
reasons concentrated almost entirely on the economic
aspects of Federation and said little about its moral and
sentimental aspects. Yet those who have been perturbed
by this have perhaps insufficiently appreciated that in the
power-struggles of a nascent federal form appeal to sentiment rarely triumphs over the vested interests of insularist
unit governments.

On the other hand, having said all this, the PNM decision had its positive elements, in that it did not turn its
back utterly, as had done Jamaica, on a future federal
endeavor. For the decision to "go it alone" did not pre-
clude, in the convention's language, "the future association in a unitary state of the people of Trinidad and
Tobago with any territory of the Eastern Caribbean whose
people may so desire and on terms to be mutually agreed,
but in any case providing for the maximum possible degree of local government"; and, beyond that, a willingness
on Trinidad's part "to associate with all the peoples of the
Caribbean in a Caribbean Economic Community and to take
such action as may be necessary for the achievement of
this objective". Trinidad was thus taking one step back-
wards in order, later, to take two steps forward. If, for

the present, that means, to put it brutally, desertion of the small and poorer islands—as, indeed, it is—the Trinidadian offense is at least mitigated by the fact that the desertion was initially that of a Jamaican leadership devoid of any real federal civic sense and of a British officialdom that permitted Jamaican secession, when secession, as a right, was unknown to the federal constitution. The Caribbean, as a whole, clearly lacks as yet the kind of bold leadership that is ready to risk all in the service of a great principle.

A final word is in order on the international implications of the election. West Indian elections, until only yesterday, concerned themselves in an insular fashion with what Adam Smith contemptuously styled "the paltry raffle of colony faction". That is no longer possible nor desirable. The growth of a Pan-Antillean nationalism, the Cuban Revolution, the changing economy of the region and its emergent status as a cockpit of international rivalries: all conspire to bring the world and its problems to the doorstep of even the smallest island. The political Balkanisation of the area—of which the breakdown of the Federation is yet another sign—aggravates all of that, since it has created, and continues to create, a political vacuum that encourages intervention by outside forces. Hence the notorious vulnerability of the Caribbean: politically, because there has been no indigenous Caribbean force capable of resisting that intervention, ever since it started with the Papal Donation of 1492; and economically, because imperial mercantilist policies have condemned it to the production of food and extractive commodities for outside consumption and over the price and sales structure of which there has been little local control.

It is within this general context that Trinidad, like Jamaica, embraces sovereign independence, with full responsibility for all of the complex problems of defense and foreign affairs hitherto looked after by London. The grim hazard of the enterprise was already underlined during the election period by, one, the British immigration control bill and, two, the British application for entry into the European Common Market. For both of those acts revealed a Britain turning her back on her Commonwealth ties and responsibilities in order to safeguard her own vulnerability in the face of an integrating European economic community. The migrant bar, as PNM pointed out, would have the effect of diverting small island migrants from Britain to Trinidad itself, thereby causing a fatal strain upon the local embryonic social services. The trade bar, even worse, could perhaps cripple the West Indian sugar, cocoa, coffee and citrus products market, protected at the moment by the system of imperial tariff preferences; for it is unlikely that the Rome Treaty members would accept terms of entry for Great Britain which would involve the possibility of privileged West Indian products crossing the Channel, once they were in the UK economy, to compete unfairly with ECM commodities. The only alternative would be for the West Indies dependencies to be accorded Associated Overseas Territories status (already enjoyed by the neighbouring Dutch Antillean economies), whereby they would obtain free entry for their products into the whole of the Common Market area but, of course, would have to face the competition on even terms of the other Associated Overseas Territories. All this explains why the PNM strove to draw voter attention to these problems, so much more urgent and potentially dangerous in their possible consequences than the usual diet of territorial elections. It explains, too, why the long-term aim of any Trinidad government must be, increasingly, the attainment of full and equal representation, as a government, in all of these international agreements that presently control the price and marketing structures of those commodities—coffee, sugar, oil, cocoa, grapefruit—in which Trinidad specialises. Since, too, in cases like coffee and cocoa the most important consumer is the United States, it means, in addition, adequate representation in Washington. It remains to be seen whether an isolated Trinidad, or for that matter an isolated Jamaica, will be strong enough to survive in that kind of international environment.[12]

The implications of all this are enormous; and it is doubtful if the average man in the West Indian street has even begun to comprehend them. In terms of independent diplomatic representation, economic and technical advisory services, foreign service missions overseas, the establishment of small but adequate defense forces—perhaps something on the model of the United States National Guard system—it means an immediate pressure on resources and manpower of no mean proportions. The recent Jamaica Ministry Paper on the establishment of a Ministry of Foreign Affairs and Commonwealth Relations and of Foreign Service Missions overseas indicates the size and character of the problems. The foreign policy problem alone is formidable; for, at the least, it means the searching out of new friends to put in the place of Britain's betrayal—as West Indians see it—of old and long ties of affection and esteem. For that reason alone, a heavy premium will be placed upon friendly relations with the United States; and the 1960 US-West Indies agreement on leased bases proved that the Trinidad PNM leadership is willing to permit the continuation of American-held bases so long as it is founded upon fair and open agreement between equals. The cry of "anti-Americanism" has been heard. But no one who knows Dr. Williams closely, and his pungent sense of practicality, is likely to believe that he would be willing to subject Trinidad to the type of massive economic embarrassments faced by Cuba, let alone risk the destruction of his own political career, by any sort of serious collision with the American power. Nor should it be overlooked, in that respect, that there has always been a tendency for West Indian politicians of the old school to concentrate upon attacking the United States rather than devoting themselves, in the PNM manner, to (for them) the less

[12] *Britain in the European Common Market: How It May Affect the West Indies,* memorandum prepared by the West India Committee, London; reprinted in the *Sunday Gleaner* (Kingston, Jamaica), February 11, 1962.

congenial task of analysing the internal problems of their own economies; with the result that, as even a leftwing French socialist like M. Guérin has pointed out in his recent volume on *The West Indies and Their Future,* they tend to make America into a scapegoat for whatever goes wrong in the Caribbean. Yet it is not enough to be against something, however justifiably. One must also be for something.[13]

That is why—to proceed to the final point—political independence must be accomplished by a positive patriotism, a new national psychology, at bottom, that is appropriate to a society that seeks to stand on its own feet. For the legacy of cultural imperialism has been the dependent colonial mentality of the Caribbean mind, what Mr. Ansell Hart, in the Jamaican case, has called the social religion of "Anglolatry", the habit of looking always to England and English ways for guidance. Here, more than anywhere else, perhaps, is the real PNM revolution, the appeal to a new West Indian pride in the hitherto repressed West Indian culture, fixed upon Captain Cipriani's *dictum* at the historic Dominica Conference of 1932 that "The Englishman has taught us that his home is his castle. We have learned the lesson well, and we must make our home our castle". West Indians will have to emancipate themselves, in their innermost selves, from the London psycho-complex; and no one who has seen how difficult it has been for Puerto Ricans, over the last two decades, to rid themselves of the Washington psycho-complex will be likely to underestimate the magnitude of the challenge, for it is always easier to change ideas than to give up feelings. Accepted and mastered, however, the challenge could be made into the foundation for a new relationship between the new world and the old. West Indians would cease to be passive recipients only of events and become active agents in their creation. They would contribute their own gifts to world civilisation in a relationship of full equality with others. Charles Kingsley saw

[13] Daniel Guérin, *The West Indies and Their Future* (London: Denis Dobson, 1961), p. 172.

something of that possibility in the thoughts that were suggested to him, some seventy-five years ago, as he watched the Negroes of Port of Spain perform their tom-tom dances in the Belmont hills. "Great and worthy exertions", he wrote, "are made, every London Season, for the conversion of the Negro and the Heathen, and the abolition of their barbarous customs and dances. It is to be hoped that the Negro and the Heathen will some day show their gratitude to us, by sending missionaries hither to convert the London Season itself, dances and all; and assist it to take the beam out of its own eye, in return for having taken the mote out of theirs".[14] It is possible that the time for that reversal of historic culture-roles has now arrived.

[14] Charles Kingsley, *At Last: A Christmas in the West Indies* (London: Macmillan, 1887), p. 308.

7.

Some West Indians, concerned that their territories might lack viability as independent states, have sought to combine autonomy with inter-island association. The historic urge toward union, culminated in the creation of the short-lived British West Indies Federation (1958–62). The federal venture is seen here through the eyes of a Jamaican nationalist who opposed it as more likely to impede Jamaican independence than to advance it. Writing just before the federation began, he found little popular sentiment for it and argued that Jamaica was too distant from the other islands to derive any tangible benefits from the connection. He envisaged Jamaica as burdened instead by caring for a number of small impoverished associates who would be unable to stand on their own feet, yet were liable to outvote Jamaica. These objections proved prophetic, going far to explain Jamaica's decision to withdraw from the federation only two years after its inception.

W. A. DOMINGO, a Jamaican nationalist long resident in New York, was a journalist and political activist who joined other emigré Jamaicans during the 1930s and 1940s in urging greater Jamaican autonomy.

British West Indian Federation—A Critique
W. A. Domingo

With practically no opposition in the territories concerned, the British Caribbean islands, with the exception
of the Virgin Islands, will be federated in 1958. The conditions under which this result was accomplished hampered
the emergence of an informed opposition. Public discussion, the necessary prerequisite of political action in democratic communities, was virtually absent when the question
of federation was considered. Supporters of federation
had the "dice loaded in their favour" and refused or
appeared unwilling to challenge dissident views. They assumed an attitude of lofty disdain for any opinion not in
harmony with their own and ignored the mutterings of
dissent which arose at a late stage. From the start the
federationists had the press and other media of publicity
and propaganda on their side. These were either controlled
by them or were generally favourable to the proposition
that it was imperative for the British Caribbean territories
to form some sort of a political union.

In one instance, the federationists went so far as to
characterize some feeble last-minute questionings as com-
munistic, implying that arguments and ideas are not to be
assayed for their intrinsic worth but on the basis of their
source.

Writing in his column in *Public Opinion*, a Jamaican
weekly newspaper, a few months before the signing of

The Gleaner Company, Ltd., Kingston, Jamaica, 1956; reprinted with permission.

the document which committed the islands to federate,
Mr. Michael Manley, journalist and prominent trade union
organizer, son of Chief Minister Manley of Jamaica, admitted with what seemed to be a touch of doubt as to
the wisdom of federation, that the demand for a federal
union had no mass basis; that it was sponsored by politicians, and when finalized will have been imposed by
them. He deplored the fact that the bulk of the people
to be affected knew very little about the subject and were
indifferent. In effect, the inhabitants of the islands were
being led, or driven, like sheep.

Because of these circumstances the British West Indian
populations have been confronted with a *fait accompli*.
How serious the result might be to them in the years ahead
is shown by the reply given by Chief Minister Manley, as
reported in *Public Opinion* of April 28, 1956. Asked if
a unit could secede if it became dissatisfied with the workings of the federation, Mr. Manley answered, "I think
not". In other words, the principal architect of federation,
an able and experienced lawyer, regards the union as indissoluble. No provision is made for a trial period of even
25 years to test the value of the union to each of its disparate units!

Although the die has been cast, final ratification is yet
to be made by the various legislatures, so an *ante mortem*
should be in order. It might be possible even at this late
date for some of the legislators who accepted the idea
without appearing to have given it any critical study or
to have made an appraisal of its possible effects on their
own country, to stop and take that "sober second thought"
considered important in personal affairs. Nothing is perfect and above critical examination. It should never be
too late to correct a mistake.

West Indian proponents of federation at no time, in
Jamaica at any rate, invited, courted or engaged in any
full dress discussions in which the pros and cons of the
subject were carefully assessed and the full play of controversy brought into operation. There was no careful,
selfish, if you will, scrutiny or evaluation of the question
from the point of view of the special interests of each

colony. Public debate on the desirability or wisdom of Jamaica entering the federation was discouraged and even resisted. The pros had a field day. Seemingly having long decided that some sort of union must *ipso facto* be beneficial to every unit, including their own, they proceeded with what was evidently their pre-determined plan.

From an unknown source this writer received a copy of "Freedom News Letter" from Jamaica by mail. In it is reported what purports to be the exact answer given by the Chief Minister of Jamaica to the question: "Don't you believe your Government enjoys sufficient prestige and goodwill to allow the people to decide by referendum whether we join such a federation without achieving independence first?" Mr. Manley is quoted as saying, "We can do anything but will not permit a referendum".

The quoted reply was made at a public lecture by Mr. Manley under the auspices of the Jamaica Manufacturers' Association at the Carib Theatre in Kingston on April 22, 1956. It leaves no conclusion but that it was his irrevocable intention to foist federation on Jamaica. Implicit in the answer to the question, which challenged the wisdom of Jamaica subordinating its own struggle for the fullest self-government in favour of federation, is the fear that public discussion, the necessary, salutary and inevitable concomitant of a referendum, might upset plans that already had been formulated. It is a sad, disheartening and revealing commentary on the trend of Jamaican politics.

From time to time this writer persistently, but vainly, tried in the Jamaican press to lure Jamaican federationists into a debate on the topic. Apparently ventilation of the subject was tabooed by them. It was not to be publicly examined in all its aspects, least of all from Jamaica's special point of view. It appears to be a case of, "We have spoken; there is no further discussion; the case is closed".

Failure to provoke open discussion leaves one alternative—analyse the arguments and try to discover the motives and influences which appear to have induced Jamaican federationists to include their country in the nascent union.

At the outset it must be made crystal clear that there is

no intention of imputing or ascribing self-serving or ignoble motives to anyone. Nor is there any purpose of applying opprobrious terms, such as "tory", "traitor", "Communist", "reactionary", etc., to the defenders of federation. Cold war epithets will find no place in this critique; but cold, dispassionate arguments will. It is only fair to assume that everyone acted and is acting in good faith.

The attitude of Jamaican federationists, in the light of available evidence, cannot be regarded as based on a respect for and acceptance of the generally observed principles governing the adoption of a programme or a course of action likely to profoundly affect a country and its future population. Facts, logic and the conclusions legitimately derivable from them appear not to be considered of the highest importance. This was demonstrated when Mr. Manley declared to a group of Jamaicans in New York last winter, shortly after he had signed the document in London which committed Jamaica to be a member of the burgeoning federation, that opponents of his action had "logic, arguments and common sense" on their side, but lacked "faith". The inescapable inference is that Mr. Manley and his supporters possess an abundance of "faith" but are perhaps destitute of sound logic and good arguments for their cause.

"Faith" is said to be necessary in matters of religion, but it is hardly a safe guide for political action of the sort envisaged by federation. A famous American orator defined faith as "belief without evidence".

The more West Indian federationists, especially Jamaicans, defend their position for an over-all federation, the less convincing their arguments become. These questions naturally arise: Why should the islands federate? Should Jamaica and British Honduras, situated as they are geographically, be part of the federation? Should federation of any sort, even if considered desirable, take precedence over the attainment of self-government by each political unit of the British Caribbean? Should federation, at best a dubious political grouping, be equated with or linked to self-government, a fundamental political and human right?

The usual glib answer is that unity means strength; that

the units are each too small in area or population to be important in world affairs; that the inhabitants are "one people".

It is not true that unity necessarily increases strength. It can seriously weaken some of its components. A chain, as is known, is as "strong as its weakest link". It does not become stronger by adding some "strong" links. The argument about size is indeed novel and will be dealt with later.

Is it true that West Indians are one people? The majority of them are of Negro ancestry with varying degrees of admixture with other races. Among these diverse peoples exist many sharp and ominous cleavages of class, colour and race. It is impossible to wish this fact away. But even if the population was homogeneous to the ultimate degree in each colony, or in the colonies as a whole, that would not be a convincing reason for them federating with their far and near, insular and continental, neighbours in the area.

The French, Germans, Italians, Poles and Spaniards occupy the same European land mass and are of the same race, meaning that by and large their observable physical resemblances are greater than their dissimilarities, but this "oneness" is not regarded by Europeans as a compelling reason for federating their nations. Similarly, the inhabitants of China, Mongolia and several Asian countries occupy the same land mass and look so much alike physically as to be virtually indistinguishable from one another, but neither geographical proximity nor physical alikeness is regarded as constituting a substantial basis for uniting the several nations into one nation.

Geographical contiguity and similarity of language and customs, as in the cases of Canada and the United States, and Mexico and Guatemala, not to mention many countries of South America, are not rational grounds for individual nations agreeing to obliterate their independent national existence.

If being of Negro descent in the Caribbean is justification for federation, Haiti and the French West Indies with their heavy Negro populations, eminently qualify for in-

clusion in any such union! The patent absurdity and unreality of this type of argument condemns it completely.
Race is not a legitimate ground for federating nations or
territories.

The British and American Virgin Islands are in the
Caribbean and the inhabitants are mostly English-speaking
Negroes, but they will not be in the federation, the former, although British, as the result of their own free
choice.

To insist that race or language should be the basis of a
federation is to accept the dangerous and discredited Hit-
lerian doctrine of "race and nation", a Nazi concept which
repudiated the principles of democracy and was itself
repudiated in a bloody holocaust. It is unbelievable that
any sane person, cognizant of the history of Latin America, where oneness of religion also exists, would seriously
suggest that these nations sink their national individualities
and federate. As a matter of history, be it noted, the Central American Republics were politically united in their
early existence, but national characteristics and conflicting
interests developed, resulting in defederation.

What, then, is the discernible driving force that actuates
West Indian politicians? That force seems to be the long
connection of the territories with Great Britain. It is significant that of all the Caribbean peoples it is only among
the British-controlled ones that there is any agitation for
regional federation. Limitation of the agitation to one segment of the peoples of the area excludes any other conclusion than that the special attitude is primarily due to
their peculiar conditioning.

An understanding of the psychological aspects of the
question offers the only feasible explanation why colonies
as far apart as 1,000 miles, separated by water, as are
Jamaica and Trinidad, were urged by their leaders and
encouraged by the British Government to federate. The
motivation could not be cultural or historical for there is
no uniform culture, if any special culture at all, in the
British West Indies. As for a common history there is none
except insofar as the islands are the colonial possessions
of England.

Dominica, St. Lucia and Grenada have been under French rule and until this day the inhabitants, as well as of Trinidad, commonly speak a French *patois* and retain vestiges of French culture and customs. Every island or colony has its own history with which the inhabitants are naturally familiar; but only a few outside scholars—specialists—are likely to be interested enough to study individual insular histories. Ignorance of Jamaica is as profound among Trinidadians as is ignorance of Trinidad among Jamaicans.

Identity of economic interests does not exist among the units. On the contrary, they produce practically the same primary agricultural commodities and seek the same foreign markets, thus in reality they are competitors. Each wants, because of understandable internal reasons, to increase its production. Competition, or the effort of each unit to sell more goods to the same customers, is likely to be intensified.

It is the natural aim of each colony to industrialize to the limit of its resources; but this normal and laudable objective will pose serious problems which must ultimately lead to friction inside the union. It seems, therefore, that the urge for federation which will soon be effectuated by West Indian politicians, rests on no firmer foundation than the fact that the colonies have been tied to Britain, their political "motherland", for a long period of time.

There are several federations extant. The United States, Canada, Australia, Switzerland, are notable examples of such political arrangements. In each of these cases the component units occupy the same land mass and are contiguous. There is no separation by water. Wherever islands are or were federated the distance between one island and its nearest neighbour in the union is relatively insignificant. This is true of the Windward and Leeward Islands in the British West Indies.

For centuries there has been considerable inter-island trade and travel between the two island-federations. Movement of peoples in and between the two groups of islands and, for that matter, in the eastern sector of the British West Indies, has been practically unhindered. On the other hand, Jamaica and British Honduras, situated far to the west, are virtually isolated from the eastern colonies, continental and insular.

There is little travel or communication between the two sectors, consequently few family ties exist between the peoples of the two areas—east and west. Because of their proximity to each other, and the movement of peoples within the eastern colonies, numerous family connections exist. Thus a Barbadian may have close relatives who were born in Trinidad, St. Lucia and British Guiana. Jamaican family ties are with Cuba, Central America and the United States.

The British Government realistically recognized the ineluctable fact of geography when it federated the Leeward and Windward Islands separately, although at one time they were federated together. The federation had the distinction of being logical and practical. It was not synthetic. It facilitated, as was doubtless intended, administration.

The second realistic recognition of the physical facts of the area was when Colonel Oliver Stanley, then Secretary of State for the Colonies, sent a Despatch to the West Indies on March 14, 1945, stating the willingness of the Imperial Government to support some sort of federation. In the document, the Colonial Office suggested consideration of one federation to include all the colonies or two federations—one, western, presumably composed of British Honduras and Jamaica, the other obviously consisting of the colonies in the east, including the mainland territory of British Guiana.

By advancing the idea of two federations the British Government clearly suggested that an over-all federation might not be desirable or be the best means of achieving unity. Obviously the British Government is not likely to sanction, unless compelled by the determined action of the inhabitants of an area, any type of political union likely to weaken the economic grip of England on her colonies. England's policy, motivated by intelligent self-interest, most naturally is to make concessions, when they are inevitable, with the objective of reducing as much of her financial responsibility as possible, while retaining the maximum economic and political advantages.

It is significant that West Indians at home and abroad completely ignored the suggestion for the creation of two federations. They argued with disarming simplicity that "the bigger the area, the better". They contended and still contend that a "new nation" of approximately 3,000,000 people is capable of cutting a more important figure in world affairs than two "new nations", each with a population of less than 2,000,000.

Only an incorrigible optimist who is oblivious of the realities of the present-day world can exaggerate into a faith the future of any small and weak nation, whether it has ten or three million people. The irrefragable fact is that a small nation can hope to make an impression on world affairs only through the skill of its statesmen or if its territory contains products vitally needed by mankind.

Evidently the leaders and perhaps the peoples of the two mainland colonies have not been impressed by the logic or wisdom of joining the federation. Neither race, language, culture nor political attachment to England has, up to now, had much weight in deciding the conduct of British Guiana and British Honduras. How long this aloofness will continue is problematical, for the British Government and the units to be federated are exerting maximum pressures on the two recalcitrant colonies in an effort to have them reverse their position.

Nothing better illustrates the indifference of West Indians in America regarding the political future of their islands than the damning fact that apart from the Jamaica Progressive League of New York there is no organization of West Indians in the metropolis dedicated solely to the task of securing self-government for any section of the British Caribbean.

There are cricket, literary and social clubs, religious and fraternal groups a-plenty, but only one political organization in a population of over 200,000 West Indians in the United States.

The Jamaica Progressive League was founded in 1936 by a group of Jamaicans in New York at the instance of

W. Adolphe Roberts, poet, historian and novelist, a Jamaican by birth.

> The objective of the League was clearly stated in its Declaration:
> "Firmly believing that any people that has seen its generations come and go on the same soil for centuries is, in fact, a nation, the Jamaica Progressive League pledges itself to work for the attainment of self-government for Jamaica, so that the country may take its rightful place as a member of the British Commonwealth of Nations."

Nothing is said about federating with any other colony or island in the Caribbean. The Declaration is a forthright statement of intention. Nothing in it is opportunistic, equivocal, apologetic or conditional. The establishment of Jamaica as a self-governing Dominion with all its attributes was the aim. For this purpose the League worked and sacrificed. Its many early drives for funds to help the People's National Party in Jamaica were unconnected with anything not contained in the Declaration. Campaign and organizational funds were collected and sent to Jamaica for that specific purpose.

At this point it should be instructive and profitable to examine the ideas of West Indians in the United States who favour federation—one federation.

The subject was not new in the eastern islands. It had often been bandied about. Discussion and advocacy of federation was a distinguishing feature of the politics of the area. That this should be so is understandable. The existence of the already-federated islands made the subject a foremost part of the political thinking of the sector.

Jamaica manifested little interest in the controversy. Relative remoteness gave no urgency to the matter in the two western colonies, so they took no active part in it.

Paradoxically, one of the high priests of federation was a Jamaican, Dr. Louis Meikle, who wrote a rambling and incoherent book on the subject some fifty years ago. Dr. Meikle had spent part of his early life in the United States at a time when annexation of the islands to the United States was being mooted for American strategic reasons.

Appalled by the prevailing racial situation in the United States, he expressed his opposition to annexation by advocating federation. Dr. Meikle spent the last years of his life in Trinidad.

The question of federation was for the first time definitely projected on the Jamaican political scene by Hon. T. Albert Marryshow of Grenada as part of a speech he delivered in Kingston in 1945. An accomplished orator, Mr. Marryshow's speech, couched in sentimental terms, evoked some emotional response, but local indifference soon reasserted itself. Mr. Marryshow had long crusaded for federation in the columns of his weekly newspaper, *The West Indian,* which circulated almost entirely in the eastern islands. He had also frequently toured those islands and British Guiana to lecture on his favourite topic. The few Jamaicans who heard of federation in their island did so only in a vague manner. To them it was remote and unrelated to their destiny.

It is beyond successful contradiction that in the islands the inhabitants, as a general rule, regard themselves as Trinidadians, Barbadians, Jamaicans, Antiguans, etc., not as West Indians. This is particularly true of Jamaicans. Separated from the other colonies under the Union Jack by relatively large stretches of water, as are Jamaica and British Honduras, development of a genuine regional national feeling was next to impossible. At best the term "West Indian", even when restricted to the British insular possessions, is geographical, not national.

British Caribbean immigrants in the United States, as well as Bahamans, Bermudans, Guianese and Hondurans, are called West Indians. The last four groups of immigrants protest the designation as inaccurate, but the American majority fixed the pattern, so most of the immigrants sensibly accept the term, even though they know that Puerto Ricans, Haitians and Dutch and French Caribbeans are, geographically speaking, West Indians.

This lumping together of all English-speaking Caribbeans in the United States has had the effect of creating a loose, superficial unity—an artificial oneness. The newborn and synthetic oneness generated an emotional support of federation. Many Jamaicans, who never heard of federation in their island, becoming "West Indians" in the United States, have been psychologized into accepting the new political concept without scrutiny. They seem to reason, if they reason at all, that since they are "West Indians", not Jamaicans, in America, it would be ideal if all the islands were united under one government.

Leadership of New York federationists is in the control of individuals from the eastern islands where the issue has been alive for generations. Many of these leaders hail from an existing federation. For the most part their islands are small (even in West Indian terms) and without any significant mineral resources. Only Trinidad, largest of the group, has any mineral wealth. Smallness of territory and lack of mineral potentialities tend to imbue the people with a sense of frustration and hopelessness. They can see no future for their countries unless they are attached to richer and larger units—hence their vehement advocacy of federating not only their closely-situated islands, but all the British Caribbean colonies, seems necessary and logical to them. They see in federation a source of borrowed strength and the means of easing population pressures through emigration to the other islands, thereby effecting their own insular improvement and salvation.

A British Colonial Office-sponsored Conference met at Montego Bay, Jamaica, in 1947 to discuss West Indian federation. Representatives from all the Caribbean colonies attended. New York federationists sent a statement to the gathering setting forth their views on the question at issue. The document contained the theory, aims and strategy of its sponsors.

The gist of the thesis is that federation and self-government are indivisible. According to its authors, federation and complete self-government—Dominion status— are inseparable and should be achieved *simultaneously*. Federation is defined as the political union of several units with the Federal Government enjoying independence. Without independence, it is argued, federation is a cruel and obvious fraud.

An examination of this view is in order. It is idealistic,

but fallacious. Federation does not operate in a vacuum and is not determined by a special or strained definition. In the world of actuality, federation means the organic combining of several units for common purposes which, it is believed, will be mutually advantageous. To this end each unit loses some of its sovereignty to the Federal Government. Independence is neither connoted nor inherent.

Federations are either voluntary or imposed. The United States, Canada, Australia and Switzerland are examples of federations which were created more or less voluntarily. The units of each nation had previously enjoyed sovereign rights to a great degree. Malaya, and the Leeward Islands, on the other hand, were federated by the British Imperial Government for colonial administrative purposes. Both types of federation are functioning realities regardless of how they came into being.

It is manifestly ridiculous to contend that the Leeward Islands are not federated because they are a Crown Colony and, therefore, not independent. Such an argument belongs to the limbo of illogicality and is an egotistical disregard of reality. It is a patent *reductio ad absurdum*.

The present writer, a Jamaican, passionately believes in self-government and democracy. He regards them as synonymous. He strongly disapproves Jamaica's inclusion in an over-all federation as artificial and fraught with the possibility of disaster for the island, especially when it is recognized that with 59% of the territory and 53% of the population Jamaica is to have only 38% of the seats in the Federal Parliament! In other words, with over half the area and the population Jamaica will have less than two-fifths of the representation! Jamaica is penalized, it seems, because of its size and the fecundity of the population!

Few Jamaicans visit or migrate to the eastern colonies. There is nothing to attract them to those territories. Most important, considering the politics of the area it must not be forgotten that Jamaicans successfully, through hard work and personal and financial sacrifices, led the fight for British West Indian democracy as expressed in universal suffrage and unitary self-government. History, honestly written, will show what part the writer played in the

political drama in shaping policies, suggesting the raising
of badly-needed organizational and campaign funds in
the United States (funds, without which, as leaders of
the People's National Party have frequently publicly testi-
fied, victory would have been impossible or long-delayed);
besides speaking and writing for years in Jamaica and the
United States for the cause nearest to his heart—the extension of democracy in the British West Indies through winning complete autonomy for Jamaica.

Without federating with any country Jamaica single-
handedly secured an advanced constitution. It is no exaggeration to claim that the success of Jamaica in wresting
political concessions from Great Britain inspired other British colonies, even in far-off Africa, to accelerate or make
demands for national freedom. After the 1944 Jamaican
constitution was won and published, members of the
British Parliament, as well as the English Press, frequently
stated that the results achieved in Jamaica would have
important effects on the future of the British Colonial
Empire. They did.

It is generally conceded by observers of the British
Caribbean scene that Jamaicans are politically more advanced, alert, aggressive and progressive than their fellow-
islanders. Existence of robust political parties in Jamaica
in contrast to the absence of such a phenomenon in the
other colonies, is striking proof of the vitality of Jamaican
politics.

But for the forensic skill and deft negotiating of Mr.
Manley at the Conferences in Trinidad and London, federation would have been a dead issue. Conflict of interests—Customs Union, inter-island immigration, tariff, etc.—
was very much to the fore. Mr. Manley succeeded in having settlement of some of the most vital and controversial
issues that will affect individual units of the "new nation"
postponed. These important matters are to be decided
AFTER the union has been in existence for FIVE years.

A heavy responsibility rests on Mr. Manley. The future
of his country has been largely determined by him. It is
true that the Jamaica Labour Party, led by Alexander
Bustamante, eventually endorsed federation, but no one

who knows the glaring limitations of the erratic labour leader would credit him with the ability to negotiate anything requiring first-class intellectual resources. However, it must not be forgotten that Mr. Bustamante's support of federation was not consistent. At one time he was against it, later he changed his mind, seemingly as he was moved by the spirit. At first he described federation as the federating of poverty and conditionally opposed it. Subsequently, with the announced ambition of becoming the first Federal "Governor General", a dream he boastfully expressed, he supported the idea.

Mr. Manley's influence on Jamaica has been powerful and largely benign. His countrymen look to him for leadership. Few care to disagree with him or to criticize him publicly. A prominent coloured American, Rev. G. Hawkins, who visited Jamaica recently, stated from the platform at a mass meeting also addressed by Mr. Manley in New York City in April, 1956, that he had noticed in Jamaica that Jamaicans mentioned Mr. Manley's name with "awe". Unquestionably Jamaica owes a debt of gratitude to Mr. Manley and the devoted army of humble organizers of the People's National Party. They roused the people out of political apathy and passivity.

The programme of social, political and economic reforms for Jamaica initiated by the People's National Party should prove of lasting benefit to the island. Its rehabilitation should be quickened. The devotion, integrity, patriotism and experience of Mr. Manley and his associates in the Government should result in an improvement of the conditions of the masses.

For the first time since the 1944 constitution Jamaica has a "clean" Government. So far, unlike its predecessor, it has been untouched by scandals of graft or ineptitude. No longer are Jamaicans embarrassed or chagrined by acts of official buffoonery and venality. Jamaicans can now be proud of their young nation.

The attitude of this writer on West Indian affairs has never been one of "narrow, insular chauvinism". On the question of federation he has endeavoured to be realistic and sensible. He believes it is naive and absurd, to use polite terms, for anyone to have thought that the British Tory Government would grant independence and favour federation simultaneously. The uneven political development and status of the units provided the Imperial Government with an ideal excuse for blocking or delaying autonomy. Any demand for both objectives to be obtained together invited failure and revealed a lack of elementary political sagacity. Experience has shown that only when pressed by more than mere words has the British Government been willing to make far-reaching concessions to any colonial possession.

The British Government, naturally thinking in terms of its national interests, can be expected always to act in a manner consistent with the protection of those interests. Federation of any sort, especially among peoples of diverse political levels and experiences, will be used to bind the area to the British as long as self-government is withheld. Once this is understood it should be obvious, to use a much-abused word, that the twin goals of federation and self-government were not likely to have been attained at the same time.

It might well be asked: If you oppose Jamaica's inclusion in the federation, do you oppose federation as such? What is your alternative for Jamaica? Reasons of a general character answering the first question have been already presented.

The first goal of every colony should be to obtain maximum self-government for itself, whether it is called Dominion status or some other name. Terms are immaterial.

The primary democratic and national desideratum is that each unit control all of its own affairs. On this there should be no compromise. Self-government is the essence of democracy. It should never be conditioned by or linked to a demand for federation. It is the peak of unreality to make the dual demand, even assuming federation to be the panacea some people appear to think it will be. Freedom, independence or autonomy is the prescriptive and indefeasible right of all peoples whether their territory or population is large or small.

As they are now governed, the British Caribbean colonies consist of seven units, including two on the mainland. Geography and history determined this arrangement. However, being under British control it was inevitable that several types of united regional activities would be encouraged or imposed. The important fact to bear in mind is that each colony is *administered separately*.

Some of the islands are semi-feudal and this condition is reflected in their politics. As a consequence, some of the colonies, even some of the islands in a colony, are more advanced than others. For administrative efficiency, as already stated, the Imperial Government at some time federated the Leeward and the Windward Islands. It did more, it attached the Cayman and the Turks and Caicos Islands to Jamaica, and Tobago to Trinidad. Proximity influenced this procedure which can be regarded as an example of British realism.

Considering the foregoing facts and the relative remoteness of Jamaica and British Honduras from the nearest islands of the eastern sector, it does not appear to be in the best interests of the western colonies to enter the federation. Such an important step should follow presentation of the most convincing arguments and evidence demonstrating that joining the union would be advantageous to them. At any rate it should not be capable of adversely affecting the units politically or economically or of retarding their individual forward march towards complete autonomy—the goal of all virile peoples. If union there be, it should be probationary, not virtually indissoluble.

Federation is no cure-all. Its most enthusiastic champions admit this. Even the most ideal federation can offer no guarantee of prosperity. Sir Hilary Blood, former Governor of Barbados, made this clear in a public statement in England.

The fallacy of the thoughtless optimism that federation will bring inter-island and big commercial benefits to Jamaica was neatly illustrated by Mr. Vere Johns in his column in the Jamaica *Star*. The official figures for the first three months of 1956 showed that Jamaica bought £227,000 of goods from the other islands while they bought only some £2,000-odd from Jamaica. In other words, Jamaica spent with them roughly £100 to every £1 she sold to them.

Federation should not be based on emotion. Nothing but cold, hard facts and logical arguments showing the definite unitary advantages possible should influence the adoption of any such policy. Searching scrutiny should precede decision. There should be no sentimental or romantic approach about helping "small brothers". Only the really rich can afford to be philanthropic in international affairs, not the poor.

Historically, federation was unpopular in some of the eastern islands. In 1876 the attempt of the British Government to federate Barbados with the Windward Islands caused the "Federation Riots" during the regime of Governor Sir John Pope Hennessy. The loss of life and property was great.

Observing how other British colonies obtained their independence, West Indians, if they are a virile people seeking what some of the most backward and illiterate peoples of Asia, Europe and Africa have gained or are about to gain, should not imagine that through some peculiar undemonstrated superiority they can evolve a new technique or tactic for becoming free—if they really desire freedom.

The experience of former colonies and the geographical realities of the British Caribbean suggest the practical strategy of forthrightly struggling, without deviation, for the major goal of self-government. With each colony enjoying self-government, federation, if shown to be necessary and capable of promoting general improvement, could be considered seriously.

Concentrating on obtaining federation or equating it with self-government obscures the real issue—the right of every colonial people to seek and win control of their political life. Juxtaposing the two ideals or goals is bad or self-defeating strategy for it balances a fundamental national and moral right with what is at best an artificial and dubious political grouping. Self-government is not dependent on federation. Each can exist alone. One is fundamental; the other adventitious—synthetic.

Acting on the principle of fighting for the basic rights of their countrymen, the Jamaica Progressive League of New York, in 1936, initiated the propaganda that mushroomed into a mass movement in the island and brought great changes in its constitution. The campaign conducted in Jamaica by the People's National Party from 1938 to 1943, considered daring and fantastic at first (and was opposed vigorously by Alexander Bustamante who formed his Labour Party after the New Constitution was proclaimed), caught the imagination of the people and today it would be impossible easily to deprive them of any of their hard-won rights. As the result of the struggle, with its sacrifices of time and money and the imprisonment of some of its active participants, Jamaica made significant democratic gains. The example acted like a catalyst and spurred other colonies to seek for themselves a similar relationship with Great Britain. The friendly competition among the Caribbean units proved beneficial and should be given credit for their recent rapid political progress.

It is fair to assume that if Jamaica had continued its battle for full self-government and had not been lured or thrust into the extraneous issue of federation, using the past as a guide, the island would in a short period of time have won Dominion status (the goal set by the Jamaica Progressive League) and furnished another example of political progress for the sister colonies to emulate.

On the point of each colonial unit obtaining self-government, some exponents of putting federation before or along with self-government make much of the size of some of the islands. They persistently misrepresent the arguments of their opponents by claiming that the demand for self-government of each colony is tantamount to asking that every island or islet in the British Caribbean become a Dominion or an independent political entity. Such a manifestly distorted presentation of the views of their opponents is naked dishonesty. No responsible person interested in the future of the islands has ever made such a demand. There is an obvious difference between a "colony" and an "island". A colony, as in the case of the Leeward Islands Federation, may consist of several islands.

Failure to grasp the simple difference between colony and island, the first a political status subject to change, the second, a permanent geographical fact, should be attributed to obtuseness, confusion of mind, or a deliberate attempt to befuddle the issue by making a straw man and claiming a great forensic victory by destroying it with senseless epithets and laboured sarcasm.

The size of a country has nothing to do with its right to be self-governing. Singapore is demonstrating this truism by demanding Dominion status. It sent a delegation to London for that purpose at about the same time the West Indian delegation was there negotiating for "federation", not for political freedom.

Singapore is only 225 square miles in area (about one-twentieth the size of Jamaica) and a half mile distant from the Malay Federation, but neither fact deterred the population from aiming at a separate political existence for their island. It is conceivable that a self-governing Singapore, guided by national or regional self-interest, might later decide to be organically linked to Malaya.

The negotiations failed, but it is significant that the British Colonial Office did not repudiate the right of Singapore to be self-governed because of its size. The reason given was that the territory is needed for British Imperial security and as a vital part of Western military defence. Implicitly the British Government recognized the inherent right of Singapore to have an independent political existence.

When it comes to Jamaica and other Caribbean colonies there can be no legitimate objection based on military necessity. The islands are far removed from the centres of Communist ferment.

The difference between the attitudes of the people of Singapore and those of the West Indies lies in the nature of their conditioning and their history and traditions.

West Indians have no traditions or ideal of independence. Their histories, which begin with slavery or more precisely since Emancipation a little over 100 years ago, is not calculated to inspire them with a strong desire for colonial liberation. Long colonial subjection and indoctrination have developed in them a feeling of dependency on outsiders. In the main, they seldom look to themselves for leadership and representation in their relations with the world. This is so because of no innate reason. It is the result of their conditioning.

The argument has been made with pontifical finality that it would be difficult, if not impossible, for each colony separately to win self-government. The contention ignores the spirit of the age and the lessons of history. Within the last three decades, especially during and since World War II, several new nations have come into being. Some are large in area but small in population; others are relatively large in population but small in area. Some are rich in natural resources while others are poor. Some are largely illiterate; others fairly literate. Size of population or area, wealth or poverty, education or illiteracy, is no criterion for denying self-government to a people demanding it.

The United Nations created Libya, a huge and desperately poor desert-nation. It created Israel which lives to a large extent off the largesse of Jews in other parts of the world. Iceland, until recently linked to Denmark, has a comparatively large area, very little cultivable land, and a population of 155,200 in 1954. Tiny Luxembourg has long been a nation. Soon Somaliland, another sparsely populated desert, will be given its independence. Mention need not be made of the other new and old, small and poor, nations in existence.

When Hitler threatened England with defeat in 1940, the United States Government prepared and circulated a document which foreshadowed the independence of each European colony in the New World in ten years in the event of a Nazi conquest of England, then the only undefeated belligerent European colonial power. Nothing in the document hinted that federation of the Caribbean colonies should be a condition of their becoming free nations. That kind of stipulation seems to be peculiarly West Indian in concept.

If Jamaica or any other colony, through struggle or negotiation, had first gained Dominion status it would have inspired the other colonies to demand a similar status for themselves. England gave freedom to rich Burma, India and Pakistan and is in process of conceding Dominion status to Nigeria and Gold Coast.

It is a gross repudiation of the rules of logic, an affront to common sense, an ignoring of recent history, and a cynical disbelief in the proclaimed official British policy to grant independence to colonies, to suggest that Great Britain, having relinquished control of its rich Asian possessions and about to concede independence to Nigeria and Gold Coast, both abounding with natural resources, would deny self-government to West Indian colonies. These territories have been often described by the British themselves as financial liabilities, so it is to be assumed that England would be more than happy to rid herself of the burden.

The West Indian islands are of no strategic value to England today. Whatever protection they may need from foreign attack will be provided by the United States—the most powerful nation in the world—through the Monroe Doctrine and subsequent inter-American Declarations which obligate the 21 American nations to defend the entire continent.

Latin America has frequently gone on record supporting the liquidation of colonialism in the Western Hemisphere, so there already exist powerful influences in favour of autonomy for the colonies.

As independent nations in the Western Hemisphere the West Indian peoples would be able to by-pass the racial inequities of the McCarran Immigration Law which do not affect the citizens of the autonomous nations of the American continent.

Many islanders support federation because they believe

it will facilitate emigration from the densely populated islands into British Guiana and British Honduras. Apart from the indisputable right of the two continental colonies to control their demographic character, it should be clear that mass migration will not be easy and may be fraught with misunderstandings, friction and disappointments.

Large numbers of people do not voluntarily move into less developed areas (even of their own country) unless it is to escape religious, racial or political oppression. They do not go into strange and undeveloped countries and endure hardships unless they are attracted by exceptionally high economic rewards. The belief and hope that the total British Caribbean Federation will provide outlets in the mainland for "surplus" populations may well be illusory—a chimera.

Conceivably, the Federation of 1958 may result in flooding less densely populated islands, like Jamaica, with immigrants from the more populous areas. Trinidad realized this and baulked at unrestricted inter-island immigration at the Trinidad Conference.

The glorious and inspiring struggle of Jamaica to rid itself of the humiliating bonds of colonialism indicates what can be done in the West Indies by determined and courageous indigenous nationalists. By deviating from the goal of self-government fixed by the Jamaica Progressive League and becoming entangled with federation, Jamaica has retarded, not accelerated Caribbean freedom.

Internal self-government of Jamaica is, admittedly, a long step in advance of what existed until recently, but the objective of colonials in this century should be for complete autonomy—control of every aspect of national activity. Less than this shows moral weakness and cowardice and reveals a sense of dependency, if not of inferiority.

The French North African possessions of Morocco, Algeria and Tunisia are contiguous. Their populations are more or less similar in race, religion, language and culture. At no time have the peoples of the region based their right to freedom on federation of their territories. Each nation fought for its own liberation. Economic considerations, no matter how alluring, have never induced North Africans to give second place to their human dignity and rights. Imbued with the ideal to be men among men in a world of really "free nations", they fought, and still fight and sacrifice, to secure their individual national autonomy—complete control of all their affairs.

Ceylon, the model of some federationists, has shown the way. Only about fifty miles from India, the Ceylonese people never agitated for union with their racial and religious brothers of the sub-continent. They never compromised their right to a free political existence. Today they are a completely independent state. Federation will hamstring or make more difficult the fight of the more progressive West Indian colonies for full control of their affairs—domestic and foreign.

Federation plays into the hands of the metropolitan power. The union may benefit some of the eastern islands, but this does not necessarily make it politically and economically desirable for Jamaica, British Honduras or British Guiana.

Inclusion of Jamaica is a great disservice to the country. Federation fosters an illusion of greatness, size, wealth, importance and freedom. Sooner or later it will intensify insular jealousies and differences. Friction seems inescapable.

"Big Brother" Jamaica can easily be out-voted with only 17 out of 45 seats although on the basis of population and area it is entitled to at least 22 seats in the Lower House of the Federal Parliament. Obviously the Jamaican delegates to the London Conference in accepting the arbitrary and unfair distribution of voting power were concerned more about federation than about their own country. With them it was federation, not Jamaica first. Federation, not colonial liberation, was their obsession, hence the amazing, dangerous and unwarranted voting concessions.

West Indian delegates apparently went to the Conferences on Federation not primarily to secure extension of the national and democratic rights of their countries, but to ensure continuation of ephemeral advantages now enjoyed in the British market. For some time the agricultural exports of the islands, especially Jamaica, have cost more to produce than similar articles in competing countries. As a consequence, British West Indian sugar, bananas and citrus fruits have had to depend on British subsidies, direct and indirect.

This fact seems largely responsible for the decision of the Jamaican delegation to join the strange and unnatural federation. Economic opportunism, not moral principles, was the dominating motive. Markets, not human rights, were the incentive. West Indians have the unfortunate habit of mixing political and economic questions in their relations with England. They attach greater importance to economic questions, even though the arrangements are subject to change, than to eternal moral and political principles, hence they subordinate the basic human rights of their people to be autonomous and temporize with open or veiled colonialism.

Seemingly they find it difficult to differentiate between moral values and opportunism. Freedom should be the uncompromising goal of subject peoples. Gained, national freedom provides its possessors with the indispensable tools for effecting their economic rehabilitation.

In concluding this analysis of the theory and possible effect of federation on Jamaica, it should be useful to quote from *The New York Times* editorial of February 22, 1956, entitled, "Caribbean Federation":

A new nation is taking form on our doorstep, one of the strangest nations, geographically speaking, in the world. . . . It will be a remarkable nation, stretching over 1,000 miles of water, which is the distance that divides Jamaica and Trinidad, the two main units. . . . The islands compete against each other with the same products—rum, sugar, bananas, citrus fruits, tobacco and spices.

There can be little disagreement with the terms "strangest" and "remarkable".

8.

The federation failed partly because the attitudes Domingo articulated were also held by the Jamaican majority. But the urge toward association had been powerful, especially in the eastern Caribbean. The growth of federal sentiment, the progress toward regional understanding, the birth of the federation, and its decline and break-up are described here by a Barbadian, himself an architect of the federation. Causes of the federal failure are multiple, stemming from the disparities of size and strength among member states, the distances that separated them, and the political exigencies that permitted small-islanders to dominate the federal government.

HUGH W. SPRINGER, born in Barbados, took an Oxford degree and became a barrister, returning to the West Indies to play major roles, first in Barbadian politics as leader of the Barbados Worker's Party and later in Jamaica as registrar and chief administrative officer of the University College of the West Indies. Sir Hugh subsequently became Chief Liaison Officer and then Director of the Commonwealth Education Liaison Office.

Federation in the Caribbean: An Attempt That Failed
Hugh W. Springer

I

Ever since World War II the United Kingdom has been
engaged in the process of withdrawal from the Caribbean
—indeed the beginnings were made before the war ended.
The clearest and most recent evidence has been the advance of Jamaica and Trinidad from colonial status to
independent membership in the British Commonwealth
and the United Nations. But this was not quite what had
been intended. The aim originally had been to make one
federal union of all the British colonies in the region. The
attempt, however, failed. British Guiana and British Honduras withdrew from the scheme at an early stage, and
the federation of the islands foundered after a four-year
period of trial.

Up to the middle of 1962 the British territories in this
area were contained within or along an arc stretching
from British Honduras in Central America, through
Jamaica and the Leeward Islands, to British Guiana on
the northern boundary of Brazil, and embracing (to the
south of the Leeward Islands) the Windward Islands, Barbados, Trinidad, and Tobago. They were among the oldest,
and some of them during the eighteenth century had been
the most valuable, of Britain's possessions overseas.

International Organization, Vol. 21, No. 4, Autumn, 1967,
pp. 758–75. Copyright 1967, World Peace Foundation, Boston,
Massachusetts. Reprinted by permission of the publisher and
the author.

Faced with the problems of administering these small, numerous, and widely scattered islands, the British government had for centuries toyed with the idea of unifying them. They were, of course, dealt with as a group in the Colonial Office, but the further idea of unifying their administrations on the spot had considerable attractions. Little was achieved, however, chiefly for two causes; firstly, the practical difficulty of communications between the islands, and secondly, insular jealousy, itself partly a consequence of the former. Governors were often shared by several islands, but the only unified government of a group was the weak and ineffective federal government of the Leeward Islands, which lasted from 1871 until it was abolished in 1957 in order to allow the islands to enter separately into the short-lived West Indies Federation of 1958–62.

This federation of the British West Indies was something of a *tour de force*. The group comprised ten island administrations with a gross population of 3,100,000 on a total of 8,000 square miles. One island alone, Jamaica, contained 1,600,000 people on 4,400 square miles of land and was 1,000 miles to the west of the others. Among these, Trinidad, with a population of 826,000 on 1,980 square miles, was as dominant as Jamaica was in the whole group. Among the rest, Barbados with 232,000 people had one-third of the remaining population on 166 square miles—one-tenth of the remaining land. The Windward Islands with 314,000 inhabitants and the Leeward Islands with 123,000 people completed the picture. The federation was made practicable by the development of air travel during World War II. Until then, facilities for travel between Jamaica and the eastern islands, a thousand miles away, were virtually non-existent. Only Jamaicans abroad, when they came into contact with other West Indians as students, soldiers, or emigrants and recognized common characteristics and experiences, shared with other West Indians the community of feeling which engenders national sentiment. The menace of enemy submarines during the war also made it necessary to organize the procurement of supplies and the movement of goods on a regional basis, and this was achieved through cooperation between the territories themselves as well as between the United Kingdom and the United States. Moreover, the recognition of the need for a dynamic policy of economic development—which had been emphasized by disturbances, strikes, and riots in the British territories during the 1930's —led to the setting up (with headquarters in Barbados) of the Development and Welfare Organization recommended by the Royal Commission of 1938–39.

This recognition, together with the experience of cooperation in the war effort, brought into existence the first international agency in the Caribbean, the Anglo-American Caribbean Commission (with headquarters in Trinidad). Soon France and the Netherlands joined the Commission, and its name was changed to Caribbean Commission. In 1944, the activity of this organization was significantly expanded when at a meeting in Barbados a series of West Indian conferences was inaugurated, in which the representatives of the territorial governments played a principal part. With the progress of decolonization during the postwar years, the Caribbean Commission was eventually succeeded in 1961 by the Caribbean Organization, in which the governments of the territories in the region have taken the place of the metropolitan governments.

The Development and Welfare Organization and the Caribbean Commission contributed indirectly to the creation of the West Indies Federation of 1958–62. The Comptroller for Development and Welfare had a staff of specialist advisers, who in their reports and in their many consultations with political leaders, senior civil servants, and leaders of commerce and industry invariably placed the problem under discussion in the regional context; their example was not without its effect on those they dealt with.

The Development and Welfare Organization also performed indispensable functions during the period between the agreement in principle to federate, made at the Montego Bay Conference in September 1947, and the coming into effect of the federal constitution in January 1958.

During those ten years this organization supplied headquarters, and often chairmen and secretariat as well, for a
number of pre-federal regional activities. Beginning with
the Standing Closer Association Committee which drew up
the first scheme for a federal constitution, these activities
included the Regional Economic Committee (which played
an important role in enabling the several governments to
arrive at common policies and courses of action in economic matters) and the Standing Federation Committee,
which served, within prescribed limits, as both constitutional convention and federal parliament between 1956
and 1958.

The Caribbean Commission, in its own somewhat different way, also helped to promote a regional outlook. Its
operation was less close and intimate than was the Development and Welfare's in the British territories. But
whereas the emphasis of Development and Welfare was on
development, the regional point of view being incidental
and limited to the British parts of the region, the Commission was regional in both name and avowed purpose,
and its scope embraced all the territories at that time flying
the flag of Britain, the United States, France, or the Netherlands. Its most effective contribution to the integration of
the region was probably through the work of its Research
Council and its Information Service. Its West Indian conferences also played their part in encouraging interest in
regional cooperation and produced, if not a sense of belonging together, at least a wider recognition of the existence of potentially friendly neighbors. Now that the federal union of the British islands has foundered, it may be
that the Caribbean Organization will be called upon to play
a different role, and a more important one than it would
otherwise have played, in the ultimate unification of the
Caribbean lands.

But the contribution of these organizations to the creation of the West Indies Federation was merely instru-
mental or ancillary. The federal movement owed its origin to the smallness and poverty of the territories and the
recognition of these facts by both the Colonial Office and

the local political leaders. Some form of unification was
the obvious answer. In the circumstances of the West
Indies, this form had to be federal, since the territories
were numerous and widely separated by sea, and most of
them were accustomed for centuries to making decisions
about their own affairs without consulting their neighbors.
The further aim of using unification as a vehicle for national independence was determined by the local upsurge
of nationalist feelings in the 1930's, combined with Britain's change of colonial policy during the war.

J. H. Proctor, in discussing the functional approach to
political union, cited the West Indies as an example of
functional cooperation making a substantial contribution
to the cause of federation.[1] He wrote before the West
Indian Federation had come into actual existence, but at
a time when it seemed certain to do so, and when its prospects seemed good. He could not have foreseen the res-
tiveness that Jamaica would exhibit from the start nor
the decisions of political leaders which would lead to the
break-up of the federation just after the first set of difficulties had been ironed out by eighteen months of study
and discussion. But even from his point in time, it was
clear that functionalism played the minor role and the
political effort he calls federalism played the major one
in bringing about political unification.

The Montego Bay decision was taken at a conference
of delegates from all the island governments and from the
mainland territories of British Guiana and British Honduras. At the conference there was a full and frank exchange of views with the Secretary of State for the Colonies, Arthur Creech Jones. Some of these delegates had
just been attending a conference in Kingston of the Caribbean Labor Congress (CLC) (which embraced the popular political parties and trade unions that had come into
being to harness the flood of political energy released

---

[1] Jesse Harris Proctor, Jr., "The Functional Approach to
Political Union: Lessons from the Effort to Federate the British Caribbean Territories," *International Organization,* Vol.
10, No. 1 (February 1956), pp. 35–48.

by the disturbances, strikes, and riots of the 1930's). These two conferences thus signified that the decision to seek national independence for the West Indies through federal union had been arrived at both by the government of the United Kingdom and by the peoples of the West Indies themselves.

The labor movement in the West Indies had become the vehicle for a nationalist spirit which had been gaining form and strength since the turn of the century and especially after the First World War. This nationalist spirit, originating largely abroad (in the reaction of West Indians to their shared experience as an unprivileged minority) readily assumed a West Indian character in the eastern Caribbean where there was intercourse between the islands at all levels; but in Jamaica nationalist feeling was confined within the shores of the island.

In 1945, however, the Jamaican labor movement became linked in part with that of the eastern group when the People's National Party, led by Norman Manley, became affiliated with the CLC. Although the other half of the movement, led by Alexander Bustamante, had at this time no links with the eastern Caribbean parties or unions, Bustamante at Montego Bay, representing the government of Jamaica, gave his approval to the principle of federation—qualified, however, by his insistence that a large financial subvention from Britain was essential to the success of any such scheme.

Manley, although present as representative not of his government but of the Caribbean Commission, expressed eloquently the sentiments of the majority of the delegates present. He appealed to "men who were unwilling to give up any local root of power for the creation of a larger centre of power" to "drop out of their minds their own security, real or apparent, and the years of power and position in their own lands, and see that this larger objective opens our horizons and gives a wider opportunity for all." He concluded with the challenge: "If we won't leave our little boats and get into that larger vessel which is able to carry us to the goal of our ambitions then I say without hesitation that we are damned and purblind and history will condemn us."[2]

The Montego Bay Conference marked the high point of West Indian unanimity and emotional fervor. It recommended the appointment of a committee of representatives of the West Indies governments to work out proposals which might form the basis of a federal government leading to West Indian independence; this recommendation was immediately implemented by the appointment of the Standing Closer Association Committee. Other committees and commissions were appointed to consider special problems. Indeed the period between September 1947 and January 1958, when the federal constitution came into force, was a period of meetings, commissions, reports, and resolutions—a period during which the West Indian leaders, instead of being involved in the unifying activity of demanding independence from Britain, found themselves engaged in long drawn-out and self-regarding negotiations with one another. The enthusiasm of 1947 was displaced by calculation; ten years later only momentum carried forward the unifying forces.

This was the case everywhere except in Trinidad. There, in September 1956, Eric Williams, at the head of the newly formed People's National Movement (PNM), in one political campaign swept not only into parliament but into power. A former professor of political science, Williams justified the case for federation by argument and appeal to history. He contrasted the seventeenth and eighteenth centuries, when small states were the rule (when England and Scotland were with difficulty united in 1707), with the nineteenth and twentieth centuries, when the industrial revolution and large-scale production on the one hand and the improvement in methods of transportation and communication on the other initiated trends toward larger units of government:

> Look around the world today and try to find a community of 700,000 people of the size of Trinidad and

[2] Conference on the Closer Association of the British West Indian Colonies, Part 2, *Proceedings* (London: H.M.S.O., 1948), Col. 218, pp. 57–62.

Tobago playing any important part in world affairs. There is none. There can be none. The units of government are getting larger and larger. Whether federation is more costly or less costly, whether federation is more efficient or less efficient, federation is inescapable if the British Caribbean territories are to cease to parade themselves to the twentieth century world as eighteenth century anachronisms.[3]

But Williams' enthusiasm evoked no response. The general attitude remained that of unemotional acceptance, accompanied in some cases by hardheaded bargaining for unit advantages. During the two-year regime of the Standing Federation Committee, its members seemed to be united chiefly in their determination to clip the wings of the federal government that was to succeed them. They were particularly ungenerous in depriving it of the modest financial leeway that the 1956 conference had left to it.

II

The course of events that led to the disruption of the federation began almost with its inauguration. The Jamaica section of the federal elections which were called for by the Governor General, Lord Hailes, soon after he took office on January 3, 1958, ended disastrously for the Federal Labor Party with which the People's National Party (PNP), in common with the ruling parties in most of the other islands, was affiliated. Of the seventeen seats available for Jamaica the PNP secured only five. This result was due in part to the fact that Norman Manley had not found it possible to stand for election. He was the elected Leader of the Federal Labor Party and had been generally expected to become the first Prime Minister of the West Indies.

This distinction fell to Sir Grantley Adams, Premier of

[3] Eric Williams, lecture delivered at Woodford Square on January 5, 1956, in *Federation, Two Public Lectures* (Trinidad: People's National Movement, 1956), pp. 11–12.

Barbados and one of the veteran leaders of the labor movement in the Caribbean, who had been President of the CLC at the height of its influence in 1947 and was now first Deputy Leader of the Federal Labor Party. He took office with a very slim majority, and had to exercise all his considerable political and parliamentary skill to keep his government from defeat during the first anxious session.

During this first session the Federal Parliament took a decision that led to a review of the constitution being initiated before the federation was two years old. Ken Hill, a Jamaican member of parliament from the opposition party, moved for the appointment of a select committee to take such steps as were necessary to achieve self-government and dominion status at the earliest possible moment. The proposal was prompted by dissatisfaction with the "colonial" limitations contained in the federal constitution, especially certain reserve powers of the Queen and certain discretionary powers of the Governor General. These were transitional provisions, but, since the major unit governments had achieved internal self-government, the transfer to the new federal government of reserve powers formerly attached to the units exposed the federal government to the imputation of being more "colonial" than its units. The logical remedy was for the Federation to move on to independence without delay.

This logic appealed strongly to the Premier of Trinidad, Dr. Eric Williams, and he and his party, the PNM, took the lead in pressing for an early advance to dominion status. Jamaica, on the other hand, was beginning to have second thoughts about its position in the Federation and was more urgently concerned about lessening the powers of the Federal Government in relation to Jamaica than with improving the status of the Federation.

A forum for debate between these points of view was provided by an intergovernmental conference convened by the Federal Government. The Federal Government had succeeded in carrying an amendment to Ken Hill's

motion by which it was agreed that, instead of a select
committee being appointed, a constitutional review conference should be summoned under Article 118 of the
constitution, "in order to achieve the goal of self government and Dominion status within the Commonwealth at
the earliest possible date." The Government later decided
to summon the unit governments to a preliminary conference. This conference met on September 28, 1959.

By this time the opposing positions of Trinidad and
Jamaica had been fully and publicly developed. The Trinidad government had published a paper entitled *The Economics of Nationhood,* in which the case for a strong
federal government was argued. It should have powers of
taxation in all fields and the final word in legislation on
all matters of planning and development. The common
purpose was to build a West Indian nation; and since the
first objective of the nation was to build a national economy, the national government must be enabled to do this
by being given "complete command of all its material
and other resources, including its perspective for the future."[4] The Trinidad proposals were debated in the legislature, and the delegates to the intergovernmental
conference were given a mandate to secure a strong independent federation vested with appropriate powers and
responsibilities.

The warmth of Trinidad's support for a powerful federal center is perhaps surprising when we consider its relatively strong economic position as a unit. Of all the islands it was the one most capable of going it alone.
Moreover Eric Williams had only recently generated a
wave of Trinidadian nationalist feeling on which the
PNM had swept into political power. But these nationalist
feelings did not at first come into conflict with the already
existing West Indian sentiment. Trinidad, unlike Jamaica,
by reason of its geographical position was well accustomed
to being one of the West Indies islands, and the habit of
intercourse with the neighboring islands in many areas

[4] *Economics of Nationhood* (Port-of-Spain, Trinidad: Office
of the Premier and Minister of Finance, 1959), p. 3.

and at all levels was of long standing. Moreover, the federal capital was not remotely situated but on its own soil. Nevertheless, Trinidadian nationalism had become strong, was growing stronger, and, as we shall see, after Jamaican nationalism had seized the opportunity given to it of plucking Jamaica from the Federation, Trinidadian nationalism, flushed with a second great victory at the polls, asserted itself and followed suit.

The Jamaican proposals were also the subject of debate in the Jamaican legislature, and the Jamaican delegates were given a unanimous mandate to press them upon the conference. Jamaica insisted that the power of the federal government to intervene in Jamaican affairs should be severely limited. In particular, the constitution should be amended to exclude the power to control industrial development and to levy taxes on income and profits. The Jamaican delegates demanded that representation in the house of representatives be on the basis of population (instead of the compromise by which Jamaica's 1.5 million people had seventeen seats; Trinidad's 750,000 had ten seats; Barbados' 230,000, five seats; and the other islands, with populations ranging from 50,000 to 80,000, two seats each, except Montserrat whose 13,000 inhabitants had to be content with one seat). The Jamaican representatives agreed to a customs union but insisted that its implementation should not be hurried. Trinidad's demand for a strong federation without delay raised no new issues of principle. But the Jamaican proposals would alter the character of the Federation.

How had Jamaica's change of attitude come about? The chief cause was the improvement in its economic position since 1947. During the ten-year period, agricultural production and income had increased. Tourism also had expanded continuously, so that by 1958 it was contributing almost as much to the national income as sugar. Bauxite production had begun in 1952, and from one million tons in 1953 had risen to nearly six million in 1958. Jamaica was also achieving an encouraging measure of success in the promotion of secondary industries. Whereas in 1947 its economic position had been such that union with the eastern Caribbean territories, including oil-rich Trinidad, seemed the best, if not the only, avenue to economic improvement, by 1958 the position had changed and Jamaica could hope with some confidence to achieve on its own the self-sustaining economic growth that would lead it eventually into the ranks of the "modernized" and "developed" countries.

In this situation it was easy for tension to arise between the West Indies federal government and the government of Jamaica, where West Indian sentiment was a plant of new and tender growth and not well nourished. The federal capital was a thousand miles away in Port of Spain. The Prime Minister was not a Jamaican. Owing to the poor showing of the PNP candidates in the federal elections, the Jamaican members of the federal cabinet were not persons of eminence. The relationship between the roles of Sir Grantley Adams as federal Prime Minister and Mr. Norman Manley as Leader of the Federal Labor Party (and at the same time Premier of Jamaica) was not an easy one for either of the two men.

Even a prime minister who had not just experienced a decade of political supremacy in Barbados, as Sir Grantley had done, might have been irked by the position of financial stringency and helplessness in which the federal government found itself. Sir Grantley's reaction was to hint publicly that the government, as soon as it had the power to impose taxation on income and profits, might do so with retroactive effect. The fact that the next general elections in Jamaica were probably less than a year away almost certainly intensified the sharpness of the public reaction to these veiled threats. Certainly Bustamante and his opposition party seized on them (as they did on so harmless and necessary a measure as the federal Compulsory Land Acquisition Act) to embarrass the Government party. Jamaican nationalism, encouraged by the PNP in the late 1930's and early 1940's but dormant since 1947, was now awakened and had become a force once more. It was, however, no longer directed against Britain but instead was aimed against the new menace that had arisen in the dim and distant regions of the eastern Caribbean—the federal government.

The realization that the federal government was a separate entity whose actions could affect Jamaica was a shocking experience for a large number of Jamaicans. Outside the small circle of those involved in the making of government policy, serious thought about the implications of federation for Jamaica's political position began with the Prime Minister's reference to retroactive taxation. Until then the Federation had been accepted as something external, and it had been assumed that nothing in Jamaica's position would be changed.

The reaction therefore was one of shock, and the language used to express it was sometimes violent. Robert Lightbourne, one of the Jamaican members of the opposition, introduced a motion in the federal House of Representatives, calling for the immediate revision of the federal constitution in order to eliminate the power of retroactive taxation and of interference with tariff structures without Jamaica's consent, and to provide for representation in the House on the basis of population. The substance of this motion, as we have seen, became eventually the unanimous mandate from the Jamaican House of Representatives to the Jamaican delegates to the intergovernmental conference in 1959.

The conference duly opened on September 28, 1959, but its deliberations were not concluded until May 1961. The first session lasted ten days and resulted only in agreement in principle that population was to be the basis of representation in the elected house of the federal parliament. The method of application of this principle, as well as the other constitutional changes and political and economic arrangements which were implied by the move to dominion status, were referred for detailed consideration to two committees of ministers assisted by working parties of officials.

It was now clear that the continuance of the federal union would depend on the possibility of the units coming to terms with Jamaica. Manley returned from the intergovernmental conference in a hopeful mood, and at the PNP annual conference a fortnight later, he described the party's policy on federation in the following words: "We conceive that in the long run there are real and great advantages in Federation but these advantages cannot be accepted at the price of anything that would destroy or injure us in a fundamental respect."[5] He took this stand in the House of Representatives also, when he introduced his government's report on the Trinidad meeting in a speech on November 3, 1959.[6] He recalled the reasons why the political parties in Jamaica had agreed "over a period of nine years, in eight full-scale debates—and on every occasion unanimously—that federation was a desirable move." In his view "the basic reasons . . . were soundly conceived and subject to certain qualifications . . . would be soundly conceived today."

Times had changed, however. The beginning of the federation "has coincided almost with the climax of the combination of activities which have been undertaken by Jamaica with a view to a transition to a higher level of economy." For this reason, "the Federation must proceed more slowly than other Federations have proceeded in the past. Jamaica," Manley said, "has the highest percentage of unemployed of any country in the West Indies . . . consequently there is no part of the West Indies in which any disruption of the forward progress could be more damaging and disastrous; and not alone for Jamaica, . . . but also for the whole future of the Federation." He believed Jamaica could become a dominion on its own, but "I know she would not have the significance in the world that the West Indies would have."

While the intergovernmental committees and working parties were doing their work behind the scenes, the Jamaican government did two things which later proved to

[5] *Gleaner* (Kingston, Jamaica), October 26, 1959.
[6] Jamaica, *Proceedings of the House of Representatives, 1959*, pp. 95 ff.

be important for the future of the Federation. In January 1960 Mr. Manley led a delegation to London to ask the Colonial Secretary what were the minimum requirements for dominion status and whether Jamaica could hope to achieve that status on its own. The answer to the latter question was in the affirmative, and this considerably strengthened Jamaica's bargaining position in the forthcoming discussions with the other West Indian governments. It was a sign of the times that no one expected Britain to intervene to save the Federation, though some hoped for this. In earlier epochs Britain's influence played an important part in leading New Brunswick and British Columbia into the Canadian federation and in preventing western Australia from seceding from the federal Commonwealth of Australia. But in our time the government of the United Kingdom has evidently not regarded it as a British interest that West Indian unity should be preserved. Its attention has been deeply engaged with more pressing problems in other places, and perhaps we should not forget that the Monroe Doctrine was invented in Britain, and that geographically the West Indies belong to the Americas.

The other thing that Mr. Manley and his government did in this connection was more difficult to explain. At the end of May 1960, the Jamaican government decided that the issue of Jamaica's remaining in the Federation or not was to be submitted to a referendum of the people. This decision was an immediate reaction to the withdrawal by Bustamante and the Jamaica Labor Party (JLP) of their candidate from the federal by-election in St. Thomas, declaring that henceforth they were opposed to federation. In an official statement Premier Manley gave the following reason for his decision:

> The official decision of the Jamaica Labour Party to oppose Federation has created a new situation in Jamaica. When both parties were acting together it was right to assume that they represented the voice of the people. Now that one party, the Jamaica Labour Party,

has officially resolved to oppose Federation, it is right
that it should come before the people for decision.[7]

This statement is to be contrasted with Manley's strong
rejection of the suggestion of a referendum in his speech
to the House of Representatives on November 3, 1959.
He had said on that occasion:

> There are men who say today, "go to the people—
> take a referendum." Maybe it will come to that, but not
> now. It would be a betrayal of responsibility to do that.
> Let me repeat. It would be a betrayal of leadership and
> a betrayal of responsibility to do that now.
> The people did not put us here to go back and ask
> them what to do. The people put us here on a stated
> policy, to fight to achieve certain ends. When we fail to
> achieve those ends, that is the time we are to go back
> to the people and say, "Look, it cannot be done, do you
> think we should turn back?" That is the time.[8]

The intergovernmental conference was resumed in Port
of Spain on May 2, 1961, and was followed by the conference for the review of the constitution which began
in London on May 31. As might have been foreseen, the
threat of secession enabled Jamaica to win agreement
from the other units on all the conditions which its legislature had unanimously required for continued membership in the Federation.

The conclusions reached at the London conference were
to be put before the island legislatures. They were undoubtedly acceptable to the Jamaican legislature, but the
ultimate decision had now been placed beyond its reach.
The referendum was held on September 19, 1961, and
resulted in a vote of 46 percent in favor and 54 percent
against Jamaica's continued membership in the Federation. The question whether Trinidad would join in a fed-

[7] *Gleaner,* June 1, 1960.
[8] Jamaica, *Proceedings of the House of Representatives,
1959,* p. 102.

eration with Barbados, the Windward Islands, and the Leeward Islands was settled in the following January, in the negative.

III

Kenneth C. Wheare has observed that in the cases of the United States of America, Canada, Switzerland, and Australia, the desire for a federal union was accompanied by six factors, and he concluded that the desire for federal union was unlikely to arise unless these factors or most of them were present. Wheare's factors were: (1) a sense of military insecurity and the consequent need for common defense; (2) a desire to be independent of foreign powers, and a realization that only through union could independence be secured; (3) a hope of economic advantage from union; (4) some political association of the communities concerned prior to the federal union, either in a loose confederation, as with the American states or the Swiss cantons, or as parts of the same empire, as with the Canadian and Australian colonies; (5) geographical neighborhood; and (6) similarity of political institutions.[9] They fall readily into two classes, which I shall call (a) predisposing conditions and (b) inducements. Previous political association, geographical neighborhood, and similarity of political institutions may properly be described as predisposing conditions. The sense of need for common defense, the desire for independence, and the hope of economic advantage are in the class of inducements.

If we take the predisposing conditions first, and begin with *similarity of political organization,* we find that even the crown colony constitutions which before the war were found in every territory except Barbados, were parliamentary in type; the postwar constitutions, like the traditional

[9] Kenneth C. Wheare, *Federal Government* (Oxford: Oxford University Press, 1946), p. 37.

Barbados one, were modeled on the British parliamentary
system.

Geographical neighborhood is not a precisely definable
concept. On the one hand, it seems safe to say that, if the
West Indian communities had been adjacent in a continuous land mass, federation would probably not have
seemed the obvious way of bringing them under one government. Three million people on 8,000 square miles of
land do not make a big country. On the other hand, in
the West Indies of actual fact, distances by sea between
the units varied from the few miles between one Leeward
or Windward island and another to the thousand miles
that separates Jamaica from Barbados or Trinidad. Some
twenty years ago the advent of air travel put Jamaica for
the first time within reach of the eastern Caribbean. The
condition of geographical neighborhood may therefore be
said to have been present during that period, though
hardly before.

The third predisposing condition, *previous political association,* may be said to be present mainly in the literal
sense that the islands were all "parts of the same Empire."
There never was a center of authority or government for
the whole of the West Indies as Lagos was for Nigeria
and Delhi was for India. The nearest thing was the Regional Economic Committee (REC) (1951–56), which
was composed of representatives of the governments of
all the territories and maintained a secretariat in Barbados
at the headquarters of the Development and Welfare Organization. But the REC, as its name implies, dealt with a
limited range of problems, and it had no decision-making
power.

All three predisposing conditions, then, are present, but
not always in great strength.

When we come to the *inducements,* which, I suggest,
are the operative factors, we shall find that they are present intermittently, weakly, or not at all. In ascending order of importance the first is the *hope of economic advantage* from union. This hope was shared by all the
islands in 1947, but by 1958 only the smaller islands firmly

retained it. In the case of Jamaica, greatly increased income from traditional agriculture, expanding tourism, and the new and rapidly expanding mining of bauxite combined with a successful start in the process of generating secondary industry to raise the question whether federal union was economically more advantageous after all than development as a separate country. Trinidad, richer and longer involved in the active process of economic modernization, might well have entertained the same doubts. But it was not yet fully moved by the island nationalism which was even then gathering force; moreover, long association and intercourse with the neighboring islands had made her more deeply committed than Jamaica to West Indian nationhood as the political goal.

The second inducement, the *desire for independence*, is, in practice, closely associated with the preceding one, since economic viability and independence are interconnected. The desire to be independent of the Colonial Office was still general in 1958, but it had been considerably weakened in some quarters by the achievement of complete or almost complete internal self-government. But the source of pressure toward independence, nationalism, was now no longer always a unifying factor. Island nationalism tended to take priority over West Indian nationalism, and where it did the conviction that only through union could independence be achieved had grown correspondingly weaker.

The third "inducement," the *need for common defense*, did not operate as a motive for bringing the West Indies together. When West Indians have thought at all about the problem of defense, they have tended to assume that the military might of Britain and the United States would always be available in time of need. It was of course recognized that an independent federal nation must have defense forces, and provision was made for them in the federal arrangements. But there was no sense of imminent danger.

It seems then that a country about to enter a federal union is inhibited by a strong psychological barrier that can be overcome only by something like what I have called the inducements among Wheare's unifying factors. It seems further, to judge from the known cases, that the sense of need for common defense is at the head of the list, the desire for independence and for common economic advantage being second and third with a close link between them. Common defense was the chief motive in the creation of the United States of America; fear of the United States united the Canadian provinces; fear of German expansionism in the Pacific was a unifying motive in the Australian case; and fear of Russia has been a decisive factor in the integration of Europe.

Fear perhaps is the only certain inducement. It is probably true that communities will *sometimes* unite with one another for economic advantage or because of the urge to independence, but that they will *always* unite if they believe that uniting will ensure their survival. Even if it is successfully initiated without the sense of danger, federal unity is difficult to preserve without it, as can be seen not only from the West Indian case but also from other postwar federations that have been created out of former empires of European countries. There has been a tendency for their component units to fall apart, as in the case of French West Africa and French Equatorial Africa. Stresses and strains have shown themselves in India and in Nigeria. If the tendency to disintegration has been up to now more marked in Africa than in Asia, this may well be because the countries concerned in Asia are more directly exposed than those in Africa to the threat of external aggression.

But the federalizing process does not end with the creation of the federal system. Carl Friedrich and others have emphasized that the creation of a federal state is not an event but a process, and is therefore subject to "the permanent give and take between the inclusive community and the component communities . . . [which] is a universal principle of political organization."[10] Thus in the

---

[10] Carl J. Friedrich, in A. W. Macmahon, ed., *Federalism Mature and Emergent* (Garden City, N.Y.: Doubleday, 1955), pp. 513–14.

United States the widening of the sphere of government in the area of the social services, the centralizing tendency induced by the imperatives of economic stabilization and control, and the requirements of national defense have led, over a period of time, to changes in the relation between the federal government and the state governments. In important areas of activity "dualism" has been increasingly replaced by "cooperation," in which the states supplied the local knowledge and the personnel, and the center supplied the funds.

In the same vein, E. B. Haas, writing about the early progress of the movement toward European integration, observed that the federalizing process was facilitated by the pressures of political parties and other interest groups (e.g., business and labor). These tended to spill over into the federal sphere and thereby added to the integrative impulse, since they sought to obtain common benefits by uniting beyond their former national boundaries. Even national governments in the long run brought themselves to defer to federal decisions, lest the example of their recalcitrance act as a precedent for other governments.

Haas thought that an external threat was a helpful but "by no means indispensable" inducement. In his view,

> The process of community formation is dominated by nationally constituted groups with specific interests and aims, willing and able to adjust their aspirations by turning to supranational means when the course appears profitable. . . . A larger political community can be developed if the crucial expectations, ideologies and behaviour patterns of certain key groups can be refocussed on a new set of central symbols and institutions.

He adds a warning to the effect that these generalizations only apply to societies where similar operative factors are to be found, where key groups exist in a sufficiently developed form, with identifiable, and competing leadership, and where there is a sufficiently well-established tradition of democracy and constitutionalism.[11]

[11] E. B. Haas, *The Uniting of Europe* (Stanford: Stanford University Press, 1958), pp. xiii–xiv.

These conditions exist in the West Indies, though to a less advanced degree than in western Europe; and over the period since 1947, when the federal arrangements began to be discussed, appreciable progress has been made in the process of integration. This progress has taken place in the areas where opportunities have been provided for cooperation or rivalry. Manufacturers from Trinidad have sought to capture a share of the Jamaican market and vice versa; unit governments and commodity associations have cooperated with each other and with the federal government in the marketing of crops. Further opportunities of cooperation have been provided by the common services operated by the federal government—the defense forces, the meteorological services, regional shipping, regional civil aviation control, and the university. Professional associations, trade unions, sporting organizations, agricultural, industrial, and commercial associations all have formed appropriate groupings at the federal level. Finally, the federal government itself exerted a unifying influence both in the thousand little ways resulting from its very existence, and also by reason of the controversies excited by the customs union recommendations, the Federal Land Acquisition Act, and the Prime Minister's veiled threat of retroactive taxation. Through these means the fact of federation was finding an increasing measure of acceptance even while the federal government was being criticized. But the process was interrupted.

IV

I have used the word "interrupted," because I believe that the world trend in the direction of larger rather than smaller entities will triumph in the long run. It is a paradox that in present day circumstances of production, trade, and communications, small countries should remain separate or amalgamations disintegrate. The explanation suggested so far has been the absence of a pressure or inducement sufficiently compelling to overcome the natural reluctance to accept subordination to a central government.

Another part of the explanation may be that the countries in question in the West Indies and elsewhere still continue to look to their former metropolitan countries for the economic and technical assistance they need if they are to survive and make progress. They do not for the moment see comparable advantages to be derived from closer association with similarly dependent countries, while they do see without enthusiasm the loss of a measure of control of their own affairs to a federal government that is new and inexperienced and with which they have not yet come to identify themselves.

With the transition from the physical comforts of colonial status to the colder and harsher realities of the world of independent nations there may well come the recognition that weak nations need to look to one another for mutual support and assistance as well as to the greater powers. In the prevailing state of national interdependence this amounts to saying that for smaller and poorer countries the chances of help from the larger and wealthier countries will be greater if they combine.

Factors favorable to amalgamation do continue to operate in the West Indies. Some of the common services—for example, the university, the shipping service, the meteorological service, and regional agricultural research—have survived the break-up of the federation. On the economic side, the need of all the islands to maintain markets and favorable prices for similar products (none of them easy to sell in the world market) is a motive for continued cooperation. The need for united action may be expected to be more keenly felt as, with independence, the former colonies are exposed to increasing economic danger without the protection and special privileges that were the reverse side of colonial status. The probable entry of Britain into the European Common Market is only the first example of this kind of danger.

The motive of defense, whose absence from the origins of the recently dissolved federation we have noted, may yet enter the picture after independence. There exist several possible causes of friction between Trinidad and Venezuela; and the danger of possible subversion will continue in Jamaica for some time to come. Indeed, thoughtful and farsighted Jamaicans began to recognize this possibility ever since the federal controversy arose in 1958 when people began to think seriously about the implications for Jamaica of being in the Federation. S. G. Fletcher, the Managing Director of the *Gleaner,* Jamaica's leading newspaper, called attention to it as early as January 14, 1959, in an article in the *Gleaner* entitled, "Recheck on Federation" in the course of which he wrote:

> A small unit on its own, under self-government, can easily become a dictatorship—witness Dominican Republic, Haiti, Nicaragua, even Cuba. A Federal Government, a Federal Army and a Federal Police Force will be a safe-guard against local dictatorship in any Unit and an influence in maintaining the rule of law. A Federal dictatorship is hard to visualise in our island-hopping context.

The editorial of December 31, 1960, in the *Gleaner* refers to Jamaica as being "no longer an isolated island in an archipelago of peace" but "now vulnerable in the sea of contention. . . . Jamaica is next door to Cuba, the focus of the Communists' entry into the new world. . . ." And the writer goes on to stress the need for a strong security force. The sense of this danger continues. Sir Alexander Bustamante, whose party was returned to power in the general election of April 10, 1962, announced on April 12 that he would seek a defense treaty with the United States "to protect us from foreign invasion."

It seems likely that any regrouping brought about by considerations either of defense or of economic advantage would extend beyond the limits of the former British possessions. This would almost certainly be the case if United States requirements for Caribbean defense were to make it necessary to press for the integration of the region. And the idea of a common economic community embracing the entire Caribbean area, which West Indians have sometimes discussed as a distant prospect, has recently been adopted as policy by Eric Williams and the PNM.[12] We should, however, recognize that the glamor of representation in foreign capitals and of participation in international activities will create vested interests in the continued separate existence of every independent nation.

Jamaica and Trinidad have shown by their postwar development that with a reasonable amount of luck they are capable of achieving self-sustaining economic growth. For the other islands some form of unification would seem to be essential—to a less extent for Barbados than for the Windwards and Leewards. Barbados has always paid its way, and the size of the market it requires for its two main exports—sugar and people—is small enough to be assured indefinitely, given a reasonable amount of good will on the part of its traditional neighbors and trading partners.

For the Leewards and Windwards some sort of unification is necessary. Proposals for a federation of these islands with Barbados are being discussed by the governments of Britain and the islands concerned. If the discussions end in a unification of the "Little Eight," the reduction of political entities in the British group from ten to three may be regarded as useful progress in the direction of regional unification.

[12] Resolution on Independence passed by People's National Movement Special Convention in Port of Spain, Trinidad, January 27–28, 1962. See also Eric Williams, *Speech on Independence* (Trinidad, 1962), p. 22.

9.

Following the Jamaican, Trinidadian, and Barbadian withdrawal from the federation, the smaller islands of the eastern Caribbean sought to regroup on their own. Beset by offers of amalgamation from Trinidad, by economic dependence on Britain, and by quarrels and rivalries among themselves, their efforts failed. Excerpts from the painful history, told here by the St. Lucia-born educator who led efforts to salvage the federal craft, illuminate both the difficulties of union and the perils of insularity.

DR. W. ARTHUR LEWIS, a renowned economist who has specialized in the economic problems of developing countries, taught at Manchester and then served as Vice-Chancellor of the University of the West Indies for several years before returning to his own discipline at Princeton. A determined West Indian federalist, Sir Arthur continues to play a major role in West Indian regional affairs as Director of the West Indies Development Bank and as Chancellor of the University of Guyana.

The Agony of the Eight
W. Arthur Lewis

If common sense were to prevail, the departure of Jamaica would be hailed as a chance to build a strongly centralised federation, to which most of them [the other islands] had at some time been committed. But common sense does not flourish in an atmosphere where everybody is angry with everybody else.

This is a personal chapter. On the night of the referendum I recalled Dr. Williams's statement that if Jamaica left the federation, Trinidad and Tobago would also leave. I therefore decided to go and see him immediately, and try to persuade him that the nine would make a nice federation, without Jamaica.

Dr. Williams and I are old friends, who have known each other since we were both students 30 years ago. We admire and respect each other, and each of us knows that he can call on the other's talents in support of national causes.

Dr. Williams was in a very bad mood. The goings-on at Lancaster House still rankled, and he was absolutely fed up with most of the principal characters. Fortunately he had already decided to lie low, and say nothing for the time being. It was clear that if forced to speak, he would simply announce that Trinidad too was coming out of the

The Agony of the Eight (Barbados: Advocate Commercial Printery, 1965), pp. 10–39. Reprinted by permission of the publisher and the author.

federation and seeking its independence. I hastily agreed
that his decision to keep silent was much the more desirable.

His mind was not yet made up. He would have nothing
whatever to do with the Grantley Adams federation; that
must pack up and its leaders disappear. Thereafter he was
attracted to the idea of a unitary state.

Part of this attraction was political. The federal government had been handicapped by the absence of organised
party support, since the so-called West Indian Federal
Labour Party was just a collection of diverse local groups.
In a unitary state there could be a unitary political party,
the PNM, functioning throughout the territory. He did not
relish the prospect of miscellaneous island parties, some
of doubtful purpose, in forming a new federal government.

On the other hand, a unitary state between such diverse
islands, cut off from each other in so many senses, is both
impossible and undesirable. Each of these islands has its
own problems, and fears, correctly, that if it were governed from some other island, its problems would be neglected.

Also, salaries and the cost of living differ greatly. A
unitary state has to have uniform salary scales. Civil servants in all the islands would have to get Trinidad salaries,
at an extra cost which, in 1961, would have come to about
W.I. $13 million a year. A federation avoids most of this
cost, since only the federal officials have a uniform scale.

The same applies to economic and social policies. In a
unitary state the standards of education, hospitalisation,
roads and such would have to be raised everywhere to
Trinidad levels, and the cost of this would fall on Trinidad
taxes. Much song and dance is made about having so many
Ministers, and so on. But the posts which a unitary state
would save come to less than two per cent of the budget,
which is negligible in comparison with what a unitary state
would cost.

A unitary state is a fine sounding idea, but neither Trinidad nor the other islands could afford it. When Grenada

opted to join in a unitary state with Trinidad, the financial arithmetic stood out as a major obstacle. Multiply by eight, and the thing is clearly impossible.

I urged on Dr. Williams that the idea of a unitary state was a non-starter. The nearest we could get to it would be the kind of federation outlined in "The Economics of Nationhood."† Now that Jamaica was out, this proposal could be revised. Did he still stand by it? If so, I would tour the islands to find out how close the remaining leaders now were to agreement on this basis.

Dr. Williams replied affirmatively. He still believed in "The Economics of Nationhood," and he would welcome my tour, on the clear understanding that he was not now committing himself to any line, and would make no decisions or announcements until after the elections of December 1961.

So I set off touring all the islands, selling "The Economics of Nationhood." This was a mistake. At that time "The Economics of Nationhood" was already impossible. In that document Trinidad had offered to bear an enormous proportion of the cost of running the islands.

The mood in which such generosity was possible had long since evaporated. I was in the position of a salesman taking orders for a product which the company had already discontinued.

Selling the product was easy. I began with Mr. Bird. I had never met him before, and had been warned that he would prove extremely difficult. Actually, we got on together like a house on fire.

Since I did not believe in a unitary state, and fully accepted his contention that Antigua would be neglected if the local leaders were deprived of the initiative in economic and social matters, we were talking the same language. I accepted some of his points and he accepted some of mine. The main framework of "The Economics of Nationhood" remained intact, on the basis that the federal government would not monopolise initiative in economic and social

† Port-of-Spain, Trinidad, Office of the Premier and Ministry of Finance, 1959.

matters, but would share it with the island governments.

I conceived an immense affection for Mr. Bird, which was for a time reciprocated. In the next two years we worked together very closely. This warmth has never diminished on my side.

Then what I had been told proved true: any federal scheme which you can sell to Mr. Bird, the others will also buy. When I returned to Trinidad I was able to tell Dr. Williams that the main framework of "The Economics of Nationhood" was acceptable to all the eight, and I had no doubt that a conference could reach easy agreement on a new federal constitution.

But the atmosphere of the two previous years was not to be cleared away so easily. From the time of the Antigua pact with Jamaica, Trinidad and The Eight had been snarling at each other.

Practically all Dr. Williams's close associates were fed up to the teeth with the small island leaders; wanted to have no more to do with them; were urging that Trinidad should go on to independence alone. "The Economics of Nationhood" stood absolutely no chance.

The reason for my mistake was ignorance. As head of the University College I had kept scrupulously out of politics; had played no part in the federal wrangle; and did not know how deep the hatreds were.

Had I known better I would have tried to stay with Dr. Williams before going on tour, and to work out first some new scheme more acceptable to his close associates. I would probably still have failed, in that angry atmosphere, but it would have been a better try.

By the end of 1961 Dr. Williams had stated repeatedly that the existing federation must be wound up, though he remained silent on what should take its place. The Secretary of State for the Colonies, Mr. Maudling, accepted this position, and announced that he would visit Trinidad and start discussions with political leaders on January 16, 1962.

The Trinidad decision was published on that morning.

Trinidad would go on to independence, taking with her any of the islands which would join her in a unitary state.

The Federal Cabinet was meeting that morning with the Chief Ministers of the eight. Neither Mr. Bird nor Mr. Barrow was present, but having spent the previous day with them in Antigua, I was able to report that their position was that, if Trinidad would not play, the eight should form a new federation. This proved to be the unanimous opinion of the Chief Ministers, so the Cabinet was authorised to report this to Mr. Maudling that same afternoon.

Mr. Maudling was astonished, and angry. He seemed to have expected the islands to be willing to become a unitary state with Trinidad, though he did not say so. He resisted the idea of a federation for several days, but was finally persuaded before he left.

One fact which persuaded him was the obvious circumstance that there was no love lost between the leaders of Trinidad and the leaders of the eight. Trinidad might refer in passing to a unitary state, but in day-to-day negotiations this seldom entered their thinking. If there was no willingness to talk federation, there was even less basis for a unitary state.

It was thus easy to see that Trinidad and the eight must be allowed to go separately; but was federation the answer for the eight?

The preferred alternative, as the Colonial Office saw it, would be a unitary state of the eight. But this was a nonstarter, for reasons we have already seen.

It would cause too much frustration, and would also cost too much, since all the other islands would have to be levelled up to Barbados, at the expense of Barbados. The answer must be federation, or else continued direct relationship of each island with the Colonial Office.

The latter was unattractive, for several reasons. First, the Colonial Office was fed up with the West Indies, especially after the islands had made such a mess of federation. It wanted to get rid of them as soon as possible.

Secondly, the maintenance of good government requires a federal structure. In a small island of 50,000 or 100,000 people, dominated by a single political party, it is very difficult to prevent political abuse. Everybody depends on the government for something, however small, so most are reluctant to offend it.

The civil servants live in fear; the police avoid unpleasantness; the trade unions are tied to the party; the newspaper depends on government advertisements; and so on.

This is true even if the political leaders are absolutely honest. In cases where they are also corrupt, and playing with the public funds, the situation becomes intolerable.

The only safeguard against this is federation. If the government in island C misbehaves, it will be criticised openly by the citizens of island E. The federal government must be responsible for law and order, and for redress of financial or other abuses.

Thus the Colonial Office could not in good conscience make each little island independent on its own. To do so would be to betray the liberties of the West Indian people.

This point was not just academic. At that moment the Colonial Office was investigating alleged financial irregularities in four of the islands, and was appointing commissions of enquiry. A federal framework was clearly needed to ensure good government.

Another argument related to the staffing of the public service. In these days there is a world-wide scarcity of good professional people, such as engineers, architects, doctors, agricultural specialists, statisticians and other technical people. A small island of 80,000 people finds difficulty in recruiting such people, and still more difficulty in holding them, since it has no ladder of promotion to offer. Service in a federal organisation is much more attractive.

The islands also get better service; federal services can hire more specialised people; duplication can be avoided; and technical services can be streamlined.

Then there is the argument of international financial assistance.

These islands, taken individually, are too small for attention by the World Bank, the United States Aid agencies, and other sources of international assistance. All the principal agencies which give aid have indicated their willingness to support generously an Eastern Caribbean federation; and their equal unwillingness to become involved with each island separately.

The same goes for borrowing power. Who will lend money to a little island of 80,000 persons, subject to no financial controls? The ability of the little islands to attract finance depends on their hanging together, and guaranteeing each other's fiscal integrity.

This may not seem so obvious today, when bananas and the tourist trade are booming. For the moment there is no end of financial braggadocio. Unfortunately in the West Indies, as elsewhere, booms tend to vanish away as rapidly as they come.

A wise government looks ahead to see who will befriend it when the lean times come again.

The decision to support a new federation of the eight was not taken lightly. The Colonial Office was reluctant to start a new federation, when the old had done so badly. It took Mr. Maudling several days to see that there was no other solution.

And it then took him several months to persuade his colleagues back home in the British Cabinet. The idea of a little eight federation was not forced on the islands by the British Government; on the contrary, the British Government resisted it until the facts could no longer be ignored.

The fundamental issues are law and order, control of the police, the independence of the civil service, the magistrates and the judiciary, financial integrity, the ability to recruit and hold good technical staff, and the ability to attract external grants, loans and investments.

The political leaders take it for granted that anything they will do is democratic and right, so they tend to ignore these issues.

They make federation a question of customs unions, freedom of movement, exclusive lists, concurrent lists and the like. All this is secondary.

The fundamental reason for federating these islands is

that it is the only way that good government can be assured to their peoples.

Mr. Maudling saw the point. A unitary state, with or without Trinidad, was neither possible nor desirable. Federation with Trinidad was the obvious solution, but if Trinidad would not play, it would have to be a federation of the eight.

Barbados was a special case. This island had always been financially independent; under the constitution financial irregularities could not arise; its secondary education was so far advanced, and the numbers returning from university education were so large, that it had no difficulty in recruiting and keeping a technical service.

Most of the arguments for federating the other islands could not be applied to Barbados.

In recent months people have been saying that Barbados wanted to get the other islands into a federation so that it could dictate to them and exploit their markets. Nobody could say this who took part in these discussions in 1962 and 1963.

Mr. Barrow was dragged into the federation of the eight. The problem arose within six weeks of his becoming Premier, when his mind was preoccupied with getting hold of Barbados affairs. He would have liked to postpone the whole question.

He came along because of a long-time friendship with some of the other leaders, especially Mr. Bird, as well as because of a life-long devotion to West Indian federation.

The people behind him were equally lukewarm. The few potential industrialists welcomed a customs union, which might benefit a few manufactures. But tourism will provide as much income and employment in Barbados as manufacturing industry, and tourism does not depend on federation.

It suits Barbados to be the capital of the eight. But if the seven Windward and Leeward Islands preferred to federate by themselves without Barbados, this would make little difference to the economy of Barbados.

The real problem which Barbados presents to the other seven is the opposite of a desire to dominate. Three hundred years of strongly insular pride make its people somewhat indifferent to what happens outside their tiny paradise. A series of baseless accusations tends to produce a reaction of weariness. "If the other seven do not want us, let them go their own way" has become a common attitude.

This can be fatal to the others. For a federation without Barbados would not seem as stable politically and financially to the outside world as a federation which included Barbados. In truth, all the eight need each other.

So before leaving Trinidad at the end of January 1962, Mr. Maudling asked the eight to prepare a plan for a federation of the eight and submit it to him.

This was done at a conference of the eight held in Barbados in March 1962. This was a good meeting. I had been asked to prepare papers, and had done so in some detail.

The Ministers took the point about law and order. They agreed to federalise the police, the magistrates and the judiciary.

Then they argued about what should be on the exclusive or on the concurrent lists, and what services should be transferred at once to the federal government.

In my eyes this argument about lists was secondary. Federations begin with limited powers. They grow stronger as the people get used to looking to a common government, and as experience shows that some problems can be solved only by the common government.

Given the preservation of law and order and financial probity, I would never make the issue of federation turn on whether this or that matter is on the exclusive or the concurrent list.

Ministers also took Mr. Maudling's financial point: political independence must carry an assurance of financial independence. The grants-in-aid towards recurrent expenditure must come to an end. They agreed that these grants should taper off within five years, on condition that an equal sum was paid into a capital fund for economic development.

Thus the islands would not lose financially from independence, but at the same time the recurrent budgets would cease to be subsidised.

The conference of March 1962 provided a firm basis for a new federation. Papers were sent to London. In due course the British Cabinet was persuaded that federalism was the right answer, and Ministers were summoned to a London conference in May 1962.

This London conference also went smoothly. Small concessions were made here and there, but essentially the framework of March 1962 was preserved. The constitution then agreed was published as Cmd. 1746.

The constitution agreed in May 1962 was an excellent foundation for a new federation. This does not mean that it was perfect. Any federal constitution embodies a whole series of compromise agreements. Any theorist can do better.

The question to ask is: Does this constitution provide the essentials for a good start? The answer is that the constitution of May 1962 would have made an excellent beginning. What then held it up?

Money. The British Treasury was not yet willing to agree to the financial formula, which would guarantee the islands the same amount of aid for the next five years as they were then receiving. It therefore played for time.

The Colonial Office announced that before this constitution could be adopted there must be further studies—a fiscal study, a civil service study, and an economic study. Heavens above! All these matters had been studied ad nauseam in recent years. The only purpose of further studies was to get the Treasury off the hook.

This error is the main reason why the islands are not already federated. Twenty-one months later the Treasury gave exactly the undertaking which it had refused to give in May 1962. But by then this was no longer adequate. Ministers were frustrated and angry, and now wanted more.

For want of a little common sense at the Treasury, the chance of federating on excellent terms was lost.

May 1962 was the high water mark of the federal scheme. From the moment the Treasury refused to play, the situation began to deteriorate.

First came the Grenada election. The pro-Trinidad party offered access to the riches of Trinidad's oil wells. The pro-federal party offered: nothing, since the Treasury would not talk. The pro-Trinidad party won.

The defection of Grenada was not of great moment to the others, except on sentimental grounds. It raised the fear that St. Vincent might follow, and thus the chain unravel. But both parties in St. Vincent held firm for federation.

It was more of a blow to the people of Grenada, who were thus launched on years of frustration, whose end is not yet in sight. A unitary state is very expensive; to get this off the ground is virtually impossible.

More dangerous to the federation was the vacuum created by postponement. The first months of 1962 were a challenge to Ministers, to which they had risen nobly. January had found them abandoned by both Jamaica and Trinidad. Mr. Maudling had promised to support them if they came up with a reasonable scheme. Putting aside insularities and petty jealousies, they had indeed come up with a scheme which Mr. Maudling himself endorsed as reasonable. Now they were told to go away and wait, with no end to the waiting in sight.

Men can live at a high emotional level only for limited periods. If they have striven and have achieved nothing, they cease to strive.

So Ministers, in the long waiting period which followed, began to have second thoughts. In the excitement of defederation they had hung together, and conceded many of their powers to the proposed federation. As the weary months dragged on, with still no word from the Treasury, anger and frustration succeeded to co-operation and creativity. Feeling sold, they began to be in a mood to take back some of what they had given.

The Commissioners came and went. Their reports were published. All but one merely dotted i's and crossed t's. The one exception, a report by Dr. O'Loughlin, sent the blood racing.

Miss O'Loughlin had been asked by the Colonial Office to estimate how much the seven islands would "need". Her answer was that they would need $215 million over the five years 1964–68, or a total of $300 million over the 10 years 1964–73.

Since the Treasury had just refused to guarantee $75 million for the first five years, this Colonial Office sponsored report, showing a need for $215 million was heady wine. Dr. O'Loughlin became the heroine of the Seven.

Ministers adjusted their sights upwards. Why be content with as much for the next five years as in the preceding five, when the Colonial Office itself had published a report showing that the need was three times as great?

When in February 1964 the Treasury at last gave the guarantee which it had refused to give in May 1962, it was rejected out of hand, as an insult to intelligence.

Meanwhile the pre-federal organisation had also got off on the wrong foot. The London conference had decided to create a Regional Council of Ministers, consisting of the Chief Minister of each island, with the Governor of Barbados in the chair. Meeting regularly, Chief Ministers would get to know each other's way of thinking, and thus prepare for an easy transition to a federal cabinet.

Two decisions set this back. At the first meeting several Chief Ministers turned up with other Ministers to function as their advisers. Instead of becoming a Cabinet, the Council became a conference. Instead of seven members, as many as twenty persons might turn up.

When seven members were expected it was feasible to say that decisions must be unanimous. When this became a meeting of up to twenty persons, the unanimity rule became a nightmare, since each Chief Minister had to satisfy his other Ministers before he could cast his vote.

This reduced decisions of the Regional Council of Ministers to the lowest level: only the most innocuous measures could be agreed to. This would prove to be fatal to attempts to secure a strong federal constitution.

By the spring of 1963 the Commissioners had all reported, and it was time to go to London again. The London meeting was set for June, but in order to reduce the time spent in London Mr. Nigel Fisher, Under Secretary of State for the Colonies, came with advisers to preside over the meeting of the Regional Council of Ministers held in Barbados in May 1963.

The atmosphere of this conference was terrible. First there was a long wrangle over the timing of independence. Jamaica and Trinidad had both achieved independence the previous August. The Seven had always said that they wanted the federation to be independent from its inception, while the British had always said that the federation would need some time to run itself in before becoming independent. The British had their instructions, and would not budge.

A conference in the West Indies with a junior Minister is bound to be a mistake. His authority to negotiate is limited. He digs in his heels on what seem to the West Indians to be negotiable points. His obstinacy irritates, and tempers flare.

Conferences with the British should always be held in London.

The atmosphere deteriorated rapidly when the conference moved on to review the proposed constitution. By now Ministers had recovered from the shock of the Jamaica referendum and the Trinidad decision, which had encouraged them to seek cover under their own federal umbrella. The Treasury's refusal to talk was also irritating.

They now began to pick at the structure which had been agreed on the previous May. The police and the magistrates were removed from federal control, and restored to the units. The administration of Income Tax was also taken away. Then the conference tripped up over the Antigua Post Office.

Mr. Bird proposed that postal services remain with the units, at least initially. He proposed a five-year stay, after which removal could be made only by invoking the procedure for amending entrenched clauses.

The West Indians did not care much about the proposal, one way or the other, but it inflamed the British. They made it an issue of principle. Who had ever heard, they asked, of a country which did not control its own post offices?

Tempers flared; names were called, and the conference broke up without issue. The proposed visit to London was postponed till "some time in the autumn", from which it was again postponed till April 1964.

It has not yet taken place.

At this point relations with London were at rock bottom. From the moment of the Antigua Pact, Ministers of the Windward and Leeward Islands had worried about finance; this loomed larger in their minds than any other issue.

They had been willing to buy the May 1962 constitution if the Treasury would guarantee the next five years. Instead, they seemed to be getting the run-around. More reports, and more dispatches from London: but not one word about finance.

It was decided to put a spoke in London's wheel. Ministers agreed amongst themselves that they would not go to London until they had previously reached unanimous agreement in the West Indies. Thus London would be faced with a united front, and be unable to dictate.

This may sound a good idea; but it is actually an error of the first magnitude. How are twenty Ministers to agree unanimously on something so essentially full of compromises as a federal constitution?

Agreement is difficult enough in London, where it is subject to pressures of various sorts, including the clock, and the prospect of a Treasury grant. To decide not to go to London without unanimous agreement was virtually to decide not to go to London at all.

Besides, this gambit could not work. Independence conferences in London are attended by both the governing and the opposition parties; whereas the Regional Council of Ministers excludes the opposition. Even if the Ministers were unanimous, the Colonial Office could reopen any issue to please an opposition party.

To get unanimous agreement before going to London, one must frame a constitution so weak that it is hardly worth having. Then, with the opposition parties in London, the whole subject is back on the table. Nothing is gained, but the chance of framing a good constitution is lost.

Ministers met again in Barbados in September 1963. From here on the proceedings can be followed in the White Paper which was issued earlier this year.

The September meeting was good. The Secretary of State produced an acceptable formula for independence. Nobody made an issue of the Antiguan Post Office. Ministers would not go to London during the winter, but they would be ready in the spring. Meanwhile Barbados would produce a new draft, based on current thinking, and Dr. O'Loughlin and a committee would produce a new budget. In due course the London meeting was fixed for April 1964.

The Barbados draft was ready by April 1964, but Ministers had not yet had time to study it, so the meeting was postponed again. The Regional Council of Ministers did not return to the subject until its meeting in October 1964.

One reason for the delay was the political crisis in St. Lucia. Mr. George Charles lost his majority in the Legislature, and in a general election was defeated by Mr. Compton, who became the Chief Minister.

The arrival of a newcomer to participate in negotiations which have been going on for years, is always fraught with danger, save in well-run countries, where foreign relations do not depend on who has won the last election. To the newcomer, a document which has emerged from years of compromise is obviously absurd; how can he be expected to accept such nonsense?

To Mr. Compton, the position reached by his fellow

Ministers in the middle of 1964 seemed obviously inadequate. The point that all federal constitutions are compromises, and that all compromises are inadequate, did not register.

He was ready to start all over again. In a moment of extravagance one of his Ministers tore up the Barbados draft in a session of the Legislative Council.

But this is running ahead. The Regional Council of Ministers studied the Barbados draft at its meeting in October 1964. The meeting made good progress. The draft was generally liked, but there were reservations. Ministers created four technical committees to which the document was referred.

These committees met at the end of 1964, and reported early in 1965. All seemed to be going well. The draft was now quite some distance from the agreed constitution on May 1962. The police and the magistrates had gone from federal control. The power of the federal government to intervene to correct financial malpractices of island governments had been whittled away almost to nothing. The number of services to be transferred was down to the barest minimum.

Still, the document represented a start on the federal road. Since there is no other solution for the islands, any start is better than none. Experience will prove that the federal government needs more power, and it will get more power as it goes along.

At this point everything was suddenly halted again by Antigua's Post Office. Mr. Bird intensely dislikes interference from London.

He has worked an economic miracle in Antigua, developing the tourist trade to the point where the island's budget has been able to dispense (defiantly) with grant-in-aid. An oil refinery is being built in the island, and a deep water harbour is not far off.

He is rightly proud of his achievements; sees Antigua as on the verge of self-sufficiency, and is in no mood to be dictated to.

One of the reservations to the federal draft was made by

Mr. Bird. It states that the federal government shall administer such services as are agreed to at the inception of the federation, but may not take over any new service from a unit without the consent of the unit concerned. So Antigua may keep its Post Office forever if it wishes to.

This is a large hammer with which to crack such a small nut. Normally federal constitutions can be amended only if a substantial majority of the units agree. Now Antigua was proposing a new category which could be amended only by unanimous agreement.

Had the matter been left to the other West Indian Ministers, it would not have blown up into a major issue. Reservations fly back and forth; negotiations occur; new compromises are made.

But the Secretary of State was asking for documents to be published, and was proposing to comment, for publication, on the documents. And so, as in some weird story by Gunter Grass, the Post Office was destined to become the locale of a major confrontation.

The Regional Council of Ministers was due to meet again in April 1965. The reports were all ready, and final agreement was in sight. The independence conference was set for London on July 1.

All this was shattered by the crisis over Antigua's Post Office. Mr. Bird's reservation demanded that the Federal Government have no power to acquire new services without unanimous consent.

The Secretary of State, in a despatch dated March 22, 1965, objected to this reservation: "I should find it very difficult to agree."

Well then, says Mr. Bird, since you and I are not talking about the same kind of federation, there is no point in my attending any further conference on federation.

Well then, retorts the Secretary of State, we will go along without Antigua.

Oh no, says Mr. Bramble. Antigua and Montserrat must stick together, so it will have to be a federation of five.

Thus, when the Regional Council of Ministers met in

April 1965, the seven were down to five, for reasons which the five could not understand, since they had no doubt whatsoever that any differences between themselves and Antigua could be resolved somehow.

Mr. Bird had made his reservation, and they had come prepared to discuss it with him, only to find that in the course of exchanges behind their backs, Mr. Bird had disappeared.

Progress could hardly be expected.

St. Kitts, Dominica and St. Vincent reiterated their desire to go forward with federation as soon as possible with whatever number could come.

Barbados and St. Lucia fell to quarrelling with each other. So the meeting broke up without issue.

Now (August 1965) Mr. Barrow has produced a White Paper.

As could be foreseen, what he says in effect is: "Enough of all this. Since London won't talk money and Mr. Compton doesn't understand the difference between a federation and a unitary state, let us wash our hands of the whole business. Barbados will go forward to independence alone."

This is indeed a low state to have reached, but it need not be the end.

Mr. Barrow is a reasonable man, and a West Indian patriot.

He knows the advantages of federation. Neither is Mr. Bird an obstacle; he has been working for federation for 14 years; the other West Indian leaders would have no difficulty in coming to terms with him once they sat round the table.

These islands did not start on the federal road in a fit of idleness. They started because it was clear that a federation is the only possible solution of their problems.

Federation is the only framework which will guarantee law and order, good government, financial stability, the recruitment and retention of good technical staff and the ability to attract financial assistance from outside, including the power to borrow, and including also the kind of stability which attracts private investment.

If each little island goes off on its own, its people must suffer.

Barbados comes nearest to being able to stand by itself in these respects.

But even Barbados is too small to go off by itself, and its people know this. They have consistently supported this federation, ever since it was mooted.

Ministers of these little islands feel overconfident now, because their economies are booming, but booms tend to vanish as fast as they come; and how will they feel then?

Other schemes besides federation are mirages.

A unitary state, with or without Trinidad, is much costlier than a federation, much harder to achieve, and simply not on the cards.

Union with Canada is not a serious proposition in Canadian circles.

Union with Britain, on such terms as Puerto Rico's union with the United States, or Martinique's with France, or Surinam's with the Netherlands, would have made excellent sense for these small islands, but the moment for it is past; it stands no chance in London.

In any case, a prior federation of these islands would be a necessary prelude to union with any other country.

Ultimately West Indians will come together again in political association, but only after the present generation of leaders is dead.

Jamaica is out forever; should never have been in, since sentiment for federation was never strong in that island.

But it is the inescapable destiny of Trinidad, British Guiana and the other British islands to link their fortunes together.

No doubt it will begin with confederation, rather than federation; a common nationality, a common currency, and common representation abroad. Once established, the links will grow like ivy. Associations should always start on a limited basis, and grow slowly with time.

The eight—or seven or six—must enter such an association as a unit, equal in numbers to the other units, and able to speak with a single voice.

The disparity in size between Jamaica and Trinidad on the one hand, and the eight on the other, was one of the obstacles to smooth working of the defunct West Indies Federation.

Meanwhile, the fact that it is obvious that the eight must ultimately unite with Trinidad and British Guiana in confederation serves to disrupt, rather than to integrate.

At the moment Mr. Burnham and Dr. Williams are not on speaking terms, so their two countries have to outsmart each other.

Instead of helping the eight to come together, each of these larger units fishes among the smaller islands, promoting disunity, and endangering the smaller federation.

Trinidad offers a unitary state, but when the offer is accepted by Grenada, stalls indefinitely.

Common decency suggests that this poor deluded island should now be released if Trinidad is not prepared to go ahead.

British Guiana fishes for Barbados and Antigua, in a Free Trade Area, thus promoting confusion, jealousy and disunion with the other islands.

Must the eight also wait until the present generation of leaders is dead before they can take an obvious step?

The biggest obstacle has been the continued silence of the British Treasury.

London has contributed nothing to federal discussions except a string of irritating pronouncements.

This is the moment for a firm statement of precisely what help it is prepared to give, and on what terms.

The other main obstacle to progress is fatigue.

These discussions have now gone around and around for three and a half years, always waiting for London to break its silence.

Ministers are frustrated, and tend to vent their anger on each other.

In this atmosphere, the proposition that agreement must

be reached in the West Indies before Ministers go to London is deadly.

A new initiative can come only from outside. But Ministers must be in a frame of mind to receive it.

There is no fundamental obstacle in the way. All the existing leaders, with the exceptions of Mr. Compton and Mr. Blaize, have been committed to this federation for the past three and a half years.

There are no insuperable differences between them.

The position on March 21, just before the Secretary of State wrote his despatch, was that they were in broad agreement with the reports which their technical advisers had produced; that they expected to reach agreement in Barbados in April 1965, and were planning to be at an independence conference in London in July 1965.

No new issue has arisen since February which interferes with this basic agreement.

The Free Trade Area with British Guiana, when extended to the whole federation, is an accession of strength.

Any one of these leaders can break the present deadlock by initiating quiet talks with the others.

Have we not this much statesmanship left in these little islands?

10.

West Indian regional cooperation requires compromises and sacrifices by all participants. Another eminent regionalist, a Guyanese of East Indian descent, here describes the progress made in the economic arena and warns that only integration will enable the West Indies completely to shake off the imperial presence. A case in point is Anguilla, which after four years of rebellion was permitted to sever itself from the Associated State of St. Kitts-Nevis and to revert to full colonial status. How far the self-determination of small islands should prevail against wider West Indian interests is the heart of the West Indian regional problem.

S. S. RAMPHAL, S.C., Attorney General and Minister of State in Guyana, was also Assistant Attorney General in the former West Indies Federation. He plays a major role in such regional agencies as the Caribbean Free Trade Association (CARIFTA).

West Indian Nationhood—Myth, Mirage or Mandate?
S. S. Ramphal, S.C.

> *I submit that the time is at hand . . . for us to com-*
> *mence a dialogue of unity in which we shall explore all*
> *the possibilities of achieving a realistic West Indian na-*
> *tionhood. And in our perspectives for the Caribbean let*
> *us anticipate that dialogue and fix on the horizon, as a*
> *distant light that beckons us—The Republic of the West*
> *Indies. Let this be our vision of the future.*

I like to think that there may be a moral in the fact that in delivering the opening lecture in this forward looking series I have come back after 12 years to this hall of the Trinidad Public Library where I had last spoken in 1959. The year before, we had inaugurated the Federation of the West Indies and I was speaking in a series that bore the title "The Federal Principle". After 10 years of discussion at Conferences and in Parliaments, of negotiation with Britain and between ourselves, the aspirations of a generation of political leaders, and of some of their people, found expression and, we believed, fulfilment in the new State we had established with its Capital here in Port-of-Spain. In the circumstances, that series of lectures in 1959 on the "Federal Principle" was, not surprisingly, an occasion for looking back. We had arrived at unity, at any

A lecture at the Public Library, Port of Spain, Trinidad, on Wednesday, May 26, 1971; subsequently published by Guyana Ministry of External Affairs, Georgetown, June 1971. Used by permission of the author.

rate we had established the institutions of unity, and we were recalling the journey—the 300 years of groping toward effective regional constitutional arrangements, years of experimentation and of frustration with experiments that failed, but years that seemed to be moving the Caribbean toward an inevitable destiny of oneness, and we were recalling also the great federal precedents, the constitutional forms that we had opted to make our own, looking into the experience of the United States, of Canada and of Australia for guidance and for encouragement as we began our own federal undertaking. How long ago now seems that moment of high expectation—for a moment, alas, in the wide span of history, it was to be—and yet, how like yesterday it is in relation to all that has happened since!

TOWARD REALISTIC PROJECTIONS

As we attempt in this series to establish our perspectives for the seventies and beyond it is both wise and necessary to draw upon the primary lesson of the Federal experience which is, to me, that we must never again mistake the forms of unity for its substance and that, by the same token, we must never dogmatise about those forms lest they become our masters and cease to be responsive to our needs and our situations. If we have learnt that lesson well we shall be better able to preserve our perspectives from distortion. But we must also seek, in more positive ways, to get our perspectives right; and it is here that our experience during the years of separatism between 1962 and 1966 and the years of regionalism between 1966 and 1971—the totality of this experience—must be drawn upon to help us make realistic projections for the years ahead.

From this experience I select three factors as those that should control our Caribbean perspectives. I do not assert that they are only factors; nor do I deny that they may be differently combined. Out of the abundance of history there are any number of variables from which to select our precepts. All we can do at any moment is to identify those that seem to have a special relevance to the principal needs of our time and our circumstance. These are the three factors I would choose:

first, the fact of independence in the four larger territories between 1962 and 1966 and the phenomenon of Associated Status between 1966 and 1967;

secondly, the experience of independence and of Associated Status amid the realities of contemporary international existence; and

thirdly, the experience of functional co-operation in regional and hemispheric terms between 1966 and 1971.

Of these three factors, the first relates to the psychological climate for unity in the post-independence period while the second and third are factors of a more practical kind which influence contemporary attitudes to unity and which must condition our perspectives—whatever our orientation.

THE PSYCHOLOGY OF INDEPENDENCE

At the London Conference of 1961, May 31, 1962, had been selected as the date for the Independence of the West Indies. Even as we ended that cheerless Conference we were conscious that it was an independence that might never dawn; and so, indeed, it was; for that day—the last day of May in 1962 which should have seen the beginning of the new West Indian Nation—was to be the last day of the dissolved Federation. Hard on the heels of the dissolution—some thought indecently soon after the funeral rites of the dismembered Federation—Jamaica embraced independence. Less than one month later, Trinidad and Tobago, pursuing an inexorable subtraction, followed suit. Four years later—years marked by bitterness and lost opportunity—Barbados moved on to independence, leaving the Leeward and Windward Islands to an uncertain and problematical constitutional end. Just six months before Bar-

bados' independence, my own country, Guyana, which had
chosen to stand aside from the Federal experiment, with
that smugness which is often the mask of indecision, itself
moved on to independence—estranged in no small measure from the Caribbean it had deserted. Belize, meanwhile,
was steadily proceeding toward self-determination, bearing
on its back the burden of an intractable boundary dispute; and the Commonwealth of the Bahamas had itself
begun to move toward truly representative Government
and a new West Indian identification.

The constitutional scene of the seventies is thus a complete transformation of that in which federalism had
emerged in the fifties as the possible answer to improbable
local self-government. The island nationalisms that had
been burgeoning since the thirties and that ultimately destroyed the Federation in its assertiveness have found fulfilment in the independence of the larger States. In the
Leeward and Windward Islands what was attainable on
an island basis was, of course, less than immediate independence, and found expression in the phenomenon of
Associated Status. But it was characteristic of the prevailing mood that this new constitutional form should have
been widely celebrated throughout the Region as the
achievement of self-determination; indeed, in one State,
it was officially proclaimed as "Independence in Association". The Bahamas is now poised for independence in its
more conventional form; as, also, is Belize. In each case
it is a matter of timing; and the timing is in the hands of
the local leadership.

It may be the case that West Indian unity can only
emerge in an effective and permanent form out of conscious sacrifice; and that, therefore, it cannot be achieved
in these terms until that autonomy which must in part
be sacrificed is itself secured. Perhaps, this was why a federated West Indies which was accepted in Montego Bay
in 1948, when it seemed to be the only means of satisfying the local national ambition, was no longer supportable
in 1961 when it could be presented as frustrating that
narrower nationalism. Now it is all different. What was

attainable as separate States has been achieved. We have been equipped with the conventional form of independence. We have acquired what Professor Gordon Lewis calls "the paraphernalia of sovereignty", and have done the fashionable and the necessary things. And to a substantial degree this is as true of the Associated States as it is of the rest of us.

To the extent, therefore, that we have needed the psychological reassurance of independence before creating that unity which Norman Manley so perceptively described as "a wider field for ambition", that need has been fulfilled. Our flags, our anthems testify to our independence. Our votes in the United Nations, our separate Embassies abroad, proclaim our sovereignty, as they do our separateness. Hereafter, the decisions are our own and we alone shall be responsible for the regional implications of those decisions that we take—as we alone shall be responsible for the local implications of those decisions that we fail to take. To those who accept a Freudian analysis of the failure of federalism in the sixties we can present today a new West Indian released from the inhibitions of a thwarted island nationalism and well equipped, or at least better equipped, to adjust to the need for a more mature West Indian nationhood. The psychological environment of the West Indies of today must, to this extent, be more propitious for the growth of an effective and a lasting unity and the acceptance of a regional identity based upon it.

DE-COLONISATION NOT ENOUGH

The next factor which I see as contributing toward West Indian nationhood is the actual experience of independence and of Associated Status. How satisfying, other than in psychological terms, has been the new status? Let it be said, straightaway, that there has been a substantial area of satisfaction. The processes of nation building which have been at work throughout the Region and which have given the West Indian a new spirit of self-reliance and

fostered a new confidence and self-respect could never
have been invoked save through the forms of self-
determination. Whatever may be our particular assess-
ments of the pace and quality of change, no West Indian
will seriously deny that important advances have been
made in the social, political and economic fields in the
post-independence period in all our States, and that they
would never have been made under Colonial auspices.
The changes have, of course, been more fundamental
in the independent States than they have been in the Associated States or in those, like Belize and the Bahamas,
that are not yet independent. In all, however, the new
constitutional status has been an effective instrument of
change.

But the new status has made a contribution, also, of
another less direct kind in that it has dispelled illusions
that self-determination, by whatever name called, provides
a magic key to a better life for our people. Side by side
with the psychological lift that the new status has given
and the new opportunities for practical change it has provided, comes the acknowledgement, however reluctant, that
decolonisation is not enough; that the reality of independence derives not from constitutions but from strength; that
while it is good to possess the right of choice it profits us
little when we are faced with barren options—when both
our freedom of choice and our range of choice are conditioned by external forces which we are powerless individually to influence, much less to control, and which we
would be foolhardy to ignore. It is ironic that while we
may have had to fragment in order to satisfy a primal in-
stinct for freedom, independence in isolation has served
to emphasise our need of each other. It is paradoxical that
we may have to contribute sovereignty in order to gain
economic independence.

THE METROPOLITAN PRESENCE

In this respect the experience of Associated Status has
been similar to that of independence; but there is an as-

pect of the former which is peculiar to that status and which raises considerations that need to be examined with greater particularity. I refer to the metropolitan presence in the Caribbean that Associated Statehood at the moment ensures. The concept of statehood in association with Britain represents an attempt to weld the principle of self-determination into the geographic and demographic realities of the Leeward and Windward Islands taken separately. Let it be conceded at the outset that the resulting constitutional formula satisfies the basic criteria of self-determination by placing in the hands of the State the option for independence as well as the machinery by which that option may at any time be exercised. True enough, there are built into that machinery procedural devices, such as special majorities and referenda, which impose restraints on the exercise of the option; but these are familiar devices whose object is to secure consensus within the State rather than consensus with the metropolitan power. A challenge that they amount to a denial of the option for independence to the people of the State could not easily be sustained. Thus, in the Fourth Committee of the General Assembly and in the Committee of 24, West Indian delegations have taken the position that these arrangements, novel, indeed, exotic though they be, fulfil the requirements of the Assembly's resolution on self-determination.

Yet it remains the case that so long as the option is not exercised Associated Status, for all its potential for self-determination, provides constitutional cover for an essentially metropolitan presence in the Caribbean. We cannot, therefore, be content with reliance on the potential so long as that potential remains unfulfilled. We cannot be content as a Region with the power to bring to an end the British metropolitan presence in the Caribbean so long as that power is not used. While the option for independence remains unexercised responsibility for the defence and external affairs of each Associated State rests with the British Government—as, apparently, does the right to determine whether a particular matter falls within the reserved category. These are substantial concessions to colonialism and for so long as they remain a part of the West Indian constitutional scene they will represent a challenge to regional ambition.

The problem is, of course, that those very realities of geography and demography that forced the compromise with immediate independence that Associated Status represents act as an effective restraint on the people of the Associated States in their exercise of the options for independence. The most ardent nationalist among us must pause before promoting independence in isolation for any of the Associated States. When communities of millions with ancient traditions of sovereignty feel it necessary to combine in order to survive, communities whose populations must be counted in tens rather than in hundreds of thousands must inevitably pause before entering the international jungle clad only in the loin cloth of notional independence. How then shall we evaluate the experience of Associated Status as a factor shaping our Caribbean perspectives?

The answer surely must lie in the frank acknowledgement that its potential for self-determination will remain unfulfilled unless and until it can be realised on the basis of such a consensus for unity among the Associated States or between them, or some of them, and the independent States as can make a living reality of independence. In short, independence will not be achieved, the metropolitan presence will not be ended unless, within the Region, there is reached such a measure of agreement on political association that the exercise of the separate options for independence by each Associated State will produce a West Indian community that not only meets the theoretical requirements of self-determination but is capable of sustaining effective independence. The challenge of nationhood is as clear as it is inescapable. But in responding to that challenge there are still further factors of which the Region must take note.

THE RATIONALE OF ASSOCIATED STATUS

I believe it is sometimes thought that the rationale of Associated Status is the inability of each State to exercise responsibility for its own defence and external affairs, and that this is why these subjects are reserved as the responsibility of Her Majesty's Government in the United Kingdom. If these responsibilities were the only impediments to the independence of each Associated State they would hardly justify the restraint of its Government and people. So far as external affairs are concerned, the problems, though serious, would not be insuperable. So far as defence is concerned, although we are still a long way off from achieving an ordered international society in which defence is an acknowledged responsibility of the world community, we have made sufficient progress for the international legal system and international political realities to exercise a substantial deterrent on external aggression. There would be few States in today's world of nuclear weapons and inter-continental missiles to deliver them that would qualify for independence if one of the criteria for it were a defence capability equal to the task of sustaining national sovereignty in the case of external aggression. Defence capability in these terms is not a valid criterion for independence in the nineteen seventies. The truth is that a need to leave responsibility for defence and external affairs with Britain is not the reason for the formula of Associated Status; that reservation is the result of a decision taken on more general grounds against the viability of independence for the islands separately. It is important to our perspectives that we appreciate this essential fact.

In no respect is this more critical than in relation to regional security. Whatever may be the case with defence, what is indispensable in any State is a capability to maintain the State intact against forces making for fragmentation and to maintain within the State peace and lawful government. Let me say at the outset that I do not speak here of a capability for repression or even imply qualification of the right of dissent. Protest movements anywhere have less to fear from a strong democracy than from a weak oligarchy. What I speak of is that capability which is essential if States are not to degenerate into anarchy or disintegrate into as many fragments as there are ambitious men. How much truer is it not the case that what stands in the way of the exercise of the option for independence by each Associated State is an often unspoken anxiety about the needs of internal security rather than of external defence? And are these considerations not relevant even to the independent States?

THE DANGER OF FRAGMENTATION

In the Caribbean, as in every democratic State, there always will be political dissatisfaction with the policies of Governments. But the geography of the Caribbean introduces two special factors. In the first place, it increases the probabilities that separate communities—which are island communities within the State—will have peculiar areas of dissatisfaction. In the second place, it makes it more likely that these differences will exert fissiparous tendencies as they become more acute. In an archipelago, the search for solutions to political problems all too readily turns to separatism and finds expression in secessionist movements. To minimise these tendencies and to prevent the further fragmentation of the Region must surely be a primary responsibility of our time. The Wooding Commission on Anguilla has rendered a valuable service by drawing attention to the consequences of further fragmentation in the Region. It is good to remember what they said:

Fragmentation would make the subversion of lawful authority on any one island easier; it would make the preservation of its sovereignty more difficult; and it would make the task of providing an acceptable standard of living for the population of the islands beyond the capacity of most. Moreover, the West Indian territories are geographically within easy reach of the great and expanding economic giants of the American mainland and for this reason are exposed to the risk of being overwhelmed by them and so losing the opportunity for political and economic self-fulfilment. This risk is increased when tiny islands, lacking the resources to support even administrative structures capable of meeting their own needs, seek to create or maintain an independent existence.

The Commission recorded the manifest concern over fragmentation and its consequences that they found among the Governments of the Region. But they also found that this expression of concern had not yet been followed by determined efforts to guard against the consequences. Unless Commissions of Inquiry into secessionist attempts are to become an annual ritual in the Caribbean it is time that we undertook such efforts and pursued them with resolution. In doing so, may I suggest two prerequisites to success. First, a regional acknowledgment that political differences and dissatisfactions do not provide justification for the overthrow of lawful government or for the disintegration of States through unconstitutional action. This is in the area of ideas. Governments, political parties, groups involved in public affairs and the people of the Caribbean generally must articulate the concept so that it becomes a part of the political ethic of the Region. Let us at least immunise ourselves from a facile romanticism that equates secessionist movements with the pursuit of self-determination and makes an appeal to the Charter of the United Nations ignoring the specific declaration of the resolution on the Granting of Independence to Colonial Territories and Peoples that "any attempt aimed at the partial or total disruption of the national unity and territorial integrity of a country is incompatible with the purposes and principles of the Charter of the United Nations".

REGIONAL PEACE-KEEPING

The second pre-requisite is that, within the Region, and available to every State, must be the means by which the violent or otherwise unconstitutional overthrow of governments, whether through secessionist movements or otherwise, can be prevented. This calls for the creation of machinery of practical co-operation in matters of security. In short, it calls for the creation of machinery for regional peacekeeping. If it be the case, as I suggest it to be, that it would impose an intolerable burden on the Associated States to carry separately a physical capability necessary for the maintenance of the State's territorial integrity the only alternatives are recourse to assistance from outside the Region in times of extremity and crisis or regional security machinery. The former is, of course, not a real alternative for such assistance will always carry with it the stigma, and the danger, of external interference. But, by the same token, if we reject that course and do nothing about assembling a regional alternative we merely pander to the forces of fragmentation and invite the dethronement of constitutionalism in the Caribbean.

It is, I suppose, conceivable, although it will surely be extremely difficult, for regional security machinery of the kind I have mentioned to be created on the basis of our present separatist political arrangements. What is obvious is that such machinery will function best if assembled under the roof of regional political unity; if, in fact, it were seen as one of the attributes of Caribbean nationhood.

THE POST-FEDERAL RECORD

In all these respects, therefore, the experience of independence and of Associated Status has served to emphasise not so much our separateness as the inadequacies of our separate existence and, with this awareness, to heighten our sense of Region. Responsive to this experience has come a truly remarkable flowering of regionalism since 1965. Who could have envisaged in those depressing days of 1962 as we went through the processes of disintegration at what came to be known as the "Dissolution Conference" (despite our efforts to hide the realities under the title "Common Services Conference") that within another decade we would have devised and implemented a programme of co-operation which in its impact upon the Region, no less than in its range and depth, would far exceed anything actually accomplished during the life of the Federation itself. Today, this post-federal regional effort presents an impressive record of functional co-operation.

Let us survey this record for a moment. At the Common Services Conference what was salvaged from the regional wreck was the University of the West Indies and the Shipping and Meteorological Services. Little else remained to mark the passing of the gallant ship or of its captain and its crew. Today, we have already celebrated the third anniversary of the Free Trade Area that spans what was the Federation and includes, as well, Belize and Guyana. Today, we have already held the First Annual Meeting of the Board of Governors of the Regional Development Bank, an institution that includes among its regional members all the Member States of the Free Trade Area together with the Bahamas; one that is controlled by the Region and charged with special responsibilities for advancing its economic development. Today, we have at work, as it has been for several years, a regional bureaucracy in the form of the Regional Secretariat administering the Free Trade Area, co-ordinating the agreed programmes of co-operation and preparing the plans for those upon which agreement is being canvassed.

And what a diversity of programmes in fact exist! On the occasion of the Seventh Meeting of the CARIFTA Council, Member Governments signed no less than six Agreements relating to such diverse subjects as legal edu-

cation, a technical assistance programme, interchange of
public service personnel, new arrangements for marketing
oils and fats, the Headquarters of the Secretariat and the
legal capacity, privileges and immunities of the Association. And these are but the latest recruits to an established
regiment that includes among its Members health, plant
quarantine, medical research, the blind, mass media,
census, veterinary control, and, of course, the University,
meteorology and shipping. Hardly a month passes but that
our circumstances dictate the need for further regional
efforts. We are about to conclude agreement on a Common Examinations Council and just this week my own
Government has been considering the establishment of a
regional centre for testing the pharmaceutical standards
of marketed drugs. The point of all this is that the experience of independence and of Associated Status has
impelled us into a major programme of regional co-
operative endeavour. But what of the experience of functional co-operation itself? How should it influence our
regional perspectives?

To answer these questions we need to look closely at
that experience or, rather—since I could not inflict such an
exposition upon you tonight, even assuming I were qualified to deliver it—at some of its relevant highlights. Successes there certainly have been. The Free Trade Association has made an effective start. Regional trade has been
liberalised and West Indian products have taken the places
of non-regional products on the shelves of our supermarkets and in our department stores. Whether it be matches
or paper bags, fruit juices or frozen foods, garments or re-
frigerators, we are increasingly buying CARIFTA. We
have enlarged the domestic market for our manufacturers
and in some, although all too few cases, we have lowered
the price to our consumers. The Regional Development
Bank has quickly established a reputation of banking integrity and is beginning to make available new financial resources for development especially in the Leeward and
Windward Islands.

Perhaps, above all, an almost constant interchange of

information and ideas through regular meetings of Ministers, of officials and of private sector personnel and the increasing regionalisation of our communication media have created an environment of intimacy and of understanding. If we seem to disagree more often than hitherto it is primarily because we have more to do with each other over an ever-widening area of accord. We have come, I believe, to respect each other more as we do business across the table from month to month; almost, from day to day. We have grown less doctrinaire in our respective policy-positions and more understanding of the social, political and economic factors that influence national policy. We have developed a new sense of Region throughout the area and strengthened a regional identity among our people.

FAILURES AND OMISSIONS

These are substantial gains; but it would be indulgence in delusion for us to engage merely in self-congratulation. There is much that we have not done well, and there is so very much more that remains unattempted. Some of our failures are obvious. In general, the full benefits of the creation of a larger domestic market have not been passed on to the West Indian consumer in the form of a better product or a lower price. Too many manufacturers, some still enjoying tax exemptions, misread the objects of the Free Trade Association as being limited to business expansion and enhanced trading profits. All too few have been enlightened enough to recognise the need to bring the employment benefits of expansion and diversification to those areas within the expanded market that have not hitherto attracted industry.

Governments, too, have failed in not ensuring the effective operation of the Agriculture Marketing Protocol whose objectives are to bring to the primary producer of the Region, and more particularly to its farmers and market gardeners, benefits comparable to those which the

CARIFTA Agreement brings to the enterpreneur. In the result, the benefits from CARIFTA have been unevenly distributed throughout the Region—not that uneven distribution was not inevitable in the early years; but enough has not yet been done in respect of the operation of the Agreement itself and the ancillary developments that should have followed to give confidence, or even hope, to the depressed areas of the Region that this imbalance will be redressed.

Let us remember that the freeing of trade was never an end in itself. If all we had set out to do at Dickenson Bay in 1965, when the Agreement was first signed by Antigua, Barbados and Guyana, was to provide a larger market for our secondary industry producers we would have little to our credit. We saw this, certainly we in Guyana saw this, as the first step in a process of economic integration—leading us, that is, to making of our scattered region at least an economic community. Much, therefore, was intended to follow. Little was spelled out as we took those first tentative steps, but by 1967 when the pebble we had thrown from the shore at Dickenson Bay had produced ripples of dialogue throughout the Region it was possible to articulate a programme, and this we did at that important Conference of Heads of Government of the Commonwealth Caribbean countries which was held in Barbados in that year.

The preamble to the CARIFTA Agreement had itself set down as our goal the ultimate creation of a viable economic community. The Resolution of the Conference in which the Governments of the Region committed themselves to membership of the Free Trade Association charted the course toward that goal. Studies were to be initiated immediately on the common external tariff; the principle of regional industries was accepted—that is, the principle of coordinated action in relation to those industries which would require the whole or a large part of the entire regional market on a protected basis if they were to be established at all. It was agreed that a regional policy of incentives to industry should be adopted as early as possible. A location of industries policy was accepted in principle designed to establish more industries in the less developed countries. We agreed to maintain and improve regional carriers within the Region. These were to be the sign-posts along the road to a West Indian economic community. The CARIFTA Agreement was merely the starting point of the journey.

Much work has been done on paper in pursuit of that Resolution. Many studies have been undertaken and some of them have been completed. However, on no single item in that programme which I have just mentioned has there been agreement to act. We have not agreed on a common external tariff. We have not even agreed that we are ready to discuss the Report on it. We have not reached agreement on regional industries or on a location of industries policy. We have not reached agreement on the harmonisation of fiscal incentives; we have failed singularly to establish a regional carrier of the Caribbean, much less to maintain and improve it. It would have been surprising if we could have completed all the necessary studies on all of these matters and had them discussed and agreed upon at a regional level and put into operation by the third anniversary of the operation of the Free Trade Association. What is disappointing, what is disturbing, is that there is not good reason to believe that agreement will be reached on any of these matters within the foreseeable future. This is a serious indictment of us all, and it is not one that I make lightly. I should be surprised, however, if any Minister, indeed, if any official, who has sat, as I have sat, at each of the eight meetings of the Council of the Free Trade Association or at the annual conferences of Caribbean Heads of Government that followed the 1967 meeting in Barbados, would dispute that prognosis.

THE TECHNICIANS ABSOLVED

Let me absolve the technicians of the Region from any responsibility for this. They have served the Region well.

Those responsible for the preparatory studies, like the economists at our Universities, like our colleagues in the Economic Commission for Latin America, have done all we have asked of them and are still at work. Our tireless and dedicated public officers in the Regional Secretariat have laboured long and devotedly in implementation of the Barbados Resolution. The irresolution has been the responsibility of Governments. Some, of course, bear this responsibility to a greater degree than others; but few of us are free of any part of it.

At one end of the scale are Governments who give the impression of being well content with the present benefits of mere free trade—of being unwilling to face even the possibility of sacrifice so that those benefits may be more evenly distributed through a progressive implementation of the Barbados Resolution, through moving on, that is, from merely opening our markets to each other's products to an integration of our economies. At the other end, territories that should be the recipients of benefits under some of these developments have grown sceptical of the programme of integration on the basis of their experience of CARIFTA itself. Some of the scepticism is understandable. Thus the Associated States may legitimately ask what is there in it for them when there is no machinery that distributes to them, directly or indirectly, the benefits of the freeing of trade which accrue to the exporting countries of the Region.

AN IDEOLOGY OF REGIONALISM

If all this is so clear, why is it that we have not made more progress or that we cannot at least hold out a reasonable expectation of progress? I suggest that the explanation lies in the fact that while we have passed resolutions that promise integration, some of us have made no national commitment to it. We have not made that commitment because we have not developed an ideology of regionalism. Pragmatism and expediency have their places in national and regional affairs; but there is a level of collective endeavour—whether at the level of the community, of the State or of the Region—that needs to be supported by belief and by faith; for it is only out of such belief, out of such faith, that will come the type of commitment that produces fundamental change. What we have lacked is that ideology of regionalism and until we develop it, or until those among us who profess it are prepared to act in its pursuit, we will fail to come to grips with the essentials of the programme of integration.

CARIFTA: UPWARD NOT ACROSS

So far I have talked of our failure to move CARIFTA upward from the Free Trade Area toward an economic community. The picture is, however, much worse than that. It would be bad enough if all we faced was delay, however avoidable, in moving upward to a more intimate economic association; but we face the real possibility that while we delay we may be encouraged to take steps that would render vertical development impossible, or at least utterly improbable. Already it has been suggested that what we should be doing is to expand the Free Trade Area horizontally—that is, to broaden its membership by going beyond Commonwealth Caribbean countries. There is more I wish to say later about our relations with Latin America. Suffice it to say at this point that in moving in a direction which dilutes the intimacy of the Association, by introducing at this formative stage States that bring to it totally different social, political and constitutional norms, a new language, a new culture and new methods of operation, we must in the nature of things enormously increase the difficulties of securing consensus for our joint progress upward toward an economic community. Here, certainly, is an important matter for open debate in the Region—for that dialogue on fundamentals which should be the very essence of regionalism.

RETENTION OF THE BANK'S CHARACTER

A not dissimilar problem has arisen in the very early
life of the Regional Development Bank. Here, proposals
for enlarging the regional membership of the Bank by including among its borrowing members Latin American
States bordering on the Caribbean raise questions of profound importance to the character of the institution. We
are at long last developing with the Republics of the Hemisphere those relationships that geography and history or-
dained but which colonialism denied us. At the United
Nations where we work together as Members of the Latin
American Group, in the Economic Commission for Latin
America where we plan together the development of the
Region, and, for those few of us who are within the Organisation of American States and have access to the Inter-
American Development Bank, in those institutions we are
constantly getting to know each other better and to work
out programmes of effective co-operation. We will be
better and more effective partners in Latin America, however, if we first strengthen our unity and consolidate those
institutions designed to promote it. It is unthinkable, certainly it is to us in Guyana, that we could contemplate
arrangements for enlarging the Regional borrowing membership of the Bank in ways that would ensure or even
facilitate a situation in which West Indian Governments
would cease to have that majority control of the Bank
which was a cardinal feature of its establishment. Latin
America will respect us more if we demonstrate pride in
our own institutions and resolution in retaining their basic
character.

Nor is this an inward looking philosophy. There should
be room in the Caribbean Development Bank for Latin
American States. We believe there is already such room;
but, certainly, new accommodation could be made if it
were needed to enable Latin American States to participate
in the Bank on acceptable terms. We would be false to our

history and blind to our future if we provide a preferred place to Britain and Canada in this Bank and deny access to friendly Latin American States. But, we would be false to ourselves and blind to the social, political and economic realities of the West Indies if we did not insist, when we make non-regional membership of the Bank more representative, that the Bank should retain its fundamental character as a West Indian institution and as a West Indian institution committed to the cause of West Indian economic integration. Likewise, I suggest, our Latin American brothers would think us lacking in self-interest, to put it no higher, if we did not seek to ensure that their participation in the Caribbean Development Bank should be on a basis of reciprocity that allows access to the Inter-American Development Bank for all Commonwealth Caribbean States.

THE DISMANTLING OF SEPARATISM

I have suggested earlier in relation to the Free Trade Area that one of the impediments to progress toward integration is the absence of an ideological commitment to regionalism. But the difficulties I have alluded to—whether they be our failure to agree on a regional air carrier or to come to grips with the common external tariff or to take decisions on fiscal incentives, or whether they concern such organic issues as the membership of the Free Trade Area and of the Bank—all these difficulties, have their origins in the realities of separatism. These realities are forever contending for supremacy over the needs of regionalism and eroding our regional commitments as fast as they are made. There is only so much that can represent a common factor of advantage in regional arrangements. Beyond that point—and it is a point that we may well be close to—beyond that point, if commitment to regionalism is to prevail, we shall have to dismantle the realities of separatism. We cannot reach our goals of integration, much less of nationhood, if each of us must weigh every regional enterprise in the scales of local self-interest. It is not, for example,

that an "open skies policy" may not promote the local
interests of a particular island; it is that what will best
serve the interest of the West Indian community should
prevail. It is not whether an enlargement of the Free Trade
Area would not assist industrial expansion in another; it
is that what maximises the benefits of free trade for the
entire Region and advances us to our agreed objectives
should predominate. But so long as our governmental
structures are separatist so long will most Governments
feel obliged to make local self-interest the touch-stone of
regional action. Here again, with the Bank as with the
Free Trade Area, there is need for us to be guided by an
ideology of regionalism. I believe that ideology will develop if we can secure more effective dialogue at all levels
within the Region. In our perspectives for the seventies
the provision of such opportunities for dialogue and the
creation of the institutions for regional decision-making
pursuant to dialogue must occupy a prominent place.

THE URGENCY FOR CHANGE

Nor can this be a leisurely pursuit. To all but those who
will not hear, the Caribbean today reverberates with a
clamant demand for social and economic change. These
voices will not be stilled while West Indian Governments
indulge the semantic luxuries of innumerable conferences
and commissions. They will not be hushed while those who
are resistant to change protract the dialogue in an intermi-
nable filibuster. For the truth is that the challenge of
change which our generation faces is itself that challenge
of nationhood and it is important that we should understand the plea for unity in these terms. Not for the first
time in West Indian history is this plea sounded in the
cause of social and economic justice—it is at one with Marryshow's cry in the nineteen thirties that the "West Indies
must be West Indian". Now, as then, it rises up out of a
ground swell of disaffection with the system and of resentment of its inequities.

Today, the demand is for economic independence at the community level and for social and economic justice at the individual level. That demand is bound up with such questions as ownership and control of West Indian resources—whether these be on or beneath our soils or in or below the waters adjacent to our coasts, our right to be more than primary producers for the industrialised societies of the world, our access to world markets on just terms for all our products, the terms of bilateral and multilateral aid in redress of our legacy of underdevelopment, and, in the end, the quality of life of all our people. Amid the harsh realities of contemporary international existence, economic integration, regionalism, and West Indian nationhood maximise our all too slender chances of success—give us some hope, perhaps our only hope, of meeting the legitimate demands for change that lie behind the protest movements of the Region. The urgency for change is our mandate for unity.

INVOLVEMENT OF THE PEOPLE

Nor must the dialogue of unity be limited to Governments; for if nationhood is to be real and lasting, indeed, if it is to be achieved, the people of the Region must themselves be involved in laying the foundations. Already much work has been done; for the people have been active in the cause of regionalism. Quite outside the range of functional co-operation between Governments, West Indians have been coming together in the conviction that common endeavour is essential to the achievement of their common objectives. Through this process of natural, almost spontaneous, co-operation has emerged a miscellany of regional non-governmental associations which, together, span a remarkable cross-section of West Indian life and activity. Our trade unions were perhaps the pioneers in this pursuit of strength through regional action. Today, they have been joined by many others—by our commercial and manufacturing communities, by our teachers, by our public serv-

ants, by our engineers, by our lawyers, by our nurses, by
our cane farmers, by our clergymen, by our musicians,
by our sportsmen, by our writers, by our broadcasters, and
now, in the year of "Women's Lib", by our women. And
this is by no means an exhaustive catalogue for no list has
yet been compiled, so natural and uncontrived has been
the growth. No less significantly, on the other side of Governments, our radical, reformist and protest groups have
themselves sought coordination and joint action in pursuit
of their "new world". The foundations of nationhood are
truly being laid by the people of the West Indies themselves; they have much to contribute to the building of the
mansion in which we must all dwell.

POLITICAL ASSOCIATION A NECESSITY

But on Governments must fall the major constructive
task. The time, I submit, has come for Governments to
build—to examine again a restructuring of our governmental arrangements so that the decisions that are important to the Region as a region are informed by the interests
of the people of the Region and not merely of its separate
parts. If our developing ideology of regionalism is to be
translated into programmes of practical endeavour, it is
necessary for us to create a governmental environment
which will be more propitious to regional decision-making
than our present arrangements. In short, I suggest the time
has come for us to face the reality that without political
association of some kind we may not be able to carry our
programme of regionalism very much further. What
forms that political association should take is a matter we
shall have to examine closely in the light of all our experience of working together; but especially in the light of the
federal experience. We need to approach this creative task
unencumbered by stereotype constitutional forms. The
uniqueness of our circumstances may well demand new
techniques and new systems. Let us not be afraid of novelty
or of experimentation; for it may be that neither federa-

tions nor confederations nor unitary states will provide satisfactory models for us. Nor should we merely think in terms of super-structures—it may well be that we shall have to dismantle before we can rebuild. I am satisfied that we have in our midst all the talents we need for this creative work; its beginning awaits only our inspiration.

UNANIMITY NOT ESSENTIAL

In saying this I am conscious that not all our Governments, not all our States, not all our people, have the same commitment and that therefore it will not be simple, and may not be possible, to achieve unanimity in the Region on the need to move beyond functional co-operation. But unanimity, while devoutly to be wished, is not essential to progress. CARIFTA would never have been, had we waited for unanimity. Nor should a decision of one or more of our brothers not to proceed at the same pace be the cause of annoyance and antagonism. We have already seen that out of the experience of independence and Associated Status, as well as out of the experience of functional co-operation, has come a closer understanding of each other. Along with this understanding must come a tolerance of a different point of view, and we must be capable not merely of acknowledging a brother's right to disagree but of respecting his judgement in so doing. Differences between us, therefore, on either the pace of the journey toward nationhood or of the journey itself must neither deter those of us who feel committed to it nor allow it to be marred by recriminations at its start.

Have we not reached a stage in our relationships in the Caribbean where we can say to each other with frankness and with mutual respect just where we stand in relation to political unity and whether we can proceed on the basis of such consensus as exists, leaving no doubt as to the welcome that awaits any West Indian State that is unwilling to proceed with us from the beginning? Unless we can be as frank as this with each other, not merely can we not

proceed further, or, at best, at the pace of the slowest, but
our existing relationships will begin to be marred by new
frustrations and our present efforts to be stultified by a
constant process of wrangling over responsibility for our
failures.

A VISION OF THE FUTURE

I submit that the time is at hand—and with so many national elections now out of the way and others soon to be,
that the time is specially propitious—for us to commence a
dialogue of unity in which we shall explore all the possibilities of achieving a realistic West Indian nationhood.
And in our perspectives for the Caribbean let us anticipate
that dialogue and fix on the horizon, as a distant light that
beckons us—the Republic of the West Indies. Let this be
our vision of the future. Some will say that our three
hundred years of inconclusive association establishes West
Indian nationhood as a part of our mythology—a myth in
the folklore of the Caribbean. Others, grown cynical with
the frustrations of the past and the particular disillusion-
ment of the federal experiment, will urge that it is no
more than a mirage, a unity that will forever be in sight
but yet ever out of reach. I suggest to you that West Indian
nationhood can be both real and attainable and that to
make it so has become a mandate of history to our generation. To the carrying out of that mandate we must
bend our energies now—without dogma, without precon-
ditions, without unalterable formulae, without non-
negotiable positions, with a willingness to search for the
right means, with patience in persuasion and with tolerance where we fail to persuade, but with a clear and un-
yielding commitment to the creation of a West Indian
Nation.

II ON BEING A WEST INDIAN

11.

For many West Indians the search for identity involves continual shifts of focus, if not of allegiance. Writing in the late 1940s, Frantz Fanon describes the French West Indian transition from identification with Europe and whiteness to Africa and blackness. This shift, earlier and more emphatic in the French Caribbean than elsewhere, owed much to the towering presence of the father of *négritude*, Aimé Césaire, and to the close association of French West Indians with Africans as students in Paris and as colonial officials in Africa. Fanon also notes the repetition of the West Indian dilemma—seeking acceptance first by Europe and then by Africa and being rejected by each. The last thing many West Indians have wished to be was themselves.

A noted Third World spokesman, FRANTZ FANON was born in Martinique, became a psychiatrist in France, and served in Algeria during the French North African rebellion. His role as a prophet should not obscure the analytic acuity of his observations and his scorn for purely romantic identifications as "solutions" to problems of racial and national identity.

West Indians and Africans[1]
Frantz Fanon

Two years ago I was finishing a work[2] on the problem of
the colored man in the white world. I knew that I must
absolutely not amputate reality. I was not unaware of the
fact that within the very entity of the "Negro people"
movements could be discerned which, unfortunately, were
utterly devoid of any attractive features. I mean, for example, that the enemy of the Negro is often not the white
man but a man of his own color. This is why I suggested
the possibility of a study which could contribute to the
dissolution of the affective complexes that could oppose
West Indians and Africans.

Before taking up the discussion we should like to point
out that this business of Negroes is a dirty business. A business to turn your stomach. A business which, when you
are faced with it, leaves you wholly disarmed if you accept the premises of the Negro-baiters. And when I say
that the expression "Negro people" is an entity, I thereby
indicate that, except for cultural influences, nothing is left.
There is as great a difference between a West Indian and a
Dakarian as between a Brazilian and a Spaniard. The object
of lumping all Negroes together under the designation of

Toward the African Revolution, New York, Grove Press,
1967, pp. 17–27. Copyright © 1967 by Monthly Review Press;
reprinted by permission of Monthly Review Press.

[1] First published in the review *Esprit*, February 1955.

[2] *Peau noire et masques blancs* [Black Skin and White
Masks]. Editions du Seuil, Paris.

"Negro people" is to deprive them of any possibility of individual expression. What is thus attempted is to put them under the obligation of matching the idea one has of them.

Is it not obvious that there can only be a white race? What would the "white people" correspond to? Do I have to explain the difference that exists between nation, people, fatherland, community? When one says "Negro people," one systematically assumes that all Negroes agree on certain things, that they share a principle of communion. The truth is that there is nothing, *a priori*, to warrant the assumption that such a thing as a Negro people exists. That there is an African people, that there is a West Indian people, this I do believe.[3] But when someone talks to me about that "Negro people," I try to understand what is meant. Then, unfortunately, I understand that there is in this a source of conflicts. Then I try to destroy this source.

I shall be found to use terms like "metaphysical guilt," or "obsession with purity." I shall ask the reader not to be surprised: these will be accurate to the extent to which it is understood that since what is important cannot be attained, or more precisely, since what is important is not really sought after, one falls back on what is contingent. This is one of the laws of recrimination and of bad faith. The urgent thing is to rediscover what is important beneath what is contingent.

What is at issue here? I say that in a period of fifteen years a revolution has occurred in West Indian-African relations. I want to show wherein this event consists.

In Martinique it is rare to find hardened racial positions. The racial problem is covered over by economic discrimination and, in a given social class, it is above all productive of anecdotes. Relations are not modified by epidermal accentuations. Despite the greater or lesser

[3] Let us say that the concessions we have made are fictitious. Philosophically and politically there is no such thing as an African people. There is an African world. And a West Indian world as well. On the other hand, it can be said that there is a Jewish people; but not a Jewish race.

amount of melanin that the skin may contain, there is a tacit agreement enabling all and sundry to recognize one another as doctors, tradesmen, workers. A Negro worker will be on the side of the mulatto worker against the middle-class Negro. Here we have proof that questions of race are but a superstructure, a mantle, an obscure ideological emanation concealing an economic reality.

In Martinique, when it is remarked that this or that person is in fact very black, this is said without contempt, without hatred. One must be accustomed to what is called the spirit of Martinique in order to grasp the meaning of what is said. Jankelevitch has shown that irony is one of the forms that good conscience assumes. It is true that in the West Indies irony is a mechanism of defense against neurosis. A West Indian, in particular an intellectual who is no longer on the level of irony, discovers his Negritude. Thus, while in Europe irony protects against the existential anguish, in Martinique it protects against the awareness of Negritude.

It can be seen that a study of irony in the West Indies is crucial for the sociology of this region. Aggressiveness there is almost always cushioned by irony.[4]

It will be convenient for our purpose to distinguish two periods in the history of the West Indies: before and after the war of 1939–45.

BEFORE THE WAR

Before 1939, the West Indian claimed to be happy, or at least thought of himself as being so.[5] He voted, went to school when he could, took part in the processions, liked rum and danced the beguine. Those who were privileged

---

[4] See, for example, the Carnival and the songs composed on this occasion.

[5] We might say: like the French lower middle class at this period, but that is not our point of approach. What we wish to do here is to study the change in attitude of the West Indian with respect to Negritude.

to go to France spoke of Paris, of Paris which meant France. And those who were not privileged to know Paris let themselves be beguiled.

There were also the civil servants working in Africa. Through them one saw a country of savages, of barbarians, of natives, of servants. Certain things need to be said if one is to avoid falsifying the problem. The metropolitan civil servant, returning from Africa, has accustomed us to stereotypes: sorcerers, makers of fetishes, tom-toms, guilelessness, faithfulness, respect for the white man, backwardness. The trouble is that the West Indian speaks of Africa in exactly the same way and, as the civil servant is not only the colonial administrator but the constable, the customs officer, the registrar, the soldier, at every level of West Indian society an inescapable feeling of superiority over the African develops, becomes systematic, hardens. In every West Indian, before the war of 1939, there was not only the certainty of a superiority over the African, but the certainty of a fundamental difference. The African was a Negro and the West Indian a European.

These are things everyone gives the impression of knowing, but which no one takes into account.

Before 1939 the West Indian who volunteered in the Colonial Army, whether he was illiterate or knew how to read and write, served in a European unit, whereas the African, with the exception of the natives of the five territories, served in a native unit. The result to which we wish to draw attention is that, whatever the field considered, the West Indian was superior to the African, of a different species, assimilated to the metropolitan. But inasmuch as externally the West Indian was just a little bit African, since, say what you will, he was black, he was obliged—as a normal reaction in psychological economy—to harden his frontiers in order to be protected against any misapprehension.

We may say that the West Indian, not satisfied to be superior to the African, despised him, and while the white man could allow himself certain liberties with the native, the West Indian absolutely could not. This was because, between whites and Africans, there was no need of a reminder; the difference stared one in the face. But what a catastrophe if the West Indian should suddenly be taken for an African!

We may say also that this position of the West Indian was authenticated by Europe. The West Indian was not a Negro; he was a West Indian, that is to say a quasi-metropolitan. By this attitude the white man justified the West Indian in his contempt for the African. The Negro, in short, was a man who inhabited Africa.

In France, before 1940, when a West Indian was introduced in Bordeaux or Paris society, the introducer always added, "from Martinique." I say "Martinique," because—as people may or may not know—Guadeloupe, for some reason or other, was considered to be a country of savages. Even today, in 1952, we hear Martiniquans insist that they (the natives of Guadeloupe) are more savage than we are.

The African, for his part, was in Africa the real representative of the Negro race. As a matter of fact, when a boss made too great demands on a Martiniquan in a work situation, he would sometimes be told: "If it's a nigger you want, go and look for him in Africa," meaning thereby that slaves and forced labor had to be recruited elsewhere. Over there, where the Negroes were.

The African, on the other hand, apart from a few rare "developed" individuals, was looked down upon, despised, confined within the labyrinth of his epiderm. As we see, the positions were clear-cut: on the one hand, the African; on the other, the European and the West Indian. The West Indian was a black man, but the Negro was in Africa.

In 1939 no West Indian in the West Indies proclaimed himself to be a Negro, claimed to be a Negro. When he did, it was always in his relations with a white man. It was the white man, the "bad white man," who obliged him to assert his color, more exactly to defend it. But it can be affirmed that in the West Indies in 1939 no spontaneous claim of Negritude rang forth.

It was then that three events occurred successively.

The first event was the arrival of Césaire.

For the first time a *lycée* teacher—a man, therefore, who was apparently worthy of respect—was seen to announce quite simply to West Indian society "that it is fine and good to be a Negro." To be sure, this created a scandal. It was said at the time that he was a little mad and his colleagues went out of their way to give details as to his supposed ailment.

What indeed could be more grotesque than an educated man, a man with a diploma, having in consequence understood a good many things, among others that "it was unfortunate to be a Negro," proclaiming that his skin was beautiful and that the *"big black hole"* was a source of truth. Neither the mulattoes nor the Negroes understood this delirium. The mulattoes because they had escaped from the night, the Negroes because they aspired to get away from it. Two centuries of white truth proved this man to be wrong. He must be mad, for it was unthinkable that he could be right.

Once the excitement had died down, everything seemed to resume its normal course . . . And Césaire was about to be proved wrong, when the second event occurred: I am referring to the French defeat.

The downfall of France, for the West Indian, was in a sense the murder of the father. This national defeat might have been endured as it was in the metropolis, but a good part of the French fleet remained blockaded in the West Indies during the four years of the German occupation. This needs to be emphasized. I believe it is essential to grasp the historic importance of those four years.

Before 1939 there were about two thousand Europeans in Martinique. These Europeans had well-defined functions, were integrated into the social life, involved in the country's economy. Now from one day to the next, the single town of Fort-de-France was submerged by nearly ten thousand Europeans having an unquestionable, but until then latent, racist mentality. I mean that the sailors of the *Béarn* or the *Emile-Bertin*, on previous occasions in the course of a week in Fort-de-France, had not had time to manifest their racial prejudices. The four years during

which they were obliged to live shut in on themselves, inactive, a prey to anguish when they thought of their families left in France, victims of despair as to the future, allowed them to drop a mask which, when all is said and
done, was rather superficial, and to behave as "authentic
racists."

It may be added that the West Indian economy suffered
a severe blow, for it became necessary to find—again without any transition—at a time when nothing could be imported, the wherewithal to feed ten thousand men. Moreover, many of those sailors and soldiers were able to send
for their wives and children, who had to be housed. The
Martiniquan held those white racists responsible for all this.
The West Indian, in the presence of those men who despised him, began to have misgivings as to his values. The
West Indian underwent his first metaphysical experience.

Then came Free France. De Gaulle, in London, spoke
of treason, of soldiers who surrendered their swords even
before they had drawn them. All this contributed to convincing the West Indians that France, *their* France, had
not lost the war but that traitors had sold it out. And where
were these traitors, if not camouflaged in the West Indies?
One then witnessed an extraordinary sight: West Indians
refusing to take off their hats while the *Marseillaise* was
being played. What West Indian can forget those Thursday evenings when on the Esplanade de la Savane, pa-
trols of armed sailors demanded silence and attention while
the national anthem was being played? What had happened?

By a process easy to understand, the West Indians had
assimilated the France of the sailors into the bad France,
and the *Marseillaise* that those men respected was not their
own. It must not be forgotten that those sailors were racists. Now "everybody knows that the true Frenchman is
not a racist; in other words, he does not consider the West
Indian a Negro." Since these men did so consider him,
this meant that they were not true Frenchmen. Who
knows, perhaps they were Germans? And as a matter of
fact, the sailor was systematically considered as a German.

But the consequence that concerns us is the following: before ten thousand racists, the West Indian felt obliged to defend himself. Without Césaire this would have been difficult for him. But Césaire was there, and people joined him in chanting the once-hated song to the effect that it is fine and good to be a Negro! . . .

For two years the West Indian defended his "virtuous color" inch by inch and, without suspecting it, was dancing on the edge of a precipice. For after all, if the color black is virtuous, I shall be all the more virtuous the blacker I am! Then there emerged from the shadows the very black, the "blues," the pure. And Césaire, the faithful bard, would repeat that "paint the tree trunk white as you will, the roots below remain black." Then it became real that not only the color black was invested with value, but fiction black, ideal black, black in the absolute, primitive black, the Negro. This amounted to nothing less than requiring the West Indian totally to recast his world, to undergo a metamorphosis of his body. It meant demanding of him an axiological activity in reverse, a valorization of what he had rejected.

But history continued. In 1943, weary of an ostracism to which they were not accustomed, irritated, famished, the West Indians, who had formerly been separated into closed sociological groups, broke all barriers, came to an agreement on certain things, among others that those Germans had gone too far and, supported by the local army, fought for and won the rallying of the colony to the Free French. Admiral Robert, "that other German," yielded. And this leads us to the third event.

It can be said that the demonstrations on the occasion of the Liberation, which were held in the West Indies, in any case in Martinique, in the months of July and August 1943, were the consequence of the birth of the proletariat. Martinique for the first time systematized its political consciousness. It is logical that the elections that followed the Liberation should have delegated two communist deputies out of three. In Martinique, the first metaphysical, or if one prefers, ontological experiment, coincided with the

first political experiment. Auguste Comte regarded the proletarian as a systematic philosopher. The proletarian of
Martinique is a systematized Negro.

AFTER THE WAR

Thus the West Indian, after 1945, changed his values.
Whereas before 1939 he had his eyes riveted on white
Europe, whereas what seemed good to him was escape
from his color, in 1945 he discovered himself to be not
only black but a Negro, and it was in the direction of
distant Africa that he was henceforth to put out his feelers.
The West Indian in France was continually recalling that
he was not a Negro: from 1945 on, the West Indian in
France was continually to recall that he *was* a Negro.

During this time the African pursued his way. He was
not torn; he did not have to situate himself simultaneously
with reference to the West Indian and with reference to
the European. These last belonged in the same bag, the
bag of the starvers, of the exploiters, of the no-goods. To
be sure, there had been Eboué, who though a West Indian, had spoken to the Africans at the Brazzaville conference and had called them "my dear brothers." And
this brotherhood was not evangelical; it was based on color.
The Africans had adopted Eboué. He was one of them.
The other West Indians could come, but their pretensions
to superiority were known. But to the Africans' great as-
tonishment, the West Indians who came to Africa after
1945 appeared with their hands stretched out, their backs
bowed, humbly suppliant. They came to Africa with their
hearts full of hope, eager to rediscover the source, to suckle
at the authentic breasts of the African earth. The West
Indians, civil servants and military, lawyers and doctors,
landing in Dakar, were distressed at not being sufficiently
black. Fifteen years before, they said to the Europeans,
"Don't pay attention to my black skin, it's the sun that has
burned me, my soul is as white as yours." After 1945 they
changed their tune. They said to the Africans, "Don't pay

attention to my white skin, my soul is as black as yours, and that is what matters."

But the Africans were too resentful of them to allow them so easy a turnabout. Recognized in their blackness, in their obscurity, in what fifteen years before had been sin, they resented any encroachment on the West Indian's part in this realm. They discovered themselves at last to be the possessors of truth, centuries-old bearers of an incorruptible purity. They rejected the West Indian, reminding him that *they* had not deserted, that *they* had not betrayed, that *they* had toiled, suffered, struggled on the African earth. The West Indian had said no to the white man; the African was saying no to the West Indian.

The latter was undergoing his second metaphysical experience. He then suffered despair. Haunted by impurity, overwhelmed by sin, riddled with guilt, he was prey to the tragedy of being neither white nor Negro.

He wept, he composed poems, sang of Africa, of Africa the hard and the beautiful, Africa exploding with anger, tumultuous bustle, splash, Africa land of truth. At the Institute of Oriental Languages in Paris he learned Bambara. The African, in his majesty, rejected all approaches. The African was getting his revenge and the West Indian was paying . . .

If we now try to explain and summarize the situation, we may say that in Martinique, before 1939, there was not on one side the Negro and on the other side the white man, but a scale of colors the intervals of which could readily be passed over. One needed only to have children by someone less black than oneself. There was no racial barrier, no discrimination. There was that ironic spice, so characteristic of the Martinique mentality.

But in Africa the discrimination was real. There the Negro, the African, the native, the black, the dirty, was rejected, despised, cursed. There an amputation had occurred; there humanity was denied.

Until 1939 the West Indian lived, thought, dreamed (we have shown this in *Black Skin, White Masks*), composed poems, wrote novels exactly as a white man would have done. We understand now why it was not possible for him, as for the African poets, to sing the black night, "The black woman with pink heels." Before Césaire, West Indian literature was a literature of Europeans. The West Indian identified himself with the white man, adopted a white man's attitude, "was a white man."

After the West Indian was obliged, under the pressure of European racists, to abandon positions which were essentially fragile, because they were absurd, because they were incorrect, because they were alienating, a new generation came into being. The West Indian of 1945 is a Negro.

In *Cahier d'un retour au pays natal* (logbook of a return to the native land) there is an African period, for on page 49 we read:

By dint of thinking of the Congo
I have become a Congo humming with forests and rivers

Then, with his eyes on Africa, the West Indian was to hail it. He discovered himself to be a transplanted son of slaves; he felt the vibration of Africa in the very depth of his body and aspired only to one thing: to plunge into the great "black hole."

It thus seems that the West Indian, after the great white error, is now living in the great black mirage.

12.

The transition from European tutelage to an awakening pride in African heritage, earlier described by Fanon, is also the theme of this essay by a young British West Indian. The author contends that efforts to evoke West Indian pride in African identity are being thwarted by a colored middle class still devoted to white and European standards.

KERWYN L. MORRIS, a graduate of the University of the West Indies, returned from Jamaica to teach in his home island, St. Vincent.

On Afro–West Indian Thinking
Kerwyn L. Morris

Vincentians like many other West Indians suffer from a very deep-seated European orientation. An orientation that is historical in origin and reflects a negative relationship. A relation that we do not want to be reminded of—a relationship between slave and master.

Such an orientation can do no good for us as Afro-West Indians. I say Afro-West Indians for that is what we are. We are a people basically of African stock whether we want to accept this or not. But it is no direct fault of ours that we, a black people, are European in our orientation. Our orientation is the product of slavery and the deliberate doings of those British imperialists who, in drawing up our education syllabuses refused to include any mention of great black West Indians like Toussaint L'Ouverture, Marcus Garvey, Sylvester Williams, George Padmore, and C. L. R. James, to name but a few. We were never told of these men, so that in our search for heroes as youngsters we found our men in imperialists like William the Conqueror, Benjamin Disraeli and Winston Churchill.

Further we were never told of the true history of the land whence we were brought—Black Africa our fatherland. We were never told that Black Africa was more civilised than Europe throughout history and so we were robbed of the black pride that our forefathers brought with them when they arrived in chains. We were never

Flambeau (Kingstown, St. Vincent), No. 4, April 1966, pp. 12–30. Reprinted with permission of the author.

told that it was as a result of contact with Europeans that the glorious path of African development was altered. We were never told that centuries before the Europeans discovered the world was round our fathers made their pilgrimages to Mecca crossing the Sahara Desert from the ancient empires of Ghana, Mali and Songhai in West Africa, using the stars for guidance. We were never told of the black kings and queens whose armies defeated early European attempts to capture us. But instead, to facilitate and prolong our subservience and oppression, to this day we were told that we were cannibals and savages. Had we been exposed to Garvey and had our parents been more attentive when he spoke at our library in Kingstown, they might have followed him up and learned from him that "when Europe was inhabited by a race of cannibals, a race of savages, naked men, heathens and pagans, Africa was peopled with a race of cultured black men, who were masters in art, science, and literature, cultured and refined." And as Garvey also said and which unadulterated anthropological history proves true,

> Out of cold old Europe these white men came,
> From caves, dens, and holes, without any fame,
> Eating their dead's flesh and sucking their blood,
> Relics of a Mediterranean flood

So that our black fathers were once great and proud men but we shall never be as great or as proud of ourselves as they were of themselves until we learn to think independently. Until we learn to think as Afro-West Indians as we truly are and not as Euro-West Indians. As Garvey further said "We have a beautiful history and we shall create another in the future that will astonish the world." West Indians need to discover their long lost black pride which was so systematically removed by the same people who have us in colonial bondage up to this day, so that there is not the remotest possibility of asserting one's West Indian personality while embracing a European orientation. The latter must be dispensed with.

There is in our midst an abundance of hypocrites and black Uncle Toms who very often cannot see any further than their noses. These are the most dangerous elements of our society and the greatest obstacles to change. The so-called middle-class or black bourgeoisie is their breeding ground. They flourish there. Lately these elements have been brandishing lip-service to West-Indianisation yet they are found to be more European than the Europeans themselves. They make their frequent trips to their "Mother Country", then stand aloft on the Swiss Alps next door and look down with disdain upon the mass of black humanity. They become white like the surrounding snow for a moment. For them the well-dressed West-Indian is one who chokes himself with a tie (the symbol of and replacement for the chains that once squeezed our necks) and suffocates in a jacket. To further express my disgust with this manner of dress and terms of reference, I shall quote a poet from French Guiana, Léon Damas who in his poem called "Balance Sheet" said:

I feel ridiculous
in their shoes, in their dinner jackets,
in their stiff shirts, their paper collars,
with their monocles and their bowler hats.
I feel ridiculous
with my toes that were not made
to sweat from morning to evening,
in their swaddling clothes that weaken my limbs
and deprive my body of its beauty.

The same reactionary elements because of their orientation and its accompanying shortcomings and pettymindedness are thus rendered grossly incapable of recognising the true and full value of a successful Afro-West Indian when they are presented with one. However, I ask those who are weathering the storm "to hold strain" for it would not be long before others return to join in the struggle against these black middle-class humbugs—the enemies of progress. Progress for them means the usage of foreign personnel in preference to nationals when nationals are available; the fools and idiots have never been taught to value anything of their own origin.

As the elections draw nigh there is talk of West Indian-ising St. Vincent through the use of text-books with a West Indian orientation. This may be adequate for those people of school age and those out of school who could actually read. But what about those who cannot read, how are they to be West-Indianised? It will have to be by action rather than by spoken or written word and I am afraid there is no half-way measure where action is concerned, for action knows no compromise. How can we talk to them of West-Indian orientation and at the same time leave the dry-rotten faded out portraits of European Governors, queens and kings in our livingrooms? How can we go to Victoria Park and present arms to the British National Anthem and still talk of West Indianisation to these peo-ple? The very name of the park must be changed, the anthem must be discarded for it was never intended to save us from damnation but only the sovereign. Can't we see it calls only for our continued subjection—"long to reign over us?" Can't we see that this is inviting continued oppression and subservience? Imagine the sons and daugh-ters of Britain's slaves singing "Rule Britannia . . . . Brit-ons never shall be slaves!" Are we out of minds or some-thing? Britain never shall be enslaved we lustily sing, while we are still held in colonial bondage by her. And we are proud to sing this for the reward of a heavy-bread and a hot sweet-drink? Poor us! Brass medals must be returned or refused or given to the 'yeah-yeah' boys, and there must be concerted efforts aimed at dispensing with the Queen's Birthday Parade. The island must be renamed Hairoun, its original name. I strongly feel that it is only by methods such as these that mass mobilisation and complete West Indianisation can be achieved. Are we prepared to use these methods? West Indianisation calls for positive ac-tion now rather than idle words.

To old colonial stooges this stinks with disloyalty and disrespect, but they must know that the concept of loyalty was one of the tools that forged a success out of colonial-

ism. The more loyal you are the more colonised and subservient you are. Are we content to remain colonised and
subservient? No! There is thus a choice to be made. One
cannot remain colonial minded and be truly West-
Indianised at the same time, and since the choice is for
the latter then the former must take its exit and the sooner
the better. We can never assert our true selves under a
colonial mentality. If we want to be true Afro-West Indians then down with colonialism and all its symbols and
stooges.

13.

This essay by a young Trinidadian of East Indian descent counterpoises the previous article. While basically sympathetic to the reformist and egalitarian aims of the current Black Power movement, the author denounces black West Indians who slight or ignore local expressions of East Indian identity. In his view, it is absurd to expect East Indians to regard themselves as "black," when black connotes "African"; he feels that East Indians can contribute most by emphasizing their cultural uniqueness and spiritual virtues.

By the Light of a Deya
K. V. Parmasad

> *If you are an East Indian*
> *And you want to be an African*
> *Just shave yuh head just like me*
> *And nobody would guess your nationality*

Lord Brynner, "our" Independence calypso King, in his winning calypso, suggests a very simple and convenient way for Indians to become Africans. He suggests that we simply shave our heads as bald as his, and no one would be able to guess our "nationality".

Though most unsatisfactory and naive, this is one solution to the problem of identity in our society. And, in spite of its superficiality, this is in no way contradictory to the belief commonly shared by many in this society. There are those who harbour the hope, the expectation and the foregone conclusive belief that Indians are the ones who must strip themselves clean of all traces of their identity—cultural, social, religious and otherwise—and submerge themselves unhesitatingly, in a social order that refuses to recognise and is openly hostile towards patterns of thought and behaviour, not in keeping with those patterns established during the colonial period.

Since the Africans, for historical reasons too well known, are the direct inheritors of this colonial order,

Tapia, No. 22, November 7, 1971, pp. 5, 8. Reprinted by permission of Tapia House Publishing Company, Tunapuna, Trinidad.

Brynner's solution is understandable. But this does not make it acceptable to the vast majority of Indians. For no solution to so noble a quest that comes so easily can be trusted to stand the ravages of time. Because identity, in the broadest sense, has to do more with how a people think than how they look. It has to do not with masquerading as someone else but discovering and revealing the true self. Especially, it has to do with how a people regard themselves in their society and the world; the particular way in which they assess their relationships individually and collectively, in the cosmos.

To boast of a national identity here, is to live in a world of make-believe. To claim that we are all one is to ignore the stark realities of the present. To ignore the presence of any one group is to sow the seeds of future conflict, discord and chaos. And the future society can afford none of these. This is why the quest must go on relentlessly. Even more so, this is why we must channel and direct our energies along such lines so that the total result of all our efforts would reflect the unified consciousness of all our peoples.

Even though we realise the inevitability of human groups learning from each other, and the necessity for this to be so, our intention is not to "Indianize" anyone. Far from it! Likewise, we will not tolerate any attempt to "ize" us in any form or fashion not in harmony with our "native selves". We will resist everlastingly, any attempts by others to deny us this sacred right of self-assertion by attempting to force us to the point of "self-denial".

Our out-moded politicians, hunting for votes through deceit and deception, trying hard but in vain to impress the hungry masses, are in the habit of speaking of the "new national identity of Trinidad and Tobago". But what national identity can we, Indians, be proud of when the culture of 40% of our people is denied its rightful place and recognition it deserves; when the vast majority of our people exist on the fringes of society and are considered as possessing nothing more than nuisance value?

The established order in this society belongs to a dying era; an era during which Indians were pushed into the background of our social life and were recognised only when it was convenient and advantageous for others to do so. Even then it was, and still is, more in the form of tokenism than genuine regard. But this never worried the Indian to any great extent. In the meantime he has been working hard and building silently but steadily from the crude earth with his bare hands. He knows overnight solutions will never work, this quality has been imbued in him by his culture. Sacrifice, self-sacrifice, is a cornerstone of Hinduism. And he is still building in spite of the odds deliberately placed in his way.

The entire social system was geared, and still is, so as to keep the Indian out, unless of course he was prepared to strip himself of his name, his religion, his culture, his language, his history and become what the system demanded—that is, Christianized, Westernized, colonized, dehumanized. Many fell, unsuspecting victims of circumstance. Many, many more stood firm, prepared to fight in their own inimitable way, the tensions and strains created by the established order.

Today, this struggle still goes on among the mass of the Indian population. Out of this struggle will emerge a new order in this land. Those who think that the Governmental, official and administrative response to the upsurge of black (African) consciousness is the making of a new social order, are sadly and tragically mistaken. No new order will ever emerge so long as the society fails to come to terms with the fact of the Indians and so long as it refuses to deal them equally the rights as citizens of this country. The new society will only come when Indians are recognised and accepted for what they are rather than for what others would want to make of them.

Every group has a part to play in forging this new identity and every group must be recognised for the part it plays. This is the level at which we must begin. However, countless occurrences every day, on an individual and

national plane provoke doubts as to whether we have
started at this level.

Merle Hodge (writing in *Tapia* of August 15) strikes
a vital note when she comments upon the "gross disrespect
and bad manners" openly displayed by members present
at the recent Chaguaramas Conference on Education when
"an intrepid Indian Trinidadian thought fit to preface his
contribution with a prayer of his religion". According to
Miss Hodge, the grand majority of those very people who
felt justified in parading their prejudices in the public but
who, "when the various Christian clergy prayed on our
behalf, bowed their heads and made their signs of the
Cross, were registering their allegiance to more than religion".

But she goes still further and sounds the heart of the
matter: "Officially, the society still recognizes only the
norms of the White Western 'Christian' world, that is
the norms overlaid on the society by its colonizers. Those
who do not necessarily subscribe in toto, that is, at least
40% of the society—at a modest estimate—are here on
sufferance, or at best occasional, condescending recognition".

This truth is so obvious that any deviation from the set
pattern is considered abnormal and out of place. When
Indians stand up and demand their rights they are branded
"racists". For fifteen years they have been totally neglected
by the government, yet, whenever an attempt is made by
Indians to help alleviate the sufferings of Indians we are
branded "separatists". But anyone can speak about better-
ing the lot of the "black man"—meaning African, ask
Wooding, not any of those advocates of "blackness" who
find it convenient and expedient to say that Indians are
included—without being a racist. But the moment one
speaks in favour of the Indian he is confronted with a
wall of hate, suspicion, indifference, contempt, hostility,
antagonism and open, brass-faced racism and discrimination.

So much so that there are Indians in this society who
are possessed by the erroneous conviction that being as

little Indian as possible and being as much Afro-Saxon, Afro-American or any other thing is being truly "Trinidadian". But this blatant denial of self is what creates the "mimic-man". Too often we think that to discard, condemn and ridicule unthinkingly and indiscriminately, every characteristic of our "native selves" is a sure sign of progress. This is not a quality of the mind that is "free and articulate". On the contrary it is an unmistakable sign of self-delusion and cultural onanism.

But let us not be disheartened and fall easy prey to the ever-present and provoking temptations that conspire against us every day, to lure us on unsuspectingly and to make us strangers unto ourselves. Let us not be too quick to discard, condemn and consider irrelevant, the religion and culture of our foreparents. Let us be sure that we do not discard the good along with the bad in exchange for something worse. Let us instead give the culture of our parents an equal chance in our lives, let us begin to study the religion of the Hindus before we feel qualified to pass judgement upon it. Let us not be fooled by the immediacy of the West that leaves us hollow inside.

No one is advocating that we return to India. But it is necessary that we, the Indians of the West—West Indians in the truest sense—should come to terms with what we have here, not discard it. We must dig deep into the farthest recesses of our consciousness as a people and discover our true selves, tapping if necessary the limitless reserve at the source of our culture. We cannot and must not deny the future social order, this, our most lasting and significant contribution in the creation of the new society.

In spite of the innumerable obstacles that will baulk our progress; in spite of the open and unofficial state-sanctioned racism practised against us, this fair land will feel and respond favourably to the full impact of Indian culture and civilization—for its own good and future progress. Time-tested virtues and ideals that have shaped the lives of so many of the greatest souls that have walked this earth, through countless ages, will sink their roots deep into our soil and fill the air with the fragrance of beautiful flowers. Christians will learn from us, Hindus, the much needed tolerance that they do not show to others who do not worship God as they do.

There is the belief among some Indians that we must protect what we have while we are unsure of what we will "get". While it is necessary and vital that we preserve and protect what we have it is no less important that our actions are the results of positive, not negative, motives. Indians must no longer be satisfied merely to accept what others throw at us. We must discard the idea of "getting". Our task must be to set out and create here a culture that we can identify with in some meaningful way. It is only when we fail to take up the challenge and refuse to face up to this vital task that we can speak in terms of what we are going to "get".

We must make of this land and its still unformed culture something that our children will be able to identify with without pawning their souls in the process. To wait submissively on what we will "get" is a defeatist position to assume. Then we will have no one but ourselves to blame if what we "get" is not what we desire. The weak are always the vanquished and Indian culture forbids us to be weak. The culture of our fathers has outlived the stresses and strains of thousands of years. Whereas other ancient cultures have disappeared under the weight of time (in Egypt only the Pyramids stand), Indian culture lives on and as Gandhi said, "though ancient it is yet not old". We in this land are the inheritors of this culture, we are the transporters of this way of life to these parts. We must not fail to nurse this land with nourishment that our infant nation hungers for.

Indians, especially the young, must take up the urgent task of re-defining their positions in this society—on all fronts. For too long have we had our positions defined for us, always to our disadvantage. With the quickening of time, if this task is not pursued with purpose and dedication, tomorrow will be worse than today. Traditional areas of involvement have to be critically re-examined and strengthened and new areas have to be explored with purpose. No aspect of our lives, collective and individual, must be spared the rigour of criticism and examination. We are extremely fortunate in that we have an unbroken and continuous flood of culture from the earliest up to the present time, from which we can draw our inspiration and strength.

If this society must be a more humane one, the colonial and materialistic systems of thought and values of the decaying and decadent West must be re-adjusted. Christianity has been the religion of the colonizers and has stained its hands with the blood of our peoples. It identified itself with, shut its eyes to, upheld and propagated many of the very values that we are now striving to shed. The Christian Church in these parts can change its garb but not its history. More and more the West is awakening to the universality, profundity and relevance of Indian religion, philosophy and culture. We are fortunate to have here the largest single group of Indians in the West. This makes our responsibility even greater yet and so also must be our influence.

To fail in this task is not simply to fail ourselves, but to fail the future West Indian peoples. We cannot fail; we must not fail, if the future society is to be strengthened not weakened by our presence in these parts. We have a sacred obligation towards the future society. To abscond is to commit a grave injustice which posterity will find it difficult to forgive.

It is customary, I know, to refer to this society as a Christian one. But this is understandable since the establishment has always been Christian and the Church always identified with the establishment. But this is as much an untruth as the dogmatic belief commonly held by those who like to consider themselves Christian, that all non-Christians are heathens, pagans and what you like and are therefore doomed to everlasting hell.

This flagrant lack of tolerance, this narrow-mindedness and even this open contempt shown by professed Christians, is reflected not only in the sphere of religion but also, more importantly, by those who administer the business of the State. But this makes the task even more urgent. Our society is not a Christian one and non-Christians have a significant role to play in ironing out the gross inconsistencies that hinder the evolution of a more humane order.

In a wider perspective ours is the struggle of the entire society. The struggle of the Indians is against an already deeply entrenched bacchanalian culture. What we must ensure is that we are not lost in it beyond recognition but that we contribute fully and fundamentally in the creation of something new, relevant and meaningful.

We must not deny the future order, the grace, the strength, the elasticity, the depth, the humility and tolerance, the wisdom, spirituality and timelessness of the culture our parents transported to these distant shores. Neither must we preserve and foster Indian culture for ourselves alone. Then it becomes useless, for one lifetime is short and fleeting and another might take us to some other shore. But society continues even after we have lived this life and man will still live on and will always seek the light.

We light our deyas not only in our homes but also in the public squares. So when we illumine our lives with the culture of our fathers, the society is illumined too. And with just one lighted deya we can light a million more. So to deprive ourselves of this light is to deprive our society of that extra light that it needs to illumine the difficult paths at night.

I have often heard it said that Indian culture bears little relevance to this society. But this statement comes more out of the depth of ignorance than unbiased conviction. I can understand if such a statement is made in terms of our education system, our economics, our politics, etc., but definitely and emphatically not when referring to Indian culture; not when more than 40% of our population are of Indian origin and relate meaningfully and unwaveringly to the basics of Indian culture.

Our religion and culture must be the supreme revolutionary force in our lives. Ours is a revolution that must begin from within our minds based on firm convictions and clear insights. From there it will make itself manifest in the wider society. Nothing, not even guns, can stall our peoples' march to liberation, if first our minds are liberated through a deep and purposeful understanding of self and an elevation of consciousness. This must be our aim.

The quick, now-for-now attempts at liberation that we see around are dangerous, not because of the violence, but because it instills in the minds of the masses, false values. It makes us believe that the change of the Head of State, the change of external structures and formulas is the answer for a better world. It tends to remove the emphasis from within ourselves and makes the external, material tools the prime movers for change and progress. Or, it throws too heavy a burden, too suddenly upon our unaccustomed shoulders, a burden which we are unable to bear comfortably for too long.

This is why such attempts at instant liberation invariably replace the order that it sought to expel by an order that is equally vicious if not more so. Liberate the mind, and external liberation follows as inevitably as the day follows the night. Liberate the externals first, and the enslaved mind will continue to apply old patterns of responses to new stimuli and the rot remains, no less stinking than it ever was.

The role of the Indian is not to deny the future society the innumerable virtues of Indian culture but to ensure that it carries unmistakable traits of the Indian character.

Africans in the West are engaged in the frantic but the vitally necessary quest for their forgotten roots. Who among us can justly and sincerely suggest that the Indian should cut his roots or be the sacrificial lamb in this quest for a highly elusive national identity? Who can rightly demand of us what they would not demand of themselves?

14.

This essay, the 1970 graduation address at the Barbados campus of the University of the West Indies, views the search for a special West Indian identity as often fruitless or misguided. While sympathizing with the desire for identity, Professor Lewis concludes that whatever may be uniquely West Indian is not worth celebrating, except, perhaps, in the realm of the arts. He argues that West Indians will do better to model themselves after what they find best in each aspect of their multifaceted heritage.

W. ARTHUR LEWIS is identified on page 214.

On Being Different
W. Arthur Lewis

A constant theme in today's West Indies is that we should stop imitating other peoples, and do our own thing. We should be different, and West Indian. It is an attractive theme; has indeed become almost a bandwagon theme; every other public speaker takes the chance of recording his adherence to it. I too want to get into this popular stream, but I am also a little more anxious to find out just what it is all about. Obviously West Indians cannot be different from other men in everything, since we all belong to *homo sapiens*, so one has to ask where we should draw the line; in what respects should we be the same as other peoples, and in what respects should we strive to be different?

My only qualification for talking about this subject is that I have probably thought about it more than most other West Indians. Since no job was available for me here when I graduated, I have had to spend most of my life out of the West Indies. And in striving to earn my living in the great wide world I have had to try to master the highly competitive skills of my profession. In the process I have become what is now called in the West Indies an Afro-Saxon. The term is meant to be abusive, but what in practice it seems to mean is a black man who can hold his own in competition with white people on their own ground.

University of the West Indies graduation address, February 5, 1971, Cave Hill, Barbados. Used by permission of the author.

Facing this difficult challenge, I have had to ask myself
over and over again over the past thirty years what sort
of person I ought to be trying to be. West Indian, yes, but
just what does this mean that is intended to distinguish
us from other human beings?

Obviously one must not take to its extreme conclusion
the proposition that West Indians must live differently
from other men. If so, it would be wrong for Barbadians
to play cricket, which is an Englishman's invention; or if
Barbadians do play cricket, they should make their own
special rules. Taken to the extreme, the proposition would
prevent Trinidadians from playing in steel-bands, since the
steel from which the instruments are made comes from
iron ores which are not found in Trinidad. Trinidadians
should make music instead exclusively from bamboos,
which grow luxuriantly in that island, and which make
splendid musical instructions.

I do not wish to make fun of the proposition that we
should be different, which, as I have said I accept: I am
merely emphasising the fact that the proposition is not as
universal as some make it out to be. There are people
who worry at the level of the commodities we use, and
insist that it is wrong to use imported materials, or to eat
imported food—which to me seems an economic question
rather than one for nationalist emotions. Other people are
het up about the clothes we wear, or about our hairstyles,
which seem to me to be trivial and ever-changing phenomena which are hardly worth the glance of the philosopher or statesman, even though I recognise that difference in these respects gives emotional comfort to a great
many people: men have fought bitterly about the wearing
of a turban. That we should be different seems to me a
good proposition, and yet one which is easily nonsensical
or trivial, unless one defines rather carefully what it is we
are to differ in.

Before I tackle this question let me first note that the
ground is not entirely occupied by Afro-Saxons and the
advocates of an exclusively West Indian culture. We have
in our midst a third group who advocate that we should

model ourselves on the Africans, since Africa is where most of our fathers came from some two centuries ago. I will leave aside the complication that there are more Indians than Africans in Guyana and nearly as many Indians as Africans in Trinidad—and follow the proponents of this idea in arguing as if West Indians were all descended from Africa.

Even with this fatal simplification, the proposition is hardly meaningful, and always bemuses Africans who make its acquaintance. In the first place, Africa is the most diversified of all the continents in terms of strictly indigenous institutions, languages, food patterns, clothes or any other index which you care to choose. There are hundreds of tribal and national groups, very different from each other, so there is no unique African model that West Indians could imitate. In the second place Africans themselves are trying hard to get into the modern world, and are in the process of shedding a great number of the characteristics which they developed in isolation. The idea that we should choose as models what they are discarding seems to them a little quaint. To use the popular jargon, the Africans are having as big a crisis of identity as we are. In stretching out to them we shall find sympathy and understanding, but hardly remedies for the condition in which we both find ourselves.

However, let me come back to my theme, the proposition that we strive to be ourselves, not Englishmen or Africans or Indians or Chinese, but West Indians.

Different in what ways? Since we are not racists, we are committed to the proposition that we are essentially the same as other men. Societies differ not in the underlying humanity, but in what they make of themselves and of their environment. What differs is the human achievement. So when we say that West Indians are to be different, we mean that they must make something different—our achievement must be unique.

In framing the problem in this way I am automatically ruling out what is in practice the most obvious difference between peoples, namely their manners and customs, especially their clothes, language, accent, mannerisms and food. Here for instance is a standard anthropological problem. When you meet your friend should you shake hands with him? The traditional answer is: If he is an American, Yes. If he is an Englishman, No. If he's a Frenchman, shake hands with him every five minutes. When we say that a man is typically German, or Chinese, or that we can always recognise a West Indian on the streets of Harlem, it is to these superficial characteristics that we refer.

Inevitably, manners have strong local roots and differ from place to place. Inevitably the local manners are menaced by foreign importations, and inevitably local conservatives and local revolutionaries get very excited with every new importation. Traditionally it used to be the most highly educated and well travelled who were least identifiable by these local mannerisms, since they tend to follow the precept that when in Rome one does as the Romans do; but today, thanks to records, television and films, it is the masses of the population who seem to be quickest in adopting the new international life styles of the world's young adults, and the whole world is now coming to look and sound alike.

No doubt West Indians will and should evolve their own ever-changing systems of manners, but this is not what we have to examine. The charge against the Afro-Saxon is not that he does not dress like a West Indian or speak with a West Indian accent, but that he does not *think* like a West Indian. Hence our question has to be: how should West Indian thinking differ from other thinking? And to answer it we have to look at the whole realm of human thought, and to ask what opportunities it offers for national characteristics. This is a very appropriate question for a university community, since thought is our stock in trade.

The human achievement is all the product of thought, applied to work. It is rather small. Man has existed for a million years, but it is only within the last 5,000 years that we have made significant progress. This is because nature is hard and cruel, and has had to be fought every step of the way. The fight has not been led by any one nation; nations have had very little to do with it, and nationalism has been more often destructive than helpful. Individuals of many nations have contributed, each building on the work of his predecessors from many different nations at many different times. What has resulted from this is a body of knowledge which is now the heritage of all mankind. This knowledge divides into three areas—first, knowledge of how phenomena work, which includes the natural and social sciences; secondly, moral knowledge, or if you like, opinion as to how human beings are to behave towards each other if human society is to be tolerable; and thirdly aesthetic knowledge, or how to be creative in the arts. Each of these three kinds of knowledge combines elements of universality with some opportunity for differences between national groups.

Let us take first science, natural and social. The evolution of natural science was delayed for a long time by prejudice, or as we would now say by lack of objectivity. Indeed the very notion that science should try to be objective was bitterly resisted, by those who thought that we should accept only results which seemed consistent with what was already revealed about God. Science was to serve religion, or as we might now say, to serve the purpose of history. The social sciences are fighting the same struggle today against those, including many social scientists, who not only deny that social scientists can be objective, but also argue that they should not try to be objective, since their science should serve the purposes of history. If they are right, social science would differ from society to society; but they are not right. Genuine social scientists, gathered together from all parts of the world, have no difficulty in understanding each others' concepts, and in my profession of economics we have found that any tool which is illuminating in one part of the world—like monetary theory or linear programming or the discounting of future returns—is equally illuminating everywhere, whether in the Soviet Union, or the U.S.A. or Tanzania.

I am of course talking about theory. The applied part
of any science is naturally environment-related. Any scientific group is bound to contribute more to the study of its
own environment, or its own history, than will be contributed by other groups elsewhere. Every colony has had
to fight the battle to have its own curriculum in its schools
and colleges. This is obviously right, but is also easily over-
done. We make progress in science not only from studying
the local environment, but also from elaborating our basic
theory. This kind of theoretical elaboration frequently
derives from wide comparison. Particularly, if you want
to be a revolutionary in science, achieving some great
new breakthrough, you have to understand the existing
system which you wish to overthrow better than it is
understood by its supporters, not less so. Keynes was able
to invent a new economics because he thoroughly understood the old. If any new physics or sociology is going to
come out of the West Indies it will be from people who
have mastered the old physics or sociology, and not just
from people who have rejected the old without really
coming to grips with it.

In sum, we will make our special contribution to applied
science, but we must first master the basic universal theoretical principles of the disciplines we use. And our chance
of contributing to those basic disciplines will depend very
largely on the excellence of our secondary schools and
the respect accorded to basic theoretical studies in our university colleges. In this respect West Indians will not differ
from other men.

I have dwelt somewhat on this point because there is a
strong current of thought that West Indians should study
only things West Indian. This is an egregious error, and
a danger to the young. The old are not so easily moved,
since we have learned each to go his own way; but the
young are very conformist, and are easily bulldozed into
acting against their better judgement.

Let me turn now to the second area of human thought,
that of morals, or of what behaviour towards each other
should be. This itself divides into two parts, personality

and social structure. Manners could also be included here, but I have already dealt with this topic.

There is a distinct West Indian personality, marked by its aggressive nature, which in turn derives from the insecure family life in which such a large proportion of our children are reared. Not all West Indians are aggressive, but it is the quality we most admire in our leaders. This aggressive personality has some advantages; it is the chief reason why West Indians figure disproportionately in the black leadership of the United States. But it also has its disadvantages. For example, as Sir John Mordecai's book on the breakdown of our federation shows, the chief reason was the inability of our three leaders in the same federal political party to maintain normal personal relations, and compromise with each other. We also make rather poor business men, compared with say the Nigerian Ibos, because unlike the Ibos we are spendthrift, and not very reliable in keeping our commitments punctually.

On the whole I do not think that it is an advantage for West Indians to have a distinct personality of our own. Philosophers and religious thinkers have meditated for five thousand years on what ideal human beings should be like, and there is no reason to believe that these ideals should differ from one country to another. For my part I think our aggressive personality makes us inferior to our African brethren, who bring up their children in warm, stable and secure family situations, and who therefore produce a stable personality. If we must imitate the Africans, this is what I would urge our countrymen to imitate. Also, if we continue to be unbusinesslike and spendthrift, our society will have no long term future, since it will not survive in this Darwinian world.

In the moral area we have also the subject of social structure—family relations, the political system, class, economic relations and so on. There is an immense variety of social structures, as one moves from place to place. None embodies perfection, and all change nowadays with unprecedented rapidity. Men have imagined and written for five thousand years about every kind of social system, and it seems highly improbable that West Indians will come up with some new kind of social structure which has never been heard of before; this is why those of us who do not like our existing structures find ourselves having to import our ideas from abroad instead of trying to invent some unique West Indian social system. If perchance we did invent something new of our own (which is admittedly possible even though unlikely) and it proved to be good, it would soon be widely imitated elsewhere, since what was good for us would be equally good for many other social groups. For my part, I believe in the open, egalitarian, raceless society which we do not now have, but to which most of our leaders are committed. But when we get there we shall find ourselves in company with many other nations.

In sum, in the area of human relations, national difference is either trivial, in so far as it relates to manners, or undesirable in so far as relates to personality or to social structure. This is because the underlying principles of ethics are of universal validity; what is good for one society is likely to be good for every other. It would be nice if West Indians could have a better community life than other nations, but there is no reason to expect our struggles to be easier than anybody else's.

Finally I come to aesthetics. Music, literature and art are as important a part of the heritage of mankind as are science and morals. They differ from science in that they do not represent what is, but are products of the creative imagination. They have therefore infinite scope for variation. And yet they tend to be distinctively national in character. This is because artists live in colonies, like ants or porpoises. Some great artistic figure attracts other artists to his school; they see or hear alike; they help and criticise each other. And their product is clearly distinct from that of other schools.

It is thus of the very nature of the game that as aesthetic activity burgeons in the West Indies, our art and music and literature will be clearly distinguishable from that of other peoples. We shall have our own schools of painting and music and poetry and drama and the rest. This is the essential and most valuable sense in which West Indians must be different from other peoples. This is the contribution which above all others we know we can make to the common human heritage.

I stress the word common to avoid misunderstanding. The human heritage includes Chinese art, European art, African art; Hindu music, which is quite different from Ashanti music, which in its turn differs from the diatonic structure of jazz and the European classics. This is our common heritage, because the civilized man learns to appreciate as many of these different styles as he can, just as he learns to like French cooking and Chinese cooking and Malay cooking, which are essentially different. For any person to wish to exclude himself from any part of the human artistic heritage, in favour of his local nationalism, is simply boorish. And what is one to say of the incident in South Africa last year where three African pianists were turned away from a Beethoven competition on the ground that Beethoven is not part of African culture? Beethoven belongs to all of us.

We must also note that it is true of the arts, as it is of science, that one learns most by comparison. Our writers must study other writers—not just in English but in other languages—when they are young, in order to have a basis for developing their own styles. Difference must be grounded in wide knowledge and not in ignorance of all except the local effort.

Fortunately we have already established the beginnings of an artistic heritage. In literature we have had the great explosion of novels since the 1950's. In art, starting also in the '50's, a steadier pace has been maintained, but we have already reached the position of having established artists who manage to make a living just by selling their works. In music we are still far behind, since despite our great contributions to popular music, we have a dearth of well trained musicians, and especially a dearth of the string players needed to maintain a symphony orchestra.

The principal handicap is of course that there are so

few people who understand and enjoy the creative arts in our communities, that our artists, musicians, writers, actors and so on, have too small a market. So they have to go abroad and scatter instead of making their little colonies here, at home, which would be very much more productive. The smallness of the market is the fault of our secondary schools, which fail to develop this part of our children's personalities. A society without the creative arts is a cultural desert. I would commend to our statesmen that they put a lot more money into the creative arts departments of our secondary schools.

To conclude, as I look ahead at the evolution of the West Indies, I see many respects in which we should strive to be like other peoples—like having a well rounded personality, or scientists and scholars of world repute—and many respects in which we will be different—like having some distinctive manners and customs, our own curricula in schools, our own applied science, natural and social, and our own musical and other artistic achievements. The main point that I would leave with you is that our chance to make something good of our own depends on our studying carefully what other peoples have done, and learning from their mistakes and their successes. If we are going to close our minds in a box of pure West Indianness, we shall achieve nothing worthwhile.

15.

Political independence in the Commonwealth Caribbean is virtually achieved, but independence has not resolved local dissatisfactions. Nor, as we have seen, has it given most West Indians a strong sense of national identification. Frustration over these dissatisfactions has led to confrontations between rich and poor, expatriate and local, and rulers and ruled all over the Caribbean. Particularly significant, in its being a largely unexpected occurrence in what was generally supposed to be the most progressive West Indian state, was the Trinidad black-power revolution of 1970, described here by a West Indian academic partisan. This revolt pitted modern West Indian radicals against the rule of Dr. Eric Williams, who only a short time ago himself symbolized the defeat of colonial authority, as his *Massa Day Done* (see first selection above) makes clear.

LLOYD BEST, born in Trinidad, took his degree at Cambridge University. He has been on the staff of the Department of Economics and the Institute of Social and Economic Research in the University of the West Indies, Jamaica, and at the Centre of Developing-Area Studies at McGill University in Montreal. Subsequently he became a leader of the New World Group, devoted to promoting West Indianization and social change through publication and proselytization; splitting with the group, he founded his own organization and newspaper, *Tapia,* in Trinidad, where he is also Lecturer in Economics at the University of the West Indies.

The February Revolution
Lloyd Best

I don't know what kind of society each of you has wanted to build in the Caribbean, but I know that all of us here this evening have dreamt of something different from the order which has existed there since the days that Columbus launched the Enterprise of the Indies.

We have in the Caribbean a kind of social order in which many of our highly trained people don't feel able to live. They don't feel they can express their creativity and humanity in that situation; and they have dreamt of a new order. And I think the significance of the last three months in Trinidad and Tobago is that, for the first time in the last 30 years or so, large numbers of people came into the streets of the country to try and mash up that old order and put something new in its place. And that is what the crisis is about.

We could start the story on another ordinary afternoon of February, February the 26th, when I think the crisis began or the conflict assumed crisis proportions, culminating, of course, in the confrontation of April 21st 1970, when the Government imposed a state of emergency and called the troops out with consequences we know. Or we could begin, and we have to begin as well—the story—on a day in October 1968 when Walter Rodney was de-

Speech to the West Indies Federation in Toronto, published in *Tapia*, No. 12, December 20, 1970. Reprinted with permission of Tapia House Publishing Company, Tunapuna, Trinidad, and of the author.

barred from Jamaica—and that is a critical date as we shall see. Or, we could take the story further back yet, to a fateful December evening in 1960, when Williams—not Sir George, Sir Eric—had had the nerve to announce to the people of Trinidad and Tobago that he had clinched a deal with the Americans over Chaguaramas for $51 million. Or we could take the story still further back yet, to the year 1629 or thereabouts when the political system of the West Indies was established. And each of these dates is significant for the story which we have to tell and for an interpretation of what we are now calling "The February Revolution" in Trinidad and Tobago, 1970.

Let us begin at the end as it were, and take the story from February the 26th, when 200 students and friends from the University of the West Indies—mainly students —embarked on what had become a routine political activity. They went into Port of Spain to hold a solidarity march with the students involved in the crisis at the University of Sir George Williams in Montreal. And they paraded around the town. They assembled on South Quay (I think it was), went to the Canadian Embassy in the Furness Withy building or somewhere about (I was out of the country at that time, I didn't actually see it); and they went up town, up Henry Street, across Park Street to the Royal Bank of Canada, back down in town to the main branch. They milled around denouncing the regime, denouncing Canadian imperialism and so on, and some of them decided to take a rest in the Cathedral on Independence Square. And that was like a match in a tinder box. The entire thing exploded. But not immediately; it took a few days.

It took, first of all, the scuffle that ensued with the police and then the arrest on the next day of 12 chaps for assembling in a place of worship and for other charges for which purpose the Attorney General reactivated a piece of legislation which, significantly, had been passed in the days just after emancipation to control the Queen's exslaves. And the country took note of that. The issue of the church and the intervention in the Cathedral, of course, ripped aside a lot of the veils with which the society had been hiding its past and disguising the old order; it introduced an element of anxiety into the situation.

The next week—that February 26th was a Thursday afternoon—the men who had been arrested were due to be tried. And on the Tuesday afternoon, I think it was, the leaders of those 200 students determined to have a solidarity march for the men who had been arrested. And lo and behold 200 students were suddenly transformed into 10,000 and the country immediately stood up and took notice. And Geddes Granger, the leader of those 200 students and of the National Joint Action Committee which had organised the thing, a man of a certain platform flair, decided to take the movement into Shanty Town. And that is exactly what he did. They began, of course, with only a few hundred and the thing that astounded the country is that those 200 became 10,000 in a matter of minutes, as they marched to the outskirts of the city. And that, Sisters and Brothers, introduced an altogether new chapter into the history of Trinidad and Tobago and the West Indies, though some of us did not know that for another week and a half or so.

In the course of that week and a half we had for the first time the emergence of popular cocktail parties, with a difference—Molotov cocktails. We also had later in that second week early in March a demonstration which went from Port of Spain to San Juan in the east and which, according to the conservative press, drew 14,000 people and which, according to the *Express*, the national paper, drew 20,000. And if the country had had any doubt about the significance of what had gone before many of its doubts were now dispelled. These marches revealed a number of important things. One, they revealed the existence in the country of a whole series of organizations of which few people had known before. Organizations appeared from San Juan in the east, from St. James in the west, from San Fernando, from Penal, from Mount Lambert, from behind the bridge, from Belmont, from every conceivable part of the country, a whole series of organizations suddenly appeared on the political stage. Then UMROBI in San Fernando, Pine Toppers from behind the bridge, etc.

It revealed that the country had been thinking about a whole range of issues: Inequality, unemployment, metropolitan domination, Afro-Indian relations and so on. In the very first week it had become clear that we had reached this new political stage. However, a whole series of incidents raised a certain scepticism in the minds of some people and opened an opportunity for some people to drive the movement back. The molotov cocktails and the arson, which appeared quite early in the game, resulted in the burning down in the first week of the Kirpalani store in San Juan. And the reactionary elements in the country, led by *The Nation,* the P.N.M.'s paper, immediately took the opportunity to interpret this as an anti-Indian act on the part of the movement which had as its banner —for reasons I shall come to later—"Black Power". And here again, the particular flair which the leadership of the National Joint Action Committee undoubtedly commands, led the movement to resolve this issue by a march. Granger proposed to his followers—by now many thousands—that they go back to the country and rally their districts and bring the people out to a march to the Indian area to establish the fact of Afro–Asian solidarity.

Everyone knows that the basis of the old political order in the West Indies is racial division, and in Trinidad and Tobago and Guyana in particular, racial division between Indians and the Africans, the major population groups. On the Caroni march with the aid of a number of fortuitous developments established the movement as a significant political force in the country beyond any doubt.

It took place exactly three weeks after the February 26th incident, on a Thursday afternoon. Some 10,000 people at least, were engaged on that march, 28 miles, ending in Chaguanas, and culminating in a massive meeting in the half light in downtown Couva, with a significant number of the local population participating. On the way, the Indian population had welcomed the marchers with iced water and orange juice and every manner of greeting, and no untoward incident had taken place. And the country realised that we were back in the 1930's in the sense that there was a scale of political protest in the country which opened the way to a new regime in the way that the demonstrations and riots of the 1930's in Trinidad, St. Kitts, Jamaica and all over the nation, had ushered in the age of decolonization starting with adult suffrage in Jamaica in 1944, and ending in some cases with independence.

That Caroni march established the movement as a serious political force and concluded, in my interpretation, the first of four phases in the development of the February Revolution. The second phase which came after that involved a wait on the part of the country to see what the Establishment would now do. How would the Big Doctor respond? How would the Little King take it? What would the "pussonal nonarch" do?

Everybody waited. They had noted, very early in the development of the crisis, his responses. He had said on the second or third day of the thing that he would have no truck with hooligans who had no respect for church and society. The day after that, I think, he had declined to go to a routine opening of a conference which he had to attend at the University of the West Indies and the country had noticed the sign of weakness. And later on, he had talked about 'upstarts'; and the country made its own judgment about the significance of these statements and waited to hear how he would move to cope with this new development which was obviously, at this point, serious. There is one more interesting thing that the country had to note: He began to build a wall ten feet high around his house.

Anyhow, for a long time he stood cowering behind these walls. And Parliament was no different! I think it met on two occasions during this period, and declined to note that thousands of people were walking up and down the streets of Port of Spain, that they had taken over the public square and were everywhere denouncing the old order. And then when he could wait no more, Williams ultimately spoke on March the 23rd. And when he spoke it was a major event in the development of the political situation in Trinidad and Tobago because for the first time large numbers of people in Trinidad and Tobago actually saw through the fraudulence of the regime which had governed them for 14 years.

Many people had suspected that the regime was bankrupt, larger numbers *still* knew that the regime was corrupt—they could see the evidence everywhere—they knew that it had not been delivering any goods for a long long time; but we had invested so much in it in the beginning and we trusted ourselves so little that many of us declined to draw the inferences. Many would say, "The men around him are empty, but the doctor is a boss." But when Williams spoke on that evening of the 23rd of March, with the nation on the height of crisis, a bigger crisis than we had had for 30 years, they knew! For what did Williams say?

Williams said that he had a feeling that people weren't aware of all the things that the Government had been doing for the country. He said many people were talking a lot of rubbish about petroleum and sugar, but could we cut our nose off to spoil our faces? he said. The country was saying: "If we cut our noses to spoil our faces, is *we* that cut it off!" *And that is what the issue was.*

Williams said that what we needed to do was to find more oil and more gas. He argued that it took time in the Parliamentary process; the democratic system which we had established involved a great deal of delay in the implementation of projects, and we couldn't run before we could walk. All, therefore, he could propose, was a tax to yield 10 million dollars and to push the revenue up from 386 million to 396 million dollars, the 10 million dollars being put into a special fund to create work for the population in mending roads and sweeping streets. And the country drew the appropriate inference and resolved that this regime had to go. And that ushered in the third phase of the February Revolution which lasted for about a month.

In this third phase it was quite clear, or it became crystal clear as the days passed, that the new movement was looking for a confrontation to bring the regime down as quickly as possible. There is no question about that! The strategy did not appeal to me, not because I did not agree with the objectives of course, or because I did not support the movement; but it is important to know what resources one has.

You can't provoke a revolutionary situation if you don't have revolutionary resources to take the power—and we did not have them, as we shall see. Nevertheless, I think this is the moment when the movement became intoxicated by its own success. It began, first of all, to radicalise the country—marches everywhere—in Penal, in Mayaro, a weekend in Tobago, a "holiday" weekend in Tobago of a kind that you would hardly imagine, four days I think it was, the biggest meeting in Scarborough ever, up and down the land terrorising the old regime, activating the population. Children were shouting "Power, Power to the People." Old women were involved, buying political papers. I myself was selling papers in Port of Spain, one hundred and twenty an hour. People were saying, "I don't know what Black Power is, but I am for it." Because people had reached a stage where it could not go on any longer. The regime had to go. Up and down the country, these young. Five, ten, fifteen, twenty thousand people, up and down, "Power to the People," everywhere!

And the high point of this, of course, was the funeral on that afternoon of April 19th. And then the thing began to escalate almost to a point of hysteria. Let me see if I can identify the incidents that led up to the final thing. The funeral of Davis took place on the 9th April and shortly after that the impending visit of Stokely Carmichael was announced; and people began to think of that as perhaps the opening for the final grand confrontation—wrongly, I thought, and so did *Tapia* at the time. Nevertheless it is indicative of the mood of the age.

On that same Thursday afternoon, the market vendors in Port of Spain declared their intention to throw their lot in with the Black Power Movement. Then came the weekend—that was the Thursday—and the police began to call up their reserves, the army began to call up volunteers, and the steelband threw their lot in with the movement. In other words, the country was beginning to polarise for the confrontation. Declare where you stand! Goddard went to the People's Parliament—Goddard who for many years had been thought to be a retainee in the stable of the establishment—went into the public square and denounced Williams and the regime.

On the Monday morning, Robinson, for whatever reasons, I don't think I would like to explore them, resigned from the Cabinet and pushed the political temperature higher. That was the 13th of April. On the Wednesday, the Government exacerbated the situation by warning the airlines against even allowing Stokely to pass through Trinidad. On that same day, work stopped among the daily-paid workers at the Water and Sewerage Authority. All of this, of course, with a chorus of arson and violence in the background.

On the Thursday, the governments of the region further exacerbated the situation and forced the temperature still higher. Barbados banned the black power leaders.

At home, the government, for its part, began now to make some vague concessions. Specifically, it conceded to the market vendors, hoping to bring some of the opposition back to the side of reaction. But on the Friday the W.A.S.A. stoppage extended itself to the monthly-paid workers, and the Transport Workers Association announced that on the Tuesday following, it would bring its workers out on the streets of Port of Spain in a solidarity march.

On the Saturday the N.J.A.C. organised a whole series of marches—quick marches throughout the country—Cedros, Mayaro, Tobago, all over, whipping up its political support. Obviously the movement and the country were moving toward some kind of political confrontation.

And the Sunday, the critical development took place, just as it had taken place in 1965 when Williams had declared—had introduced—the Industrial Stabilisation Act.

Sugar cracked—sugar on which so much of the Caribbean history is built and which engenders so many passions on the part of all the constituent groups in the region. Sugar cracked on that Sunday; 600 people stopped work —remember that strikes are illegal in Trinidad—600 people stopped work at Brechin Castle. The D.L.P. responded to that—seeing the crisis toward which we were heading —by calling for a national government. And everybody knew that we were in for trouble. Either the regime would fall, or the regime would impose its will on the population.

On the Monday morning, a development in sugar! Granger marches with a thousand workers from Couva to the factory in Brechin Castle and Williams, historian and politician that he is, and understanding the significance of this development which is building up to a crescendo, and understanding the significance of bringing sugar workers into Port of Spain in this political climate, determined to go for the confrontation himself. And that's exactly what he did, with a kind of historical irony that is brutal, when one considers it. Because on the morning of April the 21st 1970, ten years almost to the hour after he had organised his own march to put the Americans out of Chaguaramas, he had to pick the telephone up and call the American Ambassador and ask for troops.

And the confrontation had come, ladies and gentlemen! The country had been talking for many weeks about the army. Anybody who knows about the social structure of Trinidad would know that the people who are in the army are no different from those who come from behind the bridge or from the townships around San Juan or Tunapuna or Marabella or what have you, or who are in the University of the West Indies; and that we could not afford to make the same assumptions, fortunately or unfortunately, that are made in Europe.

There is no ruling class in the army, there is no ruling officer class and the country had been considering that.

What would be its significance if the confrontation came? And I think it is indicative of the extent to which the Government was cut off from information and from the population, that everybody was expecting the army to go along with the movement, everybody except the Government.

And on the morning of April 21st Williams sent the police into the homes of the leaders of Black Power—they swooped down at half-past four in the morning; he declared a State of Emergency and placed the army under the control of the police hoping to coerce the country into quiescence. And the army introduced a slight qualification.

The question we have to ask ourselves is, What is the meaning of all of this? Where does it leave us now? It is here that I must go back to the second date of the four that I identified at the start. For the events that I have just described to you very briefly, and very superficially in some way for lack of time, were merely the culmination of a long confrontation that has been going on in the political and social system of the West Indies from the very start.

And I think the important date to take second was that fateful December evening in 1960—in what was then the University of Woodford Square where luckily I happened to be present though I was not living in the country at that time. And you will remember on that evening Williams announced his plans for a Chaguaramas settlement. And for the first time in his political history he was talking and the population was not listening. And it was then that he launched the attack on Sir Gerald Wight, which ultimately led to his statement "Massa Day Done", because he felt the break in communication and had to leave his prepared text and whip up support on that evening.

But the significance of it is that Williams, at that point, threw the popular movement into disarray, threw it into disorder, and lost, as a result, his own self-confidence, if he had had any. And in the years between 1960 and 1970 we can chart a progressive degeneration of the regime.

"Massa Day Done"—quite unwarranted in terms of what Williams was in fact doing! The Commission of Enquiry into Subversive Activities in an attempt to smash the union leadership! It is interesting that on that occasion I was invited to appear before that Commission although I had only been in Trinidad for six weeks and had only written a few articles in the paper (I had no political connections then). One of the interesting things is that the statement which I gave was subsequently published in a thing called "From Chaguaramas to Slavery" which is exactly the road which we have being plodding in the years past.

Commission of Enquiry into Subversive Activities; the imposition of restrictions on C.L.R. James; the Industrial Stabilization Act; the banning of literature; the banning of people including Stokely Carmichael.

One sees the regime developing along the typical Caribbean road of caudillismo: Batista, Machado, Gómez, Marco Perez Jimenez—the whole lot of them—terrorising the Caribbean people into submission.

But Williams could be seen, looking back in retrospect, charting the road milepost by milepost from 1960 because he began systematically to fall back on external resources. Chaguaramas raised the issue for him Are you going to repose the future of the people of Trinidad and Tobago on the resources that we have in the country? Or are you going to pursue the policy of what we have called "industrialization by invitation"?—relying on external resources for capital, for aid, for technology and driving away from the country any person with any creativity, any sense of independence, because they live in a regime in which they are only rubber stamps of imperial decision.

He had to make that decision in 1960. That is what Chaguaramas meant for him. And to do it of course, it was quite clear that if we were going to take a road of independence, what he called the "Independence Highway" as distinct from the "Dirt Track of Colonialism," he had to integrate the country. That was the task facing him. Because you can't build Trinidad and Tobago, or Guyana or the West Indies, unless you bring together the elements that constitute that population. And Williams was faced with that task in 1960 and he backed out; he put his tail between his legs and he kowtowed before the imperialists, and it sent him on that road right down the line—Commission of Enquiry, C.L.R. James, Industrial Stabilization—right up to the present day.

And in those years, we had, first of all, the retreat of the Indians which came very early. The thing boiled up for a moment at the election in 1961; the population flirted with Capildeo in the hope that he would do something—he did nothing—60,000 people in the Savannah, biggest meeting ever. The Indians retreated, Williams won a racist thing. He put race on the center of the table in 1961 to start with, right in the spotlight.

The Negroes next were demobilised. The teachers that put him in power began to boil down; the civil servants began to realise that this movement didn't have what they'd hoped for it; and we see progressively over the years a descent of the movement into a state of apathy, except for the unions or the militant unions, especially the Oil Workers' Union and the Transport Union.

And the issue of those years was an attempt by the Government to smash that last remaining bastion of popular protest. The unions were the only group rich enough and organised enough and numerous enough, and forced by the circumstances of their existence to stand up against the iniquities of the regime. And he tried to smash them over those years.

And then the third important date came—October 1968. And the significance of October 1968 is that counter attack which the unions, the militant unions, had been trying to launch unsuccessfully in the years since the Commission of Enquiry into Subversive Activities—the counter attack was now reinforced by the emergence of the University as an important locus of political protest for the first time.

Rodney touched it off in Jamaica, in Barbados, in Guyana. But it was in Trinidad that the consequences were most serious. The first ever political march on the part of students! And that was the first of a whole series of incidents which constituted an overture to the symphony that we heard on February 26th 1970. Rodney in October, Michener in February—the first of the Sir George Williams' incidents. The Governor General went down there and they blocked him; at which point Granger founded the N.J.A.C. and gave it some institutional shape; then Santa Flora, Five Rivers.

Come April, the transport strike—a kind of trial run. All the opposition forces gathered in Joe Young's den, considered the problem how to deal with Williams. I remember one evening that we had a meeting there at the high point of that crisis and most of the people there determined to confront Williams in much the same way that we were to confront him in April, and I suggested to them that we put the meeting off for one night to talk about it.

I remember opening the meeting the next night and talking for an hour and outlining the options available to the country and arguing that we couldn't knock Williams out with the resources that we had. We weren't organised, we did not have a medium of communication, we didn't have the resources—military or civilian—to do it. And I suggested that we had to win on points, to get the organisation in place. The fellows voted me down, 57 to 3 on the occasion, 60 people voted. And they confronted Williams next morning. Six o'clock they went down town to throw themselves under the buses, you will remember. And we didn't learn the lesson that you have to organise in order to deal with him.

Anyhow, the transport strike was a kind of trial run. It boiled up; the population alerted itself for a few moments or a few weeks, considered the possibility and decided that we didn't have the resources to do it. And we lost, on the occasion; but it contributed to the development of the counter attack—April 1969.

And then during the course of that year, the N.J.A.C. was organising everywhere in the way it organises—not grass roots in the sense that I understand it—but stirring up the people to a certain kind of political awareness, valuable in its own way, if limited.

All over, a whole series of organisations began to become very active. Pivot, which had started in the late days of New World began to become more active in the same way, to put out a mimeograph business. Moko was on the road articulating in a certain way, subsequently joined by Tapia. And a whole lot of organisations, as we were to discover subsequently, began to spring up in the communities: Pine Toppers behind the bridge, the African Liberation Movement in St. James, in Champ Fleurs a similar thing, in San Fernando, up the road by me there in Arouca, in Sangre Grande, everywhere these organisations—people beginning to organise themselves and think about the political system in that kind of political climate.

And then we had another trial run. In October of 1969, we had the political extravaganza of the Camacho funeral, when 7-or-8,000 people were brought into the University of the West Indies for our first political funeral. They buried him on the campus and there was a quality of oratory on that occasion that the country will never forget. It escalated the sense of conflict in the country. But Camacho was not a considerable person in my opinion and a lot of people who had supported him knew that. Camacho had been in the country for 20 years. He hadn't made any impact on thought in the country. But people were so disgusted with the regime, they were so at the limit of their patience, that they were prepared to take any issue that appeared to threaten the stability of this regime. And Camacho presented that case; and the students, some members of the Faculty, and the *hommes politiques* in the country used the occasion to declare another attack on the regime. That was October.

Then came the St. Francois incident when Donald Pierre went personally to the school to chase three girls out for smoking "pot"; and that was another incident. Then

the Country Club thing about that time, inflaming the
racial climate. Two black Americans come down to the
country, staying at the Hilton hotel. The practice is for
people who are staying at the Hilton to go to the Country
Club and play tennis. And here they are, two black people
attempting to do this and they are barred for all kinds of
wishy-washy reasons. And the country notes the significance of that. Fourteen years or 13 years of P.N.M. in
power and black people can't go to places in Trinidad and
Tobago. And the political climate is affected. The thing
builds up. That was January.

February—Carnival. And they say that we are a Carnival
people. But the Jour Ouvert of Carnival this year was a
political occasion. There appeared on the public stage,
the Pine Toppers—denouncing the regime in everything
that they do. Placards of every kind denouncing Williams,
racial discrimination, church hypocrisy, every conceivable
thing. Political carnival at that time. The thing revealed
that the people of Trinidad and Tobago are not precisely
what they are thought to be. They were ready for something. February; that was early in February. And then
that afternoon on the 26th, 200 students.......starting the
ball rolling on South Quay. And that was a kind of
Serajevo. Tinderbox; they ignite it, and we are on the way.

What does it mean? What does it mean? You see the
movement of history from 1960 through the Williams attack on opposition up to 1968. You see the counter attack, the students joining, Weekes and Young and The
Transport Union. The thing building up. Trial runs. Those
last 18 months provided a banner, because it was in that
period that the movement got the banner of Black Power
which had its limitations, but had the important advantage
that it had media appeal; and the fellows—the political
fellows—saw the significance of that and took it as their
banner very early in the game. Sir George Williams helped
in that sense; it was not important, it was not really material to the developments in Trinidad; but by internation-
alizing the issue and by bringing the foreign press in and

so on, it gave the fellows a banner to mobilize. So they took "Black Power"! First thing, Banner!

Second thing, organization of a certain kind. Organization of the kind that brings people into the public square. N.J.A.C. was founded at the juncture of Michener. Thirdly, regional solidarity is built, because the thing took place at the University which is a regional institution, difficult to handle. Automatic repercussions all the time. It was like playing that pin-ball thing, just bouncing off; Guyana, Cave Hill, Mona and so on; every little incident helping along in mobilising this new force.

Next, the articulate organisations and papers—*Tapia, Moko, Pivot, East Dry River Speaks*—all of them coming on the streets. We started selling, 14,000 *Tapias* in Trinidad. Everywhere in the country people buying it. Old women, young women, everybody buying political papers.

So this critical 18 months really developed the conditions necessary for the confrontation of the two months or the two and a half months. Because in addition to that, people learnt a lot of political tricks. Every incident that produced a march taught people something about the police, about the kinds of issues to which the population responded and so on, and it taught the population something about the political climate, in Trinidad and Tobago and in the rest of the region. Everybody learnt. Trial runs, Camacho, Transport strike and so on; and everything boiled up and it was ready in February and the whole blasted thing goes up as they touched it off in February.

And we came through that two and a half months up to the 21st of April. The confrontation came, and the movement did not succeed. And the question is Why?

And for that we have to go back to the fourth date before we finish off. 1629, when James, King of England, gave letters patent to the Earl of Carlisle to establish a system in the Caribbee islands. And he establishes a system in which he places a Governor to take care of his interests in the colony; and the Governor appoints a Council in which he appoints men that he could control. And they establish a political system which has nothing to do with the interests of the large mass of people living there. It is run from outside, it is legitimated from outside. Over the next 100 years or so—160 or more than that—the planters succeed in forcing the system back just a little. They establish Assemblies in which freeholding planters are represented, but they never conceive of the idea of embracing the whole mass of the black population there.

So we grew up during our political life as a people, not knowing or not being allowed to know for a long time that our participation counts, and that organisation in the constituencies, solid permanent organisation, is important to the political process to limit the abuse of power.

The 19th century comes and the British Government imposes its will on the assemblies in order to emancipate the slave population, for whatever reasons, and they reestablish a political system not markedly different from the one which King James had established with the Earl of Carlisle in 1629. It makes the Governor the King-pin. C.L.R. James has called it "Three in one and one in three"; Father, Son and Holy Ghost!

And we go through, speaking roughly now for the whole region, 100 years or so, of our existence, with this kind of political system. But even when the black population is freed and is trying to create an independent society in which we could live as men, the political system continues to be something that is imposed upon us from outside; and we adopt a strategy—a political strategy—of beating the system by accommodating to it, by achieving mobility for our brighter sons.

And we do this by establishing ourselves as labour leaders where we could as in Barbados, Antigua and St. Kitts, producing Bird and Bradshaw and a whole generation of leaders that we know of. In Jamaica, the same phenomenon; Bustamante. Or we improve ourselves by education—as in Trinidad and Guyana; Burnham, Jagan, Williams.

This is a strategy that denies what we are because the power in the hands of the colonizer is so great we didn't think we could beat it in direct confrontation. Instead, we would beat it by accepting its rules; by the churching, the education; by becoming what we call Afro-Saxons; by taking over the European culture and imposing it on the Africans; and by exercising our influence in the professions, in the civil service, and so on. And the significance of this of course is that it doesn't put any high premium on popular organization and it produces a certain kind of charismatic leadership.

This is what I have called "doctor politics" in the Trinidad case—of bright individuals who act as the messiahs. They beat the system—Williams first in the first class, Capildeo out-einsteining Einstein; and Manley is the third best lawyer in the world (black men can't be first or second); and so on. And you have a whole range of these charismatic figures coming either through the church like Bradshaw and Bird when they don't get the chance, and I call these Sunday school doctors; they learn the rhetoric of the bible and so on; they learn to speak with beauty and power and so on; and they organise their people to beat the system in a certain way without accepting it. And you have the public school doctors like Manley, where the peasants succeed and have some sense of elegance; they have their public schools and live with a certain grace to produce the kind of person Manley was—a patrician figure. Or you have the grammar-school type of Burnham and Williams and Jagan in his own way, who are really offering their technocratic excellence as men who are brighter than the fellows on the metropolitan stage in some way.

But you have this charismatic phenomena of leaders who do not repose their political organization on what people are doing in the constituencies for themselves, but are offering really an apocalypse, a messiah who will bring the day of judgement—one of these days. And the significance of all this which I can't explore here—this is not the place—is that Williams was really the leader of this movement. He was its ultimate expression because of the particular excellence that he was thought to have or to have achieved—first in the first class, plenty doctor books, and so on. And he comes onto the public stage in the 1950's offering an apocalypse:—independence, federation, morality in public affairs, economic transformation, a better dispensation for the people. And the population invests in it, at least, the black population. Even the Indian population, suspicious and so on, but they themselves, sharing the culture in a certain way, offer Williams the best commendation they could ever offer him by attempting to bring Capildeo to imitate him. They believed in him in the same way; that is why they wanted Capildeo—he is a doctor. Bright!

So the population trusts this thing and hopes for change without their own participation. That is not wholly true, it's over simple because Williams stirred a lot of people to action though he never really questioned the fundamentals of the 19th century strategy, in my opinion. I saw it very early; I am not inventing my position for now; I have held it for nearly ten years. But Williams continues on this course and the people believe in him; and they establish a new politics which hopes that Williams will somehow transform this order which we have had in the region since 1500; an order that Enriquillo as early as 1519 stood up against—a little Caribbean boy—with some Indians and some runaway Africans, to fight, very early; and hundreds of men along the line have tried to break it up, unsuccessfully. And at last, people said in Trinidad and Tobago, Williams was the man who was going to do it.

And the crisis of the last two and a half months arose because people at long last appreciated that no such thing was going to happen. That Williams could not deliver the goods. And after many years of vacillation and hesitation and unwillingness to draw the conclusion, the arrival on the stage of a large number of young people—if you look at the population structure you will see it, 62 per cent of the population are under 25—coming on the scene and seeing this foolishness that's going on—the bankruptcy of the regime, the incompetence, the corruption, the way in which people are driven out of the country, people are driven into their shells, they don't know where to turn or what to do and they say: we go mash up this blasted thing.

And that is what happened. That is what the crisis is about.

But on April the 21st, we bungled it; we bungled it because the organisation and the apparatus were not there. The work had not been done to make it possible to deal with Williams. But the population still holds its position, you don't go back on that. If you understand that the regime is not going to deliver the goods, then it has to go. It is now driven underground by the state of emergency. Fact number one, we have learnt that!

So there are two things we have learnt: one, that the regime has got to go; and two, that we don't have the organisation for it.

Third thing is that Williams survives, but he survives on a different basis. Between 1956 and 1960 he enjoyed the confidence of large numbers of the people, and the confidence was mounting, it was growing. More people were joining and people were gaining more confidence than they had had. Then from 1960, right up to the present time, the situation degenerated until 1970 when the people began playing for a confrontation and so was Williams playing for a confrontation. He was hoping that the movement would overplay its hand and, either in desperation or in exhilaration, provoke violence on such a scale as to bring the population back, on the rebound, as we say in Trinidad, back into the arms of reaction. And that is exactly what occurred.

And the population is now with him in a certain sense, large numbers out of fear. They don't trust the capacity of the new movement to run the country in peace and therefore they are afraid to let it run it in war. The revolt is from the threat of violence.

What is the significance of this? It means that we now have a typical traditional Caribbean regime in which you have a Generalissimo—Williams—who since he doesn't have the moral authority, has to fight with the troops and the police. And since he is not sure of what the population would do, since he has seen that the population is prepared to entertain a movement that would sweep him away in a quick surgical operation of a kind that we nearly had in the past two and a half months, he can never be sure. So he has now to be looking ahead of the game to exterminate areas of possible organisation. And that is what the State of Emergency is about.

Let us look at the facts. On the morning of the 21st of April, he picks up most of the leaders of the militant group: Darbeau, Murray, Nunez and so on. In the course of the next few days he picks up the rest. Granger was somewhere in the center of the island. On the morning of the 21st, the population assembles in the public square, smashes up all the store fronts in Port of Spain, every one, on Frederick, Henry, Charlotte, Independence Square, Queen Street—a final grand romantic gesture, finish, and go home.

No leadership left. All the terror in the system is police terror, official terror. The police see a man riding on a bicycle and they say "Ay boy, turn round." He ain't turn around. Bang, they shoot him. Dead. And so on. All over the place, terrorizing people. In the University, the police were running the place. Every estate constable had the power to deal with people without questioning. We could be detained without charge; they could break up any assembly above three people, deem any publication subversive—a man was put in jail for having a copy of *Moko* published the year before. They are doing these things, I am telling you. It is a police state.

But there is no terror on the part of the population. There is no violent resistance on the part of anybody. The situation is calm as the government has been saying. There was a little incident, or a little difficulty. This is looking at it from the government's point of view now, I don't share this point of view. It is that a contingent disappeared, it appears, among the civilian population. We don't know where they are and there is a possibility of a guerilla something there; this is what the government says, and there are rumours of Cubans in the hills. Trinidad lives by rumour. But conceding that there is a possibility of some danger in that district, one can see that there should be a State of Emergency in an area where there is an emergency. But no warrant whatsoever for a state of emergency in the whole country.

Why do we have it?

I think the significance is that Williams knows that he has now to live by terror and he can't afford to allow any semblance of resistance to remain in the country. He therefore has to intimidate the organizations into putting their tails between their legs. He wants to do it in such a way that it will cost him as little as possible; and anybody who is involved in political opposition, the more sane they are, the more competent they are, the more he will need to pick them up. And that is where we are now.

We have, in fact, shattered the Westminster illusion of political democracy, and we have established a typical Caribbean caudillo regime. The last question we therefore have to face, if you agree with my analysis, is "What are we going to do about it? What are we going to do about it inside Trinidad and Tobago in the days to come, starting tomorrow? What are we going to do about it in the West Indies? In the nation? And what are we going to do in the metropolitan centers where many of us are?" I don't have the answers I must tell you to begin with. I know that in Trinidad and Tobago we have to rally the population by whatever means we can to stand up for its rights.

Franco and Salazar have had states of emergency in Spain and Portugal for over 30 years, and it is entirely possible that the population could become accustomed to this way of life—curfew, no rights of assembly, no rights to publish political newspapers. This is quite standard. It's the norm in the world. The Westminster illusion that we have a system like London, like Ottawa, and so on, is a lot of foolishness. It is an illusion, it's not true, it's not the norm at all. The world is not organised that way. In most countries that's the way people live and they adjust to it very easily. And if we want to save the political regime for something more humane, something that opens the possibility for us to live like people, like men, we have to stop it early before we get accustomed to it.

Tapia has—I can only speak for *Tapia*—continued to publish material at great risk and will continue to do so, and we have a whole programme of operations intending to keep legitimate political opposition going; in fact, to translate it into government. So I think we shall have to turn our attention for the purpose of this evening to what we do in the rest of the nation. In the West Indies and here. And the answers?— I think that you have to tell me.

But I want to suggest two things in conclusion.

One, and I have proposed this wherever I have been. I have been to Britain and I have been to the continent of Europe; and I have been to Montreal, to Ottawa, and so on. And I have made the same proposals everywhere. One, that we should start some kind of defence fund. There are over 50 people in detention, some of whom are being tried at the moment for sedition—civilians that is.

And then there are the military. That's something else again. I think that under army regulations they are entitled to get defence. But we have to get money to defend these chaps. They are going to be tried in the High Court and so on for a long time, it seems, and I hope that you will contribute what you can to such a fund; that people will come forward to start a committee for that in collaboration with the other centres—I have the names of other people in other parts of the world who have agreed to do the same thing and if people here agree I can put them in contact with those people, so as to build up a significant fund to help. I don't want the fund to be a Tapia Fund, I just want the fund to be a general fund for all the people, not merely the four people who are associated with Tapia.

The second thing which I suggest is that we found some kind of Solidarity Organisation. What precisely it's going to do over time, I don't know. It depends on how the conjuncture develops. From here on, what happens to the trials, what happens to organisations like Tapia and so on in the coming weeks. There will obviously be need for demonstrations of one kind or another, need for all kinds of acts of solidarity and certainly need for keeping in contact with those people who feel that they have bonds with the home society. More than that, I can't say. I have to leave it to you on the floor to tell me what you are proposing, depending on your individual commitment.

All I would say is this. So far as I am concerned, the dream of a more humane society in Trinidad and Tobago has not in any way disappeared with what has happened in the last two months. In fact I feel that it has vindicated my own position which I have held for many years: that it is possible in this part of the world, to build something exceptional. My feeling that there will be a certain poetry in attacking this civilization of 500 years from the Caribbean has, if anything, been strongly reinforced by the historic events of the February Revolution.

16.

The 1970 black-power confrontation in Trinidad ended in the quashing of an army mutiny. The rebels were tried by military judges brought in from Africa and Asia and found guilty. Here a plea by a local barrister for mitigating the sentence meted out to Lieutenant Raffique Shah, a principal defendant, gives a remarkable insight into the nature of Trinidadian society. He suggests that the Trinidad "army" was a fiction, invented in mimicry of the British system and intended only for pageantry; the mutiny took place in an evil fantasy world and the rebels were in fact not traitors but reformers. The son of a Trinidad East Indian cane-cutter, Lieutenant Shah was a graduate of Sandhurst who had previously been chastised for various high-jinks, including the use of obscene language in the officers' mess. During Allum's speech, Shah was rebuked by the court for laughing at his counsel's analysis of the local Establishment. Shah was sentenced to twenty years in prison for his role in the Trinidad mutiny. This was subsequently reviewed and reduced to fifteen years. He was freed on appeal in January 1972, the Trinidad and Tobago Court of Appeal finding that the original verdict was a miscarriage of justice.

Born in Trinidad, DESMOND ALLUM received his legal training in Great Britain and is now a practicing barrister in his native country. He is a member of the New World Group in Trinidad and one of the founders of the political journal *Moko*.

Legality vs. Morality: A Plea for Lt. Raffique Shah*
Desmond Allum

You have now discharged according to your best lights
the first part of the two-fold duty arising out of the assignment which you accepted to perform in our affairs. You
have made a judgment concerning the facts of this case
and you have determined that my client Lt. Shah is guilty
of mutiny as charged. It is now your responsibility before
you pass sentence upon him to make a most careful evaluation of the degree of culpability which can properly be
attached to Lt. Shah's behaviour and determine accordingly what punishment it is appropriate to order against
him. In your evaluation of the evidence of the case on
the basis of which you came to the determination that Lt.
Shah was guilty of mutiny, the fact that you are strangers
among us may not have operated very substantially as
an inhibition on your ability to arrive at a correct verdict.

In dealing with the question of punishment however, I
regret to say that you will inevitably find yourself handicapped by a great difficulty in coming to your decision.
For this reason. Every society must and does determine
for itself what type of behaviour it is capable of tolerating
and the manner in which it will punish or deter acts or
conduct which it considers that it cannot tolerate. The
laws relating to mutiny which govern the present matter
provide you with the widest possible discretion. You are

Plea to court for mitigation of sentence; published in *Moko*,
March 26, 1971, pp. 1–8. Reprinted by permission of MOKO
Enterprises, Ltd., Curepe, Trinidad.

* [Editors' title]

given a range of punishment which it is within your power to order, from a sentence of death on the one hand to the mere suspension of departmental privileges on the other.

So that the provisions of the law because they are so widely discretionary and not at all mandatory do not of themselves give you any assistance as to the severity or lightness of sentence which would be most appropriate to the circumstances of this case. In addition to this, our jurisprudence has absolutely no previous experience of how to deal with a person who has been convicted of mutiny, so that in determining what punishment may be condign in this case, you will not get any assistance from an examination of precedents. For there are none. So that you cannot avoid the necessity of examining meticulously our local culture and I use this phrase in its widest possible sense, with the intention of discovering by such an examination the extent to which our society is capable of tolerating the type of offence of which you have found Lt. Shah guilty and of arriving at an evaluation of the measure of disapproval which our society, not yours, would wish to indicate in this matter. If you had an intimate and extended experience of our way of life, of our values, of those things which we hold dear and of those things which we proscribe as taboos, in short, of our civilisation, then the task which you now have to perform might be possible of achievement but, I say this, mark you, with the greatest respect, you do not have this experience so I cannot frankly see how you can proceed to the proper discharge of this aspect of your assignment.

I use the word "assignment" advisedly in preference to "duty" for to my mind one who accepts to perform a duty must be accountable, in a measure commensurate with the gravity of that duty.

For the manner in which he discharges it, and again because you are mere visitors among us, I find it impossible to pretend that you bear any measure of accountability to our society. It was for this reason that those of us who took constitutional objections to the composition of the court when this trial began some months ago were motivated to do so. The cynics who suggested that we were merely playing for time clearly did not appreciate what we meant by accountability.

The role which you have undertaken to perform in our affairs may be judicial in form but the substance and effect of it is so essentially political in nature that we feel instinctively that it can only be properly discharged by natives of this country who can be held answerable for their performance not only in the immediate future by our actual citizens but by generations to come.

It will be absolutely improper for this court, Mr. President, to import into this situation the cultural values and norms of the societies from which you come. I make no judgment on your societies and I imply no disrespect for them but I must state categorically that they are not our society and their values may or may not accord with ours, so I repeat Mr. President you have no choice but to attempt an evaluation of us, here, in Trinidad and Tobago. If you feel that you are incapable of coming to terms with this aspect of your assignment then it is your duty to say so and renounce before it is too late the grave responsibility with which you find yourself at present saddled. This in my view would be an extremely honourable course of action on your part.

As the matter stands however, I see it now as my responsibility as an advocate in your court and as a native of this country, to offer you what insights I can in an effort to assist you in coming to a proper decision. The range of possible punishments offered to you by Section 71, sub-section (1) of the Defence Act No. 7 of 1962, allows you to choose from among 8 alternatives, as follows:

(a) death;
(b) imprisonment;
(c) cashiering;
(d) dismissal from her majesty's service;
(e) fine of a sum not exceeding the equivalent of 90 days pay;
(f) forfeiture of seniority;

(g)   severe reprimand of reprimand;
(h)   stoppages

Let me say right away that never in our history, including our pre-independence history has any person ever
suffered death at the hands of the State for any offences
other than for the felonious killing of another person. That
is to say for murder. And even in the case of murder in
more recent times there are fewer and fewer executions
recorded so that we have reached the stage where although
the death penalty is still legally available it has not in fact
been imposed since April of 1970. The death penalty in
Trinidad and Tobago therefore Mr. President can perhaps be regarded as having already entered the first stage
of its obsolescence. Forward-looking people of a humanitarian disposition certainly foster this hope and I think
our civilisation can truthfully be said to have reached
the stage of development where it is revolted by and re-
jects the idea of the ritual killing of a human being by the
State. We are further reinforced in this belief by the fact
that at present there is established and at work a parliamentary commission charged with advising on the question
of the abolition of capital punishment altogether. I am not
saying that there are not still certain reactionary elements
in our society which would seek to oppose the abolition of
the death penalty but this is to be expected and the experience of other countries and other civilisations has
shown that sooner or later the death penalty will formally
be removed from our statute books. I said before Mr.
President that death sentences have only been carried out
against people who have been convicted of murder. Here
I think you have some kind of criterion which can properly
be applied to the present case.

In the course of the mutiny at Teteron no person was
either killed or wounded, in fact no bodily harm of any
kind was inflicted as a result of the conduct of any of the
persons charged before this court. I would urge therefore
that by analogy it would be quite improper for you even to
consider a sentence of death as being appropriate to this
type of mutiny, and I suggest to you with great confidence

that were it to be passed here, it would certainly serve to provoke the revulsion and rejection of all right thinking members of our community and would in addition almost certainly precipitate the type of crisis which all responsible people, particularly at this time, must work to avoid. It might of course be argued on the other hand that the offence of mutiny in itself, even though no lives were lost in its commission, is sufficient to attract the severest of punishments. Even if this were not so at law, in order to sustain such a position, one would have to show that mutiny in our society is an offence of sufficient gravity to justify, regardless of the manner in which the mutineers conducted themselves, the severest reaction from the society. If this were the case however, our laws would not have provided a choice of punishments.

The persons who framed the Defence Act have by clear inference admitted that the genus mutiny comprises many species, that there can be mutinies and mutinies is recognised, so that the gravity of each must be separately evaluated. So let us examine what exactly mutiny means in our army as an organ of this society. And perhaps I might emphasize here again that we are not considering mutiny as an offence in vacuum and unrelated to the society in which it is committed. Nor are we to consider the offence of mutiny in relation to some society other than this.

First of all Mr. President it is interesting to note how the offence of mutiny came to appear at all within the body of our juris-prudence; the simple answer is this: the law relating to mutiny was drafted for us by the British like 99% of the current laws of our land.

The military institution which this British conceived and drafted law of mutiny was intended to regulate, was itself modelled for us by the British. The etiquette of personnel relations to be practised and appreciated in our military institution was British, the rules and regulations were British, the idiom and phraseology were British, the uniforms were British, the weapons and technology prior to the declaration of the State of Emergency were British, and to ensure that the whole operation was launched in the Brit-

ish style the original officers appointed were British. In a
word the entire and total philosophy of the Trinidad and
Tobago Regiment embodied a fully integrated British conception of military life and organisation. Had we been
British or perhaps even good British colonials, there would
have probably been no flaw in this project, but of course
this was not the case. The men who were to live this myth,
who were to endure this counterfeit and to suffer it to
function in daily life were not British.

As a matter of fact they were not even Trinidadians in
the traditional sense; apart from the highest ranking, short-
term untrained officers, they were a new generation of
Trinidadians. They were the first proud, educated, perhaps
over-romantic, representatives of a new generation of
Trinidadians who flowered into emotional and intellectual
awareness with the absolute certainty that they were not
British. They were if you wish, the sabras of our young
nation and in this they were a different quality of Trinidadians from their senior officers and most certainly a
different quality of Trinidadian from our country's policy
makers who do not, and indeed cannot reasonably be expected to share this passionate certainty that they are not
British. This prior generation, Mr. President, must at best
be ambivalent. I hesitate to say schizophrenic but I do say
ambivalent for they suffered their emotional maturity and
their cultural indoctrination at the time when we were in
fact, historically a subject people, a British colony.

So try as they might they cannot slough off the skins
and markings of their growth in a colonial condition. They
may change their spots. They may mouth platitudes and slogans about independence and nationhood and sovereignty
and so on. But they cannot change their lily white black
skins. This is what the phrase "afro-saxon" means and this
is in essence the conflict from which the mutiny at Teteron
derived. It was a conflict between one generation and another, our colonial past and our future aspirations, it was
failure of communication between the two and a rejection
of each by the other. It was of course in detail many other
things as well but in essence it was a microcosm of our

times and of our society. So that from start to finish Mr. President, members of the court, we have spent the past few months engaged in something more than a trial of individuals for acts prohibited by a military law. This trial has been from start to finish a political transaction and I use this phrase without contempt. It has been an investigation into, and an exposure of the gap that separates our generations and into which our public institutions have fallen.

What occurred across the country in February, March and April 1970 was incontrovertibly in our view, part and parcel of the same disease which afflicted the army. Society is an integrated natural whole. And all the various organs and institutions which perform its separate functions, are merely convenient administrative groupings for the management of the affairs of the whole. That you find equal measures of dis-spiritedness, despondency and disaffection in all sectors of the community at the same time is no mere coincidence. It is not by mere accident that our civil service is inefficient and unproductive, that our foreign service is demoralized, wasteful and inutile, that our medical services are crippled by strikes and walk outs, that our children cannot get into schools, that road transport is strangled throughout the country by mismanagement and that 35% of our labour force under the age of 25 is unemployed so that our young men and women roam the streets dazed and maddened by marijuana and narcotics.

It is no mere coincidence, Mr. President because the medieval attitudes and snobberies, the bureaucratic tyrannies and injustices, the cynicism of the office holders, the corruption of practice and purpose that existed in the army, the wholesale mismanagement and irresponsibility which produced such a high measure of frustration among the young officers in our army, was reflected identically throughout the nation. And so in the early months of 1970, the people took to the streets, and there was violence everywhere. This Mr. President was the state of the nation at the time when a mutiny was committed in the army.

Had the entire nation at that time been subject to military law, I think you would have found yourself sitting in judgment over some 70 or 80 thousand young men of Lt. Shah's age for the offence of mutiny. It is in this setting that you must ask yourself Mr. President to what extent the offence of mutiny is to be prohibited in our society. I have reminded the court that our army in all its essential features was modelled on the British prototype. Britain since the battle of Hastings up through the centuries, through two world wars, through the invasion of Suez right up to the invasion of Anguilla has been a warrior nation.

Throughout her long history she has used her military apparatus to "carry on her politics by other means", if I may adapt the words of Clausewitz. Her armed forces have been an active and indispensable instrument of her foreign policy, yet in her history we do not read that her armed forces ever formulated her policy or seriously contributed to her politics. The idea that certain vital organs within a body politic should maintain a total political impartiality is a peculiarly British conception so that we find that the British Monarchy and British civil service and the British judiciary and to some extent the established church in Britain are all established on and to a greater or lesser extent practice this precept. But of all these, it has been her armed forces that were forced to remain thoroughly non-political in character. I do not deny that this has been a remarkable achievement. I do question however, not only the appropriateness but even the feasibility of attempting in Trinidad and Tobago to build a non-political public institution. Let us consider how the British managed to castrate the political conscience of her armed forces and to make them the mindless instruments of her policy makers, a condition eminently to be desired by a government seeking to use her army regularly for the pursuit of her political objectives. One of the most effective methods, for the cultivation of military mindlessness was the system of laws and sanctions to which a British soldier was made subject. Within this system the law of mutiny is perhaps the most important. If you are operating a war machine that you intend to use regularly in active combat as a primary instrument of your political objectives then you had better devise ways of ensuring the total unquestioning obedience of the persons who constitute your armed forces. You must develop traditions and schools where your officers are thoroughly brain-washed and you must have laws and punishments which instil fear in your ranks. You must have courts-martial, stockades and firing squads and you must use them as industriously as you cultivate your myths of courage and heroism. Your soldiers may end up de-humanised, deprived of their critical faculties, robots unable to perceive let alone evaluate their function in their society and the world at large but they would be obedient, they would be like the Light Brigade whose thoughtless heroics were celebrated by Kipling, "theirs was not to wonder why, theirs was but to do and die". This is the type of soldier that had to be created by the British to implement British expansionist policies and defence requirements over the years and in the case of Britain it might well be argued there was ample justification for the creation of an army along these lines: strict discipline, severe sanctions for its breach, and inflexible forms of etiquette and protocol which accorded so precisely, as Lt. Shah has pointed out, with the class system so organic to the British social structure.

But to attempt to transplant such a model into another country whose military traditions are non-existent, whose culture is hybrid, dynamic and above all, unsettled, is, and has been demonstrated to be, an exercise in futility. It is to transplant a form without a content, a purpose or a justification. Consider Mr. President here in Trinidad and Tobago we have an army of 700 men in a nation of 1,000,-000 souls. We have created an army not because any one considered that we needed one, but because the British insisted that we should do so as a precondition to our independence. So we find ourselves several years later and several million dollars poorer with an army of 700 men whose only real justification is the relief of unemployment

and whose only services have been the provision of a ceremonial guard, the making of music, and the maintenance
of its own morale by the playing of sport.

To the government of our country it was, like our foreign service, a juicy grassland to which its loyal party hacks
and useless senior civil servants, might comfortably be put
out to pasture on fat salaries, and generous fringe benefits.
And the prestige of resounding ranks and titles as consola-
tion perhaps for egos, bruised by the withdrawal from
useful public service. The government of this country Mr.
President, judge for yourself could never seriously have
considered the creation of a genuine war machine as an
instrument with which to "carry on our politics by other
means". This never was nor ever could be the purpose of
the Trinidad and Tobago Regiment. Our regiment, let us
face it, was a regiment of toy soldiers, expensive toys it is
true and decorative but completely and utterly useless. The
young men who were sent to Sandhurst and Mons to be
trained as officers and gentlemen in the English fashion
were offered the prospect of a professional career in soldiering and could not be made to understand and accept
that this was neither possible nor intended, in the Trinidad
and Tobago Regiment. They found a state of affairs which
they considered to be immoral and cynical.

They found the army to be in shambles, they found discipline eroded to the bone. Favouritism and injustice
rampant. Profiteering, theft and the conversions of government property openly practised. Night clubbing, gambling
and all manner of dissolution not only condoned but encouraged as a way of life by their senior officers. They
found a total lack of professional concern on the part of
the amateurs who held the authority for reform and who
not only refused to exercise it but actively resented and
visited with victimization anyone who was unwilling to ac-
quiesce in their manner of discharging their sinecures. This
was the state of affairs which existed in the army, Mr.
President, at the time when mass demonstrations and violence erupted throughout the nation in February, March
and April of 1970. And it was this army which was called

in to control the national violence. How ironical Mr.
President that the government which had blindly created
and fostered chaos around it, which had mismanaged and
bungled the nation for 14 years, should call upon a mismanaged and bungled army to control that chaos. What
happened?

The high office holders in the army reacted predictably
to their masters' call for help. Accustomed and encouraged
to believe that their jobs were sinecures, they could not
face the challenge. So they abdicated. They simply could
not perform. Col. Johnson, the commander of the cocktail
party circuit, Col. Christopher, a sheep in wolf's clothing,
Dopwell, Spencer, Vidal, the ambiguous Captain Halfhide.
The army was leaderless in the emergency. Only the pro-
fessionally trained soldiers who, in a sense we might say,
had swallowed the romance of the Light Brigade more un-
critically than the rest, knowing intimately the condition
of the Regiment, and appreciating the impossibility of such
a Regiment performing in active duty had the courage
and initiative to act. So they took control.

And how tragically ironical that instead of being deco-
rated for their public service as the deserters were, they
are charged and convicted for the offence of mutiny. Their
real offence was that they took their training as soldiers
too literally, that they were too young and idealistic to go
along with the game of make-believe. If only, Mr. President, they had been able to accept that our army was never
really intended to be an army and the career for which
they had been trained was never intended to be a career
in soldiering. Had they been able to accept the fraudulence
of their being trained and put into costumes only to participate as minor characters in a comedy of make-believe,
then they might not have found themselves convicted
mutineers today.

I suggest to you Mr. President that not only was our
army irrelevant to the needs of Trinidad and Tobago but
that the inevitable consequence of accepting the irrelevance of the army is to accept the irrelevance of a mutiny
within it. For where its purposes are non-military and

where the ambitions of the nation creating the army have
been precluded from ever being warlike by its immutable
smallness and its poverty and where the mere ceremonial
form of an army was adopted and the content was never
either introduced nor conceived of, then the solemn offence of mutiny must logically also lack a justification and
become a mere technicality; a mere legal pedantry—in
fact, a fiction.

But even so let us consider the manner in which our
mutineers conducted themselves during the course of their
mutiny. Lt. Shah had not denied responsibility for his decision nor attempted to disavow the role he played. The
manner in which this control was exercised however is very
pertinent to the question of punishment for it throws very
considerable light on the motives and intentions of the
soldiers. When they were fired upon by the Bofors of the
Coast Guard vessel HMS Trinity, waddling as it was like a
sitting duck a few hundred yards off the coast, and irre-
sponsibly overladen with civilians, they demonstrated a
generosity of restraint, a nobility of restraint. Never a shot
was returned. And sufficient fire power was available to
them and to spare, to blast the HMS Trinity to Kingdom
Come. Never a shot was returned even though the provo-
cation was abundant. Their respect for the sanctity of human life was in the best military traditions. They behaved
like officers and gentlemen. When they held their senior
officers at their mercy they treated them with courtesy and
respect, careful even of their creature comforts, their behaviour here again was in the best military traditions. They
honoured meticulously the flag of truce, whenever it was
flown. In their negotiations with the Government they were
entirely constructive in the proposals they put forward for
the salvaging of the army. All that they took by violence,
Mr. President, was the opportunity to present to the Government their views on organisational reform within the
army. Throughout this so-called rebellion no person was
shot by, or at the order of any of its leaders. Not only was
no violence done, none was offered. For none was intended. And there was such an overwhelming abundancy

and variety of actual violence possible. The fact is that military and political objectives they sought to achieve were merely the opportunity to lead useful lives and to serve the community more constructively.

You have heard evidence from both sides, which substantially agrees, on what the soldiers' demands were at the Chagacabana meeting, when the soldiers were still in complete physical control not only of the army, but of all the nation's resources in violence and the skills to use it. These were their demands:

1. The removal of the Minister in charge of the Regiment;
2. The re-instatement of Serrette as Commander of the Defence Force;
3. The appointment of Shah and Lassalle as Co. Commanders;
4. A commission of enquiry into the Regiment;
5. The removal of Johnson as Commanding Officer, and
6. Amnesty for the soldiers.

These then were the revolutionary proposals of the "rebels"! You may judge for yourself from these proposals how innocent were the purposes of the rebellion as far as seizing political power in the country was concerned. These proposals were related exclusively to the internal affairs of the regiment, and even here they made, with respect to themselves, the most modest of assertions. Can you imagine expensively trained officers, soured by frustration, finally in total control of the army, asking merely that they be appointed company commanders? Mr. President, in a genuine revolutionary state of affairs there would, first of all have been no demands at all. There would have been simply seizure of power and the disposal of the government. But here we have so-called rebels in power who, while fully in control virtually petition the Government to effect minor reforms in their professional lives and for themselves they ask merely that they be confirmed in positions within the reorganised structure far less exalted than those that they effectively controlled at the moment. And in any events, they were perfectly qualified to hold and aspire to these functions. I said that the young officers in our Regiment were guilty merely of seizing the occasion to have their case for reforms heard by the civilian authorities who had the constitutional power to effect such reforms. In effect they were offering to the civilian authorities—the politicians—the opportunity to reform the nation's Regiment which it had always been the politicians' responsibility and duty to do anyway.

They were offering to the lawful authorities an opportunity to remedy the derelictions which they had committed and accumulated over the years of neglect and mismanagement— And the ultimate irony of it all is that the politicians, while prosecuting the soldiers for providing this opportunity, have accepted and implemented in substantial measure the soldiers' proposals. All, that is, with the exception of amnesty.

Johnson was fired. Serrette is restored. The minister responsible was fired, and the entire Ministry of Home Affairs dissolved and reorganized. Serrette did appoint Shah and Lassalle to be co-commanders when he himself was reinstated. And a commission of Enquiry was established to investigate the affairs of the army.

Now it is true that the nation and its leadership reacted to the situation with panic and fear. The nation of course could not be blamed for their reaction, they knew nothing of the conditions in the army which had been closed off to it "for reasons of security" and if there is any feeling among people of Trinidad and Tobago that the soldiers should be punished it is probably for precisely this reason: that they precipitated a state of affairs that caused alarm to a number of people. It must be a question for you Mr. President to consider how seriously one should punish soldiers who by their behaviour caused the population to go into such a state of false alarm. As I said the nation could not reasonably be blamed for their reaction for while foreigners and foreign military personnel were welcomed to Teteron with almost unrestricted access to be entertained, and to be trained, but the local community was, as a matter of policy, excluded from viewing the wastage to which our scarce financial resources were being devoted.

So the local population, learning that control has been seized by rebel officers were ready in the context of the general violence in the country at that time to believe the worst. They were encouraged to arm themselves (quite illegally, I must add) to form vigilante groups, to lock up their wives and their children, and some sections of the community I understand actually did so. But is it reasonable to blame the soldiers for this reaction? The members of the Government on the other hand knowing as they must have done where true responsibility for this dissolution in the army lay, quite understandably were petrified by fear of the vengeance of the young officers and abused "other ranks" now that they seemed to have liberated themselves. So they forgot their pride, their much touted championship of non-intervention, their inflexible opposition to the Monroe Doctrine and Gunboat diplomacy and cried like hysterical children for help to every nation within ear-shot. But they did not know the young officers as individuals. To them they had always been mere cyphers now become rebellious. It never occurred to them that all that the mutineers wished, was the occasion to present their case where it might count for organisational reform within the army.

Why then are these officers before you on trial for mutiny you might well ask. First Mr. President, they are on trial because the country and the government require scapegoats for the wave of troubles which broke over the nation at large in the first quarter of 1970. Secondly the government, after keeping the affairs on the regiment hidden from the population for years, realizes now that this policy is no longer feasible and by adopting a policy of full disclosure, is using this trial as a form of public investigation with the hope that sufficient political justification will emerge for further heads to roll, including I might add, that of the now, temporarily triumphant, Brigadier

Serrette, who now that he has lost all credibility as a witness is no longer a credible leader of men.

Another reason is that the Government judges it expedient to provide a diversion for the so-called "mob"—a diversion in the style of a Roman circus, that the people should cease to focus their attention on their legitimate grievances and be deluded into believing that the ills from which they suffer can in some mysterious way be cured by the sacrificial shedding of blood or by destruction of the lives of these young men. And you honourable members of this court have been brought here to do this job for the Government. For the Government is now without either the moral authority or even the courage to act on its own behalf or through its own discredited personnel. In its cynicism the Government knows you enjoy the sympathy of our people because you are black men from the third world. Even this sense of solidarity which exists between your people and ours is not too sacred for our leaders to abuse.

The final reason why these men are prosecuted Mr. President, is this: that having forced the government to hear their proposals for reorganization in the Regiment, having forced the government in effect to acknowledge the failure of its policy towards the Regiment, the government is politically obliged to save its face by condemning as criminals, the men who exposed their mismanagement.

It cannot seriously be argued that severe punishments, or for that matter punishment of any kind, will have a curative effect on the illnesses of Trinidad and Tobago Regiment as an institution. The Mutiny unfortunately did not occur as a result of any causes which you or this honourable court have the power to correct. While severe punishment will be useless, indeed detrimental to the weakened conditions in which our country finds itself at this time, leniency may well have a healthful and healing effect on the unstable, and nerve wracked condition to which our society has been brought.

If you pass a sentence of death, Mr. President, as you have the power to do, if you order the destruction of his useful life by ordering a long period of imprisonment, you will have come to us as visitors and struck a blow against a generation which we can ill-afford to lose or deflect from its task of salvaging us from our colonial past and the wreckage of our immediate post-colonial mismanagement. And you and your brethren, unaccountable for what you will have done, will leave us in an immeasurably more desperate condition than that in which you found us. It should not have been for you to have this awful responsibility. But you have it. If you were one of us, I would demand that you discharge it with a patriotic love for our country. You are foreigners, and I can only beg of you to use it with a great understanding and measure of care appropriate to the deep sympathy which exists between your peoples and ours.

Lt. Shah is a young man of 24 in an army controlled by tired and cynical old men. On April 21st last he conceived it to be his duty to adopt a course of action which carried him fully into the teeth of the established order. He had the courage of his convictions and he did what he felt he had to do. Such a person does not readily compromise or opt out or behave in a manner inconsistent with his manhood as so many of his colleagues did. You may question his judgment, Mr. President, but there can be no question as to the honesty of his intentions or of the fact that his behaviour was selfless and demonstrated certain qualities of courage and of nobility.

He showed also a respect for the value of human life and for the dignity of those who came under his control. In considering your sentence it is proper to recognise his very positive qualities which would be admirable in any man, but in one so young as Lt. Shah are very rare indeed.

Mr. President, members of the court, in an army such as ours, reduced to the virtual shambles in which it was, in a country such as ours it is absurd and wasteful to consider punishing a man such as Lt. Shah for having committed a mutiny such as the one for which you have found him guilty. There may be legal justification for referring to his behaviour as mutinous, but there can be no moral justification for punishing him for it. A verdict of guilty is a matter of fact and of law. The determination and imposition of sentence is a matter of moral evaluation. For his behaviour Lt. Shah does not deserve to suffer punishment. He is morally entitled to be set free. Accordingly I ask and require you to set him free.

17.

Nationalization is often considered the ultimate weapon against physical and psychological dependence on or control by the former imperial power. National control of productive enterprise is more essential where, as in the Caribbean, white expatriates formerly owned almost everything and local blacks almost nothing. In this selection, however, a Guyanese economist finds his own government's steps toward nationalization lacking in real efficacy. The take-over of the bauxite industry, heralded as a great step forward in national self-determination, hardly alters the underlying circumstances that leave Guyana at the mercy of expatriate decisions and standards. White expatriates may be less visible and foreign profits less egregious, but Guyanese employees continue to absorb expatriate perspectives, and basic management decisions are made and profits taken out, by the head offices of world-wide parent corporations. Ownership of economic resources no more means control than political autonomy means true independence.

CLIVE Y. THOMAS took his undergraduate degree at the University of the West Indies in Trinidad in 1967 and subsequently became a research associate at the university's Institute of Social and Economic Research in Jamaica. He is presently a member of the Faculty of Economics at the University of Guyana and is a founder of the political journal *Ratoon*, in which this article first appeared.

Meaningful Participation: The Fraud of It[†]
Clive Y. Thomas

The most recent slogan which has been doing the rounds is "meaningful participation." As the manufacturers of these slogans have no doubt anticipated, a great deal of energy will be spent in simply arguing about it. Arguing, in the simple sense, of either being for it or against it, with little if any effort being directed towards devising a substantive programme for ending the economic dispossession of the Caribbean peoples.

However, although this has occurred, underlining many of the comments I have heard people make on this slogan can be detected a greater sense of urgency than in many previous discussions over other slogans. The reason for this, I believe, is that participation—or rather the absence of it—has been the most fundamental factor in the history of the Caribbean.

No one can effectively interpret and therefore be in a position to devise a programme for meaningful participation in industry, unless it is first understood that the drive for meaningful participation in industry is only one element, indeed is part and parcel of a drive by the peoples of the region to have participation, *on the basis of their dominance,* in all areas of their existence—both material and cultural. All of the institutions of the Caribbean have

Meaningful Participation in Industry: Meaning and Scope. Ratoon, Occasional Paper No. 1, 1971, Georgetown, Guyana. Reprinted by permission of the author.

[†] This paper reproduces a talk given by Clive Thomas during the celebration of Critchlow Labour Week.

been created on the basis of excluding the peoples' involvement. Non-participation is the characteristic condition of the West Indies.

Some of you may feel that this is overstatement. However, if you look around you, you will observe that what I have said is true of all the major institutions we take for granted and, at the same time, assume to be "local." Take for example the established "local" church. As an institution it functions simply to preach *to* the people. To tell them what they must do to save their souls. Never to involve them in truly corporate worship. In other words, it continues to operate on the same basis as that which led to its initial establishment in the country, i.e., as a vehicle for alien cultural penetration. In the process of ensuring this it has sought to destroy all indigenous attempts to develop a peoples' religion.

The same is also true for the institution of the political party. During the 1930's and 1940's many of our most outstanding and revolutionary West Indians had hoped that the political party would have become *the* indigenous institution for involving the people meaningfully in the struggle to emancipate the region. The result is common knowledge, although we may not all care to admit it with the same degree of frankness and realism. Having set its sights only on formal political independence, the political party has become essentially an electoral organisation which springs into existence to contest an election and, after it has won or lost, merely acts as an agency for excluding, rather than involving, the people in the decisions of government. As this has continued, inevitably the electoral system has been transformed into a device for *suppressing,* not *expressing,* the will of the people. In addition, the eruption of corrupt voting practices and other irregularities has reduced the whole process to simply a means of keeping the party in office—in office. A government created in this way not only does not express the will of the people, but the party and the government together cannot be a vanguard agency in the struggle of the people for legitimate and meaningful participation in the life of the nation.

The same also holds true for the institution closest to many of you, which accounts for our presence here tonight and the courses some of you have attended during the past year—i.e. the Trade Union. No one with a sense of history can deny the role the Trade Union has played as a vanguard institution in the struggle for bringing some economic crumbs to the working class and some measure of material progress. But equally, no one should deny that as an institution, as it presently stands, the Trade Unions have become, although perhaps not irretrievably, agencies for *excluding* rather than *involving* the people in participation in their work situations. Such a development is perhaps, for a number of reasons, endemic to the structure of the trade union system itself. The trade union structure does not include two categories of the labour force which are, in terms of numbers, each as large as the working force itself. These are the twenty per cent of the labour force which are unemployed and the peasants. As a result, the Trade Unions, embracing largely the working population in organized industry, have become institutions of *relative* privilege. Certainly this is the perspective which the unemployed man in the street holds. Moreover, in so far as unemployment remains at the present inhuman levels, the strength of the Unions vis-a-vis the employer is drastically reduced. Concurrent with all this, the leadership, many of whom grew up through the ranks of the Union, has become alienated. Isolated in the material environment of the city, the air-conditioned office, the board room—the Union leader becomes the agent of compromise and conciliation. It is his fundamental task to pacify, to mollify the workers, and not to involve himself in, and be a part of, their inevitable and uncompromising struggle against the employers. Where, as in Guyana, the capitalists are largely foreign, the Union leader's alienated position in the context of the institution he leads and the society of which he is a part is cruelly exposed.

All of these institutions, the church, the party, the Trade

Union, many of you would describe as I have done, as being local. Yet we have observed their fundamental incapacities. These incapacities are most dramatically exposed in their foreign counterpart institutions and, in particular, its two most supreme forms, the plantation and the multi-national corporation. It is through these two institutions that the fundamental foreign exploitation of our material resources is organized. These institutions secure foreign domination by ensuring two things, viz:

(1)   non-participation of the Guyanese people in *ownership* of their resources.

(2)   non-participation of Guyanese in decision making on such crucial and fundamental factors of their economic lives, such as markets, prices, output, technology, investment, employment, wage rates, etc.

Around this organization of our material lives has grown up a cultural superstructure designed to service these institutions—race, colour, authoritarianism, paternalism are all cultural traits with which you are familiar. In essence, these basically express the exclusion of the people as a condition of foreign exploitation and dependence.

In light of all this, it seems to me that the true meaning and scope of meaningful participation in industry, must be nothing less than that change in industrial organization which comes about as *an integral part* of a comprehensive political, social and economic revolution, which *seeks to place* (*and to create*) institutions at the service of the people. With the perspective of this interpretation, which conforms to basic and scientific studies of the history of the Caribbean, it is easy to see that strategies which are based on anything less will end up like previous "local" efforts—i.e., as another appendage of the non-participatory system.

So far three basic strategies have been employed in order to ensure meaningful participation in industry. The first has been the Guyanization of the higher administrative structure of the foreign owned plantations and multi-national corporations. A great deal of pressure has been directed towards getting these agencies to employ more and more Guyanese. And of course they have, since we are all familiar with the fact of how quick these foreign institutions are to publicize, and to boast of, the number of Guyanese in higher administrative positions. Starting from small numbers, the rate of growth of Guyanese in higher management looks impressive. But the basic situation is not as impressive as the rates would suggest. The present situation is, as the 1966 UN Manpower survey showed, that there are 500 expatriates employed as professionals and managers in the private sector. In the six largest firms in the country, 88% of the administrators and Managing Directors are expatriate and also 58% of the managers and Senior Executives.

Despite this, the impression is a rapid replacement of expatriates by Guyanese. The question however which I am posing tonight is more fundamental. What does this mean in terms of meaningful participation? As more and more Guyanese acquire higher managerial status, two things occur. First, these Guyanese move into a particular institutional structure. They are absorbed into institutions with their own ethos, values, life styles and patterns of doing things—all of which are derived from the fundamental fact that they are here to exploit our resources for foreigners. No matter what a Guyanese may claim in this situation, he cannot deny that the basic fact of his life is that he works *all* day, devotes *all* his skill and brains to servicing an enterprise which exploits his people. This is a fundamental feature of his life. The result is that he is driven to conform to the values and pattern of behaviour of the enterprise. Instead of Guyanese making the enterprise Guyanese, they are themselves turned into an extension of the exploiting corporation or plantation.

Of course, such developments suit the owners and decision makers in these industries well. Indeed, I would go further and say that they have anticipated it and that is why they have been so responsive to the call for Guyanization. They have a lot to gain. In the first place, as we have seen, the Guyanese in higher management offers no threat to the system because of the socialisation process which leads them to accept, and execute, the values and functions of these institutions. Secondly, as this occurs the companies can still reap the advantageous publicity of saying that they are becoming more local, more Guyanese in their orientation, through simply pointing to the number of Guyanese who work for them. Thirdly, these institutions have arranged it so that the Guyanese on their staff become exposed to the public and their labour force as a sort of buffer. The white expatriate is no longer visible, only his black Guyanese image. The workers direct their grievances to the local man, and this it is hoped would divert their attention from the expatriate owner. Thus it is not surprising that whoever makes the *basic decisions* about employment, wages, output, investment, conditions of work and so on in these expatriate enterprises it is always a Guyanese who is exposed as the personnel officer, the front line man, the cannon fodder in disputes with the workers.

The second process is equally fundamental and equally undermines the significance of Guyanization. This process can be described as organisational substitution. As more and more Guyanese are taken on locally to fill positions held by expatriates, so does the firm shift the decisions which were made by expatriates back to the Head Office. The Guyanese fill the posts, they empty it of any decision-making significance. We take the form. They keep the essentials and the substance. The result of this is that Guyanization as it has been practiced does not extend any meaningful participation to the Guyanese people. It does not contribute to expanding our knowledge of the operations of these industries at the higher managerial and professional levels. It supports the non-participatory system by absorbing our skilled elites into expatriate plunder. It creates a brain-drain which takes place before our eyes. We do not see it because we associate brain-drains only with the crossing of the geographical frontier. As a consequence we are actively supporting it. Guyanization does not help to *nationalize* the companies, it serves to *denationalize* the local bourgeoisie.

The second strategy has been to encourage the expatriate industries to issue shares locally as a basis for developing local ownership. There are a number of objections to this procedure which should be noted and which would serve to indicate that such participation is equally meaningless. First, the companies which go local often offer shares in such quantities as not to put in jeopardy their control of the Company. Often, the local share issue, when it is a new company, is designed to raise enough finance to pay for the construction of the firm's operations. The rest of the shares are purchased by the parent company in exchange for technical services, patent rights, etc. This means that Guyanese money pays for the enterprise, but foreign capitalists control through their parent company. In addition, despite the wide publicity of the share issue, much of which is really designed to build an image of being local, the bulk of the local shares issued are either taken up by a regular clique of local businessmen who are offered directorships, and who tend to specialize in what they euphemistically describe as partnering local and foreign capital, or they are purchased by institutional buyers, such as banks, insurance companies etc. In both cases the broad masses of the Guyanese people do not participate meaningfully.

A second objection is that in situations where the enterprise is already a going concern, i.e, already engaged in local production, the money used to purchase any increase in their local shares also serves to provide the firm with Guyanese money for expansion, without any watering down of their control. Also, when this money is raised locally, it frees funds from the parent company for investment around the world, in the same way as profits from the local company are available for investment around the world.

Thirdly, it has always been argued that the virtue of foreign capital is that it contributes resources to the country, resources which are in short supply. But many of these procedures of issuing local shares indicate that we create situations where foreign capital comes, woos local capital, uses it, and controls it for foreign ends.

Finally, the clamour for going local has only been directed towards the foreign companies. This is understandable, since the bulk of our resources is in foreign hands. But it must not be forgotten that many of our local firms are tightly controlled within families and they also are reluctant to dilute family control by going public.

The most recent strategy is meaningful participation through government purchase of 51% of shares of the big corporations. This of course has long been in practice in many of the neo-colonial states around the world. It offers no threat to foreign capital, and, as the Vice-President of Chase Manhattan argued in his address to African industrialists, basically American capital should welcome this. It ensures greater harmony between the governments and the companies. It exposes both to each other's point of view.

The truth is that 51% does not ensure control for two basic reasons. One is, lacking adequate exposure to the technical and managerial processes of the firm, 51% has to be counteracted by engaging in management contracts with these enterprises, which only secure continued foreign control of management. Secondly, the marketing and technological processes are secret, and the expatriate enterprise through this is able to further ensure that control is not lost through a mere purchase of shares.

The problem with the 51% proposition, and many others similar to it, is a failure to understand the local expression of a multi-national corporation. It is essentially a plant. It is not a firm. It is true that there are titles such as Directors, Managers, Managing Directors, etc. But the local expression of, say, Reynolds makes no decision as regards the prices of bauxite, the output, the levels of investment, or the markets. All these are done at the Head Office where decisions which normally define a firm are made. The apparatus which exists locally is just a participation in a multiplant firm. Therefore, when we seek meaningful participation, it is not simply to acquire a share in the local apparatus, but to ensure that inroads are made into the decision making centers, which exist in the North Atlantic.

It is for this reason that meaningful participation *begins,* and I insist begins, at the point of outright ownership. It is only when we "tek all" that we are in a position to develop a strategy of control. In other words, the history of these institutions precludes a divorce of ownership and control. Foreign ownership means foreign control. Complete local control can only come about through complete local ownership. Buying 51% avoids the issue and does not confront it.

Some support for this view-point stems from the fact that although throughout the Caribbean everyone is going after 51% ownership (and we have seen Williams recently with the banks and sugar companies) not one of the proponents of this view has taken the time or the effort to involve the people, to educate them, to organize them to struggle for it. How many of you know how bauxite and alumina manufacture is undertaken? How many of you know how the industry has developed? how the products are marketed? and in what countries? how they are transported? and at what prices they are sold? If I know anything, it is only after a great deal of searching among records, since nothing can be found in a well-publicised government programme to win peoples support on the issues of life and death to the economy.

This brings us back to my earlier point, that meaningful participation in industry is only one element in a comprehensive struggle to involve the people in decision-making, ownership, and the functioning of the system. Anything less is a perpetuation of the non-participatory system. Unless this is understood and digested, no proper scheme can be devised for the new institutional frame-work to organize production, consumption, distribution, investment and utilization of our resources. Thus notions such as worker-participation mean nothing, if you continue to run a system where, through extensive unemployment, one fifth of the labour force and their dependents do not even participate in the economic life of the country through the basic necessity of a job. Similarly, forms of administration mean little until we decide to start creating a governmental apparatus which would provide for the people's participation.

In summary, then, meaningful participation means—"we do not want crumbs *we want the whole bread*!" It is not an issue where our brains match theirs at a conference table. It does not even begin with negotiations. It ends there. The power we have is measured by the degree of the people's involvement in what we are fighting for. It is *this* which confronts the companies and not our "cleverness." If we understand this, why has nothing been done so far to educate the people and the country over these issues for which they must make sacrifices? A few political statements by Big Chiefs are no substitute for education and organization.

18.

The West Indian penchant for fantasy and avoidance of reality is the underlying theme of this selection by a famous Trinidadian novelist. Naipaul sees black power in the Caribbean, otherwise imitative, as exemplifying the West Indian theater of the absurd, an acting out of frustrations engendered by smallness, isolation, and impotence behind the façade of an autonomy which can never be realized. In such a context, Trinidadians take carnival seriously, but view black-power revolt as a carnival.

A third-generation Trinidadian of East Indian descent, V. S. NAIPAUL is the most illustrious of the present galaxy of West Indian novelists. Resident in London and Paris, he has resolutely resisted being pigeonholed as a "regional" writer, but from time to time returns to focus a bleakly satirical gaze on the Caribbean, as in *The Middle Passage*. His best-known novel is *A House for Mr. Biswas*. He recounts his failure to find comfort in ancestral India in *An Area of Darkness* and explores facets of Trinidadian history in *The Loss of El Dorado*.

Power to the Caribbean People
V. S. Naipaul

The Trinidad Carnival is famous. For the two days before Ash Wednesday the million or so islanders—blacks, whites, the later immigrant groups of Portuguese, Indians, and Chinese—parade the hot streets in costumed "bands" and dance to steel orchestras. This year there was a twist. After the Carnival there were Black Power disturbances. After the masquerade and the music, anger and terror.

In a way, it makes sense. Carnival and Black Power are not as opposed as they appear. The tourists who go for the Carnival don't really know what they are watching. The islanders themselves, who have spent so long forgetting the past, have forgotten the darker origins of their Carnival. The bands, flags, and costumes have little to do with Lent, and much to do with slavery.

The slave in Trinidad worked by day and lived at night. Then the world of the white plantations fell away; and in its place was a securer, secret world of fantasy, of Negro "kingdoms," "regiments," bands. The people who were slaves by day saw themselves then as kings, queens, dauphins, princesses. There were pretty uniforms, flags, and painted wooden swords. Everyone who joined a regiment got a title. At night the Negroes played at being people, mimicking the rites of the upper world. The kings visited and entertained. At gatherings a "secretary" might sit scribbling away.

New York Review of Books, September 3, 1970, pp. 32–34. Reprinted with permission of the author.

Once, in December, 1805, this fantasy of the night over-flowed into the working day. There was serious talk then of cutting off the heads of some plantation owners, of drink-ing holy water afterward and eating pork and dancing. The plot was found out; and swiftly, before Christmas, in the main Port of Spain square there were hangings, decapita-tions, brandings, and whippings.

That was Trinidad's first and last slave "revolt." The Negro kingdoms of the night were broken up. But the fantasies remained. They had to, because without that touch of lunacy the Negro would have utterly despaired and might have killed himself slowly by eating dirt; many in Trinidad did. The Carnival the tourist goes to see is a version of the lunacy that kept the slave alive. It is the original dream of black power, style and prettiness; and it always feeds on a private vision of the real world.

During the war an admiration for Russia—really an ad-miration for "stylish" things like Stalin's mustache and the outlandish names of Russian generals, Timoshenko, Rokos-sovsky—was expressed in a "Red Army" band. At the same time an admiration for Humphrey Bogart created a rival "Casablanca" band. Make-believe, but taken seriously and transformed; not far below, perhaps even unacknowledged, there has always been a vision of the black millennium, as much a vision of revenge as of a black world made whole again.

Something of the Carnival lunacy touches all these is-lands where people, first as slaves and then as neglected colonials, have seen themselves as futile, on the other side of the real world. In St. Kitts, with a population of 36,000, Papa Bradshaw, the Premier, has tried to calm despair by resurrecting the memory of Christophe, Emperor of Haiti, builder of the Citadel, who was born a slave on the island. Until they were saved from themselves, the 6,000 people of Anguilla seriously thought they could just have a consti-tution written by someone from Florida and set up in busi-ness as an independent country.

In Jamaica the Ras Tafarians believe they are Abyssin-ians and that the Emperor Haile Selassie is God. This is one of the unexpected results of Italian propaganda during the Abyssinian war. The Italians said then that there was a secret black society called *Niya Binghi* ("Death to the Whites") and that it was several million strong. The propaganda delighted some Jamaicans, who formed little Niya Binghi play-groups of their own. Recently the Emperor visited Jamaica. The Ras Tafarians were expecting a black lion of a man; they saw someone like a Hindu, mild-featured, brown, and small. The disappointment was great; but somehow the sect survives.

These islanders are disturbed. They already have black government and black power, but they want more. They want something more than politics. Like the dispossessed peasantry of medieval Europe, they await crusades and messiahs. Now they have Black Power. It isn't the Black Power of the United States. That is the protest of a disadvantaged minority which has at last begun to feel that some of the rich things of America are accessible, that only self-contempt and discrimination stand in the way. But in the islands the news gets distorted.

The media cannot make the disadvantages as real as the protest. Famous cities are seen to blaze; young men of the race come out of buildings with guns; the black-gloved hands of triumphant but bowed athletes are raised as in a religious gesture; the handsome spokesmen of protest make threats before the cameras which appear at last to have discovered black style. This is power. In the islands it is like a vision of the black millennium. It needs no political program.

In the islands the intellectual equivocations of Black Power are part of its strength. After the sharp analysis of black degradation, the spokesmen for Black Power usually become mystical, vague, and threatening. In the United States this fits the cause of protest, and fits the white audience to whom this protest is directed. In the islands it fits the old, apocalyptic mood of the black masses. Anything more concrete, anything like a program, might become simple local politics and be reduced to the black power that is already possessed.

Black Power as rage, drama, and style, as revolutionary

jargon, offers something to everybody: to the unemployed, the idealistic, the dropout, the communist, the politically frustrated, the anarchist, the angry student returning from humiliations abroad, the racialist, the old-fashioned black preacher who has for years said at street corners that after Israel it was to be the turn of Africa. Black Power means Cuba and China; it also means clearing the Chinese and the Jews and the tourists out of Jamaica. It is identity and miscegenation. It is drinking holy water, eating pork, and dancing; it is going back to Abyssinia. There has been no movement like it in the Caribbean since the French Revolution.

So in Jamaica, some eighteen months ago, students joined with Ras Tafarians to march in the name of Black Power against the black government. Campus idealism, campus protest; but the past is like quicksand here. There was a middle-class rumor, which was like a rumor from the days of slavery, that a white tourist was to be killed, but only sacrificially, without malice.

At the same time, in St. Kitts, after many years in authority, Papa Bradshaw was using Black Power, as words alone, to undermine the opposition. Round and round the tiny impoverished island, on the one, circular road, went the conspiratorial printed message, cut out from a gasoline advertisement: *Join the Power Set*.

Far away, on the Central American mainland, in British Honduras, which is only half black, Black Power had just appeared and was already undermining the multi-racial nature of both government and opposition. The carrier of the infection was a twenty-one-year-old student who had been to the United States on, needless to say, an American government scholarship.

He had brought back news about the dignity of the peasant and of revolutions based on land. I thought the message came from another country and somebody else's revolution, and wasn't suited to the local blacks, who were mainly city people with simple city ambitions. (It was front-page news, while I was there, that a local man had successfully completed an American correspondence course in jail management.)

But it didn't matter. A message had come. "The whites are buying up the land." "What the black man needs is bread." "It became a phallic symbol to the black to be a logcutter." It was the jargon of the movement, at once scientific-sounding and millenarian. It transcended the bread-and-butter protests of local politics; it smothered all argument. Day by day the movement grew.

Excitement! And perhaps this excitement is the only liberation that is possible. Black Power in these black islands is protest. But there is no enemy. The enemy is the past, of slavery and colonial neglect and a society uneducated from top to bottom; the enemy is the smallness of the islands and the absence of resources. Opportunism or jargon may define phantom enemies: racial minorities, "elites," "white niggers." But at the end the problems will be the same, of dignity and identity.

In the United States Black Power may have its victories. But they will be American victories. The small islands of the Caribbean will remain islands, impoverished and unskilled, ringed as now by a *cordon sanitaire,* their people not needed anywhere. They may get less innocent or less corrupt politicians; they will not get less helpless ones. The island blacks will continue to be dependent on the books, films, and goods of others; in this important way they will continue to be the half-made societies of a dependent people, the Third World's third world. They will forever consume; they will never create. They are without material resources; they will never develop the higher skills. Identity depends in the end on achievement; and achievement here cannot but be small. Again and again the millennium will seem about to come.

Fifty years ago, writing at a moment when Spain seemed about to disintegrate, Ortega y Gasset saw that fragmented peoples come together only in order "to do something tomorrow." In the islands this assurance about the future is

missing. Millenarian excitement will not hold them together, even if they were all black; and some, like Trinidad
and Guyana and British Honduras, are only half black.
The pursuit of black identity and the community of black
distress is a dead end, frenzy for the sake of frenzy, the
self-scourging of people who cannot see what they will
have to do tomorrow.

In *We Wish to Be Looked Upon,* published last year by
Teachers College Press, Vera Rubin and Marisa Zavalloni
report on surveys of high-school students in Trinidad they
conducted in 1957 and 1961, at a time of pre-independence
optimism. The students were asked to write at length about
their "expectations, plans and hopes for the future."

Black: I would like to be a great man not only in
music but also in sociology and economics. In the USA
I would like to marry a beautiful actress with plenty of
money. I would also like to be famed abroad as one of
the world's foremost millionaires.

Black: In politics I hope to come up against men like
Khrushchev and other enemies of freedom. I hope I
will be able to overcome them with my words, and put
them to shame.

Black: I expect to be a man of international fame, a
man who by virtue of his political genius has acquired
so much respect from his people that he will be fully
capable of living in peace with his people.

Black: I want to be a West Indian diplomat. I would
like to have a magnetic power over men and a stronger
magnetic power over women. I must be very intelligent
and quick-witted; I must be fluent in at least seven languages. I must be very resourceful and I must say the
correct thing at the correct moment. With these qualities
and a wonderful foresight and with other necessary
abilities which I can't foresee, I would be able to do
wonders for the world by doing wonders for my nation.

East Indian: I will write a book called the "Romance
of Music and Literature." I will make this book as great

as any Shakespeare play; then I will return to India to endeavor to become a genius in the film industry.

East Indian: I want to develop an adventurous spirit. I will tour the earth by air, by sea, and by land. I shall become a peacemaker among hostile people.

East Indian: When I usually awake from my daydream, I think myself to be another person, the great scientific engineer, but soon I recollect my senses, and then I am myself again.

Colored (*mulatto*): Toward the latter part of my life I would like to enter myself in politics, and to do some little bit for the improvement and uplift of this young Federation of ours.

Colored: I am obsessed with the idea of becoming a statesman, a classical statesman, and not a mere rabble-rouser who acts impulsively and makes much ado about nothing.

White: I am going to apprentice myself to a Chartered Accountant's firm and then to learn the trade. When I want to, leave the Firm and go to any other big business concern and work my way up to the top.

White: I want to live a moderate life, earning a moderate pay, slowly but surely working my way in the law firm, but I don't want to be chief justice of the Federation or anything like that. . . . Look around. All the other boys must be writing about their ambitions to be famous. They all cannot be, for hope is an elusive thing.

White: By this time my father may be a share-holder in the company, I will take over the business. I will expand it and try to live up to the traditions that my father has built up.

Without the calm of the white responses, the society might appear remote and backward. But the white student doesn't inhabit a world which is all that separate. Trinidad is small, served by one newspaper and two radio stations and the same unsegregated schools. The intercourse between the races is easier than inquiring sociologists usually

find; there is a substantial black and East Indian middle
class that dominates the professions. When this is understood, the imprecision of black and East Indian fantasy—
diplomacy, politics, peacemaking—can be seen to be more
than innocence. It is part of the carnival lunacy of a lively,
well-informed society which feels itself part of the great
world, but understands at the same time that it is cut off
from this world by reasons of geography, history, race.

The subtitle of Rubin and Zavalloni's book is "A Study
of the Aspirations of Youth in a Developing Society." But
the euphemism is misleading. This society has to be more
precisely defined. Brazil is developing, India is developing.
Trinidad is neither undeveloped nor developing. It is fully
part of the advanced consumer society of the West; it
recognizes high material standards. But it is less than pro-
vincial; there is no metropolis to which the man from the
village or small town can take his gifts. Trinidad is simply
small; it is dependent; and the people born in it—black,
East Indian, white—sense themselves condemned, not necessarily as individuals, but as a community, to an inferiority
of skill and achievement. In colonial days racial depriva-
tion could be said to be important, and this remains, obviously, an important drive. But now it is only part of the
story.

In the islands, in fact, black identity is a sentimental
trap, obscuring the issues. What is needed is access to a
society, larger in every sense, where people will be allowed
to grow. For some territories this larger society may be
Latin American. Colonial rule in the Caribbean defied geography and created unnatural administrative units; this
is part of the problem. Trinidad, for instance, was detached
from Venezuela. This is a geographical absurdity; it might
be looked at again.

A Latin American identity is also possible for Guyana
and British Honduras. But local racial politics and colonial
prejudice stand in the way. The blacks of British Honduras,
in their one lazy, mosquito-infested town, reject "Latinization" without knowing what they are rejecting. Until

Black Power came along last year, the black flag of protest against Latinization was the Union Jack; and the days of slavery were recalled with pride as the days when blacks and their English owners, friends really, stood shoulder to shoulder against the awful Spaniards. The blacks, at the end of the day, see themselves as British, with British institutions; Latin Americans are seen as chaotic, violent, without the rule of law.

There is an irony in this. Because in these former British territories the gravest issue, as yet unrecognized, is the nineteenth-century Latin America issue of government by consent. These Caribbean territories are not like those in Africa or Asia, with their own internal reverences, that have been returned to themselves after a period of colonial rule. They are manufactured societies, labor camps, creations of empire; and for long they were dependent on empire for law, language, institutions, culture, even officials. Nothing was generated locally; dependence became a habit. How, without empire, do such societies govern themselves? What is now the source of power? The ballot box, the mob, the regiment? When, as in Haiti, the slave-owners leave, and there are only slaves, what are the sanctions?

It is like the Latin American situation after the breakup of the Spanish Empire. With or without Black Power, chaos threatens. But chaos will only be internal. The islands will always be subject to an external police. The United States helicopters will be there, to take away United States citizens, tourists; the British High Commissions will lay on airlifts for their citizens. These islands, black and poor, are dangerous only to themselves.

19.

In contrast to the bleakness of Naipaul's view, his eminent countryman C. L. R. JAMES here expresses his delight in a uniquely West Indian artistic genius, the calypsonian Sparrow. The folk tradition that Sparrow built on is a true expression of the general pattern of West Indian life and also provides a critical gloss on elite and middle-class behavior and pretensions. Whatever West Indian society may be, its calypsonians hold up a unique mirror to it. It is most appropriate that the chronicler of the first successful West Indian revolution in Haiti (see "The Slaves" in *Slaves, Free Men, Citizens*) should also be the celebrator of those forces in West Indian life that limn the ferment arising from the ceaseless search for West Indian identity.

The author, born in Trinidad in 1901, has been teacher, journalist, novelist, revolutionary, Socialist, pan-Africanist, and cricket devotee. He played a major role in anti-imperialist activities in England during the 1930s and 1940s and returned to Trinidad in the late 1950s to serve as editor of the *Nation*, organ of the People's National Movement, only to break with that party's leader a few years later. He currently teaches in New York and Washington.

The Mighty Sparrow
C. L. R. James

A NATIVE WEST INDIAN TALENT, BORN AND BRED IN THE WEST INDIES AND NOURISHED BY THE WEST INDIES. WHAT HE LACKS IS WHAT WE LACK AND IF WE SEE THAT HE GETS IT, THE WHOLE NATION WILL MOVE FORWARD WITH HIM; FRANCISCO SLINGER, OTHERWISE KNOWN AS THE MIGHTY SPARROW.

It is a great pleasure to turn to a personality analysis of the most remarkable man I have met during four years in the West Indies: Sparrow.

Sparrow is a Grenadian who lived as a youth in Grenada. Obviously he was born with an exceptional gift for music, for words and for social observation. If he had gone to America he would have sung (and composed) American songs, like Brook Benton, Ben E. King, Sam Cooke and many others. Not one of them, not one, surpasses him in anything that he does. He came to Trinidad and found in Trinidad a medium, the calypso, in which his talents could have full play.

Where have we won creative national distinction in the past? In two spheres only, the writing of fiction, and cricket. Cricketers and novelists have added a new dimension, but to already established international organizations.

Not so the Mighty Sparrow, and here he is indeed

Party Politics in the West Indies, San Juan, Trinidad: Vedic Enterprises, 1962, pp. 164–75. Reprinted by permission of the author.

mighty. His talents were shaped by a West Indian medium; through this medium he expanded his capacities and the medium itself. He is financially maintained by the West Indian people who buy his records. The mass of people give him all the encouragement that an artist needs. Although the calypso is Trinidadian, Sparrow is hailed in all the islands and spontaneously acknowledged as a representative West Indian. Thus he is in every way a genuinely West Indian artist, the first and only one that I know. He is a living proof that there is a West Indian nation.

I do not propose any critical review of his music. This is work for a trained musician. There is only one quality which I wish to elaborate here.

In the famous "Jean and Dinah," Sparrow immortalizes the attitude of the ordinary people to the Americans at the base.

> It's the glamour boys again
> We are going to rule Port-of-Spain
> No more Yankees to spoil the fete . . .

If that is not a political statement, then, after thirty years of it, I don't know what politics is.

He relates how the Yankee dollars have brought some ancient performers once more into the ring, and then:

But leave them alone, don't get in a rage
When a Yankee drunk he don't study age
For whether she is 24, 25 or 80
I am sure it would not interest a drunken Yankee
For when you drink Barbados Nectar it doesn't matter
    How old she is
As long as the Yankee get what is his.

Sparrow is uninhibited about what he sees. He doesn't get in a rage. But he views the world with a large detachment. His irony and wit are the evidence.

In strict politics he shows an extraordinary sensitivity to public moods, with the same ironical detachment; this time however, not merely as an observer but as one of the people.

He begins by rejoicing at the victory of Dr. Williams in 1956.

> For we have a champion leader
> William the Conqueror

But he believes that the victory of PNM has raised the taxi fares and the price of milk. He sings "No, Doctor, No." He philosophises on the curious behaviour of politicians in general but this verse was omitted in a later edition, so I shall leave it where it is. However, he says that he still supports PNM though he will see how things go: he has in reserve his piece of mango wood.

Then follows his superb "You Can't Get Away From The Tax." He tells the public that they must accept. He expresses popular resentment at "Pay As You Earn," but in the end his father sells the revolutionary axe to pay the income tax. Despite the pervading irony he is performing a public service. He is making the unpleasant palatable with wit and humour.

Then Sparrow expresses perfectly the attitude of the ordinary man to PNM in 1959.

> Leave the dam Doctor
> He ain't trouble all you
> Leave the dam Doctor
> What he do he well do

Not too long ago, Sparrow becomes aware that things are not going well. He blames the Opposition. What is notable is his sense of the political confusion in the country.

> The island as you see
> Suffering politically
> Because the present Government
> Have some stupid opponent
> Oh, Lord, man, they ignorant . . .
> Causing they own self embarrassment

I believe here he faithfully reports public sentiment. Things are in a mess and the reason is that the Opposition are objecting to everything.

Finally there is his magnificent "Federation" calypso, a triumph.

I was in the tent the night he returned and first sang it. When it became clear what he was saying, the audience froze. Trinidad had broken with the Federation. Nobody was saying anything and the people did not know what to think, far less what to say. At the end of the last verse on that first night Sparrow saw that something was wrong and he added loudly: "I agree with the Doctor." But the people of Trinidad and Tobago only wanted a lead. Sparrow divined their mood, for henceforth he became increasingly bold and free. When he sang at the Savannah he put all he had into it and the public made a great demonstration. They wanted, how they wanted somebody to say something, and Sparrow said something. He attacked Jamaica and Jamaica deserved to be attacked. But Sparrow said what people wanted to hear: "We failed miserably."

He went further:

> Federation boil down to simply this
> It's dog-eat-dog, and survival of the fittest

The scorn, the disappointment he poured into those words did for the whole population what it wanted done and could not do for itself. The response of the public was greater than anything I have ever heard in the West Indies.

But Sparrow is a very clever man. Note the insoluble ambiguity of the last verse. He was singing before a Trinidad audience for whom a political position on federation had been taken.

> Some may say we shouldn't help part it
> But is Jamaica what start it

There he introduces the all-important question: was Trinidad right to leave, and he says that after all it was

Jamaica which started this leaving business. He does not comment himself, but he has registered that some Trinidad people are against Trinidad leaving. Now comes a master-piece of political statement.

> Federation boil down to simply this
> It's dog-eat-dog, and survival of the fittest
> Everybody going for independence
>   Singularly
> Trinidad for instance
> And we'll get it too, boy, don't bother
> But I find we should all be together
> Not separated as we are
> Because of Jamaica

What does this verse mean? I have asked a score of people and nobody can say for certain. Let us look at it. The dog-eat-dog includes everybody, and is savage enough. Then the lines which say that everybody is "going for independence |Singularly| Trinidad for instance," can be related to dog-eat-dog. But he says quickly that we in Trini-dad will get it. Which does not modify the ferocity of dog-eat-dog by a single comma. But Trinidad will get it. There must be no doubt about that so he puts in an encouraging "don't bother." Then comes the mysterious

> But I find we should all be together
> Not separated as we are
> Because of Jamaica

It can mean "I think we should all, all of us in the British West Indies, be together, and not separated as we are be-cause Jamaica left us." But it could easily mean, "I think that we who remain behind should all be together and not be separated as we are because Jamaica left."

What do I think? I think first that politically the state-ment is a masterpiece. But I can go a little further. I cannot ignore the savage contempt of dog-eat-dog, and I find the musical tone of "Everybody going for independence |Sin-gularly| Trinidad for instance" very revealing. If Sparrow liked that move politically, or if he thought that his public liked it, he would have written and sung differently. There I have to leave it.

There is more to Sparrow, much more. There is that comic episode of the Governor who was crazy, and changed the law for a lady, the lady in the short little shorts. There is the same amused and ironical detachment as when he is describing the social tastes of the Yankees.

At times he explodes. In "Leave the Dam Doctor," there suddenly stands out this verse:

> They makin' so much confusion
> But race riot in England
> They should kick them from Scotland Yard
> We have the same question in Trinidad

That can mean a lot of things.
Then comes this skilful and ferocious verse.

> Well, the way how things shapin' up
> All this nigger business go' stop
> I tell you soon in the West Indies
> It's please Mr. Nigger please

The ways of an artist are his own. You can only judge by the result. I once told him that I thought his "Gun-slingers" was a picture of violent and rebellious sentiments simmering in the younger generation. He said he didn't think of it that way. Everybody was going around saying, "Make your play," and on that he built up the whole. This is an old problem. I told him: "I accept what you say. But that would not alter the fact that such a calypso would spring only from a feeling that similar sentiments were rife among the younger generation." He reflected a second and then said, "I see what you mean." And I had no doubt that he saw exactly what I meant: that an artist draws or paints a single episode which he sees in front of him, but that he has chosen it or shapes it from pervading sentiments of which he is not necessarily conscious.

Another more pointed instance of his attitudes is his

calypso on the marriage of Princess Margaret. It is most brilliantly done and for comic verse this one stands high on my list:

> Long ago in England
> You couldn't touch the princess' hand
> Unless, well, you able
> Like the Knights of the Round Table
> If you want she real bad
> You had to beat Ivanhoe or Sir Galahad
> Mount your horse with your spear in hand
> Who remain alive that's the princess' man

Again:

> Some people real lucky
> Take for instance Anthony

And again:

> If the Princess like you
> Boy, you ain't have a thing to do

That single word, "Boy," is loaded.

And here in my view is an example of the real social value of Sparrow. I didn't know what he was getting at until after conversations in Jamaica with ordinary citizens. Now I have been a republican since I was eight years old. An Englishman, William Makepeace Thackeray, taught it to me. But the British people respect and some even love the Royal Family, and we revolutionists don't make a fuss about it. What to my surprise I discovered in Jamaica among the ordinary people was a deep regard for the British Royal Family, combined with nationalism. How widespread that is among the ordinary people in Trinidad I do not know, but Sparrow's song on the marriage was the song of a man whose inner conceptions of royalty had received a violent shock.

For a young man he shows an exceptional maturity and detachment in the way he views the life around him. As he grows older he can become a guide, philosopher and friend to the public. Some of his songs are very improper, but the West Indian audience takes them in its stride, and I could mention some world-famous novelists who excel Sparrow in impropriety. But what attracts and holds me is his social and political sense, and his independence and fearlessness. Such men are rare. At critical moments he can say, to the people or on their behalf, what should be said. Will Rogers was such a one in the United States. But I am afraid for Sparrow, mortally afraid. Such a man should be left alone to sing what he likes when he likes; he should be encouraged to do so. But West Indian governments help those who praise them and can be as savage and vicious as snakes to those who are not helping them to win the next election.

I used to listen to Sparrow before I came here and was very much impressed with his records. As soon as I saw and heard him in person, felt his enormous vitality and gathered some facts about him I recognised that here was a man who comes once in fifty years. In November 1959 I was invited to speak at UCWI on "The Artist in the Caribbean." I want to refer to how I approach the question. I spoke of art in general through the ages, of Cezanne, of Shakespeare, of Michelangelo; of the Greek city-state, of the cities of the Middle Ages. I made it clear that while I spoke about Cezanne and Michelangelo, historical figures, I was not going to express any opinions about West Indian painters because I had no qualification for doing so.

Then I moved straight to Beryl McBurnie and Sparrow, West Indian artists playing for West Indian audiences. To that university audience, after a passage on our novelists and the need to get them home, I said finally:

"When our local artists can evoke the popular response of a Sparrow, the artist in the Caribbean will have arrived."

Everything that I really think about the West Indies, not only its art, is contained in that lecture and particularly in that sentence.

Sparrow has it in him to go much further and take the West Indian nation with him. He is fully able to carry a full-length West Indian show first all over the West Indies and then to London and New York. He could write most of it, words and music. Of that I am absolutely confident. And if he were to spend some time in England his satirical eye would not fail to add to the gaiety of nations. But that undertaking is not one to be lightly embarked upon. And I am yet to find any educated West Indians in the West Indies who are educated enough to put their education at the disposal of the Mighty Sparrow. At any rate Sparrow knows those who do not like him and when he sings he doesn't mince words about them. He knows that "*they*" will do "*anything.*" He sticks to the people. Let us hope that, difficult as it may become, he will continue to be *vox populi*.

SELECTED READINGS

Those who wish to explore West Indian themes further may find this list of selected sources useful. Intended to be exemplary rather than exhaustive, it is divided for convenience into four parts: bibliographies, basic references, fiction and poetry, and current West Indian periodicals. For reprinted early works, the original publication date appears in brackets. As availability was an important criterion, references are limited to published books; for journal articles and unpublished dissertations, readers should refer to the bibliographies cited.

I. BIBLIOGRAPHIES

BAA, ENID M., compiler, *Theses on Caribbean Topics, 1778–1968* (Caribbean Bibliographic Series, No. 1), San Juan, Institute of Caribbean Studies and the University of Puerto Rico Press, 1970.

COMITAS, LAMBROS, *Caribbeana 1900–1965: A Topical Bibliography,* Seattle, University of Washington Press for the Research Institute for the Study of Man, 1968.

JAHN, JANHEINZ, *A Bibliography of Neo-African Literature from Africa, America, and the Caribbean,* London, Andre Deutsch, 1965. Antilles and Guianas section, pp. 132–95.

LOWENTHAL, DAVID, "A Selected West Indian Reading List," in his *West Indies Federation: Perspectives on a New Nation,* New York, Columbia University Press with the American Geographical Society and Carleton University, 1961, pp. 101–35. Annotated.

RAGATZ, LOWELL JOSEPH, compiler, *A Guide for the Study of British Caribbean History, 1763–1834, Including the Abolition and Emancipation Movements*, Washington, D.C., Government Printing Office, 1932.

RENSELAAR, H. C. VAN, and SPECKMANN, J. D., "Social Research on Surinam and the Netherlands Antilles," *Nieuwe West-Indische Gids*, Vol. 47, No. 1 (September 1969), pp. 29–59. Analysis of 238 sources.

THOMPSON, EDGAR T., *The Plantation: A Bibliography* (Social Science Monographs, IV), Washington, D.C., Pan American Union, 1957.

II. GENERAL REFERENCES

ABRAHAMS, PETER, *Jamaica: An Island Mosaic*, London, Her Majesty's Stationery Office, 1957.

ACWORTH, A. W., *Treasure in the Caribbean: A First Study of Georgian Building in the British West Indies*, London, Pleiades Books, 1949.

ANDIC, FUAT M., and MATHEWS, T. G., editors, *The Caribbean in Transition: Papers on Social, Political, and Economic Development*, Proceedings of the Second Caribbean Scholar's Conference, 1964, Río Piedras, Institute of Caribbean Studies, University of Puerto Rico, 1965.

ANDREWS, EVANGELINE WALKER, with ANDREWS, CHARLES MCLEAN, editors, *Journal of a Lady of Quality: Being the Narrative of a Journey from Scotland to the West Indies, North Carolina, and Portugal, in the years 1774 to 1776*, New Haven, Yale University Press, 1921.

ARONOFF, JOEL, *Psychological Needs and Cultural Systems: A Case Study*, Princeton, N.J., D. Van Nostrand, 1967.

AUGIER, F. ROY, GORDON, SHIRLEY C., HALL, DOUGLAS G., and RECKORD, M., *The Making of the West Indies*, London, Longmans, 1960.

AUGIER, F. ROY, and GORDON, SHIRLEY C., *Sources of West Indian History*, London, Longmans, 1962.

AYEARST, MORLEY, *The British West Indies: The Search for Self-Government*, New York, New York University Press, 1960.

BACCHUS, M. K., *Education and Socio-Cultural Integration in a 'Plural' Society* (Occasional Paper Series, No. 6), Montreal, Centre for Developing-Area Studies, McGill University, 1970.

BAHADOORSINGH, KRISHNA, *Trinidad Electoral Politics: The Persistence of the Race Factor*, London, Institute of Race Relations, 1968.

BANGOU, HENRI, *La Guadeloupe, 1848–1939: ou les aspects de la colonisation après l'abolition de l'esclavage*, Aurillac, Éditions du Centre, 1963.

——, *La Guadeloupe, 1492–1848: ou l'histoire de la colonisation de l'île liée à l'esclavage noir de ses débuts à sa disparition*, Aurillac, Éditions du Centre, 1962.

BARRETT, LEONARD E., *The Rastafarians: A Study in Messianic Cultism in Jamaica* (Caribbean Monograph Series, No. 6), Río Piedras, Institute of Caribbean Studies, University of Puerto Rico, 1968.

BARTLETT, C. J., *A New Balance of Power: The 19th Century* (in *Chapters in Caribbean History*, No. 2), Barbados, Caribbean Universities Press, 1970, pp. 55–91.

BEACHEY, R. W., *The British West Indies Sugar Industry in the Late 19th Century*, Oxford, Basil Blackwell, 1957.

BECKFORD, GEORGE, *The West Indian Banana Industry* (*Studies in Regional Economic Integration*, Vol. 2, No. 3), Jamaica, Institute of Social and Economic Research, University of the West Indies, 1967.

BECKWITH, MARTHA WARREN, *Black Roadways: A Study of Jamaican Folk Life*, Chapel Hill, University of North Carolina Press, 1929.

BEGHIN, I. D., FOUGÈRE, W., and KING, KENDALL W., *Food and Nutrition in Haiti*, Paris, Presses Universitaires de France, 1968.

BELL, WENDELL, *Jamaican Leaders: Political Attitudes in a New Nation*, Berkeley, University of California Press, 1964.

BELL, WENDELL, editor, *The Democratic Revolution in the West Indies: Studies in Nationalism, Leadership, and the Belief in Progress*, Cambridge, Mass., Schenkman, 1967; New York, Oxford University Press, 1967.

BENEDICT, BURTON, editor, *Problems of Smaller Territories*, London, Athlone Press for the Institute of Commonwealth Studies, 1967.

BENNETT, J. HARRY, JR., *Bondsmen and Bishops: Slavery*

and Apprenticeship on the Codrington Plantations of Barbados, 1710–1838 (University of California Publications in History, Vol. 62), Berkeley, University of California Press, 1958.

BENNETT, LOUISE, *Jamaica Labrish*, Jamaica, Sangster's Book Stores, 1966.

BENOIST, JEAN, *Les Martiniquais: anthropologie d'une population métissée* (*Bulletins et Mémoires de la Société d'Anthropologie de Paris,* Ser. XI, Vol. 4, No. 2, pp. 241–432), Paris, Masson, 1963.

BENOIST, JEAN, and OTHERS, *L'archipel inachevé: culture et société aux Antilles francaises,* Montreal, Presses de l'Université de Montreal, 1972.

BENOIST, JEAN, editor, *Les Sociétés Antillaises: études anthropologiques,* Montreal, Department of Anthropology, University of Montreal, 1966.

BERGHE, PIERRE L. VAN DEN, *Race and Racism: A Comparative Perspective,* New York, John Wiley, 1967.

BICKERTON, DEREK, *The Murders of Boysie Singh,* London, Arthur Barker, 1962.

BLAKE, JUDITH, with STYCOS, J. MAYONE, and DAVIS, KINGSLEY, *Family Structure in Jamaica: The Social Context of Reproduction,* New York, Free Press, 1961.

BLANSHARD, PAUL, *Democracy and Empire in the Caribbean: A Contemporary Review,* New York, Macmillan, 1947.

BONE, LOUIS W., *Secondary Education in the Guianas* (Comparative Education Center, Monograph No. 2), Chicago, University of Chicago, 1962.

BRATHWAITE, EDWARD, *The Development of Creole Society in Jamaica,* London, Oxford University Press, 1971.

BRO-JØRGENSEN, J. O., *Dansk Vestindien indtil 1755: Kolonisation og Kompagnistyre* (Vore Gamle Tropekolonier, Vol. 1), Copenhagen, Fremad, 1966.

BURN, W. L., *Emancipation and Apprenticeship in the British West Indies,* London, Jonathan Cape, 1937.

BURNHAM, LINDEN FORBES SAMPSON, *A Destiny to Mould: Selected Discourses by the Prime Minister of Guyana,* Trinidad, Longman Caribbean, 1970.

BURNS, ALAN, *History of the British West Indies,* London, George Allen and Unwin, 1954; New York, Barnes and Noble (2nd revised edition), 1965.

CALLENDER, CHARLES VICTOR, *The Development of the Capital Market Institutions of Jamaica*, Supplement to *Social and Economic Studies*, Vol. 14, No. 3, Jamaica, 1965.

CAMPBELL, A. A., *St. Thomas Negroes: A Study of Personality and Culture* (Psychological Monographs, Vol. 55, No. 5), Washington, D.C., American Psychological Association, 1943.

CARLOZZI, CARL A., and CARLOZZI, ALICE A., *Conservation and Caribbean Regional Progress*, Yellow Springs, Ohio, Antioch Press for the Caribbean Research Institute, St. Thomas, U.S.V.I., 1968.

CASSIDY, F. G., *Jamaica Talk: Three Hundred Years of the English Language in Jamaica*, London, Macmillan, 1961.

CASSIDY, F. G., and LE PAGE, R. B., *Dictionary of Jamaican English*, Cambridge, Cambridge University Press, 1967.

CÉSAIRE, AIMÉ, *Cahier d'un retour au pays natal* [1939], Paris, Présence Africaine, 1956.

CHAULEAU, LILIANE, *La société à la Martinique au XVIIe siècle (1635–1713)*, Caen, Ozanne, 1966.

CLARKE, EDITH, *My Mother Who Fathered Me: A Study of the Family in Three Selected Communities in Jamaica*, 2nd ed., London, George Allen and Unwin, 1966; New York, Humanities Press, 1966.

CLEGERN, WAYNE M., *British Honduras: Colonial Dead End, 1859–1900*, Baton Rouge, Louisiana State University Press, 1967.

CLEMENTI, CECIL, *The Chinese in British Guiana*, British Guiana, Argosy Press, 1915.

COLERIDGE, HENRY NELSON, *Six Months in the West Indies in 1825*, 3rd ed., London, John Murray, 1832.

COLLINS, WALLACE, *Jamaican Migrant*, London, Routledge and Kegan Paul, 1965.

COLLIS, LOUISE, *Soldier in Paradise: The Life of Captain John Stedman, 1744–1797*, London, Michael Joseph, 1965; New York, Harcourt Brace Jovanovich, 1965.

COLLYMORE, FRANK A., *Notes for a Glossary of Words and Phrases of Barbadian Dialect*, Bridgetown, Barbados, Advocate Press, 1955.

CONNOR, EDRIC, *Songs from Trinidad*, London, Oxford University Press, 1958.

CORZANI, JACK, *Splendeur et misère: l'exotisme littéraire*

aux Antilles (Groupe Universitaire de Recherches Inter-Caraïbes, Études et Documents, No. 2), Pointe-à-Pitre, Guadeloupe, Centre d'Enseignement Supérieur Littéraire, 1969.

COULTHARD, G. R., *Race and Colour in Caribbean Literature,* London, Oxford University Press for the Institute of Race Relations, 1962.

COUPLAND, REGINALD, *The British Anti-Slavery Movement* [1933], London, Frank Cass, 1964; Portland, Oregon, International Scholarly Book Service, 1964.

COURLANDER, HAROLD, and BASTIEN, RÉMY, *Religion and Politics in Haiti,* Washington, D.C., Institute for Cross-Cultural Research, 1966.

CRAIG, HEWAN, *The Legislative Council of Trinidad and Tobago,* London, Faber and Faber, 1952.

CRANE, JULIA G., *Educated to Emigrate: The Social Organization of Saba,* Assen, Netherlands, Van Gorcum, 1971.

CRATON, MICHAEL, *A History of the Bahamas,* London, Collins, 1962.

CRONON, EDMUND DAVID, *Black Moses: The Story of Marcus Garvey and the Universal Negro Improvement Association,* Madison, University of Wisconsin Press, 1964.

CROSS, MALCOLM, editor, *West Indian Social Problems: A Sociological Perspective,* Port-of-Spain, Columbus Publishers, 1970.

CROUSE, NELLIE M., *French Pioneers in the West Indies, 1624–1664,* New York, Columbia University Press, 1940.

CROWLEY, DANIEL J., *I Could Talk Old-Story Good: Creativity in Bahamian Folklore* (Folklore Studies 17), Berkeley, University of California Press, 1966.

CUMPER, GEORGE E., editor, *The Economy of the West Indies,* Jamaica, Institute of Social and Economic Research, University of the West Indies, 1960.

CUMPSTON, I. M., *Indians Overseas in British Territories, 1834–1854,* London, Oxford University Press, 1953.

CURTIN, PHILIP D., *The Atlantic Slave Trade: A Census,* Madison, University of Wisconsin Press, 1969.

——, *Two Jamaicas: The Role of Ideas in a Tropical Colony, 1830–1865,* Cambridge, Harvard University Press, 1955.

DAVIS, DAVID BRION, *The Problem of Slavery in Western Culture*, Ithaca, N.Y., Cornell University Press, 1966.

DAVISON, R. B., *Black British: Immigrants to England*, London, Oxford University Press for the Institute of Race Relations, 1966.

DEBBASCH, YVAN, *Couleur et liberté: le jeu du critère ethnique dans un ordre juridique esclavagiste, Vol. I: L'affranchi dans les possessions françaises de la Caraïbe (1635–1833)*, Paris, Librairie Dalloz, 1967.

DEERR, NOËL, *The History of Sugar*, 2 vols., London, Chapman and Hall, 1949–50.

DELAUNAY-BELLEVILLE, ANDRÉ, *Choses et gens de la Martinique*, 2nd ed., Paris, Nouvelles Éditions Debresse, 1964.

DEMAS, WILLIAM G., *The Economics of Development in Small Countries with Special Reference to the Caribbean* (Keith Callard Lectures, Ser. 1), Montreal, McGill University Press for the Centre for Developing-Area Studies, 1965.

DESPRES, LEO A., *Cultural Pluralism and Nationalist Politics in British Guiana*, Chicago, Rand McNally, 1967.

Developments Towards Self-Government in the Caribbean: A Symposium, The Hague, W. van Hoeve, 1955.

DIEDERICH, BERNARD, and BURT, AL, *Papa Doc: The Truth About Haiti Today*, New York, McGraw-Hill, 1969.

EDWARDS, DAVID T., *Report on an Economic Study of Small Farming in Jamaica*, Jamaica, Institute of Social and Economic Research, University of the West Indies, 1961.

EISNER, GISELA, *Jamaica, 1830–1930: A Study in Economic Growth*, Manchester, Manchester University Press, 1961.

ELKINS, STANLEY M., *Slavery: A Problem in American Institutional and Intellectual Life* [1959], Chicago, University of Chicago Press, 1968.

EQUIANO, OLAUDAH, *Equiano's Travels* [1789], London, Heinemann, 1967.

FANON, FRANTZ, *Black Skin, White Masks*, New York, Grove Press, 1967.

The Federal Principle, special issue of *Caribbean Quarterly*, Vol. 6, Nos. 3 and 4, May 1960.

Federation of the West Indies, special issue of *Social and Economic Studies*, Vol. 6, No. 2, June 1957.

FERMOR, PATRICK LEIGH, *The Traveller's Tree: A Journey through the Caribbean Islands*, New York, Harper, 1950.

FROUDE, JAMES ANTHONY, *The English in the West Indies: or, The Bow of Ulysses*, London, Longmans, 1888.

GASTMANN, ALBERT L., *The Politics of Surinam and the Netherlands Antilles* (Caribbean Monograph Series, No. 3), Río Piedras, Institute of Caribbean Studies, University of Puerto Rico, 1968.

GASTON-MARTIN, *Histoire de l'esclavage dans les colonies françaises*, Paris, Presses Universitaires de France, 1948.

GERBER, STANFORD N., editor, *The Family in the Caribbean*, Proceedings of the First Conference . . . , Río Piedras, Institute of Caribbean Studies, University of Puerto Rico, 1968.

GIRVAN, NORMAN, *The Caribbean Bauxite Industry* (*Studies in Regional Economic Integration*, Vol. 2, No. 4), Jamaica, Institute of Social and Economic Research, University of the West Indies, 1967.

GISLER, ANTOINE, *L'esclavage aux Antilles françaises* (*XVIIe–XIXe siècle*): *contribution au problème de l'esclavage*, Fribourg, Éditions Universitaires, 1965.

GONZÁLEZ, NANCIE L. SOLIEN, *Black Carib Household Structure: A Study of Migration and Modernization*, Seattle, University of Washington Press, 1969.

GORDON, SHIRLEY C., *A Century of West Indian Education: A Source Book*, London, Longmans, 1963.

——, *Reports and Repercussions in West Indian Education, 1835–1933*, London, Ginn, 1968; New York, International Publications Service, 1968.

GOSLINGA, CORNELIS CH., *The Dutch in the Caribbean and on the Wild Coast, 1580–1680*, Gainesville, University of Florida Press, 1971.

GOVEIA, ELSA V., *The West Indian Slave Laws of the 18th Century* (in *Chapters in Caribbean History*, No. 2), Barbados, Caribbean Universities Press, 1970, pp. 7–53.

——, *Slave Society in the British Leeward Islands at the End of the Eighteenth Century*, New Haven, Yale University Press, 1965.

——, *A Study on the Historiography of the British West Indies to the End of the Nineteenth Century*, Mexico,

D.F., Pan-American Institute of Geography and History, 1956.

GREENFIELD, SIDNEY M., *English Rustics in Black Skin: A Study of Modern Family Forms in a Pre-Industrialized Society*, New Haven, College and University Publishers, 1966.

GREGG, A. R., *British Honduras*, London, Her Majesty's Stationery Office, 1968.

GROOT, SILVIA W. DE, *Djuka Society and Social Change: History of an Attempt to Develop a Bush Negro Community in Surinam, 1917–1926*, Assen, Netherlands, Van Gorcum, 1969.

GUÉRIN, DANIEL, *The West Indies and Their Future*, London, Dennis Dobson, 1961; New York, Hillary House, Humanities Press, 1961.

HALL, DOUGLAS, *Five of the Leewards 1834–1870: The Major Problems of the Post-Emancipation Period in Antigua, Barbuda, Montserrat, Nevis and St. Kitts*, Barbados, Caribbean Universities Press; London, Ginn, 1971.

——, *Free Jamaica 1838–1865: An Economic History*, New Haven, Yale University Press, 1959.

HAMILTON, B. L. ST. JOHN, *Problems of Administration in an Emergent Nation: A Case Study of Jamaica*, New York, Frederick A. Praeger, 1964.

HAMILTON, BRUCE, *Barbados and the Confederation Question, 1871–1885*, London, Crown Agents, 1956.

HAREWOOD, JACK, editor, *Human Resources in the Commonwealth Caribbean* (Report of the Human Resources Seminar, University of the West Indies, Jamaica, August 1970), Trinidad, Institute of Social and Economic Research, University of the West Indies, 1971.

HARLOW, V. T., *A History of Barbados 1625–1685*, London, Oxford University Press, 1926.

HARRIS, DAVID R., *Plants, Animals, and Man in the Outer Leeward Islands, West Indies: An Ecological Study of Antigua, Barbuda, and Anguilla*, Berkeley, University of California Press, 1965.

HARRIS, MARVIN, *Patterns of Race in the Americas*, New York, Walker, 1964.

HAWYS, STEPHEN, *Mount Joy*, London, Gerald Duckworth, 1968.

HEARN, LAFCADIO, *Two Years in the French West Indies,* New York, Harper and Brothers, 1923.

HEARNE, JOHN, and NETTLEFORD, REX, *Our Heritage* (Public Affairs in Jamaica, No. 1), Mona, Jamaica, Department of Extra-Mural Studies University of the West Indies, 1963.

HENRIQUES, FERNANDO, *Family and Colour in Jamaica,* 2nd ed., London, MacGibbon and Kee, 1968; New York, Humanities Press, 1969.

HENRY, FRANCES, editor, *McGill Studies in Caribbean Anthropology* (Occasional Paper Series, No. 5), Montreal, Centre for Developing-Area Studies, McGill University, 1969.

HERSKOVITS, MELVILLE J., *Life in a Haitian Valley* [1937], Garden City, N.Y., Doubleday, Anchor Books, 1971.

——, *The Myth of the Negro Past* [1941], Boston, Beacon Press, 1958.

——, *The New World Negro: Selected Papers in Afroamerican Studies,* edited by Frances S. Herskovits, Bloomington, Indiana University Press, 1966.

HERSKOVITS, MELVILLE J., and HERSKOVITS, FRANCES S., *Rebel Destiny: Among the Bush Negroes of Dutch Guiana,* New York, McGraw-Hill, 1934.

——, *Trinidad Village,* New York, Alfred A. Knopf, 1947.

HINDS, DONALD, *Journey to an Illusion: The West Indian in Britain,* London, Heinemann, 1966.

HISS, PHILIP HANSON, *Netherlands America: The Dutch Territories in the West,* London, Robert Hale, 1943.

HOETINK, HARMANNUS, *Het patroon van de oude Curaçaose samenleving: een sociologische studie,* Assen, Netherlands, Van Gorcum, 1958.

——, *The Two Variants in Caribbean Race Relations,* London, Oxford University Press for the Institute of Race Relations, 1967.

HOETINK, HARMANNUS, editor, *Encyclopedie van de Nederlandse Antillen,* Amsterdam, Elsevier, 1969.

HOROWITZ, MICHAEL M., *Morne-Paysan: Peasant Village in Martinique,* New York, Holt, Rinehart and Winston, 1967.

HOWARD, RICHARD A., *The Vegetation of the Grenadines, Windward Islands, British West Indies* (contributions from the Gray Herbarium of Harvard University, No. 174, Cambridge, Mass., 1952.

HOY, DON R., *Agricultural Land Use of Guadeloupe* (Foreign Field Research Program, Report No. 12), Washington, D.C., National Academy of Sciences-National Research Council, 1961.

HURAULT, JEAN, *Les Indiens Wayana de la Guyane française: structure sociale et coutume familiale,* Paris, Office de la Recherche Scientifique et Technique d'Outre-Mer, 1968.

JAGAN, CHEDDI, *Forbidden Freedom: The Story of British Guiana,* New York, International Publishers, 1954.

——, *The West on Trial: My Fight for Guyana's Freedom,* London, Michael Joseph, 1966; New York, International Publishers, 1967.

JAMES, C. L. R., *Beyond a Boundary,* London, Hutchinson, 1963.

——, *The Black Jacobins: Toussaint L'Ouverture and the San Domingo Revolution* [1938], New York, Random House, Vintage Books, 1963.

——, *Party Politics in the West Indies,* San Juan, Trinidad, privately published, 1962.

JAYAWARDENA, CHANDRA, *Conflict and Solidarity in a Guianese Plantation,* London, University of London, Athlone Press, 1963; New York, Humanities Press, 1963.

JORDAN, WINTHROP D., *White over Black: American Attitudes Toward the Negro, 1550–1812,* Chapel Hill, University of North Carolina Press, 1968.

KARNER, FRANCES P., *The Sephardics of Curaçao: A Study of Socio-Cultural Patterns in Flux,* Assen, Netherlands, Van Gorcum, 1969; New York, Humanities Press, 1971.

KERR, MADELINE, *Personality and Conflict in Jamaica,* London, Collins, 1963.

KESTELOOT, LILYAN, *Aimé Césaire,* Paris, Pierre Seghers, 1962.

KEUR, JOHN Y., and KEUR, DOROTHY L., *Windward Children: A Study in Human Ecology of the Three Dutch Windward Islands in the Caribbean,* Assen, Netherlands, Van Gorcum, 1960.

KLASS, MORTON, *East Indians in Trinidad: A Study of Cultural Persistence,* New York, Columbia University Press, 1961.

KLERK, J. C. M. DE, *De Immigratie der Hindostanen in Suriname*, Amsterdam, Urbi et Orbi, 1953.

LAMMING, GEORGE, *The Pleasures of Exile*, London, Michael Joseph, 1960.

LASSERRE, GUY, *La Guadeloupe: étude géographique*, 2 vols., Bordeaux, Union Française d'Impression, 1961.

LEIRIS, MICHEL, *Contacts de civilisations en Martinique et en Guadeloupe*, Paris, UNESCO/Gallimard, 1955.

LE PAGE, R. B., and DECAMP, DAVID, *Jamaican Creole*, London, Macmillan, 1960.

LEWIS, GORDON K., *The Growth of the Modern West Indies*, New York, Monthly Review Press, 1968.

LEWIS, M. G., *Journal of a West India Proprietor, 1815–17*, Boston, Houghton Mifflin, 1929.

LEWIS, S., and MATHEWS, T. G., editors, *Caribbean Integration: Papers on Social, Political, and Economic Integration*, Proceedings of the Third Caribbean Scholars' Conference, 1966, Río Piedras, Institute of Caribbean Studies, University of Puerto Rico, 1967.

LEYBURN, JAMES G., *The Haitian People*, rev. ed., New Haven, Yale University Press, 1966.

LIER, R. A. J. VAN, *Samenleving in een grensgebied: een sociaalhistorische studie van de maatschappij in Suriname*, The Hague, M. Nijhoff, 1949.

LIGON, RICHARD, *A True and Exact History of the Island of Barbadoes Illustrated with a Map of the Island, as also the Principal Trees and Plants there, Set forth in their due Proportions and Shapes, drawn out by their several and respective Scales*. . . . [1657, 1673] (Cass Library of West Indian Studies, No. 11), London, Frank Cass, 1970; Portland, Oregon, International Scholarly Book Service, 1970.

LONG, ANTON V., *Jamaica and the New Order, 1827–1847* (Special Series No. 1), Jamaica, Institute of Social and Economic Research, University of the West Indies, 1956.

LONG, EDWARD, *History of Jamaica, or, General Survey of the Ancient and Modern State of That Island*, 3 vols., [1774] (Cass Library of West Indian Studies, No. 12), London, Frank Cass, 1970.

LOWENTHAL, DAVID, *West Indian Societies*, London and New York, Oxford University Press for the Institute of Race Relations in collaboration with The American Geographical Society, 1972.

LOWENTHAL, DAVID, editor, *The West Indies Federation: Perspectives on a New Nation*, New York, Columbia University Press for the American Geographical Society and Carleton University, 1961.

MACMILLAN, W. M., *Warning from the West Indies: A Tract for the Empire*, Harmondsworth, Middlesex, England, Penguin Books, 1936.

MALEFIJT, ANNEMARIE DE WAAL, *The Javanese of Surinam: Segment of a Plural Society*, Assen, Netherlands, Van Gorcum, 1963.

MALIK, YOGENDRA K., *East Indians in Trinidad: A Study in Minority Politics*, London, Oxford University Press for the Institute of Race Relations, 1971.

MASON, PHILIP, *Patterns of Dominance*, London, Oxford University Press for the Institute of Race Relations, 1970.

MATHEWS, T. G., et al., *Politics and Economics in the Caribbean* (Special Study No. 3), San Juan, Institute of Caribbean Studies and the University of Puerto Rico, 1966. 2nd Rev. Ed. (Special Study No. 8) 1971.

MATHIESON, WILLIAM LAW, *British Slave Emancipation, 1838–1849* [1932], New York, Octagon Books, 1967.

——, *British Slavery and Its Abolition, 1823–1838*, London, Longmans, 1926; New York, Octagon Books, 1967.

MATTHEWS, DOM BASIL, *Crisis of the West Indian Family: A Sample Study*, Mona, Jamaica, Extra-Mural Department, University College of the West Indies, 1953.

MAU, JAMES A., *Social Change and Images of the Future: A Study of the Pursuit of Progress in Jamaica*, Cambridge, Mass., Schenkman, 1968.

MC CLOY, SHELBY T., *The Negro in the French West Indies*, Lexington, University of Kentucky Press, 1966.

MC FARLANE, DENNIS, *A Comparative Study of Incentive Legislation in the Leeward Islands, Windward Islands, Barbados, and Jamaica*, Supplement to *Social and Economic Studies*, Vol. 13, No. 3, September 1964.

MC INTYRE, A., and WATSON, B., *Studies in Foreign Investment in the Commonwealth Caribbean: No. 1 Trinidad and Tobago*, Jamaica, Institute of Social and Economic Research, University of the West Indies, 1970.

MC KIGNEY, JOHN I., and COOK, ROBERT, editors, *Protein*

Foods for the Caribbean, Jamaica, Bolivar Press for the Caribbean Food and Nutrition Institute, 1968.

MERRILL, GORDON C., *The Historical Geography of St. Kitts and Nevis, the West Indies,* Mexico, D.F., Pan-American Institute of Geography and History, 1958.

METCALF, GEORGE, *Royal Government and Political Conflict in Jamaica, 1729–1783,* London, Longmans for the Royal Commonwealth Society, 1965.

MIKES, GEORGE, *Not by Sun Alone,* London, Andre Deutsch, 1967.

MILLETTE, JAMES, *The Genesis of Crown Colony Government: Trinidad, 1783–1810,* Curepe, Trinidad, Moko Enterprises, 1970.

MINTZ, SIDNEY W., and DAVENPORT, WILLIAM, editors, *Working Papers in Caribbean Social Organization,* special issue of *Social and Economic Studies,* Vol. 10, No. 4, Jamaica, December 1961.

MITCHELL, HAROLD PATON, *Caribbean Patterns: A Political and Economic Study of the Contemporary Caribbean,* Edinburgh, Chambers, 1967.

———, *Europe in the Caribbean: The Policies of Great Britain, France, and the Netherlands Towards Their West Indian Territories in the 20th Century,* Edinburgh, Chambers, 1963.

MITTELHOLZER, EDGAR, *A Swarthy Boy,* London, Putnam, 1963.

———, *With a Carib Eye,* London, Secker and Warburg, 1958.

MORAL, PAUL, *Le Paysan haïtien: étude sur la vie rurale en Haïti,* Paris, G. P. Maisonneuve and Larose, 1961.

MORDECAI, JOHN, *The West Indies: The Federal Negotiations,* London, George Allen and Unwin, 1968.

MOREAU DE SAINT-MÉRY, MÉDÉRIC-LOUIS-ÉLIE, *Description topographique, physique, civile politique et historique de la partie française de l'Isle Saint-Domingue* [1797], 3 vols., Paris, Société de l'Histoire des Colonies Françaises et Librairie Larose, 1958.

MOREL, JEAN-LUC, *Jeunesse et emploi: de l'insertion des jeunes martiniquais dans le milieu social* (Cahier No. 13), Fort-de-France, Martinique, Cahiers du Centre d'Etudes Regionales Antilles-Guyane, 1968.

MÖRNER, MAGNUS, editor, *Race and Class in Latin America,* New York, Columbia University Press, 1970.

MORRELL, W. P., *British Colonial Policy in the Mid-Victorian Age: South Africa, New Zealand, The West Indies*, Oxford, Clarendon Press, 1969; New York, Oxford University Press, 1969.

MOSKOS, CHARLES C., JR., *The Sociology of Independence: A Study of Nationalist Attitudes Among West Indian Leaders*, Cambridge, Mass., Schenkman, 1967.

MURRAY, D. J., *The West Indies and the Development of Colonial Government, 1801–1834*, Oxford, Clarendon Press, 1965; New York, Oxford University Press, 1965.

NAIPAUL, V. S., *An Area of Darkness*, London, Andre Deutsch, 1964.

——, *The Loss of El Dorado: A History*, London, Andre Deutsch, 1969; New York, Alfred A. Knopf, 1970.

——, *The Middle Passage*, London, Andre Deutsch, 1962.

NATH, DWARKA, *A History of Indians in British Guiana*, London, Nelson, 1950.

NETTLEFORD, REX M., *Mirror Mirror: Identity, Race and Protest in Jamaica*, Jamaica, William Collins and Sangster, 1970.

NETTLEFORD, REX M., and LA YACONA, MARIA, *Roots and Rhythms: Jamaica's National Dance Theatre*, London, Andre Deutsch, 1969; New York, Hill and Wanz, 1970.

NETTLEFORD, REX M., editor, *Manley and the New Jamaica: Selected Speeches and Writings 1938–1968*, London, Longmans Caribbean, 1971.

NEUMANN, PETER, *Wirtschaft und materielle Kultur der Buschneger Surinames: Ein Beitrag zur Erforschung afroamerikanischer Probleme* (Abhandlungen und Berichte des Staatlichen Museums für Völkerkunde Dresden, Band 26), Berlin, Akademie-Verlag, 1967.

NEWTON, ARTHUR PERCIVAL, *The European Nations in the West Indies, 1493–1688* [1933], New York, Barnes and Noble, 1967.

NIEHOFF, ARTHUR, and NIEHOFF, JUANITA, *East Indians in the West Indies* (Publications in Anthropology, No. 6), Milwaukee, Public Museum, 1960.

NØRREGAARD, GEORG, *Dansk Vestindien 1880–1917: Reformforsøg og Salgsforhandlinger* (Vore Gamle Tropekolonier, Vol. 4), Copenhagen, Fremad, 1967.

NUGENT, MARIA, *Lady Nugent's Journal*, Kingston, Institute of Jamaica, 1966.

OLIVIER, SYDNEY, *White Capital and Coloured Labour*, London, Independent Labour Party, 1910; Westport, Connecticut, Negro Universities Press, 1910.

O'LOUGHLIN, CARLEEN, *Economic and Political Change in the Leeward and Windward Islands*, New Haven, Yale University Press, 1968.

OTTERBEIN, KEITH F., *The Andros Islanders: A Study of Family Organization in the Bahamas*, Lawrence, University of Kansas Press, 1966.

OXAAL, IVAR, *Black Intellectuals Come to Power*, Cambridge, Mass., Schenkman, 1968.

——, *Race and Revolutionary Consciousness: A Documentary Interpretation of the 1970 Black Power Revolt in Trinidad*, Cambridge, Mass., Schenkman, 1971.

PALMER, RANSFORD W., *The Jamaican Economy*, New York, Frederick A. Praeger, 1968.

PANDAY, R. N. M., *Agriculture in Surinam 1650–1950: An Inquiry into the Causes of Its Decline*, Amsterdam, H. J. Paris, 1959.

PARES, RICHARD, *Merchants and Planters*, Supplement 4 of *Economic History Review* (1960); Hamden, Connecticut, Archon Books, Shoe String Press, 1968.

——, *A West-India Fortune*, London, Longmans, 1950.

PARRY, J. H., and SHERLOCK, PHILIP M., *A Short History of the West Indies*, London, Macmillan, 1956.

PARSONS, JAMES J., *San Andrés and Providencia: English-Speaking Islands in the Western Caribbean* (University of California Publications in Geography, Vol. 12, No. 1), Berkeley, University of California Press, 1956.

PATTERSON, H. ORLANDO, *The Sociology of Slavery*, London, MacGibbon and Kee, 1967; Rutherford, New Jersey, Fairleigh Dickinson University Press, 1970.

PEACH, CERI, *West Indian Migration to Britain: A Social Geography*, London, Oxford University Press for the Institute of Race Relations, 1968.

PENSON, LILLIAN M., *The Colonial Agents of the British West Indies: A Study in Colonial Administration Mainly in the Eighteenth Century* [1924] (Cass Library of West Indian Studies, No. 16), London, Frank Cass, 1971.

PHILLIPPO, JAMES M., *Jamaica: Its Past and Present State* [1843], London, Dawsons, 1969; New York, Barnes and Noble, 1964.

PITMAN, FRANK WESLEY, *The Development of the British*

West Indies, 1700–1763 [1917], Hamden, Conn., Archon Books, Shoe String Press, 1967.

POMPILUS, PRADEL, *La langue française en Haïti*, Paris, Institut des Hautes Études de l'Amérique Latine, 1961.

POPE-HENNESSY, JAMES, *The Baths of Absalom: A Footnote to Froude*, London, Allan Wingate, 1954.

——, *Sins of the Fathers: A Study of the Atlantic Slave Traders, 1441–1807*, London, Weidenfeld and Nicolson, 1967.

PREISWERK, ROY, editor, *Regionalism and the Commonwealth Caribbean*, St. Augustine, Trinidad, Institute of International Relations, University of the West Indies, 1969.

PRICE-MARS, JEAN, *Ainsi parla l'oncle: essais d'ethnographie* [1928], New York, Parapsychology Foundation, 1954.

Proceedings of the Conference on Creole Language Studies, London, Macmillan, 1961.

PROUDFOOT, MARY, *Britain and the United States in the Caribbean: A Comparative Study in Methods of Development*, London, Faber and Faber, 1954.

QUINTUS BOSZ, A. J. A., *Drie Eeuwen grondpolitiek in Suriname*, Assen, Netherlands, Van Gorcum, 1954.

Racial Problems in the Public Service: Report of the British Guiana Commission of Inquiry, Geneva, Switzerland, International Commission of Jurists, 1965.

RAGATZ, LOWELL JOSEPH, *The Fall of the Planter Class in the British Caribbean, 1763–1833: A Study in Social and Economic History* [1928], New York, Octagon Books, 1963.

RAMCHAND, KENNETH, *The West Indian Novel and Its Background*, London, Faber and Faber, 1970; New York, Barnes and Noble, 1970.

RAMSAHOYE, FENTON H. W., *The Development of Land Law in British Guiana*, Dobbs Ferry, N.Y., Oceana Publications, 1966.

RASPAIL, JEAN, *Punch Caraïbe*, Paris, Robert Laffont, 1970.

——, *Secouons le cocotier*, Paris, Robert Laffont, 1966.

REID, IRA DE AUGUSTINE, *The Negro Immigrant: His Background, Characteristics and Social Adjustment, 1899–1937*, New York, Columbia University Press, 1939.

RENO, PHILIP, *The Ordeal of British Guiana*, Special issue

of *Monthly Review*, Vol. 16, Nos. 3 and 4, July-August 1964.

REVERT, EUGÈNE, *La France d'Amérique: Martinique, Guadeloupe, Guyane, Saint-Pierre et Miquelon*, Paris, Éditions Maritimes et Coloniales, 1955.

——, *La Martinique: étude géographique*, Paris, Nouvelles Éditions Latines, 1949.

RIVIÈRE, P. G., *Marriage Among the Trio: A Principle of Social Organisation*, Oxford, Clarendon Press, 1969.

ROBERTS, GEORGE W., *The Population of Jamaica*, Cambridge, Cambridge University Press for the Conservation Foundation, 1957.

ROBERTS, G. W., and MILLS, D. O., *Study of External Migration Affecting Jamaica: 1953–55*, Supplement to *Social and Economic Studies*, Vol. 7, No. 2, June 1958.

ROBERTS, W. ADOLPHE, *The French in the West Indies*, Indianapolis, Bobbs-Merrill, 1942.

RODMAN, HYMAN, *Lower-Class Families: The Culture of Poverty in Negro Trinidad*, New York, Oxford University Press, 1971.

ROTBERG, ROBERT I., with CLAQUE, CHRISTOPHER, *Haiti: The Politics of Squalor*, Boston, Houghton Mifflin, 1971.

RUBIN, VERA, and ZAVALLONI, MARISA, *We Wish to Be Looked Upon: A Study of the Aspirations of Youth in a Developing Society*, New York, Teachers College Press, 1969.

RUBIN, VERA, editor, *Caribbean Studies: A Symposium*, Jamaica, Institute of Social and Economic Research, University of the West Indies and New York, Program for the Study of Man in the Tropics, Columbia University, 1957.

——, editor, *Social and Cultural Pluralism in the Caribbean* (Annals of the New York Academy of Sciences, Vol. 83, Article 5), New York, New York Academy of Sciences, 1960.

RUSSELL, RICHARD J., and MC INTIRE, WILLIAM G., *Barbuda Reconnaissance*, Baton Rouge, Louisiana State University Press, 1966.

SABLÉ, VICTOR, *La transformation des isles d'Amérique en départements français*, Paris, Édition Larose, 1955.

ST. JOHN, SPENSER, *Hayti, or, The Black Republic*, New York, Scribner and Welford, 1889.

SALMON, C. S., *The Caribbean Confederation: A Plan for*

the Union of the Fifteen British West Indian Colonies. . . . [1888] (Cass Library of West Indian Studies, No. 15), London, Frank Cass, 1971.

SARTRE, JEAN PAUL, *Black Orpheus,* Paris, Présence Africaine, 1963.

SAUER, CARL ORTWIN, *The Early Spanish Main,* Berkeley, University of California Press, 1966.

SAUSSE, ANDRÉ, *Populations primitives du Maroni (Guyane française),* Paris, Institut Géographique National, 1951.

SCHAEDEL, RICHARD P., editor, *Papers of the Conference on Research and Resources of Haiti,* New York, Research Institute for the Study of Man, 1969.

SCHOELCHER, VICTOR, *Esclavage et colonisation,* Paris, Presses Universitaires de France, 1948.

SCHOMBURGK, ROBERT H., *The History of Barbados* . . . [1848] (Cass Library of West Indian Studies, No. 19), London, Frank Cass, 1971.

SCHWARTZ, BARTON M., editor, *Caste in Overseas Indian Communities,* San Francisco, Chandler, 1967.

SEGAL, AARON, *The Politics of Caribbean Economic Integration* (Special Study No. 6), Río Piedras, Institute of Caribbean Studies, University of Puerto Rico, 1968.

SEMMEL, BERNARD, *The Governor Eyre Controversy,* London, MacGibbon and Kee, 1962.

SEWELL, WILLIAM GRANT, *The Ordeal of Free Labour in the West Indies* [1861], London, Frank Cass, 1968.

SHERIDAN, RICHARD, *The Development of the Plantations to 1750,* and *An Era of West Indian Prosperity 1750–1775* (in *Chapters in Caribbean History,* No. 1), Barbados, Caribbean Universities Press, 1970; New York, Walker and Company, 1966.

SHERLOCK, PHILIP, *West Indies,* London, Thames and Hudson, 1966.

SIMEY, THOMAS S., *Welfare and Planning in the West Indies,* Oxford, Clarendon Press, 1946.

SIMPSON, GEORGE EATON, *Religious Cults of the Caribbean: Trinidad, Jamaica, and Haiti* (Caribbean Monograph Series, No. 7), Río Piedras, Institute of Caribbean Studies, University of Puerto Rico, 1970.

SINGHAM, A. W., *The Hero and the Crowd in a Colonial Polity,* New Haven, Yale University Press, 1968.

SKRUBBELTRANG, FRIDLEV, *Dansk Vestindien 1848–1880:*

Politiske Brydninger of Social Uro (Vore Gamle Trope-kolonier, Vol. 3), Copenhagen, Fremad, 1967.

SMITH, M. G., *Dark Puritan,* Jamaica, Department of Extra-Mural Studies, University of the West Indies, 1963.

——, *Kinship and Community in Carriacou,* New Haven, Yale University Press, 1962.

——, *The Plural Society in the British West Indies,* Berkeley, University of California Press, 1965.

——, *Stratification in Grenada,* Berkeley, University of California Press, 1965.

——, *West Indian Family Structure,* Seattle, University of Washington Press, 1962.

SMITH, M. G., AUGIER, ROY, and NETTLEFORD, REX, *The Ras Tafari Movement in Kingston, Jamaica,* Jamaica, Institute of Social and Economic Research, University of the West Indies, 1960.

SMITH, M. G., and KRUIJER, G. J., *A Sociological Manual for Extension Workers in the Caribbean,* Jamaica, Department of Extra-Mural Studies, University of the West Indies, 1957.

SMITH, RAYMOND T., *British Guiana,* London, Oxford University Press for the Royal Institute of International Affairs, 1962.

——, *The Negro Family in British Guiana,* London, Routledge and Kegan Paul, 1956; New York, Humanities Press, 1956.

SOBERS, GARFIELD, and BARKER, J. S., editors, *Cricket in the Sun: A History of West Indies Cricket,* London, Arthur Barker, 1967.

SPECKMANN, JOHAN D., *Marriage and Kinship Among the Indians in Surinam,* Assen, Netherlands, Van Gorcum, 1965; New York, Humanities Press, 1965.

SPRINGER, HUGH W., *Reflections on the Failure of the First West Indian Federation* (Occasional Papers in International Affairs No. 4), Cambridge, Harvard University Press, 1962.

SPURDLE, FREDERICK G., *Early West Indian Government: Showing the Progress of Government in Barbados, Jamaica, and the Leeward Islands, 1660–1783,* Palmerston North, New Zealand, privately published by the author, 1962.

STARKEY, OTIS P., *The Economic Geography of Barbados: A Study of the Relationships between Environ-

mental Variations and Economic Development, New York, Columbia University Press, 1939.

STEDMAN, J. G., *Narrative, of a Five Years' Expedition, Against the Revolted Negroes of Surinam, in Guiana, on the Wild Coast of South America; from the year 1772, to 1777: Elucidating the History of That Country, and Describing Its Productions,* 2 vols., London, J. Johnson, 1806; Barre, Massachusetts, Imprint Society, 1824 ed.

STEWART, J., *A View of the Past and Present State of the Island of Jamaica; with Remarks on the Physical and Moral Condition of the Slaves, and on the Abolition of Slavery in the Colonies,* Edinburgh, Olivier and Boyd, 1823; Westport, Connecticut, Negro Universities Press, 1823 ed.

STORM VAN 'S GRAVESANDE, LAURENS, *The Rise of British Guiana,* 2 vols., London, The Hakluyt Society, 2nd Series, No. 26, 1911.

STURGE, JOSEPH, and HARVEY, THOMAS, *The West Indies in 1837, Being the Journal of a Visit to Antigua, Montserrat, Dominica, St. Lucia, Barbados, and Jamaica, Undertaken for the Purpose of Ascertaining the Actual Condition of the Negro Population of Those Islands* [1838], (Cass Library of African Studies, Slavery Series No. 6), London, Frank Cass, 1968; Portland, Oregon, International Scholarly Book Service, 1968.

STYCOS, J. MAYONE, and BACK, KURT W., *The Control of Human Fertility in Jamaica,* Ithaca, N.Y., Cornell University Press, 1964.

SWAN, MICHAEL, *The Marches of El Dorado: British Guiana, Brazil, Venezuela,* Boston, Beacon Press, 1958.

SZULC, TAD, editor, *The United States and the Caribbean,* Englewood Cliffs, N.J., Prentice-Hall, 1971.

TAJFEL, HENRI, and DAWSON, JOHN L., editors, *Disappointed Guests: Essays by African, Asian and West Indian Students,* London, Oxford University Press for the Institute of Race Relations, 1965.

TANNENBAUM, FRANK, *Slave and Citizen: The Negro in the Americas* [1946], New York, Random House, Vintage Books, 1963.

TAYLOR, DOUGLAS MACRAE, *The Black Carib of British Honduras* (Viking Fund Publications in Anthropology

No. 17), New York, Wenner-Gren Foundation for Anthropological Research, 1951.

TAYLOR, LEROY, *Consumers' Expenditure in Jamaica: An Analysis of Data from the National Accounts (1832–1960), and from the Household Budget Surveys (1939–1958)*, Mona, Jamaica, Institute of Social and Economic Research, University of the West Indies, 1964.

THOMAS, CLIVE Y., *Monetary and Financial Arrangements in a Dependent Monetary Economy: A Study of British Guiana, 1945–1962*, Supplement to *Social and Economic Studies*, Vol. 14, No. 4, December 1965.

THOMAS, J. J., *Froudacity: West Indian Fables Explained* [1889], London, New Beacon Books, 1969.

Tourism in the Caribbean: Essays on Problems in Connection with Its Promotion, Assen, Netherlands, Van Gorcum, 1964.

Tourisme et développement en Martinique (Cahier No. 16), Fort-de-France, Martinique, Cahiers du Centre d'Études Regionales Antilles-Guyane, 1969.

Trinidad Carnival Issue, Special number of *Caribbean Quarterly*, Vol. 4, Nos. 3 and 4, Jamaica and Trinidad, March-June 1956.

TROLLOPE, ANTHONY, *The West Indies and the Spanish Main*, London, Chapman and Hall, 1860; Portland, Oregon, International Scholarly Book Service, 1968.

TYSON, J. D., *Report on the Condition of Indians in Jamaica, British Guiana and Trinidad, 1938–39*, Simla, Government of India Press, 1939.

VAISSIÈRE, PIERRE DE, *Saint-Domingue (1629–1789): la société et la vie créoles sous l'ancien régime*, Paris, 1909.

VIBAEK, JENS, *Dansk Vestindien 1755–1848: Vestindiens Storhedstid* (Vore Gamle Tropekolonier, Vol. 2), Copenhagen, Fremad, 1966.

WADDELL, D. A. G., *British Honduras: A Historical and Contemporary Survey*, London, Oxford University Press for the Royal Institute of International Affairs, 1961.

——, *The West Indies and the Guianas*, Englewood Cliffs, N.J., Prentice-Hall, 1967.

WAGLEY, CHARLES, and HARRIS, MARVIN, *Minorities in the New World: Six Case Studies*, New York, Columbia University Press, 1958.

WALLER, JOHN AUGUSTINE, *A Voyage in the West Indies*, London, Richard Phillips, 1820.

WATERS, IVOR, *The Unfortunate Valentine Morris*, Chepstow, Monmouthshire, England, The Chepstow Society, 1964.

WATTS, DAVID, *Man's Influence on the Vegetation of Barbados, 1627 to 1800* (Occasional Papers in Geography, No. 4), Hull, University of Hull, 1966.

WAUGH, ALEC, *The Sugar Islands: A Collection of Pieces Written About the West Indies Between 1928 and 1953*, London, Cassell, 1958.

WELLER, JUDITH ANN, *The East Indian Indenture in Trinidad* (Caribbean Monograph Series, No. 4), Río Piedras, Institute of Caribbean Studies, University of Puerto Rico, 1968.

West India Royal Commission Report (Moyne Report), Cmd. 6607, London, His Majesty's Stationery Office, 1945.

WEST, ROBERT COOPER, and AUGELLI, J. P., *Middle America: Its Lands and Peoples*, Englewood Cliffs, N.J., Prentice-Hall, 1966.

WESTERGAARD, W., *The Danish West Indies under Company Rule (1671–1754), with Supplementary Chapter, 1755–1917* [1917], New York, Macmillan, 1957.

WHITTEN, NORMAN E., JR., and SZWED, JOHN F., editors, *Afro-American Anthropology: Contemporary Perspectives*, New York, Free Press, 1970.

WILGUS, A. CURTIS, editor, *The Caribbean: Its Hemispheric Role*, Gainesville, University of Florida Press, 1967.

WILLIAMS, ERIC, *Britain and the West Indies: Historical and Contemporary Aspects of the Relationship Between Britain and the West Indies* (Fifth Noel Buxton Lecture of the University of Essex), London, Longmans, 1969.

——, *British Historians and the West Indies*, London, Andre Deutsch, 1964.

——, *Capitalism and Slavery*, Chapel Hill, University of North Carolina Press, 1944; New York, G. P. Putnam's, 1966.

——, *Education in the British West Indies*, New York, University Place Book Shop, 1968.

——, *From Columbus to Castro: The History of the Caribbean, 1492–1969*, London, Andre Deutsch, 1970; New York, Harper and Row, 1971.

——, *History of the People of Trinidad and Tobago*, Port-of-Spain, Trinidad, P.N.M. Publishing Co., 1962; Levittown, New York, Transatlantic Arts, 1962.

——, *Inward Hunger: The Education of a Prime Minister*, London, Andre Deutsch, 1969; Chicago, University of Chicago Press, 1971.

——, *The Negro in the Caribbean*, Washington, D.C., Associates in Negro Folk Education, 1942; New York, Haskell House, 1970.

WOOD, DONALD, *Trinidad in Transition: The Years After Slavery*, London, Oxford University Press for the Institute of Race Relations, 1968.

WRONG, HUME, *Government of the West Indies*, Oxford, Clarendon Press, 1923.

YOUNG, ALLAN, *Approaches to Local Self-Government in British Guiana*, London, Longmans, 1958.

III. FICTION AND POETRY

ABRAHAMS, PETER, *This Island Now*, London, Faber and Faber, 1966; New York, Macmillan, 1971.

ALLFREY, PHYLLIS SHAND, *The Orchid House*, London, Constable, 1953.

ANTHONY, MICHAEL, *The Games Were Coming*, London, Andre Deutsch, 1963; Boston, Houghton Mifflin, 1968.

——, *Green Days by the River*, London, Andre Deutsch, 1967; Boston, Houghton Mifflin, 1967.

——, *The Year in San Fernando*, London, Andre Deutsch, 1965; New York, Humanities Press, 1970.

BARRETT, NATHAN, *Bars of Adamant*, New York, Fleet Publishing, 1966.

BENNETT, ALVIN, *God the Stonebreaker*, London, Heinemann, 1964.

BRATHWAITE, EDWARD, *Islands*, London and New York, Oxford University Press, 1969.

——, *Masks*, London and New York, Oxford University Press, 1968.

——, *Rights of Passage*, London and New York, Oxford University Press, 1967.

CAREW, JAN, *Black Midas*, London, Secker and Warburg, 1958.

——, *The Last Barbarian*, London, Secker and Warburg, 1961.

——, *The Wild Coast*, London, Secker and Warburg, 1958.

CARPENTIER, ALEJO, *Explosion in a Cathedral*, Boston, Little, Brown, 1962.

CLARKE, AUSTIN C., *Amongst Thistles and Thorns*, London, Heinemann, 1965.

——, *The Meeting Point*, London, Heinemann, 1967.

——, *The Survivors of the Crossing*, London, Heinemann, 1964.

COULTHARD, G. R., editor, *Caribbean Literature: An Anthology*, London, University of London Press, 1966; New York, International Publications Service, 1970.

DAMAS, LÉON-G., *Black-Label*, Paris, Gallimard, 1956.

DATHORNE, O. R., editor, *Caribbean Narrative: An Anthology of West Indian Writing*, London, Heinemann Educational Books, 1966.

DAWES, NEVILLE, *The Last Enchantment*, London, MacGibbon and Kee, 1960.

DOHRMAN, RICHARD, *The Cross of Baron Samedi*, Boston, Houghton Mifflin, 1958.

DRAYTON, GEOFFREY, *Christopher*, London, Collins, 1959.

FERMOR, PATRICK LEIGH, *The Violins of Saint-Jacques: A Tale of the Antilles*, New York, Harper and Brothers, 1953.

FIGUEROA, JOHN, editor, *Caribbean Voices: An Anthology of West Indian Poetry*, London, Evans Brothers, 1971.

GLISSANT, ÉDOUARD, *La Lézarde*, Paris, Éditions du Seuil, 1958.

——, *Le quatrième siècle*, Paris, Éditions du Seuil, 1964.

HARRIS, WILSON, *The Far Journey of Oudin*, London, Faber and Faber, 1961.

——, *Heartland*, London, Faber and Faber, 1964.

——, *Palace of the Peacock*, London, Faber and Faber, 1960.

HEARNE, JOHN, *The Autumn Equinox*, London, Faber and Faber, 1959; New York, Vanguard Press, 1970.

——, *Stranger at the Gate*, London, Faber and Faber, 1956.

——, *Voices under the Window*, London, Faber and Faber, 1955.

HERCULES, FRANK, *Where the Hummingbird Flies*, New York, Harcourt, Brace and World, 1961.

The Independence Anthology of Jamaican Literature,

Kingston, Arts Celebration Committee of the Ministry of Development and Welfare, 1962.

JAMES, C. L. R., *Minty Alley* [1936], London, New Beacon Books, 1971.

KHAN, ISMITH, *The Jumbie Bird,* London, MacGibbon and Kee, 1961.

————, *The Obeah Man,* London, Hutchinson, 1964.

LAMMING, GEORGE, *Of Age and Innocence,* London, Michael Joseph, 1958.

————, *In the Castle of My Skin,* London, Michael Joseph, 1953; New York, Macmillan, 1970.

————, *Season of Adventure,* London, Michael Joseph, 1960.

LAUCHMONEN (KEMPADOO, PETER), *Old Thom's Harvest,* London, Eyre and Spottiswoode, 1965.

LOVELACE, EARL, *The Schoolmaster,* London, Collins, 1968; Chicago, Henry Regnery, 1968.

————, *While Gods are Falling,* London, Collins, 1965; Chicago, Henry Regnery, 1966.

MACINNES, COLIN, *Westward to Laughter,* London, MacGibbon and Kee, 1969; New York, Fawcett World Library, 1971.

MAIS, ROGER, *Black Lightning,* London, Jonathan Cape, 1955.

————, *Brother Man,* London, Jonathan Cape, 1954.

————, *The Hills Were Joyful Together,* London, Jonathan Cape, 1953.

MARSHALL, PAULE, *The Chosen Place, The Timeless People,* New York, Harcourt, Brace and World, 1969.

MCDONALD, IAN, *The Humming-Bird Tree,* London, Heinemann, 1969.

MITTELHOLZER, EDGAR, *The Life and Death of Sylvia,* London, Secker and Warburg, 1953.

————, *A Morning at the Office,* London, Hogarth Press, 1950.

————, *Shadows Move Among Them,* London, Peter Nevill, 1952.

MORRIS, JOHN, *Fever Grass,* Jamaica, Collins and Sangster, 1969; New York, G. P. Putnam's, 1969.

NAIPAUL, SHIVA, *Fireflies,* London, Andre Deutsch, 1970; New York, Alfred A. Knopf, 1971.

NAIPAUL, V. S., *A House for Mr. Biswas,* London, Andre Deutsch, 1961.

——, *The Mystic Masseur*, London, Andre Deutsch, 1957; New York, Vanguard Press, 1959.

——, *The Suffrage of Elvira*, London, Andre Deutsch, 1958.

NICOLE, CHRISTOPHER, *Off White*, London, Jarrolds, 1959.

——, *Ratoon*, London, Jarrolds, 1962.

——, *White Boy*, London, Hutchinson, 1966.

PATTERSON, ORLANDO, *An Absence of Ruins*, London, Hutchinson, 1967.

——, *The Children of Sisyphus*, London, New Authors, 1964.

PUISSESSEAU, RENÉ, *Someone Will Die Tonight in the Caribbean*, New York, Alfred A. Knopf, 1958.

RAMCHAND, KENNETH, *West Indian Narrative: An Introductory Anthology*, London, Nelson, 1966; New York, Barnes and Noble, 1970.

REDHEAD, WILFRED, *Three Comic Sketches* (Caribbean Plays No. 6), Trinidad, Extra-Mural Department, University College of the West Indies, 1956.

REID, V. S., *New Day*, New York, Alfred A. Knopf, 1949.

RHYS, JEAN, *Wide Sargasso Sea*, London, Andre Deutsch, 1966.

RICHER, CLÉMENT, *Ti-Coyo and His Shark: An Immoral Fable*, New York, Alfred A. Knopf, 1951.

ST. OMER, GARTH, *A Room on the Hill*, London, Faber and Faber, 1968.

——, *Shades of Grey*, London, Faber and Faber, 1968.

SALKEY, ANDREW, *Escape to an Autumn Pavement*, London, Hutchinson, 1960.

——, *A Quality of Violence*, London, New Authors, 1959.

SALKEY, ANDREW, editor, *Stories from the Caribbean: An Anthology*, London, Elek Books, 1965.

——, *Breaklight: The Poetry of the Caribbean*, Garden City, N.Y., Doubleday, 1971.

——, *West Indian Stories*, London, Faber and Faber, 1960.

SCHWARZ-BART, SIMONE, and SCHWARZ-BART, ANDRÉ, *Un plat de porc aux bananes vertes*, Paris, Éditions du Seuil, 1967.

SELVON, SAMUEL, *A Brighter Sun*, London, Allan Wingate, 1952.

——, *An Island Is a World*, London, MacGibbon and Kee, 1955.

——, *The Plains of Caroni*, London, MacGibbon and Kee, 1970.

——, *Turn Again Tiger*, London, MacGibbon and Kee, 1958.

SHERLOCK, PHILIP M., *Anansi, the Spider Man: Jamaican Folk Tales*, London, Macmillan, 1962; New York, Crowell, 1954.

——, *The Iguana's Tale: Crick Crack Stories from the Caribbean*, New York, Crowell, 1969.

THOBY-MARCELIN, PHILIPPE, and MARCELIN, PIERRE, *All Men Are Mad*, New York, Farrar, Straus and Giroux, 1970.

——, *The Pencil of God*, Boston, Houghton Mifflin, 1951.

UNDERHILL, HAL, *Jamaica White*, New York, Macmillan, 1968.

VERCEL, ROGER, *L'Île des revenants*, Paris, Éditions Albin Michel, 1954.

WALCOTT, DEREK, *The Castaway and Other Poems*, London, Jonathan Cape, 1965; New York, Farrar, Straus and Giroux, 1970.

——, *The Gulf and Other Poems*, London, Jonathan Cape, 1969.

——, *In a Green Night; Poems 1948–1960*, London, Jonathan Cape, 1962.

WAUGH, ALEC, *Island in the Sun*, New York, Farrar, Straus and Cudahy, 1955.

WOUK, HERMAN, *Don't Stop the Carnival*, New York, Pocket Books, 1965.

WYNTER, SYLVIA, *The Hills of Hebron: A Jamaican Novel*, London, Jonathan Cape, 1962.

IV. WEST INDIAN PERIODICALS

Annales des Antilles. Société d'Histoire de la Martinique. Fort-de-France, Martinique. Occasional.

Bim. Bridgetown, Barbados. Semi-annually.

Cahiers d'Outre-Mer. L'Institut de la France d'Outre-Mer de Bordeaux. Bordeaux, France. Quarterly.

Cahiers du C.E.R.A.G. (Centre d'Etudes Regionales Antilles-Guyane). Fort-de-France, Martinique. Irregular (about three times a year).

Caribbean Quarterly. University of the West Indies, Extra-

Mural Department. Kingston, Jamaica, and Port-of-Spain, Trinidad. Quarterly.

Caribbean Review. Hato Rey, Puerto Rico. Quarterly.

Caribbean Studies. Institute of Caribbean Studies, Univeristy of Puerto Rico, Río Piedras, Puerto Rico. Quarterly.

Jamaica Journal. Institute of Jamaica. Kingston, Jamaica. Quarterly.

Journal of the Barbados Museum and Historical Society. Bridgetown, Barbados. Irregular.

Journal of Caribbean History. Caribbean University Press, Barbados. Approx. two per year.

Moko. Curepe, Trinidad. Approx. two times a month.

New World Quarterly. Georgetown, Guyana, and Kingston, Jamaica. Irregular.

Nieuwe West-Indische Gids. The Hague. Three per year.

Paralleles. Fort-de-France, Martinique. Three or four times a year.

Savacou. Caribbean Artists Movement. Kingston, Jamaica, and London. Quarterly.

Social and Economic Studies. University of the West Indies, Institute of Social and Economic Research. Kingston, Jamaica. Quarterly.

Tapia. Tapia House Publishing Co. Tunapuna, Trinidad. Irregular (approximately monthly).

Timehri. Royal Agricultural and Commercial Society of British Guiana. Georgetown, Guyana. Irregular.

Trinidad Nation (formerly *P.N.M. Weekly*). Port-of-Spain, Trinidad. Weekly.

Voices. The Book Shop. Port-of-Spain, Trinidad. Triannually.

INDEX

Adams, Grantley, 144, 196–97, 200, 216
Africa, xvii, 6, 176, 185–86, 208, 264, 265–75, 277–81, 295, 299. *See also* specific areas, countries, individuals
African Liberation Movement (Trinidad), 319
African National Congress (Trinidad), 142, 149–50
Africans (Afro-Americans, Afro-West Indians), xv, xvii, 3–29 *passim*, 39–40, 55, 63, 67–69 ff., 76, 77, 79, 82, 132, 134, 135, 149–52, 161, 167–68, 264, 265–75, 277–81, 282, 283–91, 293–302, 306–29, 336–71; and carnival and fantasy, 362, 363–71; and East Indians, 67 ff., 149 ff., 282, 283–91, 309 (*see also* East Indians; specific individuals, organizations, people, places); and February (Black Power) Revolution (Trinidad), 306–29, 336–37; and *négritude*, 264, 265–75, 277–81, 293–302, 309
Afro-Saxons, 287, 293–302, 323, 336–37. *See also* Africans (Afro-Americans, Afro-West Indians)

Alcazar, Henry, 12
Algeria, 185–86, 264
Allen, Alpheus, 84
Allum, Desmond, 330, 331–48
American Virgin Islands, 168
Amerindians, 137, 143, 363
Anderson, Robert, 83
Anglin, D. G., 62
Anguilla, xiv, 236, 246, 364
Antigua, 31, 36, 41, 43, 45, 54, 217–18, 219, 227–29, 230–32, 234, 252, 322
Antilles, Netherlands (Dutch), 158
Asia, 208, 371. *See also* specific individuals, people, places
Associated Status (Associated States), 239, 240, 241–62. *See also* individual states
Australia, 169, 175, 203, 205, 238
Ayearst, Morley, 66, 67–79

Bagehot, Walter, 154–55
Bahamas, 240, 242, 249
Bambara language, 274
Barbados, Barbadians, 8, 9, 10, 16, 32, 40, 41, 48, 54, 57, 58–59, 61, 70, 78, 143, 144, 170, 180, 239–40, 252, 294, 313, 318, 322; civil service in, 94, 99, 103–4,